Women and
the Military

Recent Titles in
Women and Society around the World

Women and Violence: Global Lives in Focus
Kathleen Nadeau and Sangita Rayamajhi, Editors

Women and Health: Global Lives in Focus
AnnJanette Alejano-Steele, Editor

Women and the Military

Global Lives in Focus

Ruth Margolies Beitler and Sarah M. Gerstein

Women and Society around the World

An Imprint of ABC-CLIO, LLC
Santa Barbara, California • Denver, Colorado

Copyright © 2021 by ABC-CLIO, LLC

All rights reserved. No part of this publication may be reproduced, stored in a retrieval system, or transmitted, in any form or by any means, electronic, mechanical, photocopying, recording, or otherwise, except for the inclusion of brief quotations in a review, without prior permission in writing from the publisher.

Library of Congress Cataloging-in-Publication Data

Names: Beitler, Ruth Margolies, 1966– author. | Gerstein, Sarah M., author.
Title: Women and the military : global lives in focus / Ruth Margolies Beitler and
    Sarah M. Gerstein.
Description: Santa Barbara, California : ABC-CLIO, An Imprint of ABC-CLIO, LLC,
    [2021] | Series: Women and society around the World | Includes bibliographical
    references and index.
Identifiers: LCCN 2020036233 (print) | LCCN 2020036234 (ebook) |
    ISBN 9781440860225 (print) | ISBN 9781440860232 (ebook)
Subjects: LCSH: Women and the military. | Women soldiers. | Women and war. |
    Armed forces—Minorities—History.
Classification: LCC UB416 .B45 2021 (print) | LCC UB416 (ebook) | DDC 355.0082—dc23
LC record available at https://lccn.loc.gov/2020036233
LC ebook record available at https://lccn.loc.gov/2020036234

ISBN: 978-1-4408-6022-5 (print)
    978-1-4408-6023-2 (ebook)

25 24 23 22 21   1 2 3 4 5

This book is also available as an eBook.

ABC-CLIO
An Imprint of ABC-CLIO, LLC

ABC-CLIO, LLC
147 Castilian Drive
Santa Barbara, California 93117
www.abc-clio.com

This book is printed on acid-free paper ∞

Manufactured in the United States of America

To all my selfless colleagues with whom I have served over the years in the Department of Social Sciences, you have been my mentors, friends, and inspiration.
RMB

To my parents and sister, who never fail to encourage me in whatever I want to do and then push me to keep doing it.
SMG

Contents

Series Foreword		ix
Preface		xi
Introduction		xiii
Chronology		xxi
ONE	United States and Canada	1
TWO	Latin America and the Caribbean	31
THREE	Europe	59
FOUR	North Africa and the Middle East	97
FIVE	Sub-Saharan Africa	125
SIX	Central and East Asia	155
SEVEN	South and Southeast Asia	185
EIGHT	Oceania	207
Bibliography		237
Index		271

Series Foreword

Women's roles in society and the issues they face differ greatly from those of their male counterparts. In some corners of the world, women may manage households but are deemed unworthy of an education; in other areas, women scientists are pioneers in their fields, juggling family life and their careers. Gender inequality looms in all aspects of life, from employment to education to opportunities in sports and the military. What are the challenges, issues, and achievements women around the world face?

The *Women and Society around the World* series looks at women's lives as they pertain to various issues. The volumes cover topics such as

- Health;
- Violence;
- Religion;
- Sexuality;
- The military;
- Sports;
- Education; and
- Technology, among others.

Each volume begins with an introductory background essay on the volume's topic and is followed by a general chronology of significant world events pertaining to the topic. Eight chapters follow, focusing on the world's regions: United States and Canada, Latin America and the Caribbean, Europe, North Africa and the Middle East, Sub-Saharan Africa, Central and East Asia, South and Southeast Asia, and Oceania. All chapters include a list of further reading resources, and a selected bibliography at the end of each volume provides students with additional print and electronic resources for further research needs.

The chapters examine women in each region with broad brushstrokes, highlighting specific examples of key customs and policies in specific countries that help to illuminate cultural nuances among countries within each region. They can be read alone or be reviewed cumulatively to make cross-cultural comparisons. The volumes are ideal for high school students doing projects, undergraduate students writing research papers, and even general readers interested in learning about women's lives.

The goal of the *Women and Society around the World* series is to depict the roles of women worldwide by exploring the major issues they face and the accomplishments they have made, especially in terms of bridging the gap in gender inequality and fighting for basic human rights. While readers will learn about the challenges that half of the world's population face, they will also discover the empowering ways women succeed and overcome social and cultural barriers in their daily lives.

Preface

Exploring the role of women in militaries across the globe is a daunting task. Women who serve in the armed forces emerge from a variety of cultural, social, economic, and religious backgrounds, all factors that influence how gender roles are perceived. Couple these elements with the almost universal view that the military is a masculine domain and understanding women's incorporation into armed forces becomes even more complex. For some countries, a dearth of research exists examining women's participation in national militaries. Even when studies exist, some countries get short shrift.

To examine a topic of this magnitude in a limited amount of space, regions are discussed with some thematic generality, coupled with specific examples from several countries. Not all countries allow women in the armed forces, and in many states where women are permitted to participate, they are bounded by law or culture. By the 1980s, Canada, Denmark, Sweden, and Norway had eliminated the combat exclusion for women, while other countries have banned their access to the military in general. Understanding why women are denied equal opportunities in the armed forces stems from a variety of reasons, most common of which are political and legal barriers undergirded by cultural perspectives regarding masculinity and warfare. The book covers all continents, but out of necessity, concentrates on several key countries within each region. The goal of the book is to serve as a detailed starting point for more in-depth studies on themes pertaining to women and warfare and on specific country studies.

Women have diverse experiences related to warfare, whether as mothers or wives sending children or spouses off to war or as soldiers themselves. This book provides an understanding of women's roles as participants in their national militaries. The chapters are organized by region, exploring societal and cultural views of masculinity and war, factors influencing changing views of women and the military, including conscription, economic, and demographic trends, along with integration challenges. In many countries, arguments are explored that women's incorporation into combat units will degrade efficiency and readiness due to women's physical traits and inability to meet the standards. Most chapters also consider the difficulty of women's recruitment and retention due to family obligations and negative treatment while serving. This book will interest general audiences as a survey of women's participation in the armed forces. It will appeal to scholars with an interest in women and military studies.

Carving time out of a busy work and life schedule to take on a book project requires help from many places. Colleagues lean in, bosses turn the other way when deadlines are missed, and families accept our excuses for doing a little less at home. We are indebted to our wonderful and selfless colleagues in the Department of Social Sciences at West Point. Our Department Head, Colonel Suzanne Nielsen, and Deputy Department Head, Dr. Scott Silverstone, provide inspiration and guidance in all our endeavors. We are indebted to Colonel Tania Chacho, Director of International Affairs, who guarantees that we have time to conduct our research. We are also appreciative of the Art of War Scholars and Dr. Dean Nowowiejski, who offered suggestions and encouragement to complete the research. We are very grateful to Jen Parisi Olin, who is always willing to take on extra responsibilities when we are overwhelmed. We are thankful for the patience and assistance of our editor, Kaitlin Ciarmiello. Most of all, we are thankful to our families for their support, prodding, and patience.

Introduction

Since early times, women have engaged in combat, but their systematic incorporation into formal militaries is a more contemporary endeavor. This incorporation has not been without great controversy, leading to myriad discussions of women's role in society and the feminization of what was traditionally viewed as a male profession. There is an almost universal social construction that connects women to peace and men to war and excludes images of women as combatants. These traditional notions of gender roles make it difficult for some to conceive of women serving on the frontlines. Placing women in these traditionally masculine jobs can disrupt the male notion of masculinity (Winslow and Dunn 2002, 650). Men have customarily been associated with war based on a view that men are biologically more aggressive and women more nurturing. Both historically and currently, this perception coincides with men executing battle, while women tend to the home front and are more pacifist by nature (Jacoby 2002, 90). For those who believe that gendered characteristics are biological, then it follows logically that the concepts are universal. As the book illustrates, many societies hold clear views that war is a man's domain. Societal perceptions have been changing, but many continue to hold traditional values.

MILITARISM AND GENDER

A key question that scholars have advanced is whether men are innately more militaristic than women. Feminist scholars argue that the military's connection to masculinity is socially constructed. For others "militarized masculinity, at its most basic level, refers to the assertion that traits stereotypically associated with masculinity can be acquired and proven through military service or action, and combat in particular" (Eichler 2014, 81). Militarized masculinity refers to the connection between men and violence in warfare. Even though many militaries, especially those in the West, have incorporated women into their ranks, warfare remains associated with masculine traits. Women who join the military believe that they must adopt masculine characteristics to succeed rather than "feminizing" the military. Additionally, the dichotomy of men as the "warrior" versus women as the "beautiful soul" legitimizes unequal gender relationships (Eichler 2014, 82). According to Glick and Fiske, undergirding sexist beliefs are two conflicting perspectives, benevolent and hostile sexism. Benevolent sexism refers to an affection for women, but one with a need to protect them. Although this appears to be a positive concept, the subliminal message is that women are not able to protect themselves. As such, women's capabilities are not equal and require men's help. Hostile sexism is more overt and holds a much more negative view of women, contending that they want to diminish men's authority and power (Glick and Fiske 1996, 492). It follows that women who want military jobs typically associated with men, such as combat, diminish the importance and the masculine nature of that role. Although the concept of militarized masculinity can change across time and space, modifying traditional beliefs about gender proves challenging. With this said, some countries have permitted women in all military roles and, over time, their participation is slowly changing stereotypes. When women have proven competent in their positions, and their male military colleagues trust their abilities, the negative stereotypes connected to gender decrease (King 2015, 385).

From the time of Aristotle and Plato in ancient Greece, discussions of women soldiers have occurred intertwining militarism and men. According to scholars, both were influenced by the Periclean political culture, which held that women should remain at home and silent (Salkever 1986, 233). Pericles clearly delineated the realms of the home as belonging to women and the public arena to the men and superior to the household (Salkever 1986, 234). Taking this idea a step further, men were associated with the public realm of war and women with the family and peace. When women are permitted into the male domain, scholars argue that greater integration of women occurs in "occupational orientation," or jobs that converge with civilian society, versus "institutional orientation" or those jobs which are less aligned with civilian society (Moskos 2001, 30). In the military, women have greater acceptance rates in support services and medical occupations, which coincide more with civilian society than the military.

From anthropology and other academic disciplines, the advent of agriculture had a transformative impact on the sexual division of labor. During the preagriculture period of hunting and gathering, women gathered food as it kept them closer to home, something more compatible with child care than hunting animals. When agriculture developed, the same reason kept them closer to home, and more intense food processing required women to work harder while in the home. This explanation of why men became hunters can also explain why men became warriors. Although plenty of explanations explore the issue of physical strength and speed from a biological gender perspective, the concept of women needing occupations that were compatible with child care may also explain why men became warriors. Other theories of why men became warriors include the strength hypothesis and a tendency toward violence and aggression (Ember and Ember 2011, 179).

In other explanations, cultural traditions forcing boys into shows of strength to enhance the "cult of war" leads to a belief that war is a man's domain (Herrmann and Palmieri 2010, 19). Anthropologists have explained that although women have been warriors in several societies, this has been a rare occurrence due partially to the fact that men had almost exclusive access to weapons of war. For example, since men were usually the hunters, they familiarized themselves with bones and wood that are used to make weapons. This economy-of-effort theory argues that since men were already used to dealing with these materials, even though women can make and use weapons, it did not make adaptive sense for them to do so. Taboos also developed against women's use of these objects of war (Herrmann and Palmieri 2010, 21).

Even when women served in armies and fought in battles or as part of resistance movements, they usually did not receive better treatment during their participation in war or after the fighting ended. Women were expected to return to their roles in the home and family when the war ended, and culture dictated how they were treated. Often, women's participation in warfare has either been ignored or discounted as unimportant. For example, women insurgents have been used in many cases throughout history as weapon smugglers since they were rarely searched. Women were also used to seduce men since they gained a proximity to the enemy that allowed them to kill them. Although brave acts, they did not threaten the masculine nature of the military since these were jobs that could only be performed as a woman. As such, their importance to the mission was diminished (Degroot 2001, 30).

If the military is so intricately connected with men, why are women recruited as soldiers? In most countries, women are not conscripted, even in times of national emergencies, but are expected to participate in warfare to some degree. They are often expected to take on wartime activities such as nursing the wounded or making weapons (Mathers 2013, 132). For the most part, women's roles in the military expand or contract depending on certain variables, including cultural views, periods of shortfalls, and national emergencies; however, they are frequently restricted in their tasks. In many societies, women participated in warfare tangentially by being camp followers and providing sewing, cooking, and other logistical support. Most of the tasks that women undertook, even as military members, were considered appropriate to their gender, such as nursing or administrative tasks. Yet elements of warfare touched all members of society, and women were not completely excluded from all aspects of war. Even in very conservative societies regarding gender, women played specific roles during extraordinary circumstances and all to support the men.

CHANGING ROLES OF WOMEN IN THE MILITARY

Key factors have led to changing perceptions of women's participation in the military and warfighting. Several critical variables explaining the changed perspectives are simultaneously generalizable and culturally specific. Research reflects that moving from conscription to volunteer forces influences women's participation in the military. In many cases, creating a professional force increases the need for women to participate, especially if men do not volunteer in sufficient numbers. With this said, cultural factors in certain regions continue to prohibit women's comprehensive participation in the military, even when the draft is abolished. With globalization and the influence of international and regional organizations on national policies, many countries are moving toward more gender equality legislation. Shifting cultural perspectives and pressure from international organizations are influencing countries to reassess the role of women in society. Furthermore, a country's security environment influences women's participation in the military, whether in support roles or in more direct combat positions. When security threats are high, many states expand women's roles in their armed forces. Interestingly, in some cases, women participate when threats are low since men have less of an obligation to sign up when times are peaceful. Over the centuries, the argument that men are stronger both in body and mind than women has created the military as a masculine domain; however, the increased use of technology has diminished the need for brute strength and is eroding that physical argument against women's participation. As such, changing technology and shifting cultural perspectives with regard to gender roles and personnel requirements are increasing women's participation in national militaries (Dandeker and Segal 1996, 30).

GENDER AND EQUALITY

How societies perceive gender leads to sociocultural beliefs regarding masculinity and femininity, coupled with power dynamics. As societies' views of gender equality transformed, some militaries felt pressure to follow suit. Social groups had a strong influence on women's roles in the military. The feminist movement, which grew stronger in both North America and Europe during the 1970s, pressured the government and military to modify military policy regarding gender and further integrate women into the ranks. Feminists have varied views of women in the military. For some feminists, war itself is an antithesis to feminism, viewing a crucial interconnection between pacifism and feminism. As such, when women enlist, feminists perceive their cooptation by the patriarchal system (Mathers 2013, 135). Other feminists disagree and view military service as a move toward greater gender equality. For some feminists, women's incorporation into the military was, in part, symbolic. Even if many women did not want to fight or serve in combat, they wanted to have the choice.

Even in societies that are known for promoting gender equality, such as Sweden, studies have illustrated that the connection of the military to masculinity still exists (Mathers 2013, 127). In discussions of conscription, a concept related to both nationalism and militarism, the issue of gender arises. Since conscription implies the duty to protect and it is given only to men, it forms the military as a gendered institution (Kronsell and Svedberg 2001, 158). The military in most cultures is a gendered institution with a male warrior ethos and masculine traits emphasized as the most desired.

PROMOTING GENDER EQUALITY

Changing perspectives on women's roles in society and an increased push for gender equality have led to modifications in the security and military realm. The concept of gender equality has a variety of meanings including equal treatment and gender mainstreaming. Equal treatment refers mainly to legislative changes enacted to give women the same opportunities as men. Mainstreaming refers to an exploration of structural and implicit discrimination in institutions and a revamping of those institutions, where necessary (Skjelsbaek and Tryggestad 2009, 36). The concept of mainstreaming informed important changes that emerged in the 1990s. Organizations within the United Nations (UN) began to shift their thinking regarding peacekeeping and security. A new women's agenda was advanced, a response to the violent decade of events in Rwanda, Congo, the former Yugoslavia, and other places. After the fall of the Soviet Union in 1989, UN peacekeeping operations changed from ones that had small numbers of unarmed personnel serving as observers, to a wide spectrum of operations (Skjelsbaek and Tryggestad 2009, 39). Part of the impetus for this paradigmatic shift were challenges in the field where women could prove useful, leading to a push toward more gender equality. In other words, peace and conflict needed to be assessed along gender lines, particularly to explore how these events affected women differently than men. The UN argued that having more women in observation units facilitates sexual assault reports by local women and helps decrease the rate of sexual abuse by UN personnel, a problem that occurred in several instances (Skjelsbaek and Tryggestad 2009, 40).

In 1996, the UN Department of Peacekeeping Operations initiated a study to gain a deeper insight into understanding and implementing gender mainstreaming. There had been growing research on the topic of women's role in peace and security, particularly the impact of war on women and girls, along with the important positions that women can hold in achieving peace. Although women are victims in many conflicts, they can also play a role as agents of change, whether in national militaries or as part of peacekeeping operations. This recognition led to the passage in October 2000 of the United Nations Security Council Resolution 1325 on women, peace, and security. The resolution's goal is to mainstream issues of gender within the security and peacekeeping realm (Pratt 2013, 773). The implied message of mainstreaming is that women can offer a new perspective on dealing with war and violence. Furthermore, as women comprise more than 50 percent of the population in most locations, female peacekeepers can collect intelligence and understand networks in a way that their male counterparts cannot.

In 2007, NATO tasked its members to incorporate the resolution by developing specific plans for implementation (Dharmapuri 2011, 57). To recruit women to peace operations, the UN relies on member states' contribution of forces, and requested an increase in female personnel sent to peacekeeping operations and a doubling of the number of women in national militaries. By March 2013, women comprised just 4 percent of UN peacekeepers globally, with about 3 percent of UN military personnel and 9 percent of UN civilian personnel. While this is progress from the twenty women who served in peacekeeping missions from 1957 to 1989, it still falls short of expectations. Although there is room for progress, many countries recognize the importance of understanding gender issues and have begun to include gender advisers and new programs to advance the perspective.

The following chapters explore women's roles in militaries across the globe, paying particular attention to societal views of gender and militarism, domestic and international factors leading to changing policies regarding women's service, and challenges of integration. Since UN resolution 1325 was passed in 2000, some countries have adopted gender mainstreaming policies, while others pay lip service to the concept. Each chapter incorporates a discussion of gender equality and gender mainstreaming policies.

FURTHER READING

Dandeker, Christopher, and Mady Wechsler Segal. 1996. "Gender Integration in Armed Forces: Recent Policy Developments in the United Kingdom." *Armed Forces and Society* 23 (Fall): 29–47.

Degroot, Gerard J. 2001. "A Few Good Women: Gender Stereotypes, the Military and Peacekeeping." *International Peacekeeping* 8, no. 2: 23–38.

Dharmapuri, Sahana. 2011. "Just Add Women and Stir?" *Parameters* (Spring): 56–70.

Eichler, Maya. 2014. "Militarized Masculinities in International Relations." *Brown Journal of World Affairs* XXI, no. 1 (Fall/Winter): 81–93.

Ember, Carol R., and Melvin Ember. 2011. *Cultural Anthropology.* 13th ed. Upper Saddle River, NJ: Prentice Hall.

Glick, Peter, and Susan T. Fiske. 1996. "The Ambivalent Sexism Inventory: Differentiating Hostile and Benevolent Sexism." *Journal of Personality and Social Psychology* 70, no. 3, 491–512.

Herrmann, Irene, and Daniel Palmieri. 2010. "Between Amazons and Sabines: A Historical Approach to Women and War." *International Review of the Red Cross* 92, no. 877 (March): 19–30.

Jacoby, Tami Amanda. 2002. "Gender Relations and National Security in Israel." In *Redefining Security in the Middle East,* edited by Tami Amanda Jacoby and Brent E. Sasley, 83–104. Manchester, UK: Manchester University Press.

King, Anthony. 2015. "Women Warriors: Female Accession to Ground Combat." *Armed Forces & Society* 41, no. 4: 379–387.

Kronsell, Annica, and Erika Svedberg. 2001. "The Duty to Protect: Gender in the Swedish Practice of Conscription." *Cooperation and Conflict* 36, no. 2: 153–176.

Mathers, Jennifer G. 2013. "Women and State Military Forces." In *Women and Wars*, edited by Carol Cohn, 124–145. Cambridge, MA: Polity Press.

Moskos, Charles. 2001. "What Ails the All-Volunteer Force: An Institutional Perspective." *Parameters* 31, no. 2 (Summer): 29–47.

Pratt, Nicola. 2013. "Reconceptualizing Gender, Reinscribing Racial-Sexual Boundaries in International Security: The Case of UN Security Council Resolution 1325 on 'Women, Peace and Security.'" *International Studies Quarterly* (December): 772–783.

Salkever, Stephen G. 1986. "Women, Soldiers, Citizens: Plato & Aristotle on the Politics of Virility." *Polity* 19, no. 2 (Winter): 232–253. http://www.jstor.org/stable/3234912

Skjelsbaek, Inger, and Torunn L. Tryggestad. 2009. "Women in the Norwegian Armed Forces: Gender Equality or Operational Imperative?" *Minerva Journal of Women and War* 3, no. 2 (Fall): 34–51.

Winslow, Donna, and Jason Dunn. 2002. "Women in the Canadian Forces: Between Legal and Social Integration." *Current Sociology* 50, no. 5 (September): 641–667.

Chronology

1572
In the Netherlands, during the Spanish siege of Haarlem in 1572, Kenau Simondochter Hasselaers leads 300 women into battle.

1729
The Kingdom of Dahomey recruits women after huge losses of male soldiers.

1776
Margaret Corbin participates in the Battle of Fort Washington dressed as a man and is the first American woman to eventually receive a military pension.

1782
Deborah Sampson disguises herself as a man and fights in the Revolutionary War for over a year.

1880
During the Battle of Maiwand in Afghanistan, a woman warrior, Malalai, dies fighting the British and becomes a national hero.

1885
Canadian women are recruited into the armed forces as nurses during the North-West Rebellion of 1885.

1899–1902
Boer Wars in South Africa; Australia and New Zealand send female nurses to help care for the sick and wounded.

1914

In the United Kingdom, Mabel Stobart establishes the Women's National Service League, forming female units to administer to wounded soldiers.

Petra Herrera forms an independent brigade of female Mexican soldiers after they are denied recognition for their role in the Battle of Torreón.

1917

Russia forms the First Women's Battalion of Death to boost morale in the country; the unit is never used in combat due to Russia's exit from the war.

1920

In the United States, women get the vote. One of the more persuasive arguments that leads to women's suffrage emphasizes women's service in defense of the nation.

1927

Women join India's military, serving as nurses in the Military Nursing Service.

1934–1935

During China's Long March, women serve in stretcher teams and as nurses, medics, cooks, and engineers to help the Red Army during a series of retreats.

1939

The Soviet Union and Germany sign the Molotov-Ribbentrop Pact, guaranteeing nonaggression.

1941

Germany fails to honor the Molotov-Ribbentrop Pact, and women join the military in the Soviet Union to allow men to fight on the frontlines.

1942

The U.S. Women's Army Auxiliary Corps (WAAC) is established.

1943

Legislation signed by President Franklin Roosevelt transforms the WAAC into the Women's Army Corps (WAC) and becomes a part of the U.S. Army.

1945

The Women's Regiment of the Burma Independence Army (BIA) is established.

Mauritius deploys a contingent of women to support the British Royal Air Force during war effort.

Chronology   xxiii

1948

The Women's Armed Services Integration Act is passed in the United States.

The State of Israel is created. Israel implements compulsory military for both men and women.

1949

Women in the United Kingdom enter full military service in the Women's Royal Army Corps and receive rank commensurate with their male colleagues.

1951

U.S. Secretary of Defense George C. Marshall establishes the Defense Advisory Committee on Women in the Services (DACOWITS) to advise the military on recruiting and retaining women.

1954

Women join the Japanese Ground Self-Defense Force but are limited to certain roles.

1961

Portugal allows women to join the military with an all-female corps in the Air Force.

1962

The Jordanian military establishes the Princess Muna Nursing College.

1963

The Women Auxiliary Corps is established in the Philippines and permits women to serve in noncombat/administrative duties.

1967

Women join the Guyana Defense Force as members of the Women's Army Corps, filling a manpower shortage.

1972

The Equal Rights Amendment is passed in United States.

1973

The U.S. Supreme Court rules in the *Frontiero v. Richardson* case that military policy denying dependent benefits and equal housing allowance to female military members violates the Fifth Amendment due process clause.

xxiv Chronology

1974
Women join the Chilean Women's Service Military.

1975
Cuba passes the Family Code, recognizing women's contributions to the revolution and directing men to play an equal role in the division of labor around the home.

The U.S. Department of Defense announces that pregnancy is no longer grounds for involuntary dismissal.

1976
In Argentina, a civilian government replaces the military one and allows women to join the military.

Women join the Umkhonto we Sizwe (MK) in South Africa and serve in frontline roles.

Women are admitted to all U.S. military academies.

1978
U.S. President Jimmy Carter signs a law disbanding the Women's Army Corps and integrating women in the Army.

Libya opens the Tripoli Women's Military Academy.

Algeria's President Houari Boumediene permits women to serve in the People's National Army.

1981
Women join the professional corps of the Argentine military.

1982
Israel invades Lebanon, but female soldiers are forbidden to cross the border.

1984
Israeli women are permitted to enter Lebanon to fill medical, communications, and administrative positions.

1985
Norway allows women to participate in all military roles.

1986
Women begin serving in the Singaporean Armed Forces.

1988

The Danish military opens all jobs to women and implements gender neutral requirements.

Women join the Republic of the Fiji Military Forces.

1989

Seven hundred seventy U.S. military women deploy to Panama, and several female pilots receive medals for combat missions.

1990

The Lebanese Armed Forces Command allows women to enlist as privates in the Air Force and Navy and enroll in military academies.

1991

The United Kingdom introduces maternity leave for female soldiers.

In 1991, the United States attacks Iraq after it invades Kuwait. The United States deploys half a million troops to dislodge Iraq from Kuwait, and among the troops are 41,000 women.

The United Arab Emirates establishes the Khawla Bint al-Azwar Training College, the first Army college for women in the Gulf region.

Apartheid ends in South Africa; women are permitted to join the integrated military.

1993

In the Philippines, the first group of women enters the military academies but are limited to comprising up to 5 percent of the total number of cadets.

President Bill Clinton reopens combat aviation to women.

1994

The Rwandan genocide begins. Women participate as members of armed groups during the genocide.

Alice Miller, who immigrated to Israel from South Africa and was a civilian pilot, challenges women's exclusion from taking a military exam to qualify for military positions, specifically to become a pilot.

1996

The U.S. Supreme Court rules that women could no longer be barred from attending the Virginia Military Institute (VMI).

A Defense White Paper in South Africa emphasizes facilitating equal opportunities for women soldiers and discusses the right of women to serve in any rank or position, including combat roles.

1998

The NATO Committee on Gender Perspectives (NCGP) requests National Reports from all NATO members to explore and compile statistics and information regarding member states' policies on women in the armed forces.

1999

The Bolivarian Revolution in Venezuela helps to diversify the military, allowing men and women from lower socioeconomic backgrounds to serve in the military as officers.

Norway appoints its first female defense minister.

Japan enacts a basic law for gender equality, promoting gender equality across all sectors of society.

Arlene A. Dela Cruz graduates first in her class in Philippine Military Academy.

2000

New Zealand Defense Forces opens all combat roles to women.

Women are admitted into the Chilean Military Aviation Academy of the Air Force.

Thirteen women graduate from the Argentine military academy.

2001

Australia and New Zealand join an international coalition in Afghanistan, and women participate in combat patrols.

Khatool Mohammadzai is promoted to brigadier general in Afghanistan after the Taliban are removed from power.

Israel's Women's Corps is dissolved and women are integrated in military.

2002

The Pakistani government permits women to become pilots.

2003

Women begin serving in Bangladesh's military.

Liberian military disbands temporarily after civil war ends.

2005

The first women are inducted into the Pakistani Air Force.

Russia organizes a beauty contest for the Russian Ground Forces.

2006

Algeria makes women's status in the military equal to men.

The Liberian military is reconstituted; President Ellen Johnson Sirleaf announces a goal of a force that is 20 percent female.

2007

Botswana allows women to serve in the military, the last country on the continent to do so.

The first Indian unit arrives in Liberia in 2007 to combat the rampant sexual violence plaguing the country in connection with the civil war.

2008

Women in Argentina are allowed to serve as marines, pilots, and submariners.

Women are allowed to serve on warships in Japan for the first time.

Women from Georgia serve in the Russo-Georgian War as nurses and doctors on the frontlines.

2009

Women in China are selected to fly fighter jets; others are judged based on their talent and beauty as part of the selection process to join the People's Liberation Army (PLA).

Fatima Zohra Ardjoune is the first woman in Algeria in the People's National Army to be promoted to general.

The New Zealand Army sends officers to train first class of officers in Papua New Guinea.

2011

Nigeria integrates the national military academy.

2012

Nosiviwe Mapisa-Nqakula is elected as defense minister of South Africa.

2013

President Bashir Al Assad of Syria assembles an all-female force, known as the Lionesses for National Defense, to bolster his fighting strength.

A Philippine woman commands the peacekeeping operation in Haiti.

Australian Defense Forces guarantee that all combat roles will be open to women within three years.

Two women take command of Japanese naval destroyers.

In Myanmar, newspaper advertisements target young Burmese women to join the military's administrative, logistics, and information technology fields.

Women in Argentina are allowed to join ground combat branches.

2014
Lesotho's president signs into law an order that forbids women from becoming pregnant within the first five years of their service. This law was later overturned by the country's court.

Twenty women graduate from the Chinese Dalian Naval Ship Academy, including the first Uighur female officer.

In Nepal, the Directives on Gender Conduct and Women in Military intends to create a zero-tolerance toward violence against women and to facilitate the recruitment of more women into the military.

Miriam al Mansouri becomes the first female pilot in the United Arab Emirates and leads air strikes against the Islamic State in Syria.

2015
General Gina Reque Teran is named Bolivia's first female army general responsible for commanding combat troops, a first in the region.

In a highly publicized event, two women graduate from the elite U.S. Army Ranger School, bolstering the case that women could serve alongside men in combat.

Kazakhstan hosts Batyr Arular (Warrior Women) beauty contest, and voters from around the world decided on the winner.

North Korea makes conscription mandatory for men and women.

Japan allows women to serve as fighter pilots.

Singaporean Gan Siow Huang is appointed the first female brigadier general and becomes the head of air intelligence.

2016
Australian Defense Forces open all roles to women.

Sergeant Yesica Carolina Baires graduates from the Honduran Sapper Leader Course, the first woman to do so.

Chile opens all combat roles to women.

2017

Haiti announces that it will reinstate the armed forces with a goal of 30 percent women across the force.

The first Mongolian female noncommissioned officer, Muncunchimeg Nyamaajav, attends and completes the U.S. Army SFC Christopher R. Brevard Non-Commissioned Officer Academy, in Alaska.

An online petition in South Korea receives over 70,000 signatures advocating that conscription be extended to women in South Korea; the government does not act on this petition.

In November 2017, for the first time in Israel's history, a woman is appointed deputy commander of a combat squadron.

2018

Nigeria establishes a separate Nigerian Army Women's Corps.

Saudi Arabia announces that women may serve as soldiers in the military in the provinces of Riyadh, Mecca, al-Qassim, and Medina.

Saudi Arabia lifts the ban on women driving or attending soccer matches.

Women across the region participate in the Pacific Military Cup and discuss women's roles across the region.

Women from Russia's Strategic Missile Forces compete in a "Make-Up Under Camouflage" beauty contest.

Japan lifts all restrictions on women in combat, except where maternal protection is required by law.

Taiwan revokes unpopular conscription law; this law required women from Fuchien, a remote island, to serve in a civil defense role.

Qatar allows women to volunteer for the military after a decree by the Emir Tamim Bin Hamad Al-Thani.

Saudi Arabia announces that women may serve in the military in the provinces of Riyadh, Mecca, al-Qassim, and Medina. They are permitted to serve only if they have a male guardian living in the same province as their duty.

2019

In Saudi Arabia women above the age of twenty-one can travel without permission from male guardians.

Antonette Wemyss-Gorman becomes the first female commander of the Jamaican Maritime, Air and Cyber Command, with oversight for the Jamaica Defense Force Coast Guard, the JDF Air Wing, and the Military Cyber Corps.

ONE

United States and Canada

Women in both the United States and Canada have undergone significant transformations in societal roles in the last few decades. Both countries experienced women's movements in the 1970s, pushing for equal rights and opportunities in all aspects of society, including the military. In the United States and Canada throughout the early years of their development, women supported men during battle as camp followers providing food, cleaning, and nursing care. As societal views changed, women joined the armed services and are currently permitted to serve in all branches of the military in both countries. Challenges remain as cultural views are not monolithic, and traditional values persist in some pockets of these societies. This chapter explores women's integration into the militaries of the United States and Canada, assesses the cultural views regarding women in the armed forces, and explores factors influencing women's changing roles in the military.

THE UNITED STATES

Although women served with the Continental Army during the American Revolutionary War as nurses, seamstresses and, in rare cases, as soldiers or spies, it was not until much later that women played significant roles in the U.S. military. During the early years of the United States' existence, the concept of *coverture* defined women's roles as citizens in the new republic. Because men were considered the ones with the social contract to the government, they voted, served in militias, and on juries.

Women, however, were understood as having an obligation to the man, usually her husband, who "covers" her, subsuming her rights to his (McSally 2011, 153). Women often accompanied their husbands into war throughout history to serve as cooks, seamstresses, and nurses (Goldstein 2001, 382). During the Revolutionary War, army wives and camp followers supported the Continental Army. Despite the services they performed, General George Washington found them to be a distraction and ordered officers to expel them. The Continental Congress authorized one woman for every fifteen men to assist soldiers, although most did not adhere to this ration (Goldstein 2001, 383). Some women fought in the war, although they had to hide their gender. For example, Deborah Sampson disguised herself as a man and fought in the Revolutionary War for over a year. Margaret Corbin, who began as a camp follower, participated in the Battle of Fort Washington in 1776 dressed as a man and was the first American woman to eventually receive a military pension. The fact that women had to disguise themselves as men in the early years bolsters the argument that warfare was perceived as a man's domain in a gendered military institution (Degroot 2001, 26).

According to data from 2017, the U.S. military is 16.2 percent women, though this statistic can be further delineated into branch, officers, or enlisted (Department of Defense 2017 Demographics Report, 18). Women serve as officers more frequently than they do as enlisted members of the military, making up 17.7 percent of the officer corps and 15.9 percent of the enlisted force (Department of Defense 2017 Demographics Report, 19). Women are also more likely to serve in the Air Force and comprise 19.8 percent of service members in that branch; they are least likely to serve in the Marine Corps, with just 8.4 percent of the total force (Department of Defense 2017 Demographics Report, 20).

Overall, the U.S. military is overwhelmingly Caucasian, with almost 70 percent of the force self-reporting as White. Less than 20 percent of the force self-reports as Black or African American, with the remainder of the force self-reporting as other, American Indian, Asian, or Native Hawaiian or Other Pacific Islander. The Department of Defense also reports that over 60 percent of enlisted women are minorities. The U.S. Army has the highest numbers of Black women serving in both the officer corps and enlisted ranks with 22 percent serving in the former and 39 percent the latter (SWAN Report 2019, 37). However, women of color have served since 1862, when five African American women served aboard the USS *Red Rover* during the Civil War, providing medical care (SWAN Report

Women of color have served in the U.S. military since 1862 and comprise 22 percent of the officer corps and 39 percent of enlisted ranks. (T. Anthony Bell, Fort Lee Public Affairs)

2019, 3). Cathay Williams, a former slave, served as a Buffalo Soldier, hiding her true gender for two years before her deception was uncovered. Additionally, the percentage of women who identify as Latina has increased from 12 percent in 2011 to almost 18 percent (SWAN Report 2019, 17–18). In 2019, the U.S. Military Academy graduated one of the most diverse classes with 34 Black women graduating (Hill 2019).

Societal Views of Masculinity and Warfare

The culture in which people are socialized form a foundation on how they perceive their lives. As American society has changed its perception of gender equality, women's roles in the military have also undergone transformation. In most societies, men comprise the majority population of most militaries, if not all. Men have been associated with combat and, consequently, the military has been connected to masculinity. Combat reflects a paternalistic and protective view that some men have in society regarding women. "Both institutionally and culturally, the military's

4   Women and the Military

function of protection has been conflated with its connection to masculinity" (Nantais and Lee 1999, 182). Even the fact that women served as nurses during war reflected society's view of specific gender roles such as women as caregivers. The U.S. Army experimented with mixed-gender units in antiartillery during World War II and found that these units outperformed the male-only one, yet then-Army Chief of Staff, General George C. Marshall, ended the experiment and ordered that the results remain secret. This event implies that "the decision to keep women out of 'combat positions' (if not out of actual combat itself) is based less on women's capacities and more on gendered belief systems" (Mathers 2013, 138; McSally 2011, 154).

In World War I, approximately four hundred women died serving their country, even though they were denied suffrage (McSally 2011, 153). One of the more persuasive arguments that led to women's suffrage in 1920 emphasized women's service in defense of the nation. Although many women served in World War I, most performed clerical duties as civilian employees, although they donned a uniform (Goldstein 2001, 88). Between the wars, Anita Phillips, the director of women's relations, a newly created army position, advocated for the development of a women's corps that would be fully integrated into the military, but her effort was rejected. To relieve increasing pressure to incorporate women more fully, the War Department agreed to continued auxiliary status for women (Goldstein 2001, 88). Over 25,000 women served in World War I and by World War II, 350,000 women played peripheral roles in the military to free men for combat, most serving as nurses in the Army and Navy Nurse Corps (Schaefer et al. 2015, 7).

It was not until World War II that women became more integrated and performed more significant military roles prompted mainly by a growing personnel requirement. Over 400,000 women served, with 500 losing their lives in the war effort (McSally 2011, 153). Although women flew planes and served as instructor pilots for men, they were excluded from flying in combat. The Women's Army Auxiliary Corps (WAAC) was established in 1942 after U.S. Representative Edith North Rogers of Massachusetts introduced the legislation. The WAAC was created to afford women the same rights of service as other soldiers. By 1943, legislation signed by President Franklin Roosevelt transformed the WAAC into the Women's Army Corps (WAC) and became a part of the U.S. Army. Not long after the WAAC was established, the Navy created the Women Accepted for Volunteer Emergency Service (WAVES), but women were restricted, as they were in the Army, from serving overseas, on vessels or combat aircraft. They were also limited in the rank they could attain and exercised authority over women only (Schaefer et al. 2015, 7). Although many women left the military at the termination of World War II, some remained and were integrated into the armed forces, leading to the passage of the Women's Armed Services Integration Act in 1948. Although this act capped women's participation in the armed forces to 2 percent, the legislation also contained significant positive elements. The legislation made women's service in the armed forces permanent, as opposed to granting a temporary and emergency basis for their participation and permitted them to work in the medical field and as secretaries.

By the time of the Korean War, the government tried to recruit 500,000 women but were only able to attract 46,000 to active duty by 1952. This inability to draw large numbers of women led Secretary of Defense George C. Marshall to establish the Defense Advisory Committee on Women in the Services (DACOWITS) in 1951 to advise the military on recruiting and retaining women. By 1967, notwithstanding these recruitment efforts, and despite the lifting of the 2 percent restriction on women in the military and rank limitations, the number of women entering the military remained low until the draft's end in 1973 (Szayna et al. 2016, 18). General Eisenhower argued that women would serve important military functions in the future and advocated for their permanent place, believing that women, like men, should be subject to conscription (McSally 2011, 154).

Prior to the passage of the Equal Rights Amendment in 1972, women were required to meet higher enlistment standards than men. In the 1960s, they needed to maintain a "ladylike" appearance. After 1972, women were no longer compelled to wear skirts and apply makeup, and they began to branch out from medical and clerical jobs, working in electronics, communications, and mechanical repair (Stiehm 1985, 167). Additionally, all services increased the number of women in their ranks. While the Marines only expanded the number of women by 20 percent, the Army and Navy doubled and the Air Force tripled the number of women in uniform (Schaefer et al. 2015, 10).

Changes in American society regarding women's rights and equality had a pervasive impact on the military. During this period, legal efforts were made to increase women's rights for service in the military. The Fifth Amendment's due process clause became an important basis for significant changes regarding women's status in the military. As time continued, women

6   Women and the Military

fought for expanded rights, gender equality, and equal opportunity in the military and society writ large. The Supreme Court case *Frontiero v. Richardson* ruled in 1973 that military policy denying dependent benefits and equal housing allowance to female military members violated the Fifth Amendment due process clause (McSally 2011, 154). The Supreme Court decision awarded the same benefits to dependents of female service members as men. Although women were required to remain childless while serving, their husbands could not obtain benefits without proof that they were dependent on their wives' income, something that spouses of male military members were not obliged to corroborate (Stiehm 1985, 166).

Furthermore, with the end of the draft, the military had trouble recruiting men to serve due to a reduced birthrate in the 1960s and the negative view of the Vietnam War. It created a need for women to fill positions that had been occupied by men and began to open more opportunities for women. As part of this move toward equality and increased training for women, they were admitted to the military academies in 1976. However, traditional values perceiving warfare to be in the man's domain persisted.

Connected to the conviction that war and masculinity are intertwined, in 1979, General William Westmoreland testified that "no man with gumption wants a woman to fight his nation's battles" (as quoted in Goldstein 2001, 283). What General Westmoreland's comment reflects is the belief that having women do military jobs similar to those of men and especially those in combat diminishes a man's masculinity. Beginning in the 1970s, the courts ruled that conceptions of a woman's role in society could not be used as justification for exclusion. For some, opinions informed their view of policy without any relation to the evidence or reality. When General Merrill McPeak, the Chief of Staff of the Air Force, testified in 1991 to the Senate Armed Services Committee regarding whether to repeal the ban on women flying combat aircraft, he said that "he would pick a less-qualified male pilot over a more-qualified female pilot for a combat mission" (McSally 2011, 150). Although he conceded that the combat exclusion discriminated against women, his traditional views skewed his perspective.

It was under President Jimmy Carter, who signed Public Law 95-485 in 1978, that women were integrated into the Army and WAC disbanded (Szayna et al. 2016, 18). By the 1980s, a reassessment of women in the military was prompted, in part, by a discussion of whether women should be exempted from selective service. The Selected Service registers men from age eighteen to twenty-five, both U.S. citizens and immigrants, to be called up in case of a national emergency, ostensibly the draft. During his State of the Union address in 1980, President Carter declared his intention to reinstate the Selective Service due to the Soviet invasion of Afghanistan in 1979. The president included women in his request for funding from Congress, but the legislature provided funding for male-only registration, which was then upheld by the Supreme Court ruling of *Rostker v. Goldberg* in 1981 (Szayna et al. 2016, 19). One of the arguments advanced was that since women were excluded from combat, they did not have the same obligation as men to be drafted. However, the 1948 Military Selective Service Act upon which the Selective Service was based, did not specify that men were registering for combat-only positions and, in fact, did indicate that the purpose of the registration was to provide medical personnel and manpower in the case of a national emergency (McSally 2011, 155). Despite this clarification, women were still excluded.

Although women's participation continued to be restricted in the military, particularly with regard to combat, reality on the ground made the enforcement of exclusion policies difficult. The first Gulf War in 1990 began a process of transformation that continued to gain momentum until all military occupations were opened to women in 2016. By the time women participated in the wars in Afghanistan and Iraq, both beginning in the early 2000s, despite a written policy of combat exclusion, women were fighting and dying on the nonlinear battlefield.

In 1991, the United States attacked Iraq after it had invaded Kuwait the previous August and had lobbed SCUD missiles at Israel. The United States deployed half a million troops to dislodge Iraq from Kuwait, and among the troops were 41,000 women. Congress established a commission, the Presidential Commission on the Assignment of Women in the Armed Forces, to continue its exploration of the combat ban on women. The commission retained its policies excluding women from the Special Operations forces and service on submarines and landing craft. It also created separate physical standard tests for men and women in recognition of their physiological differences, recommended gender-neutral assignment policies, and opened noncombat flying positions to women on Navy combat ships (Schaefer et al. 2015, 13). In 1993, President Bill Clinton reopened combat aviation to women and searched for other areas in the military to increase gender equality.

For some people, women are considered less competent than men despite undergoing the same training. This attitude is found in most militaries, including the United States. In 1994 when Navy fighter pilot Lieutenant Kara Hultgreen was killed attempting to land her plane on an aircraft

8   Women and the Military

carrier, a discussion followed that Hultgreen was not sufficiently qualified, but was promoted because of her gender (Mathers 2013, 141). In 1993, after the Department of Defense lifted the risk rule and allowed women to fly combat aircraft and opened combat ships to women, the U.S. Army Chief of Staff defended the continued combat exclusion policy in the Army by asserting that the bonding needed for military effectiveness could only occur in a single-gender environment (Goldstein 2001, 195).

Several critical issues have been raised over the years pertaining to the full integration of women in the U.S. military, particularly into combat units. These arguments have included the impact of women on unit cohesion and effectiveness and physical and mental differences between the sexes negating women's ability to be effective in combat. Some of these views stem from sociocultural perspectives in the American culture regarding gender roles, militarism, and the appropriate place for women in society.

Factors Influencing Change

American society witnessed shifting attitudes toward gender equality with the end of the draft in 1973 and women's actual participation in combat, despite legal limitations. The impact of these events led to the push for a fully integrated force. Many arguments were advanced with regard to lifting the combat exclusion including that service in the military is connected to one's role as a citizen. During the battle for women and minority suffrage, arguments supporting voting rights were based on prior service in defense of the nation. Furthermore, "a military force should reflect the society it defends" (McSally 2011, 150–151). In addition to the arguments above, recruiting from the entire population allows the best qualified people to join the military, rather than confining selection to specific groups of people.

Issues of Integration: Physical

Physical differences between men and women regarding strength, endurance, pregnancy, and mental capabilities have been used to exclude women from participating in all military occupations and specialties. The Women's Integration Act of 1948 had a provision that allowed the service secretaries to terminate a woman's service "under circumstances and in accordance with regulations prescribed by the President" (Stiehm 1985, 163). This allowed the military to dismiss involuntarily women who became pregnant.

Some argue that pregnancy not only affects the length of a woman's career, but it also negatively impacts military readiness and her ability to deploy (Decew 1995, 65). Despite this view, in 1975, the Department of Defense announced that pregnancy was no longer grounds for involuntary dismissal. Although litigation against involuntary dismissal began in 1970, the military dealt with pregnancy cases individually and granted waivers to pregnant women who wanted to reenter the military after a child was born (Stiehm 1985, 167). There were several cases in the Air Force where women challenged the constitutionality of the rule. While serving on active duty in Vietnam, Captain Susan R. Struck became pregnant and the Air Force recommended an honorable discharge. Captain Struck sued the Air Force and won the right to remain on active duty (Stiehm 1985, 167).

Some argue that one's ability to execute military missions require strength and endurance. Although men are usually taller than women and have greater upper body strength, studies have shown that increased fitness training and conditioning for women, along with adaptations in equipment, can close the physical gap between men and women. Other studies have shown that an average woman today is four inches taller than an average man was during World War I (Degroot 2001, 32). What the research illustrates is that people can adapt and condition to compensate for deficiencies in height and strength. Additionally, not every military job requires the same physical standards, while the military fitness tests are not necessarily matched to specific military jobs. They are used to establish a baseline of fitness for a healthy man or woman. At West Point, data from the class of 2011 illustrated that 52 percent of women could pass the Army Physical Fitness Test using the male standards (Haring 2013, 27). Studies carried out in Canada in the 1970s exploring women's physical, mental, and social characteristics for combat, led Canada to remove the combat exclusion. Similarly, in 1978, Demark eliminated its ban, followed by Norway and Sweden. In 2020, the U.S. military adopted gender-neutral standards for all specialties. While standards might differ among jobs, everyone in the same specialty will need to meet the same requirements.

Several early documents regarding women in the military mention the physical differences as a barrier to complete integration. In 1969, an Army report noted, "Physically, the military woman is not well suited for the rigors of field duty or capable of performing fatigue details normally performed by men, and cannot be considered self-sufficient enough in this regard to perform under the conditions experienced by maneuver elements in tactical operations" (Schaefer et al. 2015, 9). Others argue that women

10   Women and the Military

are physically inferior to men and would be unable to handle the rigors of battle. If women are not up to the standards of battle, logic holds that women would make the military and its ability to fight less efficient (Decew 1995, 64). However, not all men are strong enough to be in combat units, and despite this fact they are not restricted from service in these units. "It seems that efficiency should dictate gender-neutral determinations of whether or not an individual (male or female) has the competence, skill, and strength to serve in any given position" (Decew 1995, 64). More advanced weapons systems, technological skill, and education may determine positions rather than physical strength.

In the Alternative View section of the presidential commission established in 1991, a minority opinion from the commission argued that the integration of women differs from racial integration, since "dual standards are not needed to compensate for physical differences between racial groups, but they are needed where men and women are concerned" (Schaefer et al. 2015, 14). Arguments were also advanced that women did not have the emotional strength to deal with the rigors and stresses of combat (Fitrani, Cooper, and Matthews 2016, 16).

Unit Cohesion and Effectiveness

According to Feaver and Kohn in their seminal study on the civil-military gap, civilians and military members believed that the key issues regarding women's integration into all areas of the military was connected to the role of women in combat units, sexual harassment, and discrimination (Feaver and Kohn 2001, 368). Many of those opposed to women's integration into combat arms believed that women were not physically capable of executing the necessary functions associated with combat. While the physical argument was the most common reason to exclude women, other opponents held that women would disrupt unit cohesion.

The discussion of women's effect on unit readiness and effectiveness began in earnest in the 1980s when the Army questioned the Department of Defense's desire to increase the number of enlisted women on active duty. The Army wanted to "level out" the number of enlisted women due to reports by commanders that combat readiness was impacted by issues of pregnancy, single parenthood, strength, and endurance (Szayna et al. 2016, 16). In reaction to the Army's perspective, Secretary of Defense Casper Weinberger executed a study on the impact of women on combat readiness. When the study was complete in 1982, Secretary Weinberger directed all the service secretaries to support the removal of obstructions for military servicewomen, a view that became a key aim of the Reagan administration. A major issue was raised by Lawrence Korb, an assistant secretary of defense, regarding combat exclusions. He offered that if combat exclusions are legitimate, as indicated by their very existence in the regulatory statutes, then some barriers to women's participation in the military that follow from these exclusions are also legitimate (Szayna et al. 2016, 17).

Furthermore, as a consequence of the Weinberger study, the Army reevaluated a coding system used to assess the risk to women on the battlefield, and that system determined which jobs women could occupy in the military. A new "risk rule" was implemented in 1988 barring women from some noncombat units if they would be exposed to capture, direct combat, or hostile fire. Secretary of Defense Les Aspin replaced this rule in 1988 with the "direct ground combat assignment rule," narrowing the scope of the previous exclusions (MacKenzie 2012, 32–33). In other words, more positions were opened to women.

In 1992, President George H. W. Bush established the Presidential Commission on the Assignment of Women in the Armed Forces to explore, once again, women's exclusion from combat. The commission found several factors that some believed impacted unit cohesion, including inevitable male/female relationships, a desire by men to protect women, a perception that women got pregnant to avoid deployment, and women's presence as interfering with male bonding (MacKenzie 2012, 38). According to some, sexual relationships will always develop when men and women are in mixed units, thereby disrupting order and discipline and hindering unit cohesion and effectiveness. This argument was used to maintain the combat exclusion by assuming that these relationships would occur more in combat situations than in other military situations. The underlying implication was that service members would ignore the rules against fraternization while in combat (Decew 1995, 65).

Additionally, unclear combat exclusion rules made it challenging for commanders to understand when women could participate in operations. In some cases, the exclusion rules force commanders to restructure units, and this reorganization had an impact on unit cohesion. "Shifting and disrupting a crew in wartime damages cohesiveness and military readiness" (Decew 1995, 66). In 1987, about 250 women were assigned to combat units in West Germany and, given the new rules, they needed to be transferred to different positions. In doing so, the commanders knew that the dearth of men would lead to many vacancies and as such, resisted reassigning the women. Eventually, an order from the commander of U.S. Army Europe forced the transfer of women to new positions (Szayna et al. 2016, 17).

The contention that male bonding leads to cohesiveness, an element crucial to success on the battlefield, is controversial. Trusting that your fellow soldiers can do their jobs well impacts both mission success and survival of the unit's members. Some studies argue that cohesion stems not from "intimate relations or masculine rituals but rather emphasizes interpersonal trust and teamwork" (Siebold 2007, 291). According to Anthony King, "While no one would deny the intense bonds which are often evident, scholars have increasingly argued that the performance of today's professional troops does not only, nor even primarily, depend upon their personal friendships, deep though these may be" (King 2013b, 8). The most important element in unit cohesion and effectiveness is connected to professionalism and competence. One does not necessarily need to "like" their fellow soldiers. Other studies have shown that integration increases unit cohesion by decreasing prejudice as exposure to other groups leads to less discrimination (MacKenzie 2012, 41). Scholars have found that task cohesion, the concept that a commitment to a common task is the glue that bonds individuals, leading to mission effectiveness, rather than social cohesion, is the most important bond (McSally 2011, 152).

Furthermore, research shows that groups with women have higher cognitive intelligence than groups with lower percentages of women. Higher cognitive intelligence refers to the phenomenon that groups are more intelligent than individuals. The discovery that groups with women have higher cognitive intelligence may connect with the finding that women tend to score higher than men on a trait called "social sensitivity," which measures an ability to read other's emotions. Having this ability leads to stronger group collaboration, suggesting that adding women to units could increase the team's overall cognitive intelligence (Haring 2013, 28).

Combat Arms

Integration of women into the combat arms has been a very controversial issue; however, on the ground, women were already serving in situations that exposed them to direct combat. The United States has deployed more women to combat zones than other countries and therefore has experience and data sets to explore the impact of women in combat. From 2001 to 2013, 2,333,972 military personnel deployed to combat zones of which 10 percent were women (Fitrani, Cooper, and Matthews 2016, 16).

Women in combat zones began much earlier than 2001. In Panama in 1989, 770 women deployed to the region and several female pilots received medals for combat missions, while a commander who led her team in firefights, also received commendation (McSally 2011, 155). In Desert Storm in 1991, two women were taken prisoner while serving in combat support positions, and thirteen female service members were killed (McSally 2011, 156). Women's participation in the previous operations influenced Congress to direct the DOD to lift the prohibition on women flying combat aircraft, allow them to serve on combat ships, and rescind the risk rule. Despite the recognition that women were ostensibly in combat positions, the DOD enacted a new combat exclusion policy stating in part, "Service members are eligible to be assigned to all positions for which they are qualified, except that women shall be excluded from assignments below the brigade level whose primary mission is to engage in direct combat on the ground" (McSally 2011, 156). In other words, women were still excluded from combat. Although women were banned from service in combat units, in Iraq and Afghanistan, "the need for women to work with combat units in the highly gender-segregated spaces of Afghanistan and Iraq won out" (Crowley and Sandhoff 2017, 221). After 2005, women were able to wear the Combat Action badges reflecting a recognition of the reality on the ground. Although women could not serve in, but could be attached to, a combat unit, put them in actual combat (Crowley and Sandhoff 2017, 222). As Crowley and Sandhoff explain in their article interviewing women veterans, "The army was a place where these women were promised they could be all they could be, but it was also a place where they learned that sometimes all they could be was just a girl in a man's world" (2017, 222).

Despite these negative views, the political environment has had the greatest impact on rescinding the ban on women in combat since the lines between combat and support positions became ambiguous. Not only have important military leaders changed their minds regarding the ban after witnessing women's successful performance in Iraq and Afghanistan, but the reality on the ground in these countries put women in combat situations. By 2011, the military leadership diversity commission recommended that the exclusion be lifted (MacKenzie 2012, 34).

The U.S. invasion of Iraq in 2003 led the Army to restructure some units, placing combat support companies on bases with combat units

(MacKenzie 2012, 34). The nature of warfare in the Middle East and the strict gender separation in Iraq and Afghanistan led to the establishment of female-only military teams that searched women for weapons. By 2009, the military created the Female Engagement Teams (FETs), all-women groups that conducted search and engagement missions, requiring them to leave their bases and venture into hostile territory. In Afghanistan, to meet the strategic goals of security, governance, and development, coalition forces believed that female soldiers and marines could best assist the Afghan family unit and win support (Holliday 2012, 90). The female teams provided services to women in the Afghan villages and maintained personal relationships in support of the overall counterinsurgency operations. Their reach extended beyond just those with whom the women interacted. As a patrilocal society, where sons remain in their parents' home when they marry and start their new nuclear family, positive experiences with the female soldiers can have far-reaching effects (Holliday 2012, 91).

Despite the continued ban on women in combat, the military offered combat pay to women on engagement and forward support teams, reflecting a comprehension of realities on the ground. About 78 percent of U.S. military women killed in Iraq were listed as "hostile deaths" (MacKenzie 2012, 34). This actuality led to many new policy recommendations and studies regarding combat exclusion, some paying lip service to lifting combat exclusion, while others were more substantive. For example, in 2012, the Army opened certain combat-related jobs to women, yet in actuality, jobs that women were already doing such as medic or intelligence were recategorized as combat related (MacKenzie 2012, 35–36).

Additionally, the perception that the military is a masculine job persists, leading to the view that having women in combat units distracts men from their key duty (MacKenzie 2012, 32–33). In 1991, after 41,000 women participated in Operation Desert Shield and Desert Storm, Congress repealed the combat aviation exclusion, only to have a presidential commission recommend its reinstatement in 1992. Despite this backsliding, in 1996, the Supreme Court ruled that women could no longer be barred from attending the Virginia Military Institute (VMI). The case stated that "parties who seek to defend gender-based government action must demonstrate 'an exceedingly persuasive justification' for that action" (*United States v. Virginia*, 518 U.S. 515 [1996]).

Excluding women from combat limited the pool of qualified people who could serve the nation. After the U.S. involvement in Iraq (2003) and Afghanistan (2001), with women already serving in combat, some members

Female troops serving in Operation Desert Storm. The United States deployed half a million troops to dislodge Iraq from Kuwait, and among the troops were 41,000 women. (Corel)

of Congress attempted to retain the combat exclusion clause. By the year 2005, with two wars underway in Iraq and Afghanistan, the Department of Defense rejected any attempts to close more jobs to women. Several representatives from Congress pushed a bill to exclude women from serving in some Army forward support units. With the need for more personnel to fight the wars and the military already decreasing standards to recruit more members, this attempt was defeated (McSally 2011, 156). When House Armed Services Committee Chairman Duncan Hunter introduced a bill to keep women out of units with which they were already serving in Iraq and Afghanistan, the Army opposed this move. In 2010, the Navy requested that the ban on women serving on submarines be lifted (Schaefer et al. 2015, 15).

In January 2013, U.S. Defense Secretary Leon Panetta announced that the military would gradually open all military jobs to women, including service in elite units such as Navy Seals, Army Rangers, and Delta Force (Fitrani, Cooper, and Matthews 2016, 20). In a highly publicized event in August 2015, two women graduated from the elite U.S. Army Ranger School, bolstering the case that women could serve alongside men in combat. In 2020, the first woman is expected to graduate from the elite

> ### RANGER SCHOOL FOR ALL
>
> The U.S. military opened combat arms to women in 2015 and in August of that same year, Captain Kristin Griest and Lieutenant Shaye Haver were the first women to graduate Ranger school, one of the U.S. Army's most challenging training programs. Although not required, the vast majority of infantry officers need to have completed Ranger school to compete in their branch for promotion. Captain Griest became the first female infantry officer in the U.S. Army.

Special Forces Green Beret qualification course. Despite women's success, several arguments discussed above continue to be advanced as a criticism of the decision to open all military roles to women.

Sexual Harassment

Several well-publicized events in the early 1990s led to a more intense study of sexual harassment and sexual assault in the military. Sexual harassment has intense ramifications for the individual target of the assault, which can manifest itself in both psychological and physical ways and has an impact on military readiness and unit cohesion (McCone, Thomsen, and Laurence 2018, 175). In 1991, at a Las Vegas conference of the Tailhook Association, tales of inappropriate behavior by naval officers led to the dismissal of several naval aviators. As investigations continued, it was clear that pervasive gender discrimination in the military had a long history. In 1996, reports emerged from Aberdeen Proving Ground, an Army training facility, that recruits were harassed, raped, and fell prey to inappropriate relationships. In the 1990s, there were also increased reports of sexual harassment at the U.S. Military Academies (Goldstein 2001, 97). The Department of Defense addressed these issues by creating a Joint Task Force for Sexual Assault Prevention and Response in 2004.

Sexual assault and harassment have continued in more recent years with incidents at the Naval Academy and West Point, along with many other units. In one case, an Air Force officer was convicted of aggravated sexual assault only to have the conviction overturned by the Commander of the 3rd Air Force in Germany in 2013 (McCone, Thomsen, and Laurence 2018, 175). The military has implemented programs and continues intense efforts to eradicate the problem.

CANADA

Relative to other NATO countries, Canada has progressed more quickly with regard to women in combat. Since 2000, women can serve in all positions, and Canada has reconfigured submarines to incorporate women on missions. Canadian women have deployed on peacekeeping missions around the globe, yet by 1998, made up only 11 percent of Canadian forces and 1 percent of combat troops (Goldstein 2001, 85). According to the Canadian government's website, by January 2019, women comprised 15.9 percent of the military forces, comprising 2.9 percent of the combat arms. Despite the increased number of women in the forces and more attention being paid to the issue, sexual harassment remains a challenge in the Canadian military.

Societal Views of Masculinity and Warfare

After the beginning of the American Civil War in 1861, Canada created a part-time citizen's militia, not a professional military, because the government was suspect of full-time soldiers. Canada's first prime minister commented that "regulars were useful only for hunting, drinking, and chasing women and that they possessed no useful skills" (English 2004, 87). By the twentieth century, the Canadian military created the Permanent Force and by World War II, along with its NATO participation, the professional regular Army increased its competence (English 2004, 88). Canadian women have served in the armed forces since the North West Rebellion of 1885 when nurses were recruited to the war effort (Winslow and Dunn 2002, 641). As a nurturing profession, nursing was considered an acceptable role for women outside the home. Although working in the military as nurses allowed women space in the public realm, "nursing does not expand the nature of women's social participation; it merely permits women to perform an essentially private sphere function within the public sphere" (Symons 1991, 479). Women began supporting the Yukon field force in 1898 and by 1901, during the Boer War (1899–1902), women were serving as nurses and receiving lieutenant rank and pay.

During World War I, women continued nursing, but by World War II were recruited for other support jobs to cover positions while men went to the frontlines. By World War II, over 50,000 Canadian women had participated in the women's division. Opposition to women in the Canadian military remained high due to the pervasive belief that women should remain at home and, in part, to a perception that working in a male-dominated profession diminishes a woman's femininity. Interrelated with these views was a negative contention that women who served in the military were promiscuous (Symons 1991, 479). Both the military and government conducted a public relations campaign to combat these negative stereotypes by refuting the idea that a women's place is only on the domestic front and by stifling male soldiers' discussion of the women's loose morals (Symons 1991, 480). The campaign also underscored that having women serve in the military was temporary, and life would return to "normal" at the cessation of violence. This emphasis reflected an attempt to appease certain segments of the population who supported the continuation of the traditional gender division of labor; however, although women did return home after the war, the creation of government day care centers, part-time employment agreements, and tax incentives for husbands of employed women reflected a shift in societal attitudes (Symons 1991, 480).

After the number of women was reduced in the force following World War II, the three branches—Air Force, Navy, and Army—welcomed women back into the military by the 1950s, but confined them to mostly administrative, medical, and support roles. Although women were integrated into the regular forces during the Korean War and over 5,000 women served, by 1965, the number of women was capped at 1,500, comprising only 1.5 percent of the Canadian Armed Forces (CAF) (Symons 1991, 481). Additionally, there were other constraints on women's service, including barring married women from joining. Significant changes regarding women's service in the armed forces occurred in the 1970s after the publication of the *Report of the Royal Commission on the Status of Women in Canada*. This report recommended that married women be allowed to serve, all jobs should be open to women, childbirth was not cause for release from service, service agreements should be the same length for both genders, and women should be admitted in military academies (Symons 1991, 481).

Factors Influencing Change

In 1971, women began serving in more nontraditional roles as mechanics, drivers, firefighters, and military police, among others. To procure evidence regarding the impact of women in all-male occupations and "near-combat" roles, the Canadian government began a series of experiments in the 1970s known as the Servicewomen in Non-Traditional Environments and Roles (SWINTER trials). The trials were implemented to compare mixed-gender unit performance with single-gender units. Additionally, the trials explored the impact of women in combat on public perceptions and the costs associated with expanding roles to women (Schaefer et al. 2015, 55–56). The trials lasted five years and, in some cases, placed women in an all-male station in the Arctic, along with assignments as aircrew, on ships and with combat support land forces in Europe (Symons 1991, 481–482). The results of some of these trials were overwhelmingly positive, illustrating that mixed units performed as well as the all-male ones. Despite some optimistic trial outcomes, it was clear that the military was not convinced to open all specialties to women (Symons 1991, 482). One reason why some specialties remained closed to women reflected some negative conclusions from the SWINTER trials. Further examination of the trials illustrated that women felt isolated, judged harshly, and rejected by their male colleagues (Schaefer et al. 2015, 56). Often women believed that they were blamed for failures in the unit and that the leadership was not supportive (Symons 1991, 483).

Canadian society, similar to that of the United States, underwent shifting attitudes with regard to gender equality; in the late 1970s and early 1980s, Parliament passed the Canadian Human Rights Act and the Canadian Charter of Rights and Freedoms, respectively. These documents had a significant impact on expanding the roles opened to women in the military. In 1985, another document "Equality for All" was published by the Parliamentary Committee on Equality Rights and recommended women's full integration in the military, arguing that excluding women from all military opportunities impacted their careers negatively. That document led to a government-issued report entitled "Towards Equality," which established a task force to explore the effect of opening most units to women.

Recommendations stemming from the task force led to the integration of most units and jobs in the CAF. However, several units remained closed to women or required a minimum number of men. By 1988, women were still excluded from fourteen combat units in the Army and Navy, while thirty-three military occupations and a "minimum male component" existed in fifty-two jobs (Symons 1991, 484–485). However, in 1989, all military jobs were open to women except those on submarines, which were opened in 2000. Despite the legal ruling in 1989 incorporating women into all branches of the military, creating equality of opportunity between men and women, the social culture trailed the legislation, making gender integration problematic (Winslow and Dunn 2002, 642).

Integration into Combat Arms

In 1998, *Maclean's* magazine published an article on alleged rapes in the Canadian military. The article's publication led to a national outcry and a renewed debate of women in combat, coupled with a discussion on the state of the CAF's culture of gender discrimination. Negative attitudes toward gender integration in the CAF follow patterns akin to other countries, including the United States. In the CAF, the main narrative holds that women's presence detracts from unit cohesion and male bonding, despite research illustrating that increased contact with minority groups helps decrease discrimination (Matheson and Lyle 2017, 22). In the 1985 "Policy on the Employment of Women," the Canadian military advanced several arguments to limit women's service, contentions that continued to be espoused by those opposed to integrating women into all units. A major claim was that "combat exclusion was justified . . . because only through this exclusion could 'operational effectiveness' be guaranteed" (Symons 1991, 488–489). This perspective assumes that women's presence in certain units negatively impacts the effectiveness and preparedness of the unit.

The document espouses the view that women would find the continuous pressure of combat difficult and, consequently, that weakness would harm unit effectiveness. The authors of the document contend that to be effective, the group needs to be tightly bonded and trust that all members of the team will complete their jobs. However, due to values instilled during childhood, some individuals assert that women will diminish unit cohesion reflecting the CAF's underlying assumption that even education could not reduce an individual's prejudice of sharing the battlefield with women. This line of reasoning was used to omit women from combat jobs (Symons 1991, 490).

Several other arguments as to why women should be excluded from combat emerged from the policy document. Some of the discussion was interconnected with the issue of sexual attraction, positing that fraternization would undermine cohesion by setting the stage for potential favoritism. Additionally, men's perception of women in need of protection assumes that women are weaker than men and this assessment impacts gender equality. These views promote the idea that "men will never recognize women's competence and ability to be self-sufficient" (Symons 1991, 492). According to the policy, some opponents to complete integration also claim that women lack the resolve necessary to kill during battle. This assertion ignores the effect that training plays in conditioning soldiers to perform during war. It also disregards the historical reality that women have performed well in past wars (Symons 1991, 493).

Coupled with these arguments, some scholars claim that even if women are allowed in combat, their numbers would be so small as to be token. This aspect might exacerbate problems of cohesion and integration. According to research on corporate employment, if women make up less than 15 percent of the workforce, they are considered a "token," making integration extremely challenging. Token status coupled with some traditional cultural norms that favor masculinity in corporate and military settings increase the problem of integration for women (King 2013a, 20). For women to succeed, they need a critical mass and the ability for upwards mobility (Barry 2013, 28).

In 2013, women made up 14 percent of the CAF, but only 2.4 percent of combat positions. Canadian women served in combat on the frontlines for the first time in Afghanistan (2001). During that conflict, four women died, three of those in combat (Fitrani, Cooper, and Matthews 2016, 19). According to some research, Canadian women were as effective as men on the frontlines in Afghanistan, and studies have found that contrary to a view that the public would be unprepared to lose women in combat, reality illustrated that

A female reservist in Glace Bay, Nova Scotia, Canada, stands vigil at a war memorial on Remembrance Day, November 11, 2014. Since 2000, women can serve in all positions in the Canadian military. (Groovypixs/Dreamstime.com)

22   Women and the Military

female combat deaths did not elicit an outcry to remove women from ground close combat (Fitrani, Cooper, and Matthews 2016, 19). This conclusion reflects the much larger issue connected with sociocultural changes in society regarding gender equality.

Furthermore, many Western countries are exploring the tangible impact of women in mixed-gender combat units on unit cohesion. For many years, this topic had been discussed without the backing of actual research. The Canadian Forces Leadership Institute concluded that gender diversity need not degrade military effectiveness since elements that influence operational success and cohesion are multifactorial (Fitrani, Cooper, and Matthews 2016, 19). For example, how the media portrays women in combat both reflects and impacts the sociocultural view of women in society and on the battlefield (Chapman and Eichler 2014, 595). According to some scholars, Quebec possesses a different view of defense and security than the rest of Canada by espousing a more pacifist perspective (Chapman and Eichler 2014, 596). Yet research indicates that this dichotomy might be exaggerated, and in connection with women in combat, found several similar themes in both Quebec's media and the rest of Canada, including "gender does not matter in the CAF; women are equal warriors; and, somewhat paradoxically-considering the first two—women bring gender-specific qualities and skills to their soldiering" (Chapman and Eichler 2014, 596).

Despite its progressive actions on women in combat, the Canadian Armed Forces has strained to diversify its ranks, particularly with regard to women in higher ranks, thereby affecting recruitment and retention (Matheson and Lyle 2017, 18). For some scholars, the question becomes, why is it so difficult to recruit and retain women in middle and senior leadership positions? Furthermore, is there gender bias in leadership training that would impact attracting and retaining women in these positions? Scholars found that "gender bias has become so embedded in the CAF that it is not always obvious, even to those who are experiencing it" (Matheson and Lyle 2017, 20). This pervasive bias led researchers to explore the impact of leadership training on military culture where some concluded that "the structure of achievement and advancement in leadership roles tends to favour men" (Matheson and Lyle 2017, 21). Valuing "maleness" in tandem with a lack of gender diversity leads to a belief that gender equality could be menacing to the empowered group. However, if women's numbers were to increase in key leadership positions, permitting them increased roles in decision making, the organizational culture could shift

(Matheson and Lyle 2017, 21). There have been some positive shifts in numbers with women achieving higher ranks in the military. According to the Canadian government website, by the end of 2018, there were sixteen female general or flag officers.

Other scholars have explored characteristics in the CAF that impact gender integration and ultimately recruitment and retention. According to Matheson and Lyle, the CAF is a male-dominated culture of imposed isolation, with occurrences of sexual harassment and gender discrimination, lack of work-life balance, negative attitudes toward integration, and lack of leadership support (2017, 21). Since combat arms are more alienated from civilian society than other aspects of the military, they emphasize "masculine models of the warrior, thus resisting female integration" (Winslow and Dunn 2002, 642). A male-dominated culture emphasizes competitiveness, toughness, physical fitness, and putting "service before self." Although these are respectable traits, "collectively, they can undergird a culture of masculine hegemony" (Matheson and Lyle 2017, 22). This type of environment fosters sexism and hostility toward women necessitating that those who want to succeed in this milieu shed their feminine traits and cooperate in demeaning other women, while others opt to leave the service (Matheson and Lyle 2017, 22).

Certain sociocultural factors disadvantage women in the military. Although soldiers are required to put service before self, society expects women to put family above all. Men are not held to this same familial requirement. Women who deploy or leave for training exercises usually receive more criticism than men with children as the expectation holds mothers to a different responsibility standard than fathers (Matheson and Lyle 2017, 22). Additionally, some argue that because women can become pregnant, their removal from a unit, especially a combat one, would impact that unit negatively for deployment. However, research shows that male absenteeism due to sport injuries is higher than that of women, implying that the same discussion of unit cohesion with regard to men is not discussed (Matheson and Lyle 2017, 23). A key problem leading to these negative perspectives of women's incorporation into certain units may be linked to a dearth of leadership pushing integration forward, negating male hegemony, and removing gender-based barriers in the military.

Although women make up only 13.4 percent of the military, they comprise over 50 percent of the workforce in Canada. For militaries to connect with their population, their composition should reflect that population. Although Canada is a very diverse society, in general, the CAF does not replicate this diversity. However, various branches of services do reflect Canada's diversity more than others. For example, the Air Force has more women than the Navy or Army. In 1987, the Air Force lifted all restrictions on women serving in air units with leadership contending that if women had the physical endurance and were accepted by their male peers, mixed units can be effective (Winslow and Dunn 2002, 645). The Navy and Army's experience with social integration was more challenging than that of the Air Force since many men opposed women's presence, arguing that women could not execute effectively the necessary duties.

In the military, women have greater acceptance rates in support services and medical occupations, which align more with civilian society than the military. To compare military personnel perspectives with those of civilians and to determine whether greater integration occurs with occupational orientation, Gallup Canada conducted a poll in 1977. Some scholars exploring the sociocultural environment of the CAF have illustrated that the crux of the argument to exclude women stemmed more from the impact of women's integration in the military on men's perceived masculinity, rather than a lack of capabilities (Winslow and Dunn 2002, 650). Coupled with this view, some in the CAF believe that women would degrade the effectiveness of the unit because men are naturally protective of women and would put themselves in harm's way to protect them.

These perceptions impact the differences evident between the military services with regard to their acceptance of women in their units. A 1978 questionnaire distributed to 4,314 CAF forces and their spouses indicated that sailors believed women could participate in support roles, but would have a detrimental effect serving on destroyers or submarines. Some respondents held that women could serve effectively as aircrew yet rejected them "as fighting soldiers" (Winslow and Dunn 2002, 646). Those surveyed from the land forces believed women could serve as support, although 69 percent opposed women in the combat arms (Winslow and Dunn 2002, 646). Those in the Air Force supported women as aircrew, but believed that in the high-performance aircraft, women would degrade effectiveness. Additionally, "a slight majority of the airmen sampled were against women serving as soldiers and sailors" (Winslow and Dunn 2002, 647). What this early survey indicated was that while women were accepted to serve in support positions, they were not perceived as fit for combat ones.

Prior to the case of *Gauthier v. Canada* in 1989 authorizing women to serve in all units, not only were women excluded from combat or combat-related occupations, but other occupations maintained a "minimum male requirement" so that if war erupted, there would be enough men to go to combat (Symons 1991, 478). This ruling integrating women in all units began to transform the attitudes and culture of the military and society regarding women in combat, although opposition to full integration remained.

By 2017, women comprised only 2.5 percent of the Army's combat arms. Women in the Canadian Forces comprise only 4 percent of the officers in the combat arms, which includes infantry, artillery, and armor and 1.5 percent of soldiers (Lane 2017, 467). Despite Canada's early integration efforts, few women entered the combat arms, a phenomenon that can be attributed to a lack of a clear integration plan. Furthermore, leaders ignored the issue, implementation mechanisms and follow-up were lacking, and cultural factors and resistance to women's integration continued. After 1998, an increased push for better implementation programs, which allocated funds specifically to recruit women, revised fitness standards, along with added billets to training programs for women, led to an increase in the number of women recruited and retained beginning in 1999 (Schaefer et al. 2015, 54).

Additionally, the Canadian Navy implemented a plan called VISION 2010, which focused on cultural change and eliminating negative attitudes toward women, along with revisiting policies on pregnancy, family issues, and harassment. By 2010, a study illustrated that men and women show equal satisfaction rates with their careers in the military. However, even with increased job satisfaction in the military, few women are joining the combat arms. This could be due to several factors, including an inability to meet the physical standards and a minimal desire to join the combat arms. Women who have joined combat positions have felt excluded by male colleagues and have encountered resistance to their presence and discrimination, although recent studies show that these elements are improving (Schaefer et al. 2015, 55). In 2014, after a three-year study of physical fitness standards to ensure that the military was assessing general fitness and fitness for specific positions, the Canadian Forces implemented gender-neutral standards for entry into the force and other standards depending on the needs of the specialty. The minimum test to enter the force was both gender and age neutral, and those for combat positions remained gender neutral (Schaefer et al. 2015, 57).

To help the force acclimate to women's inclusion in combat, gradual integration was introduced. Women from combat support occupations were phased into combat ones over a ten-year period to accustom men to their presence, and mixed-gender training was implemented to replace the single-gender training that had occurred prior to 1989. Although the CAF wanted to assign women in groups of ten to units to have some type of critical mass, the small number of women able to meet the standards or interested in joining the combat arms made this objective difficult to achieve. Another goal of the integration process was to put women in leadership roles and on deployments, to create mentors for younger recruits, along with a more targeted recruitment process (Schaefer et al. 2015, 57–58). High institutional support in the CAF for women's integration is important for cultural change; however, the integration process hit several obstacles over the years. At the beginning of the process, military commanders were reluctant to integrate women, which led to a difficult work environment for women. For example, on mixed-gender ships, "women's issues" were dealt with separately, making the women feel excluded from the rest of the unit (Schaefer et al. 2015, 60).

Key lessons from the CAF's integration experience illustrates that visible leadership backing and a well-supported integration program facilitates women's assimilation into combat units. According to Canada's National Defense website, more women serve in the Canadian Air Force than in other services, comprising 18.7 percent of personnel. The Navy has 18.4 percent women, with the Army at 12.4 percent. In 2016, Brigadier

---

FEMALE GENERAL COMMANDS NATO MISSION IN IRAQ

In 2016, Brigadier General Jennie Carignan became the first female commander in the combat arms. Although there were other female generals, none had emerged from combat branches. She entered the military in 1986 and trained as a fuel and materials engineer, a job that deals with demolitions and clearing minefields. Carignan was promoted to major general, and in December 2019 she assumed command of NATO forces in Iraq. The mission is a noncombat training and advisory body (Ahmed 2019).

FURTHER READING

Ahmed, Syed. 2019. "Major-General Jennie Carignan Assumes Command of NATO Mission in Iraq." *Canadian Military Family Magazine*, December 4. https://www.cmfmag.ca/operations/major-general-jennie-carignan-assumes -command-of-nato-mission-iraq

Campbell, Meagan. 2016. "Detonating the Glass Ceiling." *Maclean's* 129, no. 23 (June 13): 21–23.

General Jennie Carignan became the first female commander in the combat arms (Campbell 2016, 21). In the Canadian military, women were permitted to serve in all units since 1989, but their attrition rates in combat units is 19 percent versus 8 percent among men, with family obligations as the main reason for the difference (Barry 2013, 23).

The United States and Canada have made great strides in integrating women into all branches of the armed forces. The rise of the women's movement in the 1970s, coupled with increased legislation for women's equality, have led to women's participation, and mostly acceptance, in many military units. Despite positive results, women's percentage in the military, and in combat professions specifically, are relatively small due to issues of discrimination, harassment, and work-life balance.

FURTHER READING

Barry, Ben. 2013. "Women in Combat." *Survival* 55, no. 2: 19–30.

Campbell, Meagan. 2016. "Detonating the Glass Ceiling." *Maclean's* 129, no. 23 (June 13): 21–23.

Chapman, Krystal, and Maya Eichler. 2014. "Engendering Two Solitudes? Media Representations of Women in Combat in Quebec and the Rest of Canada." *International Journal* 69, no. 4: 594–611.

Crowley, Kacy, and Michelle Sandhoff. 2017. "Just a Girl in the Army: U.S. Iraq War Veterans Negotiating Femininity in a Culture of Masculinity." *Armed Forces & Society* 43, no. 2: 221–237. https://doi.org/10.1177%2F0095327X16682045

Decew, Judith Wagner. 1995. "The Combat Exclusion and the Role of Women in the Military." *Hypatia* 10, no. 1 (Winter): 56–73.

Degroot, Gerard J. 2001. "A Few Good Women: Gender Stereotypes, the Military and Peacekeeping." *International Peacekeeping* 8, no. 2 (June): 23. doi:10.1080/13533310108413893

Department of Defense. "2017 Demographics: Profile of the Military Community." http://download.militaryonesource.mil/12038/MOS/Reports/2017-demographics-report.pdf

English, Allan D. 2004. *Understanding Military Culture: A Canadian Perspective*. Montreal: McGill-Queen's University Press. http://www.jstor.org/stable/j.ctt80gt7.11

Feaver, Peter D., and Richard H. Kohn. 2001. *Soldiers and Civilians: The Civil-Military Gap and American National Security*. Cambridge, MA: MIT Press.

Fitrani, Randall, G. S. Cooper, and Ron Matthews. 2016. "Women in Ground Close Combat." *RUSI Journal* 161, no. 1 (February/March): 14–24.

Goldstein, Joshua S. 2001. *War and Gender.* Cambridge: Cambridge University Press.

Haring, Ellen L. 2013. "What Women Bring to the Fight." *Parameters* 43, no. 2 (Summer): 27–32.

Hill, Michael. 2019. "West Point to Graduate Record Number of Black Female Cadets." *The Army Times,* May 23. https://www.armytimes.com/news/your-army/2019/05/23/west-point-to-graduate-record-number-of-black-female-cadets

Holliday, Janet R. 2012. "Female Engagement Teams." *Military Review* (March–April): 90–95.

King, Anthony. 2013a. "The Female Soldier." *Parameters* 43, no. 2 (Summer): 13–25.

King, Anthony. 2013b. "Women in Combat." *The RUSI Journal* 158, no. 1: 4–11. doi:10.1080/03071847.2013.774634

Lane, Andrea. 2017. "Special Men: The Gendered Militarization of the Canadian Armed Forces." *International Journal* 72, no. 4: 463–483. doi:10.1177/0020702017741910

MacKenzie, Megan H. 2012. "Let Women Fight: Ending the U.S. Military's Female Combat Ban." *Foreign Affairs* 91, no. 6 (November/December): 32–42. JSTOR.

Mathers, Jennifer G. 2013. "Women and State Military Forces." In *Women and Wars*, edited by Carol Cohn, 124–145. Malden, MA: Polity Press.

Matheson, Ian, and Ellyn Lyle. 2017. "Gender Bias in Canadian Military Leadership Training." *Journal of Ethnographic and Qualitative Research* 12: 18–28.

McCone, Dave R., Cynthia J. Thomsen, and Janice H. Laurence. 2018. "Introduction to Special Issue on Sexual Harassment and Sexual Assault in the US Military." *Military Psychology* 30, no. 1: 175–180. doi:10.1080/08995605.2018.1479550

McSally, Martha E. 2011. "Defending America in Mixed Company: Gender in the U.S. Armed Forces." *Daedalus* 140, no. 3 (Summer): 148–164.

Nantais, Cynthia, and Martha F. Lee. 1999. "Women in the United States Military: Protectors or Protected?" *Journal of Gender Studies* 8, no. 2: 181–191.

Schaefer, Agnes Gereben, Jennie W. Wenger, Jennifer Kavanagh, Jonathan P. Wong, Gillian S. Oak, Thomas E. Trail, and Todd Nichols. 2015. *Implications of Integrating Women into the Marine Corps Infantry*, 43–90. Santa Monica, CA: RAND. http://www.jstor.org/stable/10.7249/j.ctt19gfk6m.13

Service Women's Action Network (SWAN). 2019. *Women in the Military: Where They Stand*. 10th ed. https://www.servicewomen.org/wp-content/uploads/2019/04/SWAN-Where-we-stand-2019-0416revised.pdf

Siebold, Guy L. 2007. "The Essence of Military Group Cohesion." *Armed Forces & Society* 33, no. 2 (January): 286–295.

Stiehm, Judith Hicks. 1985. "The Generations of Enlisted Women." *Signs* 11, no. 1 (Autumn): 155–175.

Symons, Ellen. 1991. "Under Fire: Canadian Women in Combat." *Canadian Journal of Women and the Law* 4: 477–511.

Szayna, Thomas S., Eric V. Larson, Angela O'Mahony, Sean Robson, Agnes Gereben Schaefer, Miriam Matthews, J. Michael Polich et al. 2016. *Consideration for Integrating Women into Closed Occupations in U.S. Special Operations Forces*. Santa Monica, CA: RAND. https://www.rand.org/pubs/research_reports/RR1058.html

Winslow, Donna, and Jason Dunn. 2002. "Women in the Canadian Forces: Between Legal and Social Integration." *Current Sociology* 50, no. 5 (September): 641–667.

TWO

Latin America and the Caribbean

Latin America has a history of military officers serving as leaders, often using the military to control and oppress their populations. Because of this, women were confronted with two choices. They could join in the revolutionary struggle against the military regime or conform to gender and societal norms that relegated them to the home. Women supported independence struggles throughout Latin America and eventually joined regional militaries. As militaries became more equitable, allowing women to serve in the ranks, the militaries lost their reputation for brutality. Many defense forces in the region cooperate through regional forums, sharing best practices and helping after disasters. Even though women entered the armed forces, they continue to confront barriers based on gender and societal expectations.

Women have also risen to the highest ranks of the military and defense establishments in Latin America. In 2015, General Gina Reque Teran was promoted to general in Bolivia's army and made commander of combat troops, a first in the region. Between 2002 and 2007, five countries named women as defense ministers, including Chile, Colombia, Argentina, Uruguay, and Ecuador. With these appointments and international support, many armed forces have focused on developing gender inclusion policies to understand the specific challenges women face and how they can serve their nations (Burke 2007).

Progress integrating women into Latin America's defense forces remains uneven. Hampered by societal expectations, states often confine women to largely logistical or administrative roles in the military, though others have

32 Women and the Military

opened their ranks fully. Even when women can serve in most positions, they may find their roles dictated by cultures and religions that see them as responsible for the domestic front. Other women are effectively invisible in the militaries of their nations, making up small fractions of the total force.

Most of the militaries of Latin America have allowed women to serve in the professional corps much longer than in the command corps. Cadets who attend and graduate from military academies in Latin America typically join the command corps and are on track to serve as commanding officers. Those who join the military with professional skills, such as doctors, nurses, lawyers, and other professional specialties, will typically join the professional corps of the military.

For the purposes of this chapter, Latin America and the Caribbean include Antigua and Barbuda, Argentina, Bahamas, Barbados, Belize, Bolivia, Brazil Chile, Colombia, Costa Rica, Cuba, Dominica, Dominican Republic, Ecuador, El Salvador, Grenada, Guatemala, Guyana, Haiti, Honduras, Jamaica, Mexico, Nicaragua, Panama, Paraguay, Peru, St. Kitts and Nevis, St. Lucia, St. Vincent and Grenadines, Suriname, Trinidad and Tobago, Uruguay, and Venezuela.

CENTRAL AND SOUTH AMERICA

Societal Views of Masculinity and Warfare

Societal expectations often color women's opportunities. Throughout history, young women were encouraged by their families to remain pure and virtuous, two traits that often stand at odds with the largely masculine and violent nature of the armed forces. Militaries were often used to control society and brutalized women as they did so. In many Latin American countries, women remained in their homes with their parents and siblings until they were married. In Mexico, until 1917, young women under the age of thirty could not move out of their parents' home to live on their own. The strongly patriarchal Catholic religion impacted women by dictating traditional gender roles. Historically, upper-class women were expected to remain in the home as wives and mothers, while lower-class women found themselves cleaning, selling goods, and otherwise functioning as members of the informal workforce.

Although many cultures in Latin America believe that men hold the dominant positions in society and the home, attitudes have begun to change as evidenced by the number of women in the workforce and the positions they hold. The International Labor Organization noted that women's participation in the labor force jumped from 44.5 percent in 1995 to 52.6 percent in 2015 in the region (International Labour Office 2016, 6). This increase was attributed to both improved educational access and health factors along with more subsidized child care. A study published in 2007 found that women still earned about 70 percent of what men earned, though their contribution to the family coffer was fundamental for alleviating poverty for many families (Montano and Rico 2007, 1). Even with their new responsibilities outside the home, women bear a disproportionate share of domestic requirements.

Women continue to confront violence in relationships as well as in society. A recent report by the World Health Organization indicated that between 23 percent and 40 percent of women in Latin America and the Caribbean experienced intimate partner violence and nonpartner sexual violence, often in the workplace. Many of the militaries in the region are specifically attempting to address sexual assault and harassment in their ranks (García-Moreno et al. 2013, 47). In Argentina, the armed forces have created twenty-one gender offices devoted to providing guidance on how to incorporate gender into planning and respond to complaints about gender issues like working conditions, maternity leave, and child care policies, while helping raise awareness of issues that disproportionately affect women (Badaro 2014, 88). While many initially expressed skepticism about the creation of these organizations, they have helped raise important workers' rights, concerns that were ignored previously (Badaro 2014, 95).

The military has often served as an outlet for women to challenge typical gender roles. When called upon, women have served across the breadth of military specialties, including as combat leaders and revolutionaries, usually considered to be the domain of men. They have served in functions where men could not, including as spies, unnoticed by careless combatants. They have also worked in more traditional female roles such as logistics efforts and medical positions.

In some countries, conscription served as an educational experience to build national pride though mandatory service, a requirement rarely extended to women. As such, conscription, at times, reinforced traditional gender roles. Militaries were sometimes used as equalizing forces among men, as they were compelled to serve for a bounded period of time. Both Argentina and Ecuador used their militaries to build nationalism. While Argentina made deliberate strides to attract women to service, Ecuador did not. Mandatory service in Argentina emphasized nationalist sentiments, reaching indigenous and poor segments of the population who were underserved by education systems. Men's military training reinforced traditional gender norms where women stewarded home life and men were warriors (Masson 2017, 38). The military played a major role in the daily and political life of the country, even before the 1976 coup that established the military-run government.

When the Argentinian government transitioned in 1976, many of the previously repressed Argentine citizens believed that democratizing the armed forces would be a positive step forward to heal the country and transform gender roles (Masson 2017, 33). The military academy, once considered a bastion of the upper class, was voluntarily integrated by the military and included men and women from all parts of society. This integration has been challenging. Masson found that during a routine field exercise, men virtually ignored female cadets, degrading their value to the organization (Masson 2017, 39). Men were so threatened by the inclusion of women into their previously male-only spaces that many cadets and officers believed that the future of the military was at stake. Regardless of this belief, women continue to matriculate at the military academy.

While forbidding forcible recruitment, the Venezuelan Constitution incentivizes Venezuelans to register for service, maintaining that every citizen has a duty to perform military service, either in the armed forces or militia (Strønen 2016, 20). Those individuals who do enlist are guaranteed permanent dental care and life insurance. Venezuelans who cannot prove that they have served may be penalized by restrictions on attending university, obtaining a driver's license, working for state and national governments, and competing for and earning state scholarship money.

In Ecuador, the military helped institutionalize racial and ethnic integration during the twentieth century, though this integration has not extended to women (Polga-Hecimovich 2019, 20). Women are still restricted to the Navy, and the gender imbalance remains high in the armed forces with women making up just 3 percent of the total military population. A 2013 gender policy sought to further integrate women in the military with a focus on equality and opportunities, though true progress remains slow (Donadio 2016, 159).

Revolutionary struggles in the region influenced the expansion of women's roles outside the home and societal views on gender and warfare. In Nicaragua, a strong Catholic tradition encouraged women to defer to men, though they often served as the head of the house when men left in search of work or fought as members of the Sandinista National Liberation

Front (FSLN). Women also joined the FSLN, fighting to establish a new government. After the end of the revolutionary fight, many women voluntarily returned to the home. After joining the FSLN, Gladys Baez was captured by government forces and kept in solitary confinement and forced to work, much as her male counterparts were. Interviewed later, she said that her views on women in the military had changed. "Women have proved themselves to be heroic, combative, courageous and able. But we *are* less tough, we march slower, and above all we have children. You can't have a regular army poised for instant mobilization based on a floating population" (Harris 1988, 204).

In Cuba, the passage of the Family Code in 1975 recognized the contribution that women made to the revolution (1953–1959) and directed men to play an equal role in the division of labor at home. There was little enforcement, and women still executed the bulk of domestic responsibilities but pushed for additional support through legal means (Sloan 2011, 114). Women were guaranteed six weeks of paid leave prior to the birth of a child and twelve weeks after the birth. This allowed women some flexibility to balance careers and families.

In Venezuela, before President Hugo Chavez's 1999 Bolivarian Revolution, the military attracted officers from the wealthiest neighborhoods, although some men would simply buy their way out of service. Most soldiers came from lower and middle socioeconomic classes. Both President Chavez, who served from 1999 until 2013, and President Nicolas Maduro, serving since 2013, have modified the perception that officers only come from wealthy families. By changing this view, the two leaders helped attract more men and women from minority groups and lower socioeconomic backgrounds (Strønen 2015, 10). Women in Venezuela serve as part of the Bolivarian Armed Forces, making up 21 percent of total personnel in 2016, a 5 percent increase from 2014 (Donadio 2016, 212). Women also participate in the National Bolivarian Militia. Described as people in arms, the militia was formed to support the military in situations of extreme need, like natural disasters or invasion. Strønen found that women serving in Venezuela often emphasized their dual duties as soldiers and women. Not only did they perform to the best of their abilities as members of the military, but they also maintained their roles as wives and mothers (Strønen 2015, 7).

Cooperation among states in many areas has become increasingly common in Latin America. States come together to better understand the roles that women may fill and barriers they may face. Others have formed

36 Women and the Military

cooperative defense agreements. The armed forces of Latin America organized the first international event on gender in the armed forces in the region, assisted by the United Nations in November 2007. The region also hosted Women in Military and Security Conferences (WIMCON) in conjunction with U.S. Southern Command (SOUTHCOM). These conferences engender dialogue, share best practices, and consider how to adapt military and defense practices to allow women to serve to the best of their abilities.

Factors Influencing Change

Women have fought successfully alongside men for many years in both national defense forces as well as revolutionary struggles. While valuable, their service has not always brought increased equality or respect for their contribution to society. However, expanded need for recruits due to demographic changes are shifting women's roles in the military. Additionally, the changing nature of warfare has impacted the need for women to fill the ranks. In some cases, war is not always executed on a traditional battlefield, with a frontline and rear area. This aspect affects the concept of combat and where women serve. Additionally, militaries are reimagining their roles in society and have embarked on more peace and humanitarian operations. As such, militaries are recognizing women's value in a variety of military operations.

Another factor that has led to governments increasing the number of women in their ranks relates to women's past successful performance. Even without formal government support, women served effectively during struggles for independence. During the long Mexican Revolution (1910–1920), female rebels on both sides of the fight followed their husbands into battle, serving as medical attendants or as quartermasters, obtaining food and ammunition (Fuentes 1995, 528). Other women joined the Federal Army and catered food to troops who lacked families nearby (Jensen 2012, 217). During the second revolutionary wave in 1913, women were drafted into service in the state-controlled powder mills or as cooks near the front (Fuentes 1995, 533). Even after this conscription, women and men still occupied very distinct roles with women providing food and other logistical support, while men fought. Women smuggled arms and ammunition from the United States, using special slings set up under their skirts. Others dressed like local women, moving through enemy ranks to collect intelligence while ostensibly distributing food.

In addition to their support roles during the revolution, some women served as leaders of combat units. Rosa Bobadilla attained the rank of colonel after the death of her husband and was known for the "unyielding discipline of the troops under her command" (Fuentes 1995, 536). Margarita Neri was known for her readiness to torture and kill. One account suggests that she stoned a man to death to escape punishment after she was discovered to have killed her own husband before joining the army. In the Constitutional armies, women were motivated to fight by patriotism and love of their country. Women were shown in images "fitted out with horses, rifles, and cartridge belts," suggesting that their roles were more than just those of support (Fuentes 1995, 540). In 1914, Petra Herrera formed an independent brigade of female soldiers after they were denied recognition for their role in the Battle of Torreón (Jensen 2012, 218). As a commander, Herrera forced men to leave her camp at night in the interest of protecting her soldiers. By the end of the Mexican Revolution, the new war minister, General Joaquin Amara, banned female soldiers from the army barracks, believing that they detracted from good order and discipline (Jensen 2012, 218). Women were often overlooked after hostilities ended, though some earned pensions if their commanding officers would vouch for their contributions (Jensen 2012, 223).

It was not until 2000 that women could attend Mexico's military academies, allowing them to earn places in the command corps; women still serve overwhelmingly in the professional corps. Women have joined in increasing numbers after one of the military's key functions became fighting organized crime. Currently, women make up around 6 percent of Army and Air Force and 16 percent of the Navy (Donadio 2016, 186). While men are required to serve, women may volunteer and their participation numbers doubled in just one year from 2008 to 2009 (Moyano 2011, 18). Still banned from infantry roles in the Army, women are fully integrated across the Navy.

Women participated in revolutionary struggles in several other countries including Cuba, Nicaragua, El Salvador, and Colombia, and their performance has influenced their position in society. Celia Sanchez organized the first battalion of female combatants, the Mariana Grajales Brigade in 1958, and was also the first woman to fire a weapon in battle in Cuba (Thomas-Woodward 2003, 156). Women who served in the Mariana Grajales unit remained in the military after the end of the revolution, many as officers. Today, women, unlike men, are not required to serve in the Cuban military, though the Cuban government hopes that guaranteed

Women participate in operations in northeastern Mexico, February 24, 2018. Women joined the Mexican military in increasing numbers to help fight organized crime, though are still barred from direct ground combat. (Roberto Galan/Dreamstime.com)

admittance to university after service will attract women. While many serve in lower ranks, some women do hold significant responsibility. Lieutenant Colonel Victoria Arrauz Caraballo served as the second in command of the Border Guard Battalion, near the U.S. Naval facility at Guantanamo Bay in 2006 (Puebla 2003).

In Nicaragua, women fought in the FSLN, with estimates suggesting that at least 30 percent of the fighting force was comprised of women, reportedly the highest proportion of any previous Latin American liberation struggle (Harris 1988, 191). Many older Sandinista men proudly commented that "las mujeres pelearon como varones" or "women fought as men" during the revolutionary struggle (Mulinari 1998, 158). How women were portrayed was an important factor in their service. They were often depicted in one of three ways: the woman guerrilla fighter, the woman mother, and the woman revolutionary. These images showed that women's roles in the revolution were important, giving them a level of equality with men. Indeed, some women rose to the highest ranks of the organization. As women joined guerilla life,

Female soldiers march in the Salvadoran military Independence Day parades in Paseo Escalon, San Salvador. While women also served in the Farabundo Marti National Liberation Front (FMLN) during the Salvadoran Civil War, they have not enjoyed full integration in the military. Women are limited to noncombat roles. (Stuart456/Dreamstime.com)

sometimes serving on the frontlines, the gender divisions blurred and "there were no men, no women, only fighters" (Harris 1988, 194).

In a 1980 speech, a founder of the FSLN, Commander Tomas Borge, announced that "women were in the front line of battle, whether they threw homemade bombs or were in the trenches. They were in the leadership of military units, on the firing line during the war, and therefore have every right in the world to be in the front line during the period of reconstruction" (Harris 1988, 194). However, after the end of the revolution, many women were pushed out of combat roles into administrative and logistical positions. Currently, Nicaragua has an all-volunteer force and women may serve in the command corps, allowing them the opportunity to serve in leadership potions, rather than simply as professional lawyers, doctors, and other health care professionals.

40 Women and the Military

In El Salvador, women played especially valuable roles as members of the Farabundo Marti National Liberation Front (FMLN) as skilled medics and radio operators between 1979 and 1992. They had these opportunities because of their time in the refugee camps after the outbreak of the Salvadoran Civil War, where they learned to read and received training (Darden 2015, 457). Their service in the struggle for independence has not translated to full integration in the military, comprising only 5 percent of the total military population. They are largely limited to noncombat roles and serve only as junior officers.

While women were actively recruited to support the Revolutionary Armed Forces of Colombia (FARC), Colombia's national armed forces only require women to serve in times of national emergency, while men are required to perform two years of military service. Donadio found that even if women were conscripted, their service would be in support roles, rather than frontline combat (Donadio 2016, 141). Women were allowed to matriculate at the defense academy starting in 2008, expanding their possible roles in the military from professional to other logistics and administrative-based roles (McNeish, Andrade, and Vallejo 2015, 20).

Many women were victimized by the FARC as a result of the ongoing civil war; others ignored this abuse, choosing to enlist and prove their worth as women (Kazman 2019, 6). In the FARC, women shared the same responsibilities as men, sometimes serving as active combatants, mine layers, or workers around the camp. Kazman noted that women joined the FARC because of a commitment to the cause, an interest in weapons and the military, and a desire for power (Kazman 2019, 11). Others joined to remain with family or improve their standing in the country. She also found that women left the FARC for a variety of reasons. Often, their gender and the children they bore while members of the group forced them to leave to provide a better life for their families. While the FARC purported to advocate for gender equality, deserters from the organization and academics suggest that women faced many of the same issues as in the national defense forces, with few able to rise above junior officer ranks (Kazman 2019, 22).

Continued Successes in the Military

Regardless of why women join the military, many have largely succeeded in their roles, and this fact is changing attitudes regarding women's service in the military. In 2015, Gina Reque Teran was named Bolivia's first female army general. Though Venezuela had both a female general and admiral prior to her rise through the ranks, she is the first to command combat troops (Tegel 2015). The first group of forty-seven female army officers graduated during the 1980s. Until 2017, women were only allowed to serve as officers in the Bolivian army, forbidden from serving as soldiers.

Belizean Lieutenant Alma Pinelo earned the title of honor graduate after graduating from the four-month International Maritime Officer Course at the U.S. Coast Guard Training Center in Virginia. She is the first Belizean and woman to receive this award (*The San Pedro Sun* 2019). Shortly after her return to Belize, she was promoted to lieutenant commander in a ceremony attended by the commandant of the Belizean Coast Guard. When interviewed, she advocated for continued integration because "women think differently, and that reflects in military operations. Our different focus from that of men yields good results, and now it's valued" (Dussán 2018). The country is capitalizing on her success with a recruiting video for the Belizean Coast Guard, specifically targeting women with strong leadership skills for accessions and training with partner nations (Ministry National Security 2019).

Furthermore, in Belize, women have served in both regular and volunteer forces, since 1980, when thirty women volunteered as part of the first female platoon (Phillips 2002). In 2019, Nefretery Marin, the leader of the Belizean People's Front, advocated for the creation of an elite female special forces unit in the military (Marin 2019). Citing the example of the Russian Women's Battalion of Death, a World War I unit, and the Norwegian all-female special forces unit, she noted that training, discipline, and leadership would help to overcome the risks associated with women in the military, including injury, sexual harassment, and violence.

Women in the Belizean Police Department, Defense Force, and National Coast Guard participate in an annual "Wonder Woman Competition" during which teams of women compete over a three-day period to showcase the contributions made through their service ("Belize Super-Women Compete in Grueling Match" 2019). The teams take part in an eight-mile march, a cross-fit competition, and an ocean swim.

Women's success in Honduras is reflected in their ability to perform at the same levels as men in a variety of areas. In 2016, Sergeant Yesica Carolina Baires graduated from the Honduran Sapper Leader Course. Even after discouragement from men in her unit and hearing that only men could graduate from the school, she persevered, becoming the first woman to graduate from the school (Spero 2016). Despite their success, women still comprise less than 5 percent of the overall force in Honduras and have not yet achieved higher ranks of command (Donadio 2016, 177). Honduras provides personnel for missions in Haiti and the Western Sahara, and while women are technically permitted to participate in peacekeeping operations, they have not done so (Donadio 2016, 179).

In contrast to Honduras's small number of military women, about 20 percent of Uruguay's armed forces are female, and women may serve in any role, including infantry and armor, if they can meet the standards (Donadio 2016, 207). Uruguay's military is one of the highest per capita contributors to peacekeeping operations around the world, and women have served in the Uruguayan contingent in both Haiti and the Democratic Republic of the Congo. Economic despair and an opportunity to learn military skills have led rural women, with few prospects in the countryside, to join the military (Gallardo 2016). To better integrate women across the force, the military has modified equipment to fit smaller statures before women can join new branches, suggesting that some perceptions of women's abilities may still hamper women's integration across the armed forces (Dialogo 2013).

Some militaries need women to augment shortfalls in the ranks, and this fact has offered women increased opportunities in the armed forces. In Barbados, the deputy chief of staff, Commander Errington Shurland, announced that due to challenges in filling its ranks with qualified and eligible applicants, it would lift restrictions on the numbers of women serving. His efforts were rewarded when the country had to temporarily reject new applications from women because of the large number received (Cox 2016).

Women first joined the Guyana Defense Force in 1967, as members of the Women's Army Corps. This unit was designed to fill a manpower shortage in the face of the Venezuelan seizure of Ankoko Island in the Corentyne River in 1966. Four women participated in a one-week orientation course at Atkinson Field, forming the cadre for the other fifty-six women who would later join them. All sixty women practiced drill, field craft, shooting, and physical fitness, formally joining the military on March 12, 1967, creating the first detachment of women established in the Anglophone Caribbean States (*Kaieteur News* 2017). In the early years of women's integration, they often served in communications, administrative, and domestic duties, to free men for service elsewhere. However, at a service to mark the fifty-two years of service to the nation, Chief of Staff Brigadier Patrick West challenged women to "seek education gains in areas of technology," announcing that women who aspired to join the GDF must be able to join technical units (*Guyana Times* 2019).

Changing Battlefield

The character of warfare has changed with an increased focus on peace-keeping rather than traditional combat. In many countries, women were first allowed entry into military academies after the end of the Cold War, when international security trends appeared to shift away from large-scale combat to security cooperation, confidence-building measures, and peace operations around the world. By graduating from the military academies, women earned admittance into most specialties in the combat corps, though some countries still prohibit women from serving in infantry and armored forces.

Most observers believe that the traditional battlefield with a distinguishable front is no longer the norm and this lack of a linear battlefield impacts women's service. Preventing women from serving in combat roles hampers their promotion and potential in the military (Kussrow 2018, 35). Furthermore, the regional security focus has also shifted from one of defense against external enemies and internal coups, to cooperation, peace operations, and support to public security. Defense forces are increasingly involved with stabilization efforts after natural and human-made disasters. Participation in United Nations peace operations has led militaries to emphasize different capabilities than previously and foster an ability to adapt to social, cultural, and political changes. With a broadened focus on public security, states are recognizing that women bring unique skills to experiences that strengthen peace efforts. Military-led governments, once the norm in Chile, Argentina, and many other states in the region, have now become the exception with guerrilla fighters integrated into more democratic states and societies. As the role of the armed forces in Latin America has changed, so too has the role that women can play (Kussrow 2018, 34).

The largest country in the region, Brazil, has failed to make substantial progress on integrating women into its peacekeeping operations. With one of the largest militaries in Latin America, Brazil has fewer women participating in peacekeeping operations than Argentina, Peru, and Uruguay (Hirst and Nasser 2014). The Brazilian military has debated what type of weapons experience, training, and rank a female officer would need to join peacekeeping operations. This deliberation has limited the number of women who serve in these missions, with most coming from the Navy. Since 2006, at least 124 women from the Brazilian Army have deployed to Haiti as dentists, nurses, translators, and engineers, though at any given time, only about 1 percent of the 1,678 troops deployed from Brazil globally are women (Giannini, Lima, and Pereira 2016, 183). In 2016, almost a third of new recruits for the armed forces were women, although women only comprise about 7 percent of all the people serving in the country's armed forces (Giannini, Lima, and Pereira 2016, 180). While women have served in the command corps since 2012, they are confined to medical and logistics roles. They remain banned from most frontline combat roles, except in the Air Force, where they can serve as aviators. Brazil still maintains a Women's Corps for both the Navy and Air Force.

Created in 2009 to serve as a military coordinating body for the Union of South American Nations, the South American Defense Council conducted several studies on women's roles in Brazil, Argentina, and Chile. The council noted that women have not yet attained the highest ranks of leadership and attributed this finding to the short time women have served in particular roles. As a result, the council concluded that women should not face policy

---

BRAZIL

Lieutenant Commander Marcia Andrade Braga received the United Nations (UN) Military Gender Advocate of the Year Award in 2019 for her role in promoting the principles of women, peace, and security. As part of her role in the peacekeeping operations in Central Africa, she created a network of gender advisers to share best practices. She also advocated for mixed-gender teams to allow the teams to better access all parts of the population and provide help where it is needed the most. The Brazilian military has a mixed record of integrating women into peacekeeping operations, and this award speaks to the progress the country has made.

FURTHER READING

"Brazilian Woman Wins UN Military Gender Advocate Award." 2019. *Agencia-Brasil*, March 28. http://agenciabrasil.ebc.com.br/en/internacional/noticia /2019-03/brazilian-woman-wins-un-military-gender-advocate-award

barriers to hamper their ability for promotion, though unofficial societal imposed barriers may still exist (Frederic and Calandron 2015, 12).

The shift to civilian-controlled governments in Latin America has also come with a move toward democratizing the military forces of the countries in the region. By opening their ranks to women and other previously disenfranchised populations, the militaries want to recover from previous experiences with military dictatorships (Giannini, Lima, and Pereira 2016, 180). These militaries had to earn the trust of both their people and the international community. Some militaries were completely disbanded after the end of regimes, while others were restructured, with new recruits brought into the ranks. Chile and Argentina have both made substantial progress in democratizing their armed forces.

In Chile, the Women's Service Military allowed women to serve in 1974. The military encouraged women to join as volunteers in the 1990s when the country moved away from conscription. Women were still confined to support and administrative roles. They were admitted into the Military Aviation Academy of the Air Force, placing them one step closer to the frontlines in 2000, with three times the number of applicants as slots allocated. Chile advanced a set of guiding principles to level the playing field for women. These policies included integrating teams and equal treatment based on which professional skills each participant possessed (Frederic and Calandron 2015, 3). Just three years later, women competed for engineer and signal roles though remained banned from frontline combat. By 2004, women made up a fifth of new recruits annually, a huge step for them. Finally, in 2016, Chile opened all combat and frontline roles in the Chilean Army (Ross 2005).

In contrast to Brazil, the Chilean Ministry of Defense has actively established goals to increase the number of women who serve in peace operations. The country identified all positions available to women candidates for peace support operations and removed many restrictions on the deployment of female staff in the mission area. The military also maintains records on where women serve in peace operations to monitor and analyze women's experiences. Chile was among the first countries in Latin America to launch a National Action Plan to implement UN Resolution 1325. Importantly for the region, Chilean officers have worked with other regional militaries, including Ecuador and Paraguay, on best practices to integrate women into the defense forces. In 2014, of the 425 Chilean security personnel in Haiti, fifteen were women (Van Meter 2014). They supported ground units through reconnaissance efforts and repairing roads.

A female soldier rehearses for the annual military parade, held every September, to commemorate the independence of Chile. Women joined the Chilean military in 1974 and may now serve in all jobs. (Luis Sandoval Mandujano/Dreamstime.com)

Argentina also opened its military to women, with an eye toward recovering from years of military rule. Women joined the Army's professional corps in 1981, though had to wait until the mid-1990s before they could attend Colegio Militar de la Nacion (CMN), the military academy for the Argentine Army (Kussrow 2018, 37). Argentina allowed women to enter technical schools to become noncommissioned officers in the Army in 1996, though they were already integrated in the Air Force and Navy in 1980.

The thirteen women who graduated from the Argentine military academy in December 2000 were trailblazers and served as the first female military officers in the command corps in Latin America (Badaro 2014, 87). The military used the integration of the academy to improve its international image. The government initially developed quota systems, limiting the number of women who could serve to around 15 percent of the total force (Frederic 2015, 3). These quotas were soon lifted as military service gained popularity among women. Women earned the right to serve

ARGENTINA

In 2018, an Argentine Air Force second lieutenant was selected to participate in an exchange program with the United States. Sofia Vier spent a year improving her English skills as well as undergoing flight training, including simulator training. Argentina increased their efforts to recruit women to the military, opening the military academies, including the Cordoba Flight School, where Vier graduated after a year of training. She is the first Argentine pilot to be selected for this exchange.

FURTHER READING

"Argentine Female Pilot Participates in U.S. Exchange Program." 2018. U.S. Embassy in Argentina, April 13. https://ar.usembassy.gov/argentine-female -pilot-participates-in-u-s-exchange-program

---

as marines, pilots, and submariners in the Navy and Air Force in 2008 and, by 2013, they joined the Army ground combat branches. Argentina has also made strides in peacekeeping efforts with a recent contingent made up of 23 women and 417 men (Frederic and Calandron 2015, 13).

As the first Argentinian female minister of defense, Nilda Garre continued earlier reform efforts in the military by instituting the Observation on the Integration of Women in the Armed Forces in 2005. This organization was designed to understand how women were being received and treated in the military. She also created a Gender Policy Council for Defense (GPC) to serve as an adviser to the Ministry of Defense. This council included officers, noncommissioned officers, representatives from NGOs, and from other interested parties (Masson 2017, 33). This policy council recommended many reforms to balance service with protection. It noted that ingrained cultural norms presented barriers to service for women. Since military members were forbidden from joining unions, the council discovered that military workplace standards were below the rest of Argentine society. As such, the GPC standardized issues of sick and paid family leave, issues that benefited both men and women (Frederic 2015, 13). Women had very little formal protection from participating in combat, close order drill, and shooting requirements while pregnant, relying on commanding officers' judgement regarding women's participation. Since these events posed potential health problems for mother and child, the GPC implemented positive changes (Frederic 2015, 12).

48   Women and the Military

Argentine military culture demands that soldiers work as many hours as their superior commanders. This expectation often resulted in shifts that extended over twenty-four-hour periods over the course of a month. Members of the GPC presented the minister of defense with a document that reduced the working hours, in conjunction with international and national norms, allowing both men and women to maintain a more stable personal life (Frederic 2015, 17). The measure distinguished between war and peacetime service, allowing all military members to benefit from regulated working hours.

Women who join the Argentine military claim to be aware of the gendered reality of the military. With this knowledge, some explain that they want to be "just one of the guys" (Badaro 2014, 87). This perception results in the acceptance of inappropriate treatment. For example, the GPC highlighted that women were often reluctant to complain about harsh treatment, even when some conduct would be considered sexual harassment in other professions. Badaro found that the women who join "enact a paradoxical individuality that destabilizes traditional conceptions of military individuality and can operate as a source of individual agency" (Badaro 2014, 87). In this way, military women often challenge the norm of what it means to be a soldier, while redefining what a woman can do and how they can act. Badaro interviewed several female cadets at the academy. Stressing that they preferred to be treated as cadets, they noted femininity had no place in the barracks. However, they also described how they continued to dress up in their free time, maintaining some individuality. Though they wanted to be perceived as cadets, the women complained that they were required to present a traditionally feminine appearance donning earrings, makeup, skirts, and heels for parades, regardless of the weather, causing them to stand out from the rest of the cadets (Badaro 2014, 93).

A recent study found that many senior ranking officers in the Argentine military believed that the experience of fatherhood, combined with military experience, made an officer ready to assume positions of command in regiments, ships, and squadrons (Frederic and Masson 2015, 76). While mothers also have responsibilities to the children, it is unclear if senior officers will credit motherhood as a similarly qualifying preparation period for the assumption of command. Ingrained cultural norms may prove stronger than policy for women in Argentina.

The Guatemalan army recently established a Female Engagement Team platoon preparing women to serve more effectively in humanitarian and peace operations (Ramos 2019). About 10 percent of the total Guatemalan service members in the land, sea, and air forces are women. Army Captain Andrea Araujo noted that "We train to perform any mission, and soon we'll reach all ranks and positions. It's clear that our commanders identified the advantages of our skills: discipline, concentration, precision, organization, and sensitivity. Our inclusion is necessary to achieve better results" (Dussán 2018).

Peru and Paraguay provide few options for women in the services. While women in Paraguay have served as nurses in the professional corps since 1932, they are restricted to administrative and logistics roles in the command corps (Donadio 2016, 197). They have yet to break into the midgrade ranks of the officer corps and are banned from serving as soldiers and noncommissioned officers. Women have only been able to serve in Peru's military since 1998 and the Company of Non-Quarterly Active Women's Service (SANAF) allows work in administrative roles in Army Command Headquarters. They are still restricted from serving in combat weapons, special forces, and diving specialties, significantly limiting their options for promotion.

CARIBBEAN FORCES

Many countries in the Caribbean rely on small armed forces for defense and disaster relief. These countries allow women to serve mostly in support roles. Several countries lack traditional military forces, instead relying on police forces and coast guards. With an estimated 250 members of their armed forces, the Antigua and Barbuda Defense Force recruits men and women between the ages of eighteen and twenty-three who have finished their secondary school education. Though women are welcome, a report from 2003 notes that only thirty-six women serve and just two of them as officers (Osoba 2003). The country also has a National Cadet Corps, a high school group that trains young men and women to be members of the military and instills discipline, loyalty, leadership, and citizenship. There are about 180 men and women in this organization (Donadio 2016, 90).

The Royal Bahamas Defense Force is responsible for the defense of the Bahamas, aiding law and order and assisting with humanitarian tasks with local and international partners. About 30 percent of the 1,300-member Defense Force, primarily a naval organization, consists of women. With so few people serving, the force has established cooperative training efforts

50   Women and the Military

with the United Kingdom as well as the United States, and men and women train abroad for service (Donadio 2016, 90).

Women had once served as members of the West Indies Regiment in Jamaica, but were forbidden from service after independence in 1962. Women joined the Jamaican Defense Forces (JDF) in August 1976, with just five potential officers serving as members of the JDF Women's Unit, a sub-unit of the Support and Services Battalion. Many of these women broke barriers, becoming parachutists and divers. Heather George became a member of the Jamaican military parachuting team, despite her fear of heights. Kathleen Joy Rowe joined the Coast Guard, becoming the first female diver in the Jamaican Coast Guard (Ford 2012, 213). In February 2019, Antonette Wemyss-Gorman became the first female commander of the Maritime, Air and Cyber Command, with oversight for the Jamaica Defense Force Coast Guard, the JDF Air Wing, and the Military Cyber Corps. She was also the first woman to go to sea with the JDF after she completed the International Midshipman Course at Britannia Royal Naval College in the United Kingdom in 1994 ("Four JDF Senior Officers Promoted" 2019).

Women make up 20 percent of the Jamaican Defense Forces and the chief of staff's goal is to "create a force in which there will be no reference to quota" (Wilson-Harris 2019). Instead, he would like to build a competence-based force, rather than one based on a required composition. He acknowledged the difficulty of recruiting women to the force with the level of physical demands placed on all who join the JDF.

Women serve in the St. Kitts-Nevis Defense Force and the Coast Guard Unit with few restrictions on their service. A woman has commanded the basic training unit where civilians train to be soldiers, completing tasks like map reading, field craft, physical fitness, drill, and shooting courses. The country is also part of the Regional Security System (*St. Kitts & Nevis Observer* 2017).

In the Suriname Defense Organization, women make up 6 percent of the forces and typically hold work in administrative, logistical, health care, and intelligence positions. They remain barred from combat units because of their perceived physical, tactical, and psychological weaknesses (Lodge and Bak 2015). Of the 243 women serving, 18 of them are officers. The Deputy Director Ministry of Defense of Suriname, Danielle Veira, notes that the country wants to eliminate quotas, though recruiting efforts are still heavily geared toward attracting women. Two members of the South Dakota National Guard partnered with twenty-two women from the Suriname Defense Force to discuss gender equality, education and training, and career management (U.S. Embassy Paramaribo 2015). In 2018, Suriname held a Women in the Military Conference to help the commander of the Suriname Defense Force, Colonel Robert Kartodikromo, understand how he could improve the working conditions and opportunities available to women in the SDF.

In 1980, women joined the Women's Detachment in the Trinidad and Tobago Defense Force (TTDF), part of the Service and Support Battalion (Phillips 1997). Women held traditional roles in communications and administrative positions and served as bodyboards to government officials. Currently, they may now serve in any branch and military occupational specialty and have equal access to education, training, and promotion opportunities. Women are 14 percent of the overall force and about 16 percent of the officers (Donadio 2016, 97). A clinical psychologist and consultant for the Military Community Support Service, Dianne Douglas noted that with only 14 percent women, they are often showcased for special events. However, when they are not needed for publicity, their concerns are ignored (Augustine 2019). The TTDF signed onto the HeForShe Campaign, a UN Women's Campaign aimed at strengthening gender equality efforts to counter this perception.

Countries without Traditional Military Forces

Several countries in Latin America do not have traditional defense forces, instead relying on police forces, coast guards, or international stabilization efforts to maintain order. After a series of bloody and violent coups, Haiti's military was disbanded in 1995. The Haitian National Police and Haitian Coast Guard were created in their stead, and the UN Stabilization Mission to Haiti (MINUSTAH), a disarmament and demobilization effort, started to maintain public order and prepare for a transition to democracy.

In 2017, the Haitian minister of defense announced that the country would reinstate the armed forces. Many of the men who make up the leadership ranks also served in the disbanded military. Concerned that this new army may perpetuate many of the same crimes as the last, domestic and international critics perceive the organization as a reconstituted army, rather than a new, changed army (Johnston 2018). The minister of defense conveyed that the military would be primarily responsible for responding to earthquakes, contraband, and poverty. The amended charter for the

52   Women and the Military

military requires the military to contain 30 percent women, although they are currently confined to the engineering, medical, and logistics corps. The Haitian military is heavily dependent on external militaries for training, and women have traveled to other countries in the region for military exercises and training.

In both Costa Rica and Panama, national police forces replaced militaries. The Costa Rican Public Force and Coast Guard, established in 1948, maintain national sovereignty and ensure security, peace, and public order, functioning much as a military might. Panama disbanded its military after 1994 with women comprising just 8 percent of the overall force. By 2016, no women had been promoted above the rank of major in the national police (Donadio 2016, 109).

The countries of the Caribbean generally share a common agenda and participate in regional forums, dating back to their cooperation as part of the West Indies Regiment, an infantry unit for the British Army between 1795 and 1927. Many of these nations, including Dominica, Grenada, St. Lucia, and Saint Vincent and the Grenadines, do not have militaries, instead relying on small police forces and Coast Guards to maintain security. These organizations often cooperate on humanitarian relief efforts in the region. Dominica is one of the four founding members of the Regional Security System, an organization designed for collective response to threats impacting the stability of the region. It maintains a police force, which acts to defend the state when required. Grenada has a small police force and a Coast Guard. As of 2014, the highest-ranking woman in the police force, Inspector Rebecca Jones, was tasked with forming a "Women's Arm" with the RGPF, the Royal Grenada Police Force. There are no laws prohibiting women from joining the RGPF, though domestic violence and gender-based violence remain common. Women have served in the Royal St. Lucia Police Force since 1958, when Veronica Adley joined the service. She served for thirty-one years before retiring as the assistant superintendent. St. Vincent and the Grenadines has a Special Services Unit as part of its police force that protects the state against external military threats and insurrections.

Other Issues

A recent study conducted among the defense forces of the Dominican Republic, Belize, and Barbados noted that high rates of mental health issues, substance abuse issues, and the stressors of military life may be associated with higher rates of risky sexual behavior (Asefnia, Cowan, and Werth 2017, 154). Women serve in each of these countries but are limited in how they contribute. In the Dominican Republic, women make up over 21 percent of the total armed forces in the country, though have only achieved junior officer ranks of the command corps. Women make up at least 10 percent of the armed forces in Barbados.

In these countries, military personnel may be responsible for "bridging contact" between high-risk populations, including sex workers (Asefnia, Cowan, and Werth 2017, 154). The study found that the personnel serving in the Dominican Police Force were likely to report inconsistent condom use, even with multiple sexual partners in a year. Similarly, in the Barbados Defense Force, both men and women reported increased rates of sex without condoms, even with multiple sexual partners (Asefnia, Cowan, and Werth 2017, 155). While HIV-positive recruits are forbidden from joining the military, current levels of HIV infection are in line with the population of these three countries, suggesting that men and women serving have a higher prevalence of infection while on active duty. In addition, the researchers found that men and women participated in this study voluntarily, although several declined to participate after disclosing their HIV-positive status.

Additionally, men and women who serve in the Dominican Republic and Barbados were more likely to report mental health conditions, including depression and post-traumatic stress disorder (PTSD). While members of these forces do not usually serve outside their countries, they often participate in border protection, disaster relief programs, emergency response operations, drug interdiction efforts, and police assistance (Asefnia, Cowan, and Werth 2017, 157). Many of the service members report that they were personally affected by natural disasters or by violent crimes. In addition to incidents with mental health impacts, the service men and women surveyed admitted to disordered alcohol use, including excessive alcohol consumption. The researchers found that alcohol consumption is "framed as a component of military culture" (Asefnia, Cowan, and Werth 2017, 158).

In many countries in Latin America, women have progressed, but have a long way to go to achieve equality. However, over the past thirty years, women have broken new barriers, often proving their worth in international training and peacekeeping operations. Social and cultural expectations are changing slowly with women who choose to serve in the militaries frequently at the forefront of this change.

FURTHER READING

Asefnia, Nakisa, Lisa Cowan, and Rose Werth. 2017. "HIV Risk Behavior and Prevention Considerations among Military Personnel in Three Caribbean Region Countries: Belize, Barbados, and the Dominican Republic." *Current HIV Research* 15, no. 3: 154–160. https://doi: 10.2174/1570162X15666170517121316

Augustine, Marlene. 2019. "Defence Force Needs More Women." *Trinidad and Tobago Newsday*, February 15.

Badaro, Maximo. 2014. "'One of the Guys': Military Women, Paradoxical Individuality, and the Transformations of the Argentine Army." *American Anthropologist* 117, no.1: 86–99. https://doi.org/10.1111/aman.12163

"Belize Super-Women Compete in Grueling Match." 2019, March 25. http://www.reporter.bz/2019/03/25/belize-super-women-compete-in-grueling-match

"Bronze Medal for BDF." 2019. *BDF,* October 30. https://www.bdfbarbados.com/cism-games

Burke, Hilary. 2007. "Women Defense Ministers Chip at Latin America's Macho Image." *Reuters*, January 31: 1.

Cox, Ashlee. 2016. "Female Quota Full." January 23. https://www.nationnews.com/nationnews/news/76989/female-quota

Darden, Jessica Trisko. 2015. "Assessing the Significance of Women in Combat Roles." *International Journal* 70, no. 3: 454–462. https://doi.org/10.1177/0020702015585306

Dialogo. 2013. "Uruguay: Women Make Great Strides in Military." *Dialogo: Digital Military Magazine*, October 8.

Donadio, Marcela, ed. 2016. *A Comparative Atlas of Defence in Latin America and Caribbean: 2016 Edition.* Ciudad Autonoma de Buenos Aires: RESDAL.

Dussán, Yolima. 2018. "WIMCON 2018: Armed Forces Need More Women in All Branches." *Diálogo Digital Military Magazine*, December 21.

Ford, Stanley P. 2012. *Core Values: A Soldier's Story.* Bloomington, IN: iUniverse.

"Four JDF Senior Officers Promoted." 2019. *Jamaica Observer,* February 8. http://www.jamaicaobserver.com/news/four-jdf-senior-officers-promoted-rocky-meade-antonette-wemyss-gorman-create-history_156671

Frederic, Sabina. 2015. "Women's Integration into the Argentine Armed Forces and Redefinition of Military Service. What Does Military

Democratization Mean?" *Dynamiques Internationales Revue de Relations Internationales* 11: 1–23.

Frederic, Sabina, and Sabrina Calandron. 2015. "Gender Policies and Armed Forces in Latin America's Southern Cone." *Res Militaris Ergomas issue, Women in the Military*: 1–15.

Frederic, Sabina, and Laura Masson. 2015. "Profession and the Military Family in the Argentine Armed Forces." In *Military Families and War in the 21st Century: Comparative Perspectives*, edited by Rene Moelker, Manon Andres, Gary Bowen, and Philippe Manigart, 73–84. New York: Routledge.

Fuentes, Andres Resendez. 1995. "Battleground Women: Soldaderas and Female Soldiers in the Mexican Revolution." *The Americas*, April: 525–553. https://www.jstor.org/stable/1007679

Gallardo, Natalia. 2016. "A Committed Peacekeeper Woman from Uruguay." United Nations Organization Stabilization Mission in the DR Congo. May 26. https://monusco.unmissions.org/en/committed-peacekeeper-woman-uruguay

García-Moreno, Claudia, Christina Pallitto, Karen Devries, Heidi Stöckl, Charlotte Watts, and Naeemah Abrahams. 2013. *Global and Regional Estimates of Violence against Women: Prevalence and Health Effects of Intimate Partner Violence and Non-Partner Sexual Violence*. Geneva: World Health Organization.

Giannini, Renata, Mariana Lima, and Pérola Pereira. 2016. "Brazil and UN Security Council Resolution 1325: Progress and Challenges of the Implementation Process." *PRISM*, March 1: 178–197.

Guyana Times. 2019. "GDF Women's Corp Celebrates 52nd Anniversary." February 2.

Harris, Hermione. 1988. "Women and War: The Case of Nicaragua." In *Women and the Military System*, edited by Eva Isaksson, 190–209. New York: St. Martin's Press.

Hirst, Monica, and Reginaldo Mattar Nasser. 2014. *Brazil's Involvement in Peacekeeping Operations: The New Defence-Security Foreign Policy Nexus*. Oslo, Norway: Norwegian Peacebuilding Resource Centre.

International Labour Office. 2016. *Women at Work: Trends 2016*. Geneva: International Labour Office.

Jensen, Kimberly. 2012. "Volunteers, Auxiliaries, and Women's Mobilization." In *A Companion to Women's Military History*, edited by Barton Hacker and Margaret Vining, 189–231. Leiden, Netherlands: Brill.

Johnston, Jake. 2018. "Meet the New Haitian Military—It's Starting to Look a Lot Like the Old One." *Center for Economic and Policy Research,* March 16. https://cepr.net/meet-the-new-haitian-military-it-s-starting-to-look-a-lot-like-the-old-one

Kaieteur News. 2017. "Women's Army Corps Celebrates Golden Jubilee." February 6.

Kazman, Mia. 2019. *Women of the FARC.* Perry Center Occasional Paper. Washington, DC: William J. Perry Center for Hemispheric Defense Studies, National Defense University.

Kussrow, Samanta. 2018. *Primary and Secondary Roles of the Armies: Comparative Case Studies from Latin America.* Buenos Aires, Argentina: RESDAL.

Lodge, Alyssa, and Simone Bak. 2015. "The Role of Female Personnel in National Security and Peacekeeping: Alumni Share Their Perspective." August 25. Washington, DC: International Student Management Office, National Defense University. https://ismo.ndu.edu/About/News/Article/614630/the-role-of-female-personnel-in-national-security-and-peacekeeping-alumni-share

Marin, Nefretery. 2019. *Military Strategy to Fully Include Women,* March 22. https://liberationvoice.com/belize-politics/no-excuses-military-strategy-to-fully-include-women/

Masson, Laura E. 2017. "Women in the Military in Argentina: Nationalism, Gender, and Ethnicity." In *Gender Panic, Gender Policy,* edited by Vasilikie Demos and Marcia Texler Segal, 23–43. Victoria, Australia: Emerald Publishing.

McNeish, John-Andrew, Gabriel Rojas Andrade, and Catalina Vallejo. 2015. *Striking a New Balance? Exploring Civil-Military Relations in Colombia in a Time of Hope.* CMI Working Paper, Bergen: CMR Michelsen Institute.

Ministry National Security. 2019. "Belize Coast Guard Recruiting Women for Leadership Positions." *Ministry National Security,* December 5. https://mns.gov.bz/press-releases/belize-coast-guard-recruiting-women-for-leadership-positions

Montano, Sonia, and Maria Nieves Rico. 2007. "Women's Contribution to Equality in Latin America and the Caribbean." *Economic Commission for Latin America and the Caribbean (ECLAC).* ECLAC, 1–130.

Moyano, Inigo Guevara. 2011. Report. Strategic Studies Institute, US Army War College. http://www.jstor.org/stable/resrep11788

Mulinari, Diana. 1998. "Broken Dreams in Nicaragua." In *The Women and War Reader*, edited by Lois Ann Lorentzen and Jennifer Turpin, 157–163. New York: New York University Press.

Osoba, Ermina. 2003. "Women in Management and Decision-Making Processes in Antigua and Barbuda: A Statistical Analysis." *Antigua and Barbuda Country Conference*. University of West Indies.

Phillips, Dion E. 1997. "The Trinidad and Tobago Defence Force: Origin, Structure, Training, Security and Other Roles." *Caribbean Quarterly* 43, no. 3: 13–33. https://doi.org/10.1080/00086495.1997.11672099

Phillips, Dion E. 2002. "The Military of Belize." *Belize Country Conference*. University of West Indies.

Polga-Hecimovich, John. 2019. *Ecuadorian Military Culture 2019*. Miami: Florida International University Steven J. Green School of International & Public Affairs.

Puebla, Teté. 2003. *Marianas In Combat: Teté Puebla and the Mariana Grajales Women's Platoon in Cuba's Revolutionary War, 1956–58*. eds. Mary-Alice Waters, Luis Madrid, and Martín Koppel. Atlanta, GA: Pathfinder.

Ramos, Alex. 2019. "SOCSOUTH, Guatemalan Female Engagement Platoon Exchange Information." *U.S. Southern Command,* October 1. https://www.southcom.mil/MEDIA/NEWS-ARTICLES/Article/1975846/socsouth-guatemalan-female-engagement-platoon-exchange-information

Ross, Jen. 2005. "In Traditional Chile, Meet the Soldiers with Pearl Earrings." *The Christian Science Monitor*, November 7.

The San Pedro Sun. 2019. "Belizean Coast Guard Female Lieutenant Makes History." June 21. https://www.sanpedrosun.com/community-and-society/2019/06/22/belize-coast-guard-lieutenant-alma-pinelo-receives-honor-graduate-award-at-us-training-center

Sloan, Kathryn A. 2011. *Women's Roles in Latin America and the Caribbean*. Santa Barbara, CA: ABC-CLIO.

Spero, Kerri. 2016. "Honduran Sapper Leadership Course Graduates First Female Combat Engineer." *Joint Task-Force Bravo,* December 21. https://www.jtfb.southcom.mil/News/Article-Display/Article/1036269/honduran-sapper-leadership-course-graduates-first-female-combat-engineer

St. Kitts & Nevis Observer. 2017. "The St. Kitts-Nevis Defence Force Adds 19 Recruits." August 19.

Strønen, Iselin Åsedotter. 2015. *Servants of the Nation, Defenders of la patria: The Bolivarian Militia in Venezuela*. CMI Working Paper, Bergen: Chr. Michelsen Institute (CMI)/ University of Bergen.

Strønen, Iselin Åsedotter. 2016. *"A Civil-Military Alliance": The Venezuelan Armed Forces before and during the Chávez Era*. CMI Working Paper, Bergen: Chr. Michelsen Institute/University of Bergen.

Tegel, Simeon. 2015. "A Bolivian Is Thought to Be the First Woman General in Latin America Commanding Combat Troops." *www.pri.org*, March 17.

Thomas-Woodward, Tiffany A. 2003. "'Towards the Gates of Eternity': Celia Sánchez Manduley and the Creation of Cuba's New Woman." *Cuban Studies* 34: 154–280. doi:10.1353/cub.2004.0030

U.S. Embassy Paramaribo. 2015. "Military Women Exchange Experiences during International Women's Week." *U.S. Embassy in Suriname,* March 20. https://sr.usembassy.gov/military-women-exchange-experiences-international-womens-week

Van Meter, Spencer. 2014. "Partnering with Chile to Strengthen International Peacekeeping." *U.S. Department of State Official Blog,* June 4. http://2007-2017-blogs.state.gov/stories/2014/06/04/partnering-chile-strengthen-international-peacekeeping.html

Wilson-Harris, Nadine. 2019. "JDF Focuses on Recruiting More Women." *The Jamaica Gleaner,* March 19. http://jamaica-gleaner.com/article/news/20190319/jdf-focuses-recruiting-more-women

THREE

Europe

Women are playing a larger role in militaries across the globe, but especially in the West. This phenomenon can be explained by a range of variables, including sociocultural attitudinal shifts regarding gender roles, demographic changes, reduction of militaries following the end of the Cold War, changes from conscription to volunteer forces, and an increase of women in most labor forces (Harries-Jenkins 2002, 745). Many European countries have expanded women's participation in military jobs and units. By 2001, in France, the United Kingdom, and the Netherlands, women comprised almost 8 percent of their armed forces; however, this number was significantly below the 14 percent in the United States and 11.4 percent in Canada (Nielsen 2001, 31). By 2001, France allowed women in combat but curtailed the number of women serving in combat positions. During the same time period in Norway, Spain, the Netherlands, and Belgium, women were permitted to serve in most military units, but few women actually served in ground combat.

In 1998, the NATO Committee on Gender Perspectives (NCGP) requested National Reports from all NATO members to explore and compile statistics and information regarding member states' policies on women in the armed forces. This committee was based on United Nations Security Council Resolution (UNSCR) 1325 on women, peace, and security that had as its priorities gender mainstreaming and an integration of gender perspectives in the armed forces. According to the summaries of the NATO reports, women comprise an average of 10.9 percent of militaries in NATO member countries. Hungary, Slovenia, Latvia, the United States,

60 Women and the Military

A French officer in 2011. By 2001, France allowed women in combat but curtailed the number of women serving in combat positions. Women make up 19 percent of the French Army and, although they are allowed in all branches, only comprise 1.7 percent of infantry soldiers. (Suryo/Dreamstime.com)

and Greece had the highest rates of women serving in the military (NATO Summary of the National Reports 2016, 10). Greece, the United States, the Czech Republic, Canada, and France had the highest percentage of female applications to serve relative to the total number of applicants. In all nations, applications from men were higher than women. Greece and the United States had over 35 percent of applications from women, while the Czech Republic and Canada had over 30 percent (NATO Summary of Reports 2016, 13).

More specifically, most European countries allow women to serve in the armed forces, but their percentage in national forces differs significantly from country to country as do the units in which women may serve. The small country of Luxembourg has only 900 service members, with 6.6 percent women. As the country has no Navy and a very small Air Force, most women serve in the Army and military band, although all positions are open to women (NATO Summary of the National Reports 2016, 147). Women in Belgium and Lithuania make up only 7.8 percent of the military. In the Belgian Armed Forces, most women serve in the Army (43 percent), although they may serve in all positions (NATO Summary of the National Reports 2016, 53). Women in the Netherlands comprise 9.5 percent of military personnel and

11 percent in Croatia and can serve in any military occupational specialty (MOS). In Portugal and Slovakia, women comprise about 10 percent of the military, although women are not permitted in the Slovakian infantry. In Romania, women comprise only 5.9 percent of the military, whereas in Latvia and Slovenia, women comprise 16 percent of the armed forces, with women in Latvia allowed to serve in any job and participate in all operations. In the Slovenian military, 83 percent of women serve in the Army, and the remaining 17 percent are civilian personnel (NATO Summary of the National Reports 2016, 183).

This chapter examines women's role in the European militaries, where women serve in almost every country. It explores the historical context for women's incorporation into the military, along with the societal views, key factors for change, integration of women into the regional militaries, and examines other issues including sexual harassment. The discussion focuses on the United Kingdom, France, Germany, Sweden, Norway, and Denmark, but provides information on many other countries in the region.

SOCIETAL VIEWS OF MASCULINITY AND WARFARE

In exploring the militaries of the United Kingdom, Germany, and France, "the social and political life of these countries deeply revolves around a commitment to 'equality' and 'justice' while accommodating sex distinction is one of their constitutive paradoxes" (Eulriet 2012, 29). This concept can be applied to many other European countries. In other words, most Western European countries hold the liberal ideals of equality and justice as sacred, but different public cultures allow for various outcomes regarding gender roles in their respective militaries. As such, it is important to explore specific histories of several European countries' integration of women into their militaries founded on various societal views on gender equality. Additionally, the differentiated integration pace and recruitment and retention strategies are interconnected with societal views on gender and the military.

EARLY HISTORY TO WORLD WAR II

There are many examples of women's participation in war throughout European history, whether as fighters, camp followers, or in administrative positions. From the fourteenth to the nineteenth centuries, women played

62   Women and the Military

vital roles for European militaries. According to Barton Hacker, "armies could not have functioned as well, perhaps could not have functioned at all, without the service of women" (1981, 644). In the nineteenth century when many militaries incorporated support services under military control, women who had provided these amenities lost their place in history. During the thirteenth to fifteenth centuries, the dividing lines between the military and society at large were not clear cut. "Military units themselves were profit-making ventures; a company was the business of its captain, raised and directed in hope of gain, as a regiment was of its colonel, and even an army of its general" (Hacker 1981, 647). Many of the camp followers and those in need of being fed were women. Some soldiers used their wives to increase their meager salaries by having them do laundry, clean, and sew (Hacker 1981, 650).

British camp followers were an important component of the military during the French and Indian Wars, which took place in North America from 1756 to 1763. One follower, Martha May, wrote to her husband's commander after she was accused of insubordination. Although she was a camp follower, the accusation that she was guilty of insubordination reflected that she was subject to military discipline and perceived herself as part of the Army, blurring the lines between the military and society (Degroot 2001, 24). Camp followers performed support and logistical functions; however, when militaries were professionalized in the nineteenth and twentieth centuries, men replaced women in these roles, consequently affording the jobs a significance and acceptability that they did not have when women performed them. When men executed support functions in the military, they were perceived as soldiers, yet women always struggled to gain that title, exposing society's perception that war and masculinity were intertwined (Degroot 2001, 24). Similarly, in the Netherlands, there are examples of women serving in the military, as reported during the Spanish siege of Haarlem in 1572, when Kenau Simondochter Hasselaers led 300 women into battle (Moelker and Bosch 2008, 91). Although there were few women in battle in the seventeenth through nineteenth centuries, camp followers had their place in the Netherlands as they had in most other Western countries.

When women joined the military, they performed jobs that extended traditional gender roles to warfare. In the United Kingdom in 1914, Mabel Stobart established the Women's National Service League forming female units to administer to wounded soldiers (Degroot 2001, 31). In Britain during World War I, women who wanted to volunteer for noncombatant roles during the conflict faced opposition. Britain created a women's paramilitary volunteer corps in 1914 where women became drivers, performed clerical duties, and recruited for the military. Despite the resistance, by 1916, there were 10,000 volunteers and over 90,000 women serving in the auxiliaries of the Women's Services (Robert 2013, 319). They served as part of the Women's Royal Naval Service (WRNS), Women's Auxiliary Air Force (WAAF), and Auxiliary Territorial Service (ATS). Women overcame antagonism to their participation in the war effort, but had difficulty surmounting the concept of gendered space that was part of the cultural milieu during that time period. In other words, women were to remain on the "home" front, while men moved into the military space. With small changes in spatial discourse due to the war's impact, women were accepted into various positions supporting the war (Robert 2013, 321).

During World War II, women who enlisted in the British military remained on the home front by joining the auxiliary corps and performing administrative, communication, medical, and other noncombatant functions. By the end of World War II, women in the United Kingdom comprised more than 10 percent of the armed forces (Hermann and Palmieri 2010, 24). In some cases, women did fly planes and drive or

A woman reenacts the role of a member of the Women's Auxiliary Air Force (WAAF) on the Severn Valley Railway in Shropshire, England, on June 3, 2011. The WAAF was established in 1939 during World War II and joined other auxiliary forces in which women served. (Brett Critchley/Dreamstime.com)

64   Women and the Military

operate antiaircraft guns during World War II (King 2013, 9). Despite their service during wartime, women were reminded of their "natural role" as mothers and nurturers when they were given time off for lessons in "mothering" (Degroot 2001, 30).

In Germany, during World War I and World War II, like other militaries in the region, women entered industrial jobs and served in the military as civilian employees doing manual labor, medical, and administrative work. Women stayed away from the frontline and, during the war, according to Nazi ideology, their main job was to create German children (Goldstein 2001, 71). The German Armed Forces were created in the 1950s during the Cold War hostilities, but women were not included among their ranks.

Unlike in Germany and most other European countries during World War I, some Russian women did serve in combat, although there was no clear policy regarding women's roles. Many served, as they had in the United States, disguised as men (Goldstein 2001, 72). When Alexander Kerensky served in the provisional Russian government in 1917 as the minister of war, he allowed a female soldier to organize the Battalion of Death. The Germans ended up surrendering to the all-female battalion, which was a grave humiliation (Degroot 2001, 27). However, because the combat taboo with regard to women was prevalent in most societies, even the Russians camouflaged women's participation. During World War II, almost a million women comprising 8 percent of Soviet forces were in combat or in combat support positions such as fighter pilots and were reported to have fought bravely (Herrmann and Palmieri 2010, 22). After the war, these women were prevented from continuing their military careers and were told that having a family would provide greater service to the country (Degroot 2001, 27).

POST–WORLD WAR II TO PRESENT

It was only after World War II that women in the United Kingdom entered full military service in the Women's Royal Army Corps (WRAC) created in 1949 and received rank commensurate with their male colleagues (Fitrani, Cooper, and Matthews 2016, 14). However, women continued to perform administrative and clerical duties and were constrained by rules forbidding their involvement in any combat role. At that time, societal norms restricted women's participation in most military positions with both women and men holding traditional views of gender roles (Dandeker and Segal 1996, 31–32).

In 1961, Portugal allowed women to join the military with an all-female corps in the Air Force with very constrained roles. Most of those women were nurses, some trained in parachuting, to provide services in Africa where Portugal was involved in wars for control of its colonies of Angola, Guinea-Bissau, and Mozambique. However, only fifty nurses graduated from the parachuting course, and only sixteen remained on active duty after the war (Carreiras 2002, 687). This reflected a familiar pattern visible in other militaries; women were recruited during wartime and dismissed or ignored afterward. By 1988, when many other European countries were opening their militaries and more jobs to women, Portugal followed suit and two women were admitted to the Air Force Academy to become pilots. The other academies opened their doors soon after this event (Carreiras 2002, 687).

The Women's Corps of the Royal Netherlands Indian Army operating in colonial-controlled Indonesia served in administrative, medical, and secretarial positions. This unit was established in March 1944, but the Women's Assistance Corps, allowing the first women to serve in the Royal Netherland Armed Forces, was created a month later, on April 25, 1944 (Moelker and Bosch 2008, 92). The separate women's corps was disbanded in 1982, but women had begun to be admitted to all military institutes and training centers in 1978, except for the Royal Netherlands Naval Academy, where women were admitted in 1983. The government's goal was to have 12 percent women in the military by 2010, a goal it had not yet achieved by 2016 (Moelker and Bosch 2008, 93; NATO Summary of the National Reports 2016, 151). Women are not represented evenly in Dutch military ranks and are underrepresented in higher officer ranks. This situation began to change in 2006 with forty-one women serving in the Army, forty-nine in the Air Force, and forty-two in the Navy in the rank of major or higher (Moelker and Bosch 2008, 95).

By 1980, the Women's Royal Army Corps became a more significant part of the British Armed Forces and by 1982, it became one of the five colleges of Sandhurst, the academy that trains British officers. During this time, women also began weapons training, while the armed forces implemented some joint training and management. The British Army adopted gender-neutral physical tests, although by 1991, only 100 of 134 military occupational specialties (MOS) in the Army were opened to women. The military introduced maternity leave in 1991, whereas prior to that year, pregnant women were required to leave the service (Dandeker and Segal 1996, 32). During the first Gulf War in 1991, women made up 2.8 percent of the British troops who contributed to the war effort. Contrast that statistic with women in the U.S. military who comprised 6.2 percent of the forces in the Gulf (Dandeker and Segal 1996, 32). After the war, the United Kingdom disbanded the WRAC, and all recruits, men and women, faced a joint commissioning board.

In addition to the Army, women have served in the British Royal Air Force since World War I with 32,000 serving during that time period. Similar to the militaries of other countries, more women serve in the Air Force than in the other branches of service. This is due, in part, to the technological nature of the Air Force and its organizational structure. According to Dandeker and Segal, the RAF has few personnel in combat, and even when they do participate, they are far from the combat zone (1996, 34). Despite these factors, from the post-1945 period until 1979, women were underrepresented in the RAF, due to a perspective by some military and political leaders, that they were expensive to train relative to men since their retention rate was lower. By 1986, men served on average 14 years, while women remained in service for 6.9 years (Dandeker and Segal 1996, 34–35). In the United Kingdom, by 1995, women comprised 8.8 percent of the Air Force personnel. By 2016, women were 10 percent of the UK forces with 14 percent in the RAF, 12 percent in the Royal Navy, and 9 percent in the Army. The military's goal is to increase the percentage of women to 15 percent by 2020 (Brooke-Holland 2016).

The Nordic countries have a strong culture of egalitarianism that impacts their view of women's roles in the military, although generational differences exist. In a study regarding men's attitudes toward women in the Swedish military, the research concluded that men of a younger age, higher education, increased contact with women, and higher rank held more positive attitudes toward women (Ivarsson, Estrada, and Berggren 2005, 269). Although men's attitudes toward women in the Swedish military were somewhat positive, the authors were surprised, given the nature of Swedish society and its emphasis on gender equality, that the views were not even more optimistic (Ivarsson, Estrada, and Berggren 2005, 278). A key predictor of men's more positive views of women in the military was the quality of contact with them (Ivarsson, Estrada, and Berggren 2005, 276). Women began serving in selected areas of the Swedish Armed Forces in the 1980s and, by the 1990s, all restrictions on where women could serve were removed. For some men who hold more traditional values, sexist beliefs guide interactions between men and women. For them, women who work in male-dominated environments threaten men's power and roles within traditional institutions, such as the military.

Since researchers did not find a higher rate of positive attitudes toward women in Sweden's military, they surmised that there may be a "universality of the military experience across cultures" (Ivarsson, Estrada, and Berggren 2005, 278). In other words, most cultures might hold the view that the military is a male domain and men who hold sexist views are less likely to accept women in the military. Even if society is egalitarian, men with more traditional values might populate the military and thereby impact negatively the integration of women in the armed forces.

Women who find a hostile or difficult environment might leave the military, and this phenomenon works in contrast to the findings that increased contact between military men and women bolster positive attitudes toward women in the military (Ivarsson, Estrada, and Berggren 2005, 270). These results imply that both having a "critical mass" of women in the military and gender integrated training can have positive effects on men's attitudes toward women in the nontraditional environment of the military (Ivarsson, Estrada, and Berggren 2005, 279–280).

Like Sweden, a key element of Norwegian culture is the concept of egalitarianism. In 1984, Norway allowed women to participate in all military roles, if they could obtain the position's standards. Prior to integration, Norway conducted studies regarding integration and examined how to modify standards and infrastructure to facilitate the change; however, the military did not conduct pilot studies and did not follow a well-executed and gradual integration plan (Schaefer et al. 2015, 67). As a result, although the military has tried to recruit more women and has offered incentives, it has fallen short of its goal, with women comprising less than 9 percent of service members. Additionally, women above the rank of colonel only comprise 1.5 percent of officers (Gustavsen 2013, 362). To attract more women, the Norwegian military attempted to ease women's entry into service by deferring the signing of a binding contract for three months so they could decide if they wanted to remain. They also held meetings for women to discuss issues relating to their service. Despite Norway's egalitarian approach to the military, the institution continues to be dominated by the male conscript culture (Mathers 2013, 139).

People implement different cognitive frames to assess their environs. Contrasting views are grounded in varying cultural perspectives that impact how people perceive the world around them, including gender issues. In an exploration of how various cultures frame the question of

68   Women and the Military

women in the military, a study comparing views of Norwegian and U.S. military men found that Norwegians concentrated on women's equal treatment, while American men emphasized equal opportunity. In other words, the two differed in ideas regarding outcome and opportunity. The Norwegian men surveyed believed that women have skills that elude most men, such as being more socially adept, strong thinkers, good confidants, and having the ability to multitask. Although the American soldiers also perceived women in a positive light, they concentrated on unique advantages that women bring to the military. They offered that women were nurturing, thought differently than men, and added diversity (Gustavsen 2013, 364–365).

Arguments advancing the central role of women in the family structure are prominent in many parts of the world in a variety of cultures and impact perceptions on women serving in the armed forces. Women who wanted to join the British Home Guard during World War II argued that it fulfilled their role as guardians of their home. This claim resonated in many societies since it was culturally acceptable for women to defend their homes, but not to be sent abroad to fight (Degroot 2001, 29). In 1985, the French military opened all military specialties to women, including engaging in combat, although scholars argued that women were not as integrated into the military as they were in the civilian sector (Boulègue 1991, 343). A study group, the Collège Interarmeés de la Défense (CID), issued a report in 1999 exploring professional requirements and family obligations and concluded that although family obligations can interfere with a woman's military responsibilities, it is a challenge that needs to be "fixed" rather than used as an argument to exclude women from military duties (Eulriet 2012, 96).

Women make up 19 percent of the French Army, and although they are allowed in all branches, only comprise 1.7 percent of infantry soldiers. While some women can meet the physical requirements for combat units, challenging standards keep women from serving in those units. Additionally, some women elect not to serve in these units, concerned with the ramifications for family life given the long hours of training and deployments (Barry 2013, 23). Clearly, various societies' views of women's roles in both the labor force and family life impact perceptions of women in the military. The level of women's integration into European national militaries is intertwined with these views, along with beliefs that integrating women is detrimental to unit cohesion and operational effectiveness.

VIEWS OF INTEGRATION

In the 1980s, the Danish military integrated women in some land and sea combat roles as an experiment to explore their performance. The results of those early trials convinced the Danish military that women could perform as well as men and consequently, by 1988, the military opened all jobs to women and implemented gender-neutral requirements (Goldstein 2001, 85). Danish women served in Bosnia in the 1990s as part of tank crews, placing them in intimate settings with men. Similarly, Sweden implemented a gradual approach to opening positions to women with a three-step program. By 1983, most specialties accepted women except as fighter pilots, submariners, infantry, armor, and cavalry (Harries-Jenkins 2002, 747). By the end of the third phase of gradual integration, despite the Swedish supreme commander's opposition to women's service in all specialties, citing economic and medical justifications, the government found it unconstitutional to deny women access to any military positions, including combat specialties (Harries-Jenkins 2002, 747).

In Norway, women were permitted to serve on submarines, prior to any other European country and opened all combat jobs to women in 1985. By 1999, Norway appointed its first female defense minister and, in 2000, the country debated making military service compulsory for both men and women. Despite its openness, by 2001, women made up only 5 percent of Norway's armed forces, and that number was only 3 percent in Denmark (Nielsen 2001, 30–31). One reason for low female participation is connected to maternity leave and its impact on a women's job trajectory. Many women transfer into administrative jobs, rather than remaining operational after maternity leave. This affects promotion opportunities since chances of studying at military academies are reduced, an important step toward a higher rank. Norway's first female colonel was only promoted in 1999 (Nielsen 2001, 31). Studies have found that men in the Norwegian military who have served with women are more accepting of their integration (Schaefer et al. 2015, 68). To assist with integration, the European Union (EU) has created the "gender force" initiative, funding advisers who serve as a resource for women and educate and train senior leaders on gender issues (Schaefer et al. 2015, 69).

In some units, such as the Norwegian Royal Guard, women adopted masculine traits such as cursing to become "one of the boys" (Ellingsen, Lilleaas, and Kimmel 2016, 153; Schaefer et al. 2015, 68). Aside from women's personal attempts to acclimate, the Norwegian military integrates barracks and rooms. The military followed an example set by the Swedish Army in having mixed-gender rooms, consisting of six to ten soldiers with at least two women. Norway adopted room integration based on reports that women felt isolated and excluded from their unit when they were in single-sex rooms (Schaefer et al., 70). The Norwegian Military of Defense funded a study of mixed-gender rooms to assess their success in addressing women's feelings of being isolated and unwelcome (Ellingsen, Lilleaas, and Kimmel 2016, 152). Scholars argue that the mixed rooms promote gender equality since genders interact with one another as "buddies" (Ellingsen, Lilleaas, and Kimmel 2016, 155).

In Sweden, a key argument for women's integration into combat occupations was that during peacekeeping operations, female soldiers interact with other women on a level closed to men, while also contributing important communication skills. Furthermore, Swedish success in integration came from strong senior level commitment to opening the combat arms to women, leadership support that is necessary for effective integration. The support occurred in conjunction with gender initiatives to help commanders integrate women (Schaefer et al. 2015, 74).

In comparison with Canada, the United States, and Nordic countries, the United Kingdom held tight on restricting women in combat. In the United Kingdom, by the early 1990s, women served on ships and in all aircrew jobs, but were still excluded from submarines. At that stage, the British rejected women's service in ground close combat, which includes armor, infantry, and the Royal Marines, although women were encouraged to serve in the Special Reconnaissance Regiment, which conducts covert surveillance (Barry 2013, 24). This exclusion from ground close combat was confirmed by the European Court of Justice in 1999, which ruled that women could be prohibited from certain positions when it was deemed that they would impact combat effectiveness (Cawkill, Rogers, Knight, and Spear 2009, 7).

Over the years, Britain commissioned several reports to explore lifting the combat exclusion. A 2002 report exploring the physical and psychological differences between men and women concluded that with the proper training, women could become more aggressive and close the gap between genders. The study also concluded that leadership is more important to unit cohesion than its gender composition (Eulriet 2012, 62). *The Employment of Women in the Armed Forces Steering Group* responded that the findings did not reflect what might occur in actual combat since research was not conducted in a combat environment. The government asserted that testing women in combat was an extreme risk that outweighed the benefit of integrating women in ground close combat (Barry 2013, 25). As a result of the 2002 report and the Steering group's response, Secretary of State for Defense Geoff Hoon concluded that the combat exclusion should remain.

Given the United Kingdom's participation in both Iraq and Afghanistan, by 2010, women's role in war had changed on the ground, impacting cultural perceptions of women in combat. Although still restricted from combat roles, women served on the frontlines in combat support, on ships, and as pilots. Female artillery soldiers or engineers served with infantry units and experienced the same combat as infantry soldiers. As such, the lines of women serving in combat were already blurred (Barry 2013, 26–27). In actual battles in Iraq and Afghanistan, women exhibited courage under fire. In interviews with men who worked with women in the field, some argued that women did not detract from unit cohesion, although the majority were uncomfortable with women in infantry or armor. Others believed that all-male teams were more cohesive than mixed teams. Interestingly, few of the women interviewed were interested in serving in a direct combat role (Barry 2013, 25).

A 2010 study conducted by the Berkshire Consultancy found that the connection between leadership and cohesion played a smaller role than discussed in the 2002 report. The 2010 report concluded that some issue, unrelated to gender, fostered cohesion more than leadership. Some of these factors included working in small teams, knowing team members well, and sharing past operations over a longer time span. Another report finding reflected a need for women to overcome stereotypes to be fully accepted in their units. These conclusions led to increased communications and media highlighting women's contribution to the military and military operations (Eulriet 2012, 64). Despite the 2010 report, the British Ministry of Defense argued that the findings were not strong enough to warrant lifting the combat exclusion ban.

Opposition to full integration came from a variety of military members. A large percentage of British infantry soldiers emerge from the least educated parts of society, along with corporals and sergeants, who are the lowest level of army leadership. With this knowledge, the UK chiefs of staff explained their rejection of women's integration into the combat arms in 2010. They argued that they did not want to add additional challenges to these units "in an environment that is most unforgiving of mistakes" (Barry 2013, 26). This statement implies that women are excluded because

72   Women and the Military

infantry culture reflects traditional gender views. However, many other European countries had already integrated women into the combat arms, and the United States was close to modifying its policies. Although the United Kingdom changed its policies in 2011 to allow women to serve on submarines, they retained the ban on ground close combat. Their case was bolstered when in 2014, another study by the British Ministry of Defense concluded that only 4.5 percent of women had reached the standards to train for the infantry.

The deliberations continued with the United Kingdom turning to U.S. studies, particularly because the United States deployed more women to combat zones than the United Kingdom (Fitrani, Cooper, and Matthews 2016, 16). The British military examined both U.S. Army and Marine experiences, specifically the U.S. Marine's combat effectiveness study, testing the hypothesis that mixed-gender infantry units perform as well as single-gender ones (Fitrani, Cooper, and Matthews 2016, 17). In a well-publicized and highly criticized study released in 2015, the U.S. Marine Corps found that single-gender units outperformed mixed-gender ones (Seck 2015). Despite this, the United States did not reversed its decision to allow women in all branches and all jobs in the military.

Britain followed suit and in 2016, chief of staff, General Nick Carter, recommended to the defense and prime ministers that women serve in ground close combat roles. When Prime Minister David Cameron announced that women would be allowed in the infantry, Colonel Richard Kemp, a former commander in Afghanistan, argued that due to this "experiment" the price would be "paid in blood" (Lusher 2017). Predictions assert that only 5 percent of the Army's 7,000 women could pass the physical standard for those units ("Women to Serve in Close Combat Roles in the British Military" 2016). In Europe, despite similarities among countries, NATO policy makers recognized that states integrate at various speeds due to "unique environments of different nations and the different stages at which the advancement of gender equality are at among nations" (Ishaq 2014, 602).

Other countries in Europe also increased women's roles in the armed forces and lifted previous bans. Polish women had a history of service during peacekeeping operations. In 1973, a Polish military contingent participated in United Nations Emergency Forces II (UNEF) in the Middle East with women working predominantly in the medical field (Kozerawski 2017, 57). The Polish military worked with other NATO contingents where women held more positions than those in the Polish armed forces. Although women were banned from Polish units that participated in combat in the past, guidelines calling for equal promotion of men and women have led to the removal of restrictions on where they may serve. In 2003, Poland permitted women to attend military schools and, by 2004, all military posts were opened to women (Fitrani, Cooper, and Matthews 2016, 20). Currently, women comprise 12.6 percent of the Polish military and may enter into any branch and job (NATO Summary of the National Reports 2016, 85).

PHYSICAL ISSUES, RECRUITMENT, AND RETENTION

Arguments for excluding women from specific military jobs include discussions of physical attributes and capabilities. These views affect the ability of militaries to recruit and retain women. Some scholars insist that the military's feminization denotes a weakening of the state and advance many oft-heard contentions that women are not genetically programmed for violence due to physical and emotional weakness. Others argue that social, not biological factors, influence women's warrior ethos (Degroot 2001, 23).

The issue of pregnancy inevitably arises in a discussion of the physical differences between the genders. In the United Kingdom, by 1988, women were no longer forced to leave the service when pregnant. The British government commissioned a study in 1998, the Manning Report, to explore fairer employment. The findings led to more jobs opened to women, along with the introduction of an antiharassment policy. Despite these positive steps for women's integration, the report supported the military ban on women in combat positions. The study claimed that women's physical limitations preclude a blanket policy removing the ban (Fitrani, Cooper, and Matthews 2016, 14). The UK Ministry of Defense believed it was required to protect servicewomen who could be adversely affected by carrying heavy loads. Furthermore, the MOD claimed that physical distinctions between men and women, including less dense muscles and smaller hearts, lead to less explosive power and diminished upper body strength, Accordingly, the argument continues, this physical difference impacts women's effectiveness (Fitrani, Cooper, and Matthews 2016, 15).

In Sweden, at the close of the 1960s, questions arose regarding the incorporation of female officers and conscripts into the military with the proposition being strongly opposed by both politicians and armed forces (Kronsell and Svedberg 2001, 168). However, a shortage of male officers in the Swedish Air Force prompted the service to request permission to recruit women for both civilian and military positions. When debates ensued, they centered on the biological differences between the sexes, emphasizing that women's bodies were not effective for military requirements. When asked to produce evidence for the assertions, opponents of women in the military switched to economic arguments (Kronsell and Svedberg 2001, 168).

Beginning in 1998, the UK Armed Forces implemented gender-free tests, which were important to create a work environment of professionalism, judging members on their competence. Men and women underwent similar physical tests, which reflected individual competences rather than average physiological abilities of their sex. The tests were devised to represent the needs of a specific military job, rather than a general test for all military personnel. Over time, the gender-free tests led to increased injuries for women, particularly pelvic stress injuries (PSIs), fostering a renewal of segregated gender training (Eulriet 2012, 58). Despite the separate training, physical requirements for specific military jobs remain the same for men and women. The UK chiefs of staff reviewed the restrictions on women in combat several times, and most held that women's inability to meet the physical requirements for specific units kept them out. In the early 2000s, a study concluded that only 0.5 percent of women of recruitment age could meet the infantry's physical standards (Barry 2013, 24). The report also cited evidence from sports medicine that women are more easily injured than men and take longer to recover. However, researchers in this study rejected the argument that physical differences justified excluding women from combat units.

Most countries in Europe have different physical requirements for men and women to enlist in the military and annual fitness tests to remain. For example, to enlist in Portugal, the requirements not only differ by gender but also by service. The annual physical fitness tests have the same requirements or events, but the standards for each gender differ. This is similar to Romania, Lithuania, Latvia, Croatia, and Slovakia. In the Netherlands and the Czech Republic, physical fitness tests to enlist are the same for men and women, yet the annual fitness test has different requirements for each gender. However, to become a marine or diver in the Dutch Armed Forces, all candidates must meet the same standards. As for enlistment requirements, in Bulgaria, there are different physical tests for men and women and for those applying to military colleges or academies.

Only a few countries have completely gender-neutral physical fitness tests for enlistment and annual tests, including Belgium, Norway, Sweden, and Turkey. Other countries have gender-neutral standards for anyone entering certain specialties, including the infantry or Special Forces (NATO Summary of the National Reports 2016). For example, Denmark has permitted women in close combat since 1988. It conducted combat trials in 1985 and 1987, and research concluded that women perform as well as men in combat roles. Although Denmark has differentiated physical standards for each gender in the armed forces, women are expected to perform the same functions and duties as their male counterparts in the more physically demanding roles (Cawkill, Rogers, Knight, and Spear 2009, 21).

There are differing views regarding the equity of having differentiated physical standards for men and women. Some believe that having two standards is unfair. Militaries with gender-specific standards argue that they account for differences in muscle mass and physical structure. The Norwegian cultural frame of perceiving equal treatment between men and women as most important is logical if women and men are executing the same job. If this is the case, standards should not vary (Gustavsen 2013, 366). In some units, the Norwegian military retains gender-neutral standards for physical training, while in others, differentiated requirements for running or strength training are applied. Military leaders who opted for differentiated standards assert that unless they equalize the playing field, women are disadvantaged, leading to their lower recruitment. Many in Norway hold that gender is not a sufficient reason to implement varied physical standards in the military. For some Americans, the concept of equal opportunity weighed heavily on decisions regarding military physical standards. Consequently, the military implemented two different standards to level the playing field, given the physical differences between men and women (Gustavsen 2013, 366). But for some, applying differentiated standards detracts from a woman's worth in the military by portraying her as a "weak link" unable to do the same things as men (Gustavsen 2013, 367).

Coupled with the physical issue, women lack critical mass in some units, complicating women's recruitment and retention. In Norway, for example, women comprise about 9 percent of the Norwegian military, but only 2 to 3 percent of combat arms (Schaefer et al. 2015, 68). Although women are permitted to serve in close combat operations, none had done so by 2015. In European countries that permit women in combat branches, few women select these jobs due to time away from home for training and other operations. Furthermore, high physical standards are an impediment for some women, along with a concern of being isolated in their units (Schaefer et al. 2015, 68).

76   Women and the Military

The Norwegian military has tried to create a critical mass of women, which they define as 20 percent. Military researchers hold that below this number, women hold less job satisfaction and feel excluded from the unit. Most combat-related specialties have been unable to recruit 20 percent women. To increase their numbers, the Norwegian military allowed 400 women to go through Special Forces basic training in 2014. Only 50 women remained at the most rigorous part of the training, and all the women returned to the conventional forces at the training's conclusion (Schaefer et al. 2015, 70–71). Some Norwegians believe that recruiting more women into the military reflects the egalitarian nature of Norwegian society and increasing the military's diversity is a security imperative. People with different backgrounds bring various competencies to their job (Skjelsbaek and Tryggestad 2009, 48).

To recruit and retain both women and men in the military, many governments offer incentives and benefits. Compared to the United States, most European countries have very generous parental leave policies, which also extend to military members. Service members are granted parental leave, flexible hours, and accommodation for dual military families. These policies are detailed in the NATO Summary of the National Reports from 2016, but a few examples are given below.

Norway's legislation encouraging egalitarianism impacts both public and domestic life. Norwegians receive one-year parental leave after the birth of a child. Mothers are entitled to the first six weeks, while the rest of the year can be divided between the parents, with the father taking a minimum of ten weeks. However, reality illustrates that women take most of the time. Several governmental groups have issued reports recommending that the parental leave be divided more equitably between parents, allowing men more time at home and granting women opportunities for public roles. A former chief of staff, Brigadier General Robert Mood, argued that "the military must appear as a much more modern organization if it is to appeal both to women and to men" (Skjelsbaek and Tryggestad 2009, 45–46). In Belgium parents are permitted up to seventeen weeks of parental leave, with women receiving up to fifteen weeks and men up to two weeks. The Belgian Armed Forces allows for flexible hours with unit commander's approval and the military accommodates dual military families, especially if one partner is deployed (NATO Summary of the National Reports 2016, 55). Lithuania allows 160 weeks for parental leave, which is transferable between parents. In Latvia, parental leave is seventy-eight weeks; however, like Lithuania, there are no flexible hours, part-time work opportunities, or specific programs for dual military parents (NATO Summary of the National Reports 2016, 139). The Dutch Armed Forces offers up to twenty-nine weeks of parental leave and permits thirteen weeks to be taken before the child is eight years old, allowing for flexibility in parenting needs. In Poland, the military allows for up to twenty-eight weeks in parental leave and provides flexible hours if needed for child or elder care and other personal situations. Estonia allows up to twenty weeks of maternity leave, which is transferable between parents (NATO Summary of the National Reports 2016, 99). In Turkey, women are given eight weeks maternity leave prior to the child's birth and then three weeks after. Women may decide to take leave without pay for six months, while men receive one week of paternity leave (NATO Summary of the National Reports 2016, 197).

Bulgaria has one of the most generous parental leave policies, granting 410 days to women and fifteen to men after the child is born. Since the leave is transferable and equal in total to eighty-four weeks, men are permitted to have up to thirty-two weeks after the baby is six months old. The Bulgarian military considers work-life balance and allows flexible work hours for parental leave and elder care (NATO Summary of the National Reports 2016, 61). Other benefits are used to make military life more attractive. For example, the Bulgarian military incentivizes retention for both men and women with increased salaries, free medical care, additional leave days, and other benefits depending on length of service. The military also has special incentive programs to retain women through the Labor Code, which provides protections for women, and through a special agreement with the Bulgarian Armed Forces Women's Association (BUAFWA), an NGO that promotes the social status of women in the military and pushes the implementation of the women, peace, and security agenda. BUAFWA can advise the minister of defense regarding discrimination and can provide statements on a variety of issues (NATO Summary of the National Reports 2016, 61).

Although 78 percent of NATO member states have retention policies, only 19 percent have specific policies that target the retention of women (NATO Summary of the National Reports 2016, 16). Those five countries include Bulgaria, Germany, Spain, Turkey, and the United Kingdom.

The Croatian Armed Forces provide incentives to retain pilots, doctors, professors, and computer specialists, but do not have special programs to retain women. The Slovenian military offers financial incentives to retain its personnel, including low-cost rent, military vacation rentals, and financial awards. The Portuguese Armed Forces implements retention policies for men and women including continuing education, increased compensation and social support, and in 2008, a special office was established to ease transition from military to civilian life (NATO Summary of the National Reports 2016, 168).

The Norwegian military faces challenges in both recruiting and retaining women, not only in combat-related forces. Although Norwegian women comprise a large proportion of the labor force, they are only 9 percent of the military. This disconnect can be explained by several factors. A close inspection of labor statistics in Norway reveal that "its labor force is the most gender-segregated in Europe" (Skjelsbaek and Tryggestad 2009, 45). While men hold most jobs in the private and technical sector, women work in education and health care and comprise the majority of part-time labor. This is due, in part, to their desire to work in jobs that allow them time with the family. Furthermore, Norway has increased its participation in international peacekeeping missions, necessitating foreign deployments. This fact might affect women's recruitment (Skjelsbaek and Tryggestad 2009, 45).

Norway has made several attempts through "a fragmented series of initiatives and measures" to increase diversity and gender equality in the armed forces, yet their participation has not risen significantly (Steder 2014, 294). Seventy-five percent of seventeen-year-old women surveyed regarding military service claim they have no interest in a military career (Steder 2014, 295). On retention, women leave the military at a higher rate than men.

Some studies report that approximately 40 percent of women leave the Norwegian military to enter the police force. Aside from feeling excluded and token in military units, reasons why women leave include family considerations or continuing education. Other women left because of bullying and sexual harassment (Schaefer et al. 2015, 71). In 2007, Anne-Grete Strom-Erichsen, the Norwegian minister of defense, raised the question of women's underrepresentation in the military, part of a debate that had been circulating in Norwegian society (Skjelsbaek and Tryggestad 2009, 34–35). The military has explored ways to ameliorate women's experience in the armed forces. In 2014, Norway created a new Special Forces troop, the Jeggertroppen (Hunter Troop), which became the world's first all-female training program to attract more women (Braw 2016). Additionally, the military has instituted several programs to assure equality in promotion and recruitment, although the military has avoided quotas that

WOMEN IN THE SPECIAL FORCES

Norway is the first country to create an all-female Special Forces unit. This unit was established in 2014 and reflects Norway's egalitarian approach to women in the military. Norway's *Jegertroppen* or "Hunter Troops" were created in response to Norway's participation in operations in Afghanistan. In these more conservative societies, interactions between men and women are curtailed. Norway recognized a need for female soldiers to interact with women in these societies to enhance opportunities for intelligence gathering and productive community building. The unit requires women to endure challenging training, which includes parachuting, skiing in the Arctic, fighting urban areas, and navigating harsh terrain (Angerer 2017).

FURTHER READING

Angerer, Carlo. 2017. "Inside the World's First All-Female Special Forces Unit: Norway's Jegertroppen." *NBC News,* April 16. https://www.nbcnews.com /news/world/inside-world-s-first-all-female-special-forces-unit-norway -n746041

might be perceived as giving women an advantage over men (Schaefer et al. 2015, 69). Despite the avoidance of quotas, the leadership has "targets" to raise the number of women in combat-related specialties. It has also explored ways to modify equipment and uniforms for women, but has not made much progress in this area (Schaefer et al. 2015, 72).

In 1988, a survey in Sweden indicated that women left the military due to a lack of support from superiors, whose attitudes have a critical impact on their subordinates (Kronsell and Svedberg 2001, 169). By 1989, Sweden had lifted the combat ban on women and like Norway, has had difficulty recruiting and integrating women into these units. Despite continued reports by women of sexual harassment and discrimination, some soldiers in integrated units report increased operational effectiveness and shifting attitudes toward women (Schaefer et al. 2015, 74).

External events have also influenced recruiting efforts by some countries. In 2016, due to heightened tensions between Russia and the Ukraine, increased refugee activity in Europe, and the continuing terror threat, Austrian Defense Minister Hans-Peter Doskozil announced his intention to recruit 9,800 people to the Austrian Armed Forces by 2020 (Weissensteiner 2016). The Defense Ministry is investing 1.7 billion euros to update infrastructure and equipment and increase salaries to incentivize recruitment. Women comprise 2.8 percent of the Austrian military with 55 percent serving in the Army, 32 percent in logistics, and 13 percent in other units (NATO Summary of the National Reports 2016, 221). As part of this military recruitment campaign, the Ministry of Defense is committed to increasing the proportion of women serving to 10 percent. As such, the military has specific recruitment policies targeting women, including special events for women, physical fitness guidance, and weekend sessions to prepare for enlistment (NATO Summary of the National Reports 2016, 222). To support women in the service, the military holds a three-day annual conference to facilitate networking among women.

In Turkey, the military has held an honored role in society since the founding of the Ottoman state in the thirteenth century. In contemporary times, the military has professional officers, NCOs, and specialists coupled with conscripts. In the 1990s, Turkey began to reduce the number of conscripts to keep up with the changes in technology and the need for more specialized training (Varoglu and Bicaksiz 2005, 583). Turkish society holds the military in high regard as evidenced by the reference to military conscription as *vatani gorev* or "duty for the motherland" (Varoglu and Bicaksiz 2005, 585). As evidence of the esteem in which Turkish society holds the military, two of the main celebrations for life events in Turkey are the entrance and the return from military service.

Only 1.3 percent of Turkey's military are women and can only serve as NCOs or officers. With that said, in 2016, Turkey had the lowest percentage of women leaving the military of all NATO member and partner nations (1.6 percent). This fact might be attributed to its targeted policies to retain women, including part-time work, having child care centers at headquarters, and allowing for flexible hours, part-time work, and parental leave. Additionally, the Turkish Armed Forces has retention policies for all members, which includes military housing and salary increases. If a spouse is assigned abroad, a female service member may take a leave of absence, without pay, to accompany her husband to maintain family unity. In a situation where a dual military couple belongs to different services, the woman will be transferred to her husband's service (NATO Summary of the National Reports 2016, 196). These policies may reflect the perception that men hold more important roles than women in the military and the primary role of the family in Turkish society. Despite Turkey's ability to retain its female personnel, it bans women from serving in the infantry, armor, Special Forces, and on submarines. It does not have future plans to integrate them into combat positions or put them on the frontlines (NATO Summary of the National Reports 2016, 195).

FACTORS INFLUENCING CHANGE

What causes women's military roles to change over time? Several variables are key to exploring this question, including changes in conscription policies, gender equality legislation, a country's security environment, changing technology, shifting cultural perspectives with regard to gender roles, and personnel requirements (Dandeker and Segal 1996, 30). Throughout Europe, these changes led to more militaries incorporating women into their organizations.

The concept of conscription connects the ideals of citizenship and patriotism. In 1793, France called for the conscription of all citizens into the military, and this move influenced other countries to follow suit, although women had no such obligation to enlist in any country. Mass conscription followed in Belgium and the Netherlands, yet universal conscription ended in these countries in 2002. Several scholars have argued that the end of mass armies stemmed from industrialization and an increase of living standards leading to professional specialization and an "erosion of the norm of compulsory military service" (Haltiner 1998, 7–8). With the advent of advanced technology, militaries needed fewer personnel. Whatever the causes of conscription's demise, the advent of volunteer militaries did necessitate an opening to more women to fill the gap in personnel.

In 2000, a debate began as to whether women should be conscripted into the Swedish Armed Forces. With changes in Swedish culture espousing gender equality, retaining the military as an all-male domain was unrealistic. The Swedish government never implemented universal conscription, and by 2010 Sweden eliminated compulsory military service. Only 5,000 soldiers were being drafted with conscription perceived as a relic of previous times (Chandler 2017). However, by 2017, the Swedish government announced the reinstatement of conscription due to Russian activity, including its aggressive behavior in Ukraine and the annexation of Crimea. Sweden also accused Russia of breaching its airspace and executing cyberattacks in Sweden (Chandler 2017). The draft includes both men and women.

Norway introduced conscription for men in 1897, but women were excluded from this national obligation. During World War II, Norway conscripted women from 1942 to 1945, and those who were living abroad were required to return home to serve. This temporary move did not reflect profound societal changes regarding gender equality, but rather fulfilled a security need. In fact, the Parliament only permitted women to occupy civilian positions in the military (Skjelsbaek and Tryggestad 2009, 41). After the war, women were no longer required to serve. However, the Norwegian Parliament revised this decision, and by 1977 the first woman attended officer training (Steder 2014, 293). By 1984, Norway opened all areas in the military to women, although men were drafted, and women served voluntarily. In the mid-2000s, the Norwegian government debated gender-neutral conscription, but the proposal was withdrawn by 2008. Instead, the government passed a law in 2009 requiring women to attend military assessment sessions (Skjelsbaek and Tryggestad 2009, 41). In Norway, despite its egalitarian culture, few women join the military, and it recruits and retains below the average number of women in many NATO forces (Steder 2014, 294).

After the fall of the Soviet Union in 1989, the Netherlands restructured its military by reducing its personnel and abolishing conscription in 1996 (Moelker and Bosch 2008, 86). As in other countries, transformation from a conscript to a volunteer military impacts the role of women in several ways. First, the number of women in the military usually increases to fill the gap in personnel. Second, women's participation in the military is also dependent on the perceived threat level. According to Moelker and Bosch, when a threat to the country is high, women's participation increases. When there is a medium threat, women's military participation is lower, and when the threat is low, women's participation increases most likely due to men's decreased participation since they are no longer conscripted (Moelker and Bosch 2008, 89).

Women were allowed into all units of the German military by the year 2001. Since men were still conscripted into the German military at that time, a discussion emerged regarding women's conscription relating to an article of the constitution that forbids women from using firearms. During the discussions, there was expansive agreement among most political groups that an amendment allowing women to bear arms would only occur if women joined the military voluntarily. In other words, political support for conscripting women was low (Eulriet 2012, 73). During the following years, a debate ensued regarding applying conscription unequally and "granting voluntary access to women on the basis of 'professional equality,' whilst imposing military service on men in the name of national security" (Eulriet 2012, 75). Alexander Dory brought a case against the German government claiming that his military obligation or conscription advantaged women, who could serve on a voluntary basis and not interrupt their civilian employment (Eulriet 2012, 34).

Although women were not conscripted, the German government wanted to facilitate their recruitment by introducing part-time work in the military. German political culture reflects why women's conscription was rejected and why part-time work was implemented. German society, like many others, elevates women's role within the family structure, particularly their responsibility in child care. Simultaneously, society's views were shifting toward greater professional equality, including in the military. Consequently, to accommodate a woman's ability to serve and maintain an important role in family life, the Bundeswehr recommended the idea of part-time work (Eulriet 2012, 80). The issue of conscription became moot since the government decided to end male conscription in 2010.

Additionally, for countries that moved from conscription to volunteer forces, governments needed to consider expanding women's roles in the armed forces to compete with labor markets (Carreiras 2002, 689). The Portuguese Armed Forces opted for a volunteer force and began that process of professionalization when it moved to a hybrid system in 1991. It had a mix of volunteer and contracted service members to gradually replace conscripted soldiers. The Portuguese constitution of 1997 eliminated all references to conscription (Carreiras 2002, 692). A key challenge of a volunteer force, especially within the Portuguese army, was recruitment. Although legal changes took some time to occur, policy modifications followed the reality on the ground. In 1988, two women requested admission to the Air Force Academy and were permitted to attend. The actual legal changes to integrating the all-male academy followed. In fact, many policies that were enacted in the 1990s affecting women were merely reactive with regard to uniforms, pregnancy, physical fitness tests, and maternity leave. This same reactive policy making applied to the lifting of the combat ban on women in 1996. This move followed a woman's admission to the military academy's artillery course which had never been open to women (Carreiras 2002, 695). By the year 2000, almost 3,000 women served in an army of 44,000 with the army showing the most growth (Carreiras 2002, 697). Most of the functions that women performed in all the services were logistical, administrative, personnel, and finance. Interestingly, by the year 2000, women made up around 20 percent of the Air Force Academy, but only 11.3 percent of military academies overall (Carreiras 2002, 699).

84   Women and the Military

Some countries with conscription did not allow women to volunteer in the noncommissioned officer or enlisted rank and only had female officers. These countries included Poland, Hungary, the Czech Republic, Greece, and Turkey. The countries with conscription had no recruitment issues, and some applied quotas or ceilings on the number of women who could serve. In Greece, women could not make up more than 10 percent of the military academy population, and Turkey limited women to 4 percent (Carreiras 2006, 102). Italy allowed for 20 percent of students in military academies and 30 percent in enlisted ranks to be women. By the year 2000, almost all NATO countries eliminated the quotas; however, the restrictions on where women could serve and in which units, acted as a different type of constraint. In NATO countries with conscription, women served on a voluntary basis. For several countries, the connection between conscription and the obligations of citizenship emerged as an important topic in the context of gender equality.

CULTURE CHANGE AND LEGISLATION

Aside from the issue of conscription and professional militaries, other factors led to changing gender roles in the military, including culture shifts and the passage of legislation dealing with gender equality. Societal views toward gender roles and women's place in the economy was also transforming, leading to legislation affecting women's role in the labor market. In 1975, the British Parliament introduced the Sex Discrimination Act, which was also impacted by the European Community's legislation regarding equal opportunities for women. These legal changes led to the British military's reassessment of its policy toward pregnant service members. Two pregnant nurses from the auxiliary corps of the Royal Navy were discharged with the option of returning in the future. However, due to a 1976 European Community directive, women could only be disqualified from employment for a lack of operational effectiveness and not for issues related to gender. Although the military policy of compulsory discharge of pregnant service members was not changed until 1991, an interim policy granting twenty-nine weeks of unpaid leave for members with at least two years of prior service was granted (Dandeker and Segal 1996, 39).

The UN's adoption of UN Security Council Resolution 1325 in 2000 pushed most international organizations dealing with security issues, such as the European Union and the North Atlantic Trade Organization (NATO), to prioritize gender mainstreaming and the integration of women into militaries across the globe. When exploring Europe, it is critical to examine how the European Union impacts its member states' armed forces, particularly with regard to security and gender. Each member state has different political institutions and public cultures that influence their policies on gender (Eulriet 2012, 30). At times, the legal structure of regional and international organizations affects the legal structure of states.

The UN secretary general requested that member states create National Action Plans to enforce UN Security Council Resolution 1325 within their own militaries. In 2004, the European Union Ministers on Gender Equality declared that EU gender policy should be in line with the UN resolution. The United Kingdom created a national plan in 2006 and interpreted Resolution 1325 as allowing for some exclusionary policies toward women in the military (Eulriet 2012, 37). The United Kingdom's approach highlights the complex relationship between member states and the EU. Although EU policies can influence what states do on a national level, states remain critical decision makers in recruitment and retention policies regarding women in the military. However, EU law forces member states to reassess and justify their exemptions on a periodic basis (Eulriet 2012, 52).

In the 1990s, issues pertaining to women in the British military, including abandoning the discharge of pregnant service members, led the way for the opening of more military jobs for women. With this said, the military retained combat exclusion and was required periodically to justify its position to the EU. In one instance, the Equal Opportunities Commission argued that the exclusion of women from combat hampered their promotion and career opportunities, thereby preventing them from attaining the highest level of service. This aspect "found them at a disadvantage on the military labour market" (Eulriet 2012, 55).

Similar to the United States, by the 1970s, many countries in Europe were experiencing pressure from their populations for increased gender equality. Despite changes in legislation, attitudinal change takes more time to adjust. For example, French women's roles were unequal to men in a variety of ways, including their numbers in the force. In 1991, women made up 1.6 percent of officers, 8.3 percent of NCOs, and 1.8 percent of enlisted soldiers. Although men were conscripted, women were exempt and their numbers in both the officer corps and as NCOs were created by quotas (Boulègue 1991, 344). In 1996, Claire Aldige, a qualified candidate to become an officer in the Supply Corps, was not considered for the position since the 20 percent "women's quota" had already been reached (Eulriet 2012, 86). Aldige contested the decision to the Administrative Tribunal of Paris and the *Conseil d'etat* (the highest administrative court in France)

86   Women and the Military

WOMEN CHALLENGE FRENCH GOVERNMENT

In 1996, Claire Aldige, a qualified candidate to become an officer in the Supply Corps, was not considered for the position since France had a quota on how many women could serve. Aldige contested the decision in the highest administrative court in France, which ruled in her favor in 1998. Her case reflected a larger issue of equal access for women and men in public employment and led to a law, which ended the quota system for women in the French military in 1998.

FURTHER READING

Eulriet, Irene. 2012. *Women and the Military in Europe: Comparing Public Cultures.* New York: Palgrave.

---

ruled in her favor in 1998. Her case reflected a larger issue of equal access for women and men in public employment and prompted a law, which ended the quota system for women in the French military in 1998. A 1972 French law, which mandated equality between the sexes, but had left the door ajar to justify quotas, was replaced with the requirement that the secretary of defense is obligated to list specifically those positions only open to men (Eulriet 2012, 89).

In the 1960s, German groups began demanding equal rights and access in employment and other realms of society. In 1973, the German government established the Women and Society Commission, which ultimately allowed women into the German Armed Forces or *Bundeswehr* in 1975 (Kummel 2002, 555). The German Parliament plays a large role in the military by providing input to decisions made in the field. Beginning in 1987, a political party proposed legislation advocating the opening of all military jobs to women, but the proposal was defeated in the Parliament after a first reading (Eulriet 2012, 72). At that time, military women worked in medical fields, which were suffering from deep recruitment issues (Kummel 2002, 556). By the 1990s, women served in all medical careers and musical services, with the first woman becoming the surgeon general in 1994. At that time, women comprised only 1.2 percent of German soldiers (Kummel 2002, 556).

Cases have been brought to the European Court of Justice based on an EU directive that requires states to implement equal opportunity for men and women with regards to employment, promotion, and vocational training

(Harries-Jenkins 2002, 748). In 1996, Tanja Kreil, an electrician, applied to serve in maintenance, a combat support function of the German Armed Forces. German Basic Law excluded women from positions working directly with arms, something required in this position, and Kreil was denied the job. She appealed the military ruling, and eventually the case was referred to the European Court of Justice. Since European law forbids any type of gender-based employment discrimination, Germany's Basic Law conflicted with the European law. After the Kriel case went to the European Court of Justice, it ruled that the EU directive applied to national armed forces and overturned German law pertaining to the military (Harries-Jenkins 2002, 750).

After the ruling came down in 2000, Rudolph Scharping, then Germany's secretary of state for defense, announced the opening of all military jobs to women and their recruitment into all ranks beginning in 2001. As such, German Basic Law was revised, and although women were permitted in all military positions, the military refused to conscript them as required for men (Fitrani, Cooper, and Matthews 2016, 20). The military also implemented the policy of "equality of treatment," which meant that all military members needed to meet the requirements of their position to be accepted to that job (Kummel 2002, 558). These legal changes led to women entering military professions that had been closed to them previously, although there were still constraints.

Similarly, in 1999, Angela Maria Sirdar challenged the UK Royal Marines' decision not to employ her as a cook based on the "interoperability" rule in this unit, which holds that all members of the unit must be able to be in combat. Due to the combat ban on women, Sirdar was denied a place in the unit, and this ruling was upheld by the European Court of Justice (Harries-Jenkins 2002, 751–752).

German society and culture are changing with regard to gender equality, inevitably affecting military perspectives. To assess the level of impact of changing sociocultural attitudes of the larger society on the military, scholars explored male soldiers' views of women's integration. Some studies show conflicted and diversified views of women's integration. Almost 70 percent of soldiers interviewed believe that integrating women affords the German Armed Forces greater legitimacy in society. However, many soldiers retain traditional views of gender roles in society with 33 percent arguing that life in the field is too challenging for women and two-fifths contending that women lack the appropriate physical fitness levels for certain military jobs (Kummel 2002, 563). Adhering to the traditional belief

88   Women and the Military

of men as defenders and women in need of protection, 45 percent of men surveyed do not believe women can protect them, and 25 percent contend that women need to be defended (Kummel 2002, 563). The survey did reflect a belief by 66 percent of those surveyed that women's communication skills in reducing tense situations reflects an advantage that women have over men (Kummel 2002, 563).

Furthermore, a majority of men surveyed thought that women can serve in leadership positions without degrading operational effectiveness. Despite these views, over 65 percent of men perceived the integration of women as impacting their daily work life negatively, and this percentage rose with regard to problems related to sexuality. Some men fear reverse discrimination and underscore that the military must implement equal treatment, implying that women should not be given any preferential treatment (Kummel 2002, 563).

In the United Kingdom, during the 1990s, as societal views on gender roles changed and women exhibited greater interest in joining the British Royal Air Force, the service embraced opening more roles to women, recognizing that the larger pool of qualified recruits increased options for the military. In 1945, women comprised 17 percent of the Air Force, but by 1948, this number decreased to 11 percent, and by 1979 was only 6 percent (Dandeker and Segal 1996, 35). A pervasive view existed that women were more difficult to retain than men and therefore not cost effective to train. In 1986, women served an average of 6.9 years compared to 14 years for men. However, research indicated that women's attrition in training was half that of men's and that women scored higher on professional abilities and personal qualities. By 1988, women's retention increased to 10 years and a year later, the RAF began recruiting female fighter pilots and navigators. The first female fighter pilot, Jo Salter, began her duties in 1994 (Dandeker and Segal 1996, 35). Similarly, in Denmark, women trained as fighter pilots in the 1990s; however, the first Danish female fighter pilot was assigned to an F-16 only in 2006.

In the Netherlands, when the Positive Plan of Action for the Integration of Women was implemented in 1989, the objective was to increase the percentage of women in the military to 8 percent by 1993. Women were not interested in military jobs, in part, due to the military's masculine culture. When the government advanced another policy document in 1997, it concentrated on increased recruitment and devoted only one paragraph to mutual acceptance between genders (Moelker and Bosch 2008, 97). The Working Conditions Act of 1994, pressing Dutch employers to protect their employees from sexual harassment, influenced the military to modify their policy documents. The Defense Women's Network, a policy action group pushing for change for women in the Dutch armed forces, aligned with members of Parliament to address gender issues. Additionally, in 2001, the Dutch Ministry of Social Affairs and Employment implemented gender mainstreaming and established a committee to evaluate all ministries in this area (Moelker and Bosch 2008, 98). These actions forced the military to pay more attention to the cultural environment.

Eastern Europe has seen extraordinary political and cultural changes, since the fall of the Soviet Union in 1989. Albania has transformed from a communist country to a member of NATO and an EU candidate. Although Albania has been reforming its security sector, it has paid scant attention to gender equality and gender mainstreaming in the security sector. To achieve the level of democracy necessary to be admitted to the EU, Albanian society needs to transform with regard to gender equality. The Albanian constitution stipulates that discrimination due to gender, religion, or race is illegal. Other laws including one passed in 2008, the Law on Gender Equality in Society, espouses gender equality and establishes a 30 percent quota for women in the legislative, judicial, and executive branches. However, this quota has not been enforced uniformly in various institutions (Llubani 2014).

In 2014, Albania appointed its first female minister of defense, a big achievement considering there were only seventeen female ministers of defense across the globe in 2014 (Llubani 2014). In 1993, Albania ratified the Convention of Elimination of Discrimination Against Women (CEDAW), which pushes for gender equality in all domains including employment, politics, and education. A report issued in 2010 identified employment as an area of consistent concern and recommended that implementing paternity leave can alleviate some of the challenges for women in the workplace (Llubani 2014).

One of the main areas in Albania that needs improvement includes the military. The Center for Personnel Recruitment has among its main responsibilities, the recruitment of soldiers and officers. In 2012, it began to promote gender equality by creating the Sector of Equal Opportunity and pushing the recruitment of women. The military's goal was to have women comprise 15 percent of the forces. However, by 2013, women comprised only 11.2 percent, a decrease from 12.3 in 2011 (Llubani 2014). In Albania, attitudes towards women in the military are mixed. In a survey from 2010, when asked whether women are as capable as men to serve in

90   Women and the Military

the military or police, 85 percent of male respondents answered in the affirmative. However, when asked if these professions would be appropriate for the women and their families, 65 percent answered "no" and held that these are male professions (Llubani 2014).

DEMOGRAPHIC, ECONOMIC, AND TECHNOLOGICAL CHANGES

Not only have legal and cultural shifts influenced the trajectory of women's military service, but also demographic, economic, and technological changes impact women's military service. With regard to demographic transformations, from 1982 to 1994, the United Kingdom experienced what is known as the "demographic trough," referring to a decrease in population between the ages of 15–19 (Dandeker and Segal 1996, 38). This population decline of approximately 30 percent impacted the military's ability to recruit. As the largest branch of the services, the Army was most affected and conducted a study exploring both the causes and potential responses to the demographic trough. To ameliorate the effects of the population decline, the military opted to open more positions to women (Dandeker and Segal 1996, 38).

Furthermore, technological change has made the ban on women in combat and other positions unnecessary, as it can level the playing field with regard to physical demands, although the impact of technology differs depending on the specialization. The interplay between societal demands in a democracy and the specific needs of the military with regard to its war-fighting function is complex and differs from the requirements of the civilian labor market. As such, the military needs to justify "any significant divergence from wider civilian values and styles of life . . ." (Dandeker and Segal 1996, 40). A country's economic situation also impacts women's participation in the military. When the economy is strong, fewer men want to join the service, leaving the military to recruit women (Degroot 2001, 28).

REALITY ON THE GROUND AND SUCCESS

Another issue affecting women's service in the armed forces throughout Europe that has shifted some traditional views of gender is women's actual participation in war zones, even when legislation prohibited their participation. By 1990, women were permitted on British navy ships and served in the Gulf War in 1991, but participation with units that would be in direct combat, such as the Royal Marines, were closed to women. Beginning in 2001, many women had served in Afghanistan and Iraq and, although some combat positions were closed to them, many of these women had been in actual combat situations.

Due to realities on the ground, societal views are changing. As Western forces served in Muslim countries, increased operational responsibilities were transferred to women because of the cultural limitation of men interacting with women who are not family members. Female soldiers were required to search Muslim women for weapons or explosives in combat zones. Indeed, although other factors impacted this increase, several militaries experienced a spike in female participation. In Denmark, which participated in both wars in Iraq and Afghanistan, from 2007 to 2011, women's participation increased from 5 percent to 6.4 (Fitrani, Cooper, and Matthews 2016, 17).

SEXUAL HARASSMENT

Although formal barriers to women's participation in all military roles exist in many militaries, informal obstacles such as discrimination and abuse prevent women from serving or remaining in service. In a study of sexual harassment in the Swedish Armed Forces, the authors explore the impact of harassment on women's psychological and physical health, along with the impact on the job. Although there are some similarities between Anglo cultures (United States, Canada, and United Kingdom) and the Nordic (Denmark, Sweden, Norway, and Finland) particularly with regard to the concept of individualism, there are key differences in beliefs toward gender work roles, with the Nordic cultures being more egalitarian (Estrada and Berggren 2009, 167). However, researchers found similar beliefs in the U.S. and Swedish Armed Forces concerning the masculine warrior culture. Research shows that sexual harassment has a strong negative effect on job satisfaction, commitment to work, and psychological and physical health (Estrada and Berggren 2009, 179).

Some countries have not yet put in place personnel and processes to deal with sexual harassment. The NATO Summary of the National Reports (2016) provide insights into how countries approach sexual harassment. A few examples follow.

92   Women and the Military

Although the Albanian military has some training to prevent sexual harassment and abuse, they have not designated personnel to deal with the issue, but they have formal mechanisms for reporting (NATO Summary of the National Reports 2016, 50). In contrast, the Estonian military lacks a training program to deal with sexual harassment or abuse, although it has personnel to examine reports of sexual harassment, but without formal procedures in place for reporting. Along these same lines, the Estonian military does not have specific gender training programs or advisers in either the military or Estonian Ministry of Defense (NATO Summary of the National Reports 2016, 100). In the Bulgarian Armed Forces, women comprise 15.1 percent of all active duty personnel and can serve in all jobs. The Social Policy Directorate of the Bulgarian Ministry of Defense is responsible for implementing gender and equality policies along with the protection of human rights in the military. A gender policy adviser in the rank of lieutenant colonel was appointed to the adviser position in 2016 (NATO Summary of the National Reports 2016, 59). Although there are no appointed personnel in Bulgaria dealing with sexual harassment or abuse, formal mechanisms exist by which people can report with sexual harassment being treated as a crime under the Penal code. The Croatian Armed Forces has designated personnel for sexual harassment reports and the CAF has trainings, specifically in predeployment courses and in military education programs dealing with sexual harassment and abuse. The military and Ministry of Defense have six gender advisers, who receive specific training courses to prepare them for their duties.

The Greek Armed Forces have a Gender Equality Office that is responsible for gender integration and equality in the Greek military, EU, and NATO. Although the Polish Armed Forces have at least six gender-related trainings, there are no formal procedures to report sexual harassment. The Polish military and MOD also have nine trained gender advisers (NATO Summary of the National Reports 2016, 166).

The Belgian Armed Forces has specific training for the prevention of sexual harassment and abuse called the Joint Individual Common Core Skills (JCCS) and has specific personnel to take reports, along with formal procedures for reporting (NATO Summary of the National Reports 2016, 56). There are sixteen trained gender advisers for the Belgian Armed Forces and the Ministry of Defense, but they are part of the Information Operations Group and not part of a staff department. Lithuania has designated one officer in the Joint Staff Headquarters of the armed forces the additional duty of gender adviser. In 2016, the Romanian MOD implemented new guidelines to fight sexual harassment and discrimination. The military has a specific group that addresses gender issues, every unit appoints someone to deal with gender issues, and the MOD has a gender adviser (NATO Summary of the National Reports 2016).

In Europe, shifting cultural views regarding gender equality, coupled with the influence of regional and international organizations on gender policy, have affected important changes in connection to the role that women play in their national militaries. Many countries in the region allow women access to all military positions and are working toward greater gender equality throughout society.

FURTHER READING

Barry, Ben. 2013. "Women in Combat." *Survival* 55, no. 2: 19–30.

Boulègue, Jean. 1991. "Feminization and the French Military: An Anthropological Approach." *Armed Forces and Society* 17, no. 3: 343–362.

Braw, Elizabeth. 2016. "Norway's 'Hunter Troop.'" *Foreign Affairs*, February 8.

Brooke-Holland, Louisa. 2016. "Women in Combat." Briefing Paper Number 7521, March 4. https://researchbriefings.files.parliament .uk/documents/CBP-7521/CBP-7521.pdf

Carreiras, Helena. 2002. "Women in the Portuguese Armed Forces: From Visibility to 'Eclipse.'" *Current Sociology* 5, no. 5 (September): 687–714. https://doi.org/10.1177/0011392102050005005

Carreiras, Helena. 2006. *Gender and the Military: Women in the Armed Forces of Western Democracies.* London: Routledge.

Cawkill, Paul, Alison Rogers, Sarah Knight, and Laura Spear. 2009. "Women in Ground Close Combat Roles: The Experiences of Other Nations and a Review of the Academic Literature." *Defense Science and Technology Laboratory.* https://assets.publishing .service.gov.uk/government/uploads/system/uploads/attachment _data/file/27406/women_combat_experiences_literature.pdf

Chandler, Adam. 2017. "Why Sweden Brought Back the Draft." *The Atlantic*, March 3. https://www.theatlantic.com/international/archive/2017 /03/sweden-conscription/518571

Dandeker, Christopher, and Mady Wechsler Segal. 1996. "Gender Integration in Armed Forces: Recent Policy Developments in the United Kingdom." *Armed Forces and Society* 23 (Fall): 29–47.

Degroot, Gerard J. 2001. "A Few Good Women: Gender Stereotypes, the Military and Peacekeeping." *International Peacekeeping* 8, no. 2: 23–38.

Ellingsen, Dag, Ulla-Britt Lilleaas, and Michael Kimmel. 2016. "Something Is Working—But Why? Mixed Rooms in the Norwegian Army." *Nordic Journal of Feminist and Gender Research* 24, no. 3: 151–164.

Estrada, Armando X., and Anders W. Berggren. 2009. "Sexual Harassment and Its Impact for Women Officers and Cadets in the Swedish Armed Forces." *Military Psychology* 21: 162–185. https://doi.org/10.1080/08995600902768727

Eulriet, Irene. 2012. *Women and the Military in Europe: Comparing Public Cultures.* New York: Palgrave.

Fitrani, Randall, G. S. Cooper, and Ron Matthews. 2016. "Women in Ground Close Combat." *RUSI Journal* 161, no. 1 (February/March): 14–24.

Goldstein, Joshua S. 2001. *War and Gender.* Cambridge: Cambridge University Press.

Gustavsen, Elin. 2013 "Equal Treatment of Equal Opportunity: Male Attitudes towards Women in the Norwegian and US Armed Forces." *Acta Sociologica* 56, no. 4: 361–374.

Hacker, Barton C. 1981. "Women and Military Institutions in Early Modern Europe: A Reconnaissance." *Signs* 6 (Summer): 643–671.

Haltiner, Karl W. 1998. "The Definite End of the Mass Army in Western Europe?" *Armed Forces and Society* 25, no. 1 (Fall): 7–36.

Harries-Jenkins, Gwyn. 2002. "Women in Extended Roles in the Military: Legal Issues." *Current Sociology* 50, no. 5 (September): 745–769. doi:10.1177/0011392102050005008

Herrmann, Irene, and Daniel Palmieri. 2010. "Between Amazons and Sabines: A Historical Approach to Women and War." *International Review of the Red Cross* 92, no. 877 (March): 19–30.

Ishaq, Mohammed. 2014. "Advancing the Equality and Diversity Agenda in Armed Forces: Global Perspectives." *International Journal of Public Sector Management* 27, no. 7: 598–613.

Ivarsson, Sophia, Armando X. Estrada, and Anders W. Berggren. 2005. "Understanding Men's Attitudes towards Women in the Swedish Armed Forces." *Military Psychology* 17, no. 4 (October): 269–282.

King, Anthony. 2013. "Women in Combat." *The RUSI Journal* 158, no. 1: 4–11. doi:10.1080/03071847.2013.774634

Kozerawski, Dariusz. 2017. "The Gender Issue in the Polish Armed Forces on the Example of Peace and Stabilization Operations." *Science and Military* 1: 55–60.

Kronsell, Annica, and Erika Svedberg. 2001. "The Duty to Protect: Gender in the Swedish Practice of Conscription." *Cooperation and Conflict* 36, no. 2: 153–176.

Kummel, Gerhard. 2002. "Women in the Bundeswehr and Male Ambivalence." *Armed Forces and Society* 28, no. 4 (Summer): 555–573.

Llubani, Megi. 2014. "Women Representation in the Security Sector in Albania." *Albanian Institute for International Studies.* Downloaded October 2014. https://dgap.org/sites/default/files/article_downloads/policy_brief_aiis_albania_-_women_representation_in_the_security_sector.pdf

Lusher, Adam. 2017. "RAF Regiment Starts Accepting Women for Ground Close Combat Roles." *Independent*, September 1. https://www.independent.co.uk/news/uk/home-news/women-in-combat-roles-british-armed-forces-raf-regiment-first-to-recruit-ban-lifted-frontline-a7924701.html

Mathers, Jennifer G. 2013. "Women and State Military Forces." In *Women and Wars*, edited by Carol Cohn, 124–145. Malden, MA: Polity Press.

Moelker, Rene, and Jolanda Bosch. 2008. "Women in the Netherlands Armed Forces." In *Women in the Military and in Armed Conflict*, edited by Helena Carreiras and Gerhard Kümmel, 81–127. Wiesbaden: VS Verl. für Sozialwiss. doi.org/10.1007/978-3-531-90935-6_5

NATO Summary of the National Reports. 2016. Accessed September 18, 2018. https://www.nato.int/nato_static_fl2014/assets/pdf/pdf_2017_11/20171122_2016_Summary_of_NRs_to_NCGP.pdf

Nielsen, Vicki. 2001. "Women in Uniform." *NATO Review* (Summer): 30–33.

Robert, Krisztina. 2013. "Constructions of 'Home,' 'Front,' and Women's Military Employment in First-World-War Britain: A Spatial Interpretation." *History and Theory* 52 (October): 319–343.

Schaefer, Agnes Gereben, Jennie W. Wenger, Jennifer Kavanagh, Jonathan P. Wong, Gillian S. Oak, Thomas E. Trail, and Todd Nichols. 2015. "Lessons Learned from the Experiences of Foreign Militaries." In *Implications of Integrating Women into the Marine Corps Infantry*, 43–90. RAND. http://www.jstor.org/stable/10.7249/j.ctt19gfk6m.13

Seck, Hope Hodge. 2015. "Mixed-Gender Teams Come Up Short in Marines' Infantry Experiment." *Marine Corps Times*, September 10. https://www.marinecorpstimes.com/news/your-marine-corps/2015/09/10/mixed-gender-teams-come-up-short-in-marines-infantry-experiment

Skjelsbaek, Inger, and Torunn L. Tryggestad. 2009. "Women in the Norwegian Armed Forces: Gender Equality or Operational Imperative?" *Minerva Journal of Women and War* 3, no. 2 (Fall): 34–51.

Steder, Frank Brundtland. 2014. "Is It Possible to Increase the Share of Military Women in the Norwegian Armed Forces?" *International Relations and Diplomacy* 2, no. 5 (May): 293–309.

Varoglu, A. Kadir, and Adnan Bicaksiz. 2005. "Volunteering for Risk: The Culture of the Turkish Armed Forces." *Armed Forces and Society* 31, no. 4 (Summer): 583–598.

Weissensteiner, Nina. 2016. "Austrian Army Aims to Recruit Up to 10,000 Volunteers by 2020." *BBC Monitoring European*, September 16. Proquest.

"Women to Serve in Close Combat Roles in the British Military." 2016, July 8. BBC. https://www.bbc.com/news/uk-36746917

FOUR

North Africa and the Middle East

In the Middle East, women's participation in warfare, whether as part of national militaries or insurgent roles, has not translated into gender equality in either civilian or military life (Degroot 2001, 31). The region is complicated by many elements of diversity, including ethnicity, language and dialects, social class, and geography. Yet key unifying components exist including a shared colonial history and religion. Many Middle Eastern and North African (MENA) countries suffer from a lack of liberal democratic values, and this aspect impacts individual rights including those of women and minorities. Most MENA countries have majority Arab and Muslim populations and in most, Islamic law, also known as Sharia law, plays some part in the governance or social aspects of society. Although Sharia law does not necessarily dictate that women cannot participate in certain aspects of political life, traditional gender views and division of labor are discussed. Defining which countries comprise the Middle East is also a debated issue, as the term itself stemmed from the colonial period from the perspective of the British, who viewed India as the "Far East" and the area in close proximity to Europe as the "Near or Middle East." For this chapter, the following countries are included in the Middle East and North Africa: Iraq, Iran, Israel, Lebanon, Syria, Jordan, Egypt, Saudi Arabia, Bahrain, United Arab Emirate, Oman, Qatar, Algeria, Morocco, Tunisia, and Yemen.

An oft-cited United Nations Development Report issued in 2002, the Arab Human Development Report (AHDR), explored the developmental challenges of the Arab world and highlighted women's empowerment as a

98   Women and the Military

key deficiency. The eruption of the Arab Spring in Tunisia in December 2010 rebelling against authoritarian persistence, affected many countries in the region. Soon after Tunisia's longtime leader Zine al-Abidine Ben Ali (he ruled from 1987), was ousted, other rulers from Egypt, Yemen, and Libya were also overthrown. Many scholars hoped that a democratic dawn was taking place in the region and asserted that women would be empowered when political rights improved for the entire population. However, as time progressed, no country affected by the Arab Spring transitioned to democracy save Tunisia, although its fledgling democracy continues to be challenged by state building. Furthermore, expanded political rights for women have not materialized across the region.

The MENA region is extraordinarily diverse and includes Israel, which is both a Jewish state (majority of citizens are Jews) and a democracy. Israel's Declaration of Independence promulgated in 1948 establishes gender equality. Additionally, Israel's history of almost constant war with its neighbors necessitated that women participate in the military and has led to an experience incorporating women in the armed forces that differs significantly from its Arab and Muslim neighbors. This chapter explores the variety of perspectives in the region regarding masculinity and war and examines several countries that allow women to serve in the military.

SOCIETAL VIEWS OF MASCULINITY AND WARFARE

According to Haleh Afshar, throughout Islamic history, women have occasionally been active combatants as opposed to only camp followers. Even prior to the advent of Islam in the seventh century BCE, women participated in wars. During the Prophet Muhammed's time (570–632 CE), women accompanied him into battle and after his death, his youngest wife, Aisha, led an army against Ali, whose followers believed should have become the leader after Muhammed's death (Afshar 2003, 178). Although there are instances of women participating in warfare in the Middle East and Islamic world, these were the exceptions. In Iran, during the Iran-Iraq War (1980–1988), women were photographed on the frontlines covered by their chadors or modest Islamic dress, but never actually participated in active combat. These photographs were used as a "propaganda ploy" (Afshar 2003, 180).

Some scholars argue that even when women participated in formal or informal militaries, their social roles remained connected to their gender.

Portraying women as peaceful, in contrast to the more violent men, reflects elements of the patriarchy. Although during war women might fill certain more masculine roles, many people assume that women will return to traditional gender patterns at the cessation of war, reflecting the belief that women and feminists are pacifists (Shehadeh 1999, 146). Despite the stance in much of the Middle East and Muslim world that women's main role is to educate children and run the household, some countries allow women to participate in warfare in a variety of positions. As countries modernize and globalization impacts the Middle East and North Africa, women's education, role in the workforce and, consequently, in the military has begun to change. Several cases below illustrate the military roles that women have played and continue to play in the MENA region, along with an exploration of factors leading to change.

FACTORS INFLUENCING CHANGE

The history of North Africa includes examples of women who have participated in battle and have set examples for contemporary women. Tin Hinan, a Berber resistance leader in the fourth century CE, united warring Tuareg tribes and created a kingdom in the Algerian mountains. Another woman warrior, Kahina, in the seventh century led a resistance movement against the Arab armies of the Caliphate spreading Islam (Cheref 2006, 64). Although Tunisia lacked robust human rights prior to the Arab Spring in 2010, the country was in the forefront of women's rights in the Arab world. Women had many career and educational opportunities and, by 2011, comprised 50 percent of university students and served in the military (Arieff 2011, 274). The 2014 Tunisian constitution, similar to the one promulgated in 1956, requires both men and women to serve in the military. However, fewer than 10 percent of those required to enlist appear for conscription. Although the police have forced people to serve, they have done so by coercing those in the lower socioeconomic sectors of society to fulfill the commitment (Meddeb 2015). In November 2018, the Tunisian defense minister, Farhat Horchani, again considered enforcing conscription of women into the military since the constitution calls on all citizens to perform national service (Ghanem 2018). Currently, several women hold high-ranking positions in the Navy, and more than forty women serve as fighter pilots, although they make up less than 7 percent of the Tunisian military. For the most part, women serve in jobs considered more common

100   Women and the Military

for their gender, including medicine, translation, and as secretaries. Furthermore, their impeded access to combat positions has hampered their ability to acquire real decision-making roles (Ghanem 2018).

Although women played support roles in Algeria's war of independence from 1954 to 1962, many in society were reluctant to include women in the military, and society's views toward women were much less liberal than Tunisia's (Ghanem 2015). Over 10,000 women participated in medical work during the independence war, in some cases as spies. Women expected to be incorporated as equal partners in society after liberation from the French, a dream that did not come to fruition (Cheref 2006, 64). Despite their participation in the fight for independence, photos portraying women in uniform holding machine guns were implemented more for propaganda than as a realistic reflection of an egalitarian society. During the war, the National Liberation Front (FLN) openly illustrated their rejection of incorporating women into their ranks by publishing directives that stated: "it is strictly forbidden for all women to join our ranks; if they try to join, they should be turned back to their original destination" (Ghanem 2015).

After independence, the FLN became the only party in government and pushed for Islamic values. When Houari Boumediene became Algeria's president in 1965 after overthrowing Ahmed Ben Bella, he implemented relatively liberal views on women in society and permitted women to serve in the People's National Army (PNA) following the promulgation of a decree in 1978. However, in 1986, Algeria suspended the recruitment of women into the military, reflecting an unclear and debated policy. By 2001, women were again allowed to serve. An ordinance in 2006 made women's status in the military equal to men, yet the policy of equal opportunity is not reflected in the reality of the PNA. Women are "sexualized and marginalized" and serve in support roles subordinate to men, reflecting the traditional gender roles of Algerian society. With that said, the PNA retains a contradictory view of women that "is neither systematically inclusive nor wholly exclusive" (Ghanem 2015). Despite some progress in women's recruitment and an opening of all branches of the armed forces to women, they continue to serve in lower level positions and are excluded from combat.

Notwithstanding the fact that women do not serve as equals with men, positive transitions are occurring for a more inclusive Algerian military. In 2009, Fatima Zohra Ardjoune, who served as director general of the Ain Naadja military hospital, was the first woman in Algeria in the PNA to be promoted to general (Ghanem 2015). She set the stage for Fatima Boudouani to become a general in 2012 and three more women to attain the rank in 2015. By June 2014, Algeria had the greatest number of high-ranking female army commanders in the Arab world (Moghadam 2014, 73).

In another North African country, Libya, which gained its independence from Italy in 1951, women's rights were dictated by Islamic law with their primary role to reproduce. As such, strict segregation laws ensued along with early marriage and polygamy (Arabsheibani and Manfor 2002, 1009). President Muammar Qaddafi rose to power in Libya after the Free Officer's Revolution in 1969. When Qaddafi assumed power, he wanted to modernize society, allowing women to travel without permission from a male relative and by establishing a military academy for women (Londono 2011). The Tripoli Women's Military Academy, opened in 1978, had trained over 7,000 women by 1986, although in 1984, the People's Congress halted women's training (Miller 1986). President Qaddafi overturned that ruling and continued a policy that was radical for the traditional Middle East. Qaddafi demanded the full participation of women in all aspects of life, including military service.

In 1986, Qaddafi called on women in the Arab world to take up arms (Parmelee 1986). Although society incorporated more women in the workforce, the percentage of women serving in the military was small. This small number was in contrast to women's roles in some civilian jobs in specific areas of Libya. By 2011, 40 percent of lawyers in Benghazi were women, although only two women of forty members served in the recently formed Benghazi National Transitional Council (Marlowe 2011, 64). During the Arab Spring, which erupted in Libya at the beginning of 2011, President Qaddafi needed more soldiers to fight for his retention of power against the revolutionaries. To increase his support, Qaddafi turned to women, arming them to participate in the battles (Londono 2011). President Qaddafi was murdered by rebels in October 2011, and Libya fell into disarray with several rebel groups continuing to battle for control. During this period of chaos, women's rights have been severely curtailed. Human Rights Watch reported that on February 16, 2017, the forces controlling eastern Libya issued an order that women under sixty could only travel abroad with a male guardian (*Libya: Discriminatory Restriction on Women* 2017), a law that Qaddafi had dismissed.

In some parts of the Middle East, at times, women have fared slightly better in their quest for equality. Lebanon's heterogeneous religious and ethnic society has led to various women's roles in their communities and

102   Women and the Military

the military. The country's historical relationship with France, its large Christian community, and its connection to the Arab world have impacted women's roles in society. Lebanese women have had access to education and the workforce, but as demographics shifted in favor of the more conservative Shia population, women's roles in society also changed. From 1975 to 1991, the Lebanese experienced a violent and bloody civil war exacerbated by external players, including Israel and Syria. Many women supported the war efforts and believed that sending their sons to battle was a righteous calling (Shehadeh 1999, 147). Although few, if any, women were involved in the political and economic debates initiating the civil war, they could not escape the devastating consequences of the chaos surrounding them. As Shehadeh explains, the home front became the frontline along with the merging of public and private spaces (1999, 149).

Women in Lebanon, although mostly noncombatants during the civil war, cooked, sewed, and tended to wounded fighters. Some women, however, participated as active fighters for militias with whom they shared ideology. These female fighters were few and far between with most performing administrative and caretaking functions. Some women, desiring to guide Lebanon's future, participated more actively in the fighting. One of the Shia militia groups, *Amal*, which means hope, mobilized women to join its cause. *Amal*'s leader, Musa al Sadr, encouraged women to participate in the resistance in a variety of ways. Al Sadr relied on his sister, Sayyidah Rahab, to mobilize women by providing an example through her public participation. However, even Sayyidah's public functions remained confined to women's traditional roles since al Sadr held to the notion espoused in the Quran that women were subordinate to men. *Amal* maintained a Women's Affairs Department to deal with women's issues; however, the department received instructions from a male liaison officer to retain a strict separation of sexes (Shehadeh 1999, 152–153).

In another Shia-dominated militia group in Lebanon, *Hezbollah* or Party of God, women supported men in their war tasks, but also cared for needy families in the community to persuade them to support *Hezbollah*'s cause. Marrying *Hezbollah*'s political ends with social services for the community remains a significant part of the party's ideology. According to Shehadeh, one reason that women did not fight in *Amal* or *Hezbollah* was due to a belief that a woman's capture would dishonor and humiliate the organization (154).

The Lebanese Forces, a militia group established in 1976 and comprised mainly of Maronite Christians from the lower and lower-middle classes, incorporated women and girls who participated in traditional activities such as preparing food and administrative work, but also became fighters in mostly female units. Between 1975 and 1976, there were three all-female units operating in Beirut and its environs. Many women trained in light arms due to the scarcity of heavy weapons, along with the belief that a woman's military participation was temporary (Shehadeh 1999, 156). Over 3,000 women and girls trained for combat, although only around 250 took part in actual battles (Karamé 1995, 379).

According to the Lebanese Armed Forces website, women entered the LAF in the 1980s, serving predominantly in medical and administrative roles similar to most other militaries across the globe. In 1989, Resolution 376 was passed containing provisions regarding women's service in the Lebanese Armed Forces. Following this resolution, on January 9, 1990, the LAF command issued a memorandum allowing women to enlist as privates in the Air Force and Navy, along with enrollment at military academies. According to Shehadeh, when the Lebanese Forces allowed women to enter the Lebanese Military Academy, the first class was comprised of 20 percent women. Although men performed better physically, all women in that class finished the course, with a woman, who had fractured her pelvis, graduating second (Shehadeh 1999, 158). Lebanon has continued to increase the number of women in the Lebanese Armed Forces, reaching 3,000 by 2018, and has enacted a policy to integrate women with men on the frontline (Ghanem 2018). However, their numbers in the military are still small, and traditional views regarding women persist in society. In 2017, the commander of the Armed Forces, General Joseph Aoun, announced his prioritization of expanding women's military roles, including their participation in combat (Arakji 2019).

Positive changes for women's roles in both society and military have also been occurring in some of the Arab Gulf States. In 2003, women comprised over 70 percent of students in technical colleges and 60 percent in the Emirates University in Al Ain, the UAE's main institution of higher education (Salloum 2003, 101). Since 2011, the UAE has been granting women increased political rights exemplified by the appointment of the deputy federal national council speaker. Women serve in high level business positions and have a literacy rate of 89 percent. Prior to 2001, no women served in the diplomatic corps, whereas by 2015, 10 percent of diplomats were women (Katzman 2015, 102).

The United Arab Emirates, which is made up of a federation of seven states, established the *Khawla Bint al-Azwar* Training College in 1991, the

WOMEN FIGHT ISLAMIC STATE

In 2007, Miriam al Mansouri graduated from flight training and was one of three women to join the Emirate Air Force when it opened the branch to women. She had been in the Army prior to her service in the Air Force. In 2014, she led air strikes against the Islamic State in Syria in conjunction with the United States and other Arab states.

FURTHER READING

"ISIS Fight: Mariam Al Mansouri Is First Woman Fighter Pilot for U.A.E." 2014. *NBC News,* September 25. https://www.nbcnews.com/storyline/isis-terror /isis-fight-mariam-al-mansouri-first-woman-fighter-pilot-u-n211366

---

first army college for women in the Gulf region. In 1992, fifty-nine women graduated from the institution to form the basis of the UAE women's corps (Salloum 2003, 103). In 2014, Miriam al Mansouri became the first female pilot in the United Arab Emirates and led air strikes against the Islamic State in Syria (Zraick 2014). The number of female pilots has continued to grow with one qualified on the US F-16 (Katzman 2015, 102).

The small Gulf state of Qatar has also made some important changes regarding women's roles in society. Qatari women made some of their earliest advances in education. In the 1940s, a private school for girls was opened in Qatar, which began the transformation of women's education in that country. By 1955, after Qatar was profiting from oil, it offered public education to girls and, by the 1970s, girls' enrollment in schools was surpassing boys (Bahry and Marr 2005, 105). When a university was opened in Qatar, soon after its establishment, women comprised 70 percent of those enrolled. Part of the gender imbalance was connected to the fact that women were restricted from leaving the country to go abroad to study as men could do. Additionally, men had better opportunities for work, even without a university education (Bahry and Marr 2005, 106). In 2014, Qatar announced that it would consider allowing women to enlist in the military, although in certain instances, women had already been serving in administrative positions in the armed forces. In 2018, Qatar permitted women to volunteer for the military after a decree by the Emir, Tamim Bin Hamad Al-Thani, declared that women over the age of eighteen can serve. Beginning in 2013, men between the ages of eighteen to thirty-five were required to serve at least three months, but a new law increased that service to one year (Dalton 2018).

Women have participated in the Bahrain Defense Forces for over thirty years, but it was only recently that women received training and more opportunities to serve. In 2001, Awatef Al Jishi was appointed the commander of the Women Police Directorate and then in 2004, two female doctors were appointed colonels in the military (Nonoo 2012).

Saudi Arabia continues to be one of the most traditional countries in the region regarding women's rights, especially in the public realm. In February 2018, Saudi Arabia announced that women may serve in the military in the provinces of Riyadh, Mecca, al-Qassim, and Medina. They will be permitted to serve only if they have a male guardian living in the same province as their duty and would not be allowed in combat ("Saudi Arabia Allows Women to Join Military" 2018). The move to allow women into the armed forces reflects other modifications that King Salman Bin Abdul Aziz and his son, Crown Prince Muhammed Bin Salman, have made regarding women's rights. In June 2018, Saudi Arabia lifted the ban on women driving or attending soccer matches. Since August 2019, women above the age of twenty-one have the right to travel without permission from guardians (Rashad and Kalin 2019). Despite these changes, the cultural milieu concerning gender roles and social customs will take time to adjust. Women are still required to remain covered in public spaces while interacting with men.

Syria had been a trading civilization and as such, has a heterogeneous population comprised of various religious and ethnic groups. Syria gained its independence from French rule in 1946, and following many years of instability, President Hafiz al-Assad assumed power in 1970. In 2011, protests began in the city of Daraa, Syria, against his son, President Bashar al-Assad, and occurred in the context of the Arab Spring that began in Tunisia in December 2010. During this period, the Syrian government trained women to fight the rebels, who were working to topple Assad and his regime. The women were trained to fire Kalashnikov weapons, handle grenades, and attack and control checkpoints (Sly and Ramadan 2013). By 2013, Assad's power was waning amid military defections and casualties; as such, he assembled an all-female force, known as the Lionesses for National Defense, to bolster his fighting strength (Sly and Ramadan 2013). For the most part, the women were responsible for controlling checkpoints, but given the civil war, those positions constituted a "frontline."

Women's roles in society and the military in Syria differed depending on the culture and beliefs of its minorities. Syria has a minority Kurdish population that gained some autonomy in the Rojava region after the Kurds wrested control of the area from Islamist rebels. Kurds are spread among four countries—Syria, Iran, Turkey, and Iraq—each with its own characteristics. Additionally, differences exist between Kurdish women in urban or rural settings. According to scholars, Kurdish culture, although fostering traditional gender roles, affords women gender equity. According to Meral Düzgün, the Kurdish Worker's Party (PKK), a Kurdish militant and political organization founded in Turkey, has the largest contingent of armed female fighters in the world (Düzgün 2016, 284).

Women have assumed many leadership roles in Rojava, a province in Syria, including that of prime minister in 2014 in the Afrin Canton (Bengio 2016, 38). Aside from assuming higher political roles, women have gained increased access to the security realm. Women who served in the People's Protection Units (PYD) shielding the population from radical militant groups, such as Al Qaeda and the Islamic State (IS), formed an all-women's militia called the Women's Protection Unit or YPJ (Bengio 2016, 39). This group not only fights for its national group, but also challenges the traditional gender structure in the quest for gender justice (Düzgün 2016, 284).

The protection units participated in battles to remove the militant Islamic State from Syria, particularly from the city of Raqqa where the group had gained a strong foothold and named the city its capital. According to one Kurdish spokesperson, women participated in the battle against the Islamic State not only to liberate their lands, "but also a liberation of mentality and thoughts. War is not only a liberation of land. We are also fighting for the liberation of women and men. If not, the patriarchal system will prevail once again" (McKernan 2017).

In 1980, Syrian president, Bashar al-Assad, welcomed to Syria Abdullah Ocalan, a Kurdish leader from Turkey who founded the Kurdistan Workers' Party (PKK) in 1978 and consequently was forced to flee Turkey. Ocalan transported his ideas regarding gender equality and the role of women in Kurdish society to Syria. This led to the arrangement in the Kurdish-controlled region of Syria that every government institution must have both a man and woman as copresidents or chairpersons and that all committees must have an equal mix of genders. Ocalan's attitude toward governance extended to the battlefield as well. When the America-backed Syrian Democratic Forces captured the city of Raqqa from the militant Islamic State group in 2017, the overall commander was a woman from the YPJ (Nordland 2018).

Although still patriarchal and traditional in its outlook regarding gender, Kurdish women have played critical roles in politics and the military compared with some of their Arab counterparts. Intense scholarship on Kurdish women only began in earnest around 2001. Some scholars contend that early depictions of Kurdish women as freer than other women in the Middle East reflected a romanticized version of reality or served as an attempt by Kurds to advance their nationalist agenda by appearing more modern with regard to women's rights (Bengio 2016, 30). For example, Kurdish women are not required to cover their hair, can wear colorful clothing, and can dance with men in mixed settings. Yet Kurdish women of a specific class, time period, and region did, in actuality, possess more rights than other women in the region, including Arabs and Turks (Bengio 2016, 31).

With the advent of the Arab Spring, a Kurdish Spring occurred simultaneously and has led to an empowering of Kurdish women. Part of women's motivation for increased rights stemmed from the history of illustrating crucial leadership roles that Kurdish women have played in society. For example, during the seventeenth century, a Jewish Kurdish woman, Asenat Barzani, the daughter of a prominent rabbi, learned Torah and the mystical branch of Judaism called the *Kabbalah*. Her father made sure to stipulate in her wedding contract that she would be free from domestic work to continue her religious studies and, when her husband died, she became the head of a men's religious school (Bengio 2016, 31–32). In another example of Kurdish women's leadership, during the period of the Ottoman Sultan Murad IV (1623–1640), a woman, Khanzad, assumed leadership in battle and led armies into raids in Iran. The Kurdish Regional Government (KRG) in Iraq even erected a statue honoring her contributions to the nation. In a more contemporary example, during World War I, Adile Xanim headed the Jaf tribe in the Halabja region of current day Iraq and is recognized for saving British soldiers stationed in that area (Bengio 2016, 33). Most women are still subordinate to men in the male-dominated society; however, the historical examples of women in leadership positions reflect that, under particular circumstances, men would accept being led by dynamic and charismatic women (Bengio 2016, 34).

Kurdish women's experiences in Turkey influenced Kurdish women in other countries. Despite the cultural context of the Middle East and the traditional patriarchal system, Kurdish women in Turkey spearheaded the role of women in politics, social endeavors, and the military. Women participated in the Kurdistan Workers' Party (PKK), established in 1978 and

108　Women and the Military

outlawed by the Turkish government, and in legal Kurdish parties. The PKK espoused gender equality, mainly due to the Marxist views and personal history of its leader, Abdullah Öcalan. In fact, one of the movement's founders, who worked closely with Ocalan, was Sakine Cansiz, head of a PKK squad in Iraqi Kurdistan. Additionally, in the legal Kurdish party established in 1990 and currently known as the Peace and Democracy Party, an established quota gives women 40 percent of positions, including leadership ones (Bengio 2016, 35–36). Kurdish women's roles in the political system reflect the more accepted position of women in Kurdish society than in other countries in the Middle East.

The British controlled Iraq indirectly until 1958, although Iraq gained formal independence in 1932. In the 1930s, women fought against the British by providing food for soldiers and gathering donations. By 1959, a personal status law was enacted that was liberal compared to the rest of the Arab world. It gave women more power with regard to divorce, inheritance, and child custody, by removing power in these areas from the religious authorities (Brown and Romano 2006, 52). Kurdish women in Iraq also participated in the women's movement beginning in the 1920s. After Turkey's establishment in 1923, Kurdish women from Turkey moved into Iraqi Kurdistan to activate the women's movement, which led to the opening of a girls' school in Sulaymaniyya. Margaret George Shello, an Assyrian from Iraqi Kurdistan, became the first female fighter in the *Peshmerga* (Kurdish guerrilla forces) in 1960 and led battles against the Iraqi Army (Bengio 2016, 40). It was only after the Gulf War in 1991, when the Kurds created an autonomous regional government, that the women's movement flourished with many participating heavily in state building. By 2011, women comprised 29.7 percent of the KRG's Parliament compared with only 5.7 percent in 1992 (Bengio 2016, 41–42).

With the advent of the Arab Spring and the growth of the Islamic State in Iraq and Syria, the *Peshmerga* engaged in battles to push IS out of Iraq. In the 2nd *Peshmerga* Battalion established in 1996, 550 women train and fight against the Islamic State. There are approximately 15,000 Kurdish women fighters comprising almost 35 percent of Kurdish forces, especially in YPJ. They are known as fierce warriors and frighten Islamic State members, who believe that if they are killed by a woman, they will not enter paradise (Fitrani, Cooper, and Matthews 2016, 17).

The Qajar Dynasty ruled Iran from 1779 to 1925 and opened the first girls' school in 1907. When Reza Shah Pahlavi assumed power in 1925, ending the Qajar's hold on power, he forced women to remove their veils, permitting them to work in the public domain in many occupations. In 1941, Reza Shah Pahlavi abdicated the throne to his father, who continued to secularize society and forced both men and women to adopt Western clothing. Kurds, a minority also present in Iran, created the Republic of Kurdistan in 1946, which lasted approximately a year. During that time, the Republic's leadership supported women's participation in both politics and national movements (Bengio 2016, 42). Once the Republic of Kurdistan collapsed, Kurdish women's progress in Iran trailed behind other Kurdish women, especially those in Turkey.

In recent years, Jordan has shifted its perspective regarding women's roles in the security sector due to the changing nature of warfare and attitudinal adjustments regarding women in the workforce. Women began to serve in the Jordanian military in education and medical positions in the 1950s. By 1962, the military established the Princess Muna Nursing College, and in 1965 its eight graduates were commissioned as second lieutenants. In the 1970s, women were then recruited to several administrative positions, including computer programmers, accountants, secretaries, and typists, all positions conventional for women. After members of the royal family, Princesses Aisha Bint Al-Hussein and Basma Bint Ali Bin Nayef, requested that King

An Iraqi Army woman, one of thirty-eight women in the second class of recruits, conducts basic training at the Jordanian Royal Military Academy on June 22, 2004. Women began to serve in the Jordanian military in education and medical positions in the 1950s. (Department of Defense)

JORDAN SENDS FEMALE OFFICER TO SANDHURST

In 1995, the Jordanian government created the Directorate of Women's Affairs, which became the Directorate of Women's Military Affairs dealing with women's issues, including maternity leave, skill advancement, wearing of the hijab, and increased education. Princess Aisha Bint Al-Hussein, a member of the royal family, rose to the rank of major general and was the first woman in the Middle East to attend the Royal Military Academy Sandhurst in the United Kingdom.

FURTHER READING

Kawar, Jumana. 2017. "Jordanian Women's Evolving Role in the Armed Forces." In *Women in International Security,* November 28. http://wiisglobal.org /2017/11/28/jordanian-womens-evolving-role-in-the-armed-forces

Hussein increase women's participation in the Jordanian Armed Forces, in 1995, his government created the Directorate of Women's Affairs, which became the Directorate of Women's Military Affairs (DWMA) dealing with women's issues, including maternity leave, skill advancement, wearing of the hijab, and increased education (Kawar 2017). Princess Aisha rose to the rank of major general and was the first woman in the Middle East to attend the Royal Military Academy Sandhurst in the United Kingdom. In 1995, she became the head of the Directorate of Women's Military Affairs.

In 2005, Jordan experienced a series of suicide bombing terrorist attacks, including one involving a female suicide bomber, whose explosive belt did not detonate. For the security sector, the attack demonstrated a requirement for more women in counterterrorism and intelligence forces, and within a year, opportunities expanded for women in the military police, as bodyguards in special protection units, and in military intelligence (Kawar 2017). In addition, women trained to execute counterterrorism and crisis management operations, protect personnel, and provide security at airports and conferences. This shift occurred at a time when Jordanian women were increasingly participating in UN peacekeeping operations and other NATO missions. As trainers for the missions, their participation is essential to communicating important cultural and religious perspectives for women, consistent with intent of UNSCR 1325. Women's prominence is expanding and enhancing Jordan's ability to deal with emerging security threats such as radicalization and terrorism.

Female Iraqi Army trainees learn proper breathing techniques while firing an AK-47 on June 22, 2004, in Jordan. The trainees are in basic training at the Jordanian Royal Military College. Although the percentage of women serving in the Jordanian military is relatively low, 5 percent of Jordanian Air Force pilots are women. (Department of Defense)

Jordan also created the Jordanian Armed Forces Quick Reaction Force Female Engagement Team (QRF), a special-missions platoon composed entirely of female soldiers. It functions to enable operations and activities within specific cultural norms and contexts, providing expanded cultural access that its male counterpart units cannot gain. In April 2018, the team conducted *Exercise Eager Lion* with units from the United States. The team integrated with and assisted an infantry company, where it responded to refugee incidents and conducted personnel searches on females. The QRF addressed cultural considerations while conducting security operations. The goal of the Female Engagement Team is to enhance gender integration into the Jordanian Armed Forces, while improving operational effectiveness ("Improving Security through Female Engagement within the Jordanian Armed Forces" 2018).

Although Jordanian women have a literacy rate of almost 97 percent, they play a small role in the workforce due, in part, to cultural beliefs that a woman's priority should be her family (Kawar 2017). Women make up about 45 percent of public employment, yet only comprise 13 percent of the private sector. They have difficulty competing with men since some employers fear that women's obligations at home might curtail hours at work and that pregnancy will affect their ability to work (Kawar 2017). Some unemployed women with a university education have begun to apply to the Jordanian Armed Forces (JAF), which offers several benefits to women. The JAF offers equal pay and promotion commensurate with seniority and qualifications. The military also offers three months of maternity leave with the Directorate of Women's Military Affairs' (DWMA) objective to have at least 3 percent female officers in nonmedical fields, along with expanding job opportunities to women (Kawar 2017). The Air Force has also been increasing women's training; 5 percent of the Jordanian Air Force pilots are women. Several female pilots trained in the United States to fly Blackhawk helicopters (Frantzman 2018).

Israel

Israel is often held up as the example of an egalitarian country with an equally egalitarian fighting force due to women's conscription into the military and their perceived role as fighters during Israel's War of Independence in 1948. Israel has a compulsory military system requiring both men and women to serve in the Israel Defense Forces (IDF). Since the country's founding in 1948, men were required to serve for three years, while women serve for two, although recent changes have begun to equalize the time. Married women are not required to serve, but can do so voluntarily, while the ultraorthodox community, both men and women, along with most Palestinian citizens of Israel, have been exempt from service. A recent law in 2014 requires ultraorthodox men to serve, but exemptions remain the norm.

The Israel Defense Forces (IDF) was established in 1948 after Israel declared its independence. Prior to 1948, several paramilitary and self-defense groups existed with the earliest being *Hashomer* established in 1908, to protect early Jewish settlements in rural areas. Since its inception, women participated in this defense organization and, although women had weapons' training, most were relegated to support roles by working in communication, first aid, and medical care (Jacoby 2002, 88).

During World War I, the Ottomans, who controlled the area of Palestine, suspected members of *Hashomer* of collaborating with the British and consequently arrested and tortured both men and women, ultimately dispersing the organization. After the Ottoman defeat, the British gained

North Africa and the Middle East   113

the mandate over Palestine, although the Labor Federation (*Histadrut*) became the Jewish representative entity in Palestine and created the *Haganah* to deal with defense. While women were granted many rights in the Jewish community, the *Haganah* excluded them from most tasks in the organization. The prestate period reflected an ideology of gender equality, but the reality was a "the domestication of women within key structures of Israeli society" (Jacoby 2002, 88). In some cases, women did provide crucial benefits to the security establishment. Since the British prohibited women from being searched, women in the *Haganah* were able to smuggle weapons, while others operated signaling equipment or served as nurses (Van Creveld 2000, 84).

In 1941, when fear that the Germans were going to invade Palestine emerged, the Jewish community received permission from the British to establish a full-time volunteer force called the *Palmach*. The majority of those who enlisted in the *Palmach* were in their late teens, including women who comprised 15 percent of the 6,000 members in 1947. When the German threat subsided, the *Palmach* increasingly directed its operations against the British. Although women did not participate in combat operations against the mandatory power, the *Palmach* "was perhaps the most sexually integrated armed force in history where men and women lived in neighboring tents and trained together" (Van Creveld 2000, 85). Aside from participating in the *Palmach*, young Jewish men and women were encouraged to join the British Army during World War II to defeat the Nazis and acquire military experience that they could eventually bring back to Palestine. Over 30,000 volunteers served, 3,000 of whom were women serving in the women's corps (Van Creveld 2000, 85). In November 1947, the United Nations voted to partition Palestine into a Jewish and Arab state, raising tensions in the region. A week later, a mixed-gender *Palmach* squad on patrol was captured and murdered by Arabs. Following this event, the *Haganah* leadership decided to remove women from combat units, although local leaders did not always obey the rule, and several women died in battles in 1948 (Van Creveld 2000, 85–86).

When the Israel Defense Force was established after the declaration of the Israeli state, the *Palmach* was disbanded and women were then put into *Chen*, the women's corps, serving in mostly support functions. *Chen* means grace and the lack of "linguistic coincidence" reflected the societal view that women in the military should retain their feminine qualities. Indeed, included in their basic training was an encouragement to emphasize their feminine appearance and "cosmetic guidance" (Sharoni 1995,

114 Women and the Military

127). Women's separation from men in an autonomous unit reinforced traditional societal gender roles.

After the creation of Israel, over the protestations of religious Jews, the IDF recognized the numeric disadvantage Israel faced compared to the Arab states and conscripted women into the military, in part, to allow men to go to the frontlines (Van Creveld 2000, 87). However, as a concession to the religious population, religious, pregnant, or married women were exempted from military service. During the Suez Campaign in 1956, a war that Israel fought with France and Britain against Egypt, some women had flown transport aircraft. After this conflict, very few women held combat-related positions, despite several attempts to incorporate them into those roles. Women were permitted to become NCOs and officers but were trained separately, and most positions to which they were assigned commanded other women. Because women were not incorporated into commanding or training, but were in staff positions, they were at a disadvantage for promotions. Although Israeli society was somewhat egalitarian due to its socialist foundations, the IDF retained a masculine culture. According to Van Creveld, even though the IDF was successful in its military campaigns, the military "in its treatment of women was retrograde rather than forward-looking" (Van Creveld 2000, 90).

The Yom Kippur War in 1973 changed Israel in a variety of ways. While Israel emerged victorious from the war, the country sustained high rates of casualties and the IDF was no longer viewed, as it was after the Six-Day War in 1967, as the invincible Israeli army. Following the 1973 war when Egypt led a surprise attack on Israel, the IDF had a manpower shortage and explored options for expanding women's participation. During that war, women served as clerks, nurses, and in communications. While in 1974 only 210 military specialties were open to women, by 1976 that number reached 296 (Van Creveld 2000, 91). Women remained under the women's corps leadership, but with new positions opened to them, they increased their opportunities to teach skills such as firing weapons, tank driving, and launching artillery. Even though women were instructors in using artillery, some argued that since women were unable to carry the heavy loads of the artillery, their incorporation into this specialty put an undue burden on their male counterparts (Van Creveld 2000, 92). As a country in almost a constant state of combat, where serving in the military came with societal and economic benefits, excluding women from combat affected women's prestige and ability to lead.

During the 1982 Israeli invasion of Lebanon, women were forbidden to cross the border. However, the war in Lebanon was extremely controversial and perceived by many Israelis as a war of choice rather than one for Israel's survival, as previous wars were viewed. Accordingly, some men were reluctant to serve in this war, consequently impacting the IDF's policies toward women. In 1984, women entered Lebanon to fill medical, communications, and administrative positions. There were no female casualties during this war as the IDF took special care to protect women, believing that a public relations disaster could emerge from female deaths (Van Creveld 2000, 93). As the security environment shifted in the 1980s, Israeli society reflected on issues of civil society and an individual's role within the security realm (Jacoby 2002, 84). Although women fought during Israel's War of Independence, some scholars view that period as exceptional since the creation of the IDF prohibited women in combat. By 1991, the number of occupation specialties opened to women increased 60 percent, and this transformed the composition of the officer corps by doubling the number of female officers. Even with these changes, by 1994, 33 percent of women in the IDF served in clerical or service positions under a male commander (Jacoby 2002, 91). In 1994, Alice Miller, who immigrated to Israel from South Africa and was a civilian pilot, challenged women's exclusion from taking a military exam to qualify for military positions, specifically to become a pilot. Due to her challenge, a bill was advanced changing the Defense Service Law and allowing women to take qualification exams for certain military positions. Additionally, the Supreme Court forced the Air Force to accommodate women to train as pilots. In 1999, the first woman completed the pilot's course and joined an F16 squadron, and by 1998 women were permitted in antiaircraft defense units (Jacoby 2002, 91).

By the year 2000, women in the IDF filled any military position so long as they were "capable" (Fitrani, Cooper, and Matthews 2016, 20). In the IDF, women do not serve in close combat, but serve in other combat positions, comprising 20 percent of the professional military and 33 percent of conscripts. Women began their integration in the combat arms around 2000, due to a personnel shortage, a desire by commanders to use women more flexibly, and both legal and public pressure for equal rights and responsibilities (Schafer et al. 2015, 62). In November 2017, for the first time in Israel's history, a woman was appointed deputy commander of a combat squadron.

116 Women and the Military

Societal Views on Masculinity and the Military

Although 80 percent of Israel is Jewish with a large Arab minority, the country is comprised of large immigrant communities leading to a heterogeneous society with a variety of views on gender equality. As a liberal democracy, Israel's push for gender equality sometimes conflicts with its more traditional gender values, positing that women's focus should be family and children. In Western countries, serving in the military reflects a citizen's role in maintaining a state's sovereignty and participation in the political realm. For Israelis, serving in the military reflects a commitment to state and "civic virtue is constructed in terms of military virtue" (Sasson-Levy 2001, 9). On a more practical level, service in the military offers people access to benefits and other services in civilian life. Those who do not serve are perceived as less than full citizens.

Although Israel is a liberal democracy, in 1948, it adopted a "status quo" arrangement to appease the religious who opposed a secular constitution. Consequently, Israel has no written constitution, but has a series of Basic Laws, which serve as the constitution. As such, although Israel has religious freedom for all, the concept of secularism was not enshrined in the constitution, thereby allowing religious and secular communities to adjudicate any issues that arise on a case-by-case basis. This status quo arrangement has given the religious establishment control over personal status laws, which include aspects of marriage, divorce, and child custody. Particularly in marriage and divorce, women are relegated to traditional roles as wives and mothers, thereby increasing gender differences. Due to this status quo arrangement, religious or married women are exempted from conscription but may volunteer to serve.

Furthermore, because of the predominance of warfare in Israel and the country's concern for security, the security apparatus reflects a masculine, patriarchal structure that pervades all aspects of Israeli society (Jacoby 2002, 84). As warfare has historically been a masculine endeavor, men were the decision makers in both war and national security. As such, Israel's security situation and men's prominent role in the security realm impact gender relations in the state. There is a gender equality myth with regard to Israel since women are conscripted into the army, fought in Israel's War of Independence, and had a female prime minister, Golda Meir, who served from 1969 to 1974 (Jacoby 2002, 87). However, since women were not considered strong enough for combat, their relegation to the sidelines permeated their roles in civilian society as well (Levy 2010, 187).

Additionally, the volatile security situation led to a veneration of masculine traits, marginalizing women and forcing them into the more traditional feminine spheres of child rearing (Jacoby 2002, 87).

Notwithstanding that Israel's declaration of independence granted gender equality, the military rules reflect a much more gendered hierarchy. Exemptions for pregnancy, marriage, and religious beliefs are easy to obtain, despite the almost constant state of war in Israel and its need for personnel. Men and women are required to serve annually in the reserves after their compulsory military service, although women are often exempted. For women, more masculine roles in the military offer higher prestige, yet the military structure emphasizes women's lower status in the organization.

Although Israeli women have compulsory military service, for much of the IDF's existence, a strict gender division of labor was enforced, reflecting Israeli cultural norms. Within the last decade, as in many other Western countries, people recognized that women's opportunity for complete societal equality was hampered by its exclusion from all aspects of military service. In Israel, military service impacts job opportunities, important networking, and other advantages. Israeli women began to demand being drafted into combat positions. After both Israel's Parliament and Supreme Court's intervention in 1995, the military opened several opportunities for women, including as pilots, in the border police, antiaircraft, and naval commando. By January 2000, the Knesset (Parliament) approved a law allowing women to serve in any military position, although this depended on military requirements. The dismantling of *Chen*, the women's corp, followed in June 2000, placing women under the command of their units rather than under a separate women's command (Sasson-Levy 2001, 7). By 2001, the first female combat pilot graduated from the pilot's course, and a female border police was wounded in action.

Integration continues to have its challenges. According to Sasson-Levy, some women adopt three types of roles to integrate into the IDF's masculine hegemony, including distancing themselves from femininity, trivializing sexual harassment, and emulating combat soldiers' patterns of comporting themselves. Some women adopt men's mannerisms by learning to walk in a "masculine" way, increasing their use of curses, modulating the pitch of their voices, avoiding makeup, and wearing uniforms that androgenize them (Sasson-Levy 2001, 11–12). Furthermore, women's incorporation into combat roles did not diminish the interconnection between combat and masculinity; nor did it elevate women's lower status (Sasson-Levy 2001, 9).

118   Women and the Military

Factors Influencing Change

Although Israel is part of the Middle East, it is a Westernized democracy and has experienced pressures for equality similar to North American and European countries, along with attitudinal and demographic shifts regarding military service. In 1975, the Israeli government created the Commission on the Status of Women to explore gender inequality, yet issues of the military were not central to its exploration (Levy 2010, 188). In 2000, the government modified the Security Service Law to implement equality throughout the IDF. This meant that women could serve in combat roles, although they had to volunteer, whereas many men were forced to serve in those roles. Additionally, in 2003, women in combat roles were required to serve thirty-six months, the same time as men are required to serve, while most female soldiers only serve twenty-four months. Some scholars argue that equalizing military service will have ripple effects in the civilian sphere, granting women more equality overall. However, despite sociocultural attitude changes in Israeli society, the IDF opened these positions to address a manpower shortfall (Levy 2010, 188). The IDF maintains the chief of staff's adviser on women's issues to assess gender inequality in the Israeli military.

By 2013, women comprised "16 percent of artillery jobs, 15 percent of field intelligence; 21 percent of nuclear, biological and chemical (NBC) occupations; 14 percent of the Commando K9 Oketz (Israeli special forces canine) unit; and 68 percent of light infantry" (Schaefer et al. 2015, 62). Despite increased integration, women comprised only 3 percent of combat soldiers (Barry 2013, 23).

The example of the IDF's integration of women into parts of the combat arms is instructive. Although women seemed to have more injuries than men and a higher burnout rate, commanders note that they are motivated, organized, disciplined, talented in shooting abilities, and professional in their use of weapons (Schaefer et al. 2015, 62). It illustrates that with appropriate training and equipment modifications, women can perform as well as men. Additionally, mixed-gender training improves women's physical performance, while combined accommodations bolster unit cohesion (Schaefer et al. 2015, 64).

The IDF has strived to integrate women by modifying equipment to fit physical differences and implementing quotas. The IDF has also created the Women's Affairs division and "cohesion days" to deal with obstacles that women face in the military (Schaefer et al. 2015, 64). Aside from

North Africa and the Middle East   119

facing opposition and discrimination from men in the military, women also encounter discrimination from the religious conservatives who hold traditional views about a woman's role in society. With the forced incorporation of the ultraorthodox into the IDF, women have begun to feel increased discrimination.

As both women and religious groups are increasingly integrated into the military since the year 2000, the two are coming into conflict. Yagil Levy argued in 2010 that the IDF had been experiencing two social revolutions, feminism and religiosity, and that these are headed toward a confrontation (2010, 185). This perspective became even more evident when the Knesset passed a universal conscription law in 2014 that required ultraorthodox Jews to serve in the IDF. Previously, religious Jews could gain an exemption or deferral from military service if they were registered to study in a religious institution. Men who were already exempted under the old law would not be forced to serve, but a three-year transitional period ended in 2017, necessitating that most religious Jews serve. Several challenges with regards to gender relations have arisen with the incorporation of this group into the military. For religious men, strict separation of the sexes is required to maintain the laws of modesty, while the IDF has been steadily expanding integration, particularly in combat units. Rabbis have increased their requests for gender separation, and the IDF has responded by advancing rules of integration that require separate living arrangements, a requirement that women dress modestly, and a "prohibition on physical contact" between the sexes (Levy 2010, 186). Despite these requirements, the rabbis have continued to press for more stringent separation, clearly limiting women's increased acceptance and integration into combat units. Levy argues that given the structure of Israel's institutions and symbols, the conflict between feminists and religious groups "is an asymmetric conflict in which the religious groups have a definite advantage" (Levy 2010, 186). In one case, when a female instructor was teaching paratroopers, thirty religious men in the course turned their backs on her, while another instructor allowed the men to lower their heads when the female instructor was speaking (Kobavitz 2018).

There are many religious Jews, both men and women, who willingly serve in the military. To accommodate religious-nationalist Israeli Jewish women who serve in the IDF, yet also want to continue their Jewish studies, the IDF has created the *garin* program. This program allows women to study in a religious Jewish academy, and after they complete that program be conscripted into the IDF (Stollman 2009, 159).

SEXUAL HARASSMENT AND ASSAULT

Some Israeli scholars claim that women in the military are marginalized due to the masculine nature of the institution and therefore do not benefit from military service, while others hold that women gain advantages despite the "gendered construction of military roles" (Dar and Kimhi 2004, 434). Due to a gendered division of labor in the IDF, and since men occupy the more elite and coveted positions, women hold an inferior status (Dar and Kimhi 2004, 435). This inferior status is connected to potential sexual abuse or a diminished social capital that men receive when they seek civilian employment (Dar and Kimhi 2004, 435).

Given the patriarchal structure of Israeli society due to both the preeminent role of the military and religion in some parts of society, gendered violence has been tacitly condoned in the IDF over the years, along with sexual harassment (Jacoby 2002, 92). After the women's corps was dissolved in 2001, a gender adviser position was created. In 2006, the chief of staff of the IDF, Dan Hulutz, decided to merge the gender adviser position with another, ostensibly abolishing it. His decision was almost simultaneous with the release of an internal report revealing that women in the IDF face discrimination and obstacles to advancement. Despite the outcry by many in Parliament, the chief of staff refused to reverse his decision (Prince-Gibson 2007). When a new chief of staff, Gabi Ashkenazi, was appointed in 2007, he reversed his predecessor's pronouncement. According to an internal IDF survey in 2016, one in six women in the IDF reported being victims of sexual harassment with women describing an environment conducive to harassment (Ahronheim 2017).

FURTHER READING

Afshar, Haleh. 2003. "Women and Wars: Some Trajectories towards a Feminist Peace." *Development in Practice* 13, no. 2/3: 178–188. http://www.jstor.org/stable/4029590

Ahronheim, Anna. 2017. "1 in 6 Female Soldiers Report Sexual Harassment in IDF." *The Jerusalem Post,* September 10. Proquest.

Arabsheibani, G. Reza, and Lamine Manfor. 2002. "From Farashia to Military Uniform: Male-Female Wage Differentials in Libya." *Economic Development and Cultural Change* 50, no. 4 (July): 1007–1019.

Arakji, Dina. 2019. "Females in the Ranks." *Carnegie Middle East Center,* June 19. https://carnegie-mec.org/diwan/79306

Arieff, Alexis. 2011. "Tunisia: Recent Developments and Policy Issues." January 18. Accessed November 7, 2019. https://digital.library.unt.edu

Bahry, Louay, and Phebe Marr. 2005. "Qatari Women: A New Generation of Leaders?" *Middle East Policy* 12, no. 2 (Summer): 104–119. EBSCO HOST.

Barry, Ben. 2013. "Women in Combat." *Survival* 55, no. 2: 19–30.

Bengio, Ofra. 2016. "Game Changers: Kurdish Women in Peace and War." *The Middle East Journal* 70, no. 1: 30–46. https://dx.doi.org/10.3751/70.1.12

Brown, Lucy, and David Romano. 2006. "Women in Post-Saddam Iraq: One Step Forward or Two Steps Back?" *NWSA Journal* 18, no. 3: 51–70. http://www.jstor.org/stable/40071181

Cheref, Abdelkader. 2006. "Engendering or Endangering Politics in Algeria? Salima Ghezali, Louisa Hanoune and Khalida Messaoudi." *Journal of Middle East Women's Studies* 2, no. 2: 60–85. https: doi:10.2979/mew.2006.2.2.60

Dalton, Jane. 2018. "Qatar Allows Military Women to Do Service for the First Time." *The Independent*, April 6. https://www.independent.co.uk/news/world/middle-east/qatar-women-military-service-allow-gender-saudi-arabia-a8291451.html

Dar, Yechezkel, and Shaul Kimhi. 2004. "Youth in the Military: Gendered Experiences in the Conscript Service in the Israeli Army." *Armed Forces and Society* 30, no. 3 (Spring): 433–459.

DeGroot, Gerard J. 2001. *International Peacekeeping* 8, no. 2 (Summer): 23–39. doi:10.1080/13533310108413893

Düzgün, Meral. 2016. "Jineology: The Kurdish Women's Movement." *The Journal of Middle East Women's Studies* 12, no. 2 (July): 284–287. Project Muse.

Fitrani, Randall, G. S. Cooper, and Ron Matthews. 2016. "Women in Ground Close Combat." *RUSI Journal* 161, no. 1 (February/March): 14–24.

Frantzman, Seth J. 2018. "Jordan's First Female Black Hawk Pilots Meet U.S. General Vote." *Jerusalem Post,* January 29. http://www.jpost.com/Middle-East/Jordans-first-female-Black-Hawk-pilots-meet-US-General-Votel-540154

Ghanem, Dalia. 2015. "Women in the Men's House: The Road to Equality in the Algerian Military." November 4. https://carnegie-mec.org/2015/11/04/women-in-men-s-house-road-to-equality-in-algerian-military-pub-61463

Ghanem, Dalia. 2018. "Women at Arms," December 3. https://carnegie-mec.org/diwan/77852

"Improving Security through Female Engagement within the Jordanian Armed Forces." 2018. *The Maple Leaf.* Accessed September 2, 2019. https://ml-fd.caf-fac.ca/en/2018/06/14778

Jacoby, Tami Amanda. 2002. "Gender Relations and National Security in Israel." In *Redefining Security in the Middle East,* edited by Tami Amanda Jacoby and Brent E. Sasley, 83–104. Manchester, UK: Manchester University Press.

Karamé, Kari. 1995. "Girls Participation in Combat: A Case Study from Lebanon." In *Children in the Muslim Middle East,* edited by Elizabeth Warnock Fernea, 378–391. Austin: University of Texas Press.

Katzman, Kenneth. 2015. "The United Arab Emirates: Issues for US Policy." *Current Politics and Economics of the Middle East* 6, no. 1: 89–129.

Kawar, Jumana. 2017. *Jordanian Women's Evolving Role in the Armed Forces.* November 28. http://wiisglobal.org/2017/11/28/jordanian-womens-evolving-role-in-the-armed-forces

Kobavitz, Yaniv. 2018. "Israeli General: Army Should Have Reacted Stronger When Paratroopers Turned Back on Female Instructor." *Haaretz,* August 9. https://www.haaretz.com/israel-news/.premium-israeli-general-army-should-react-stronger-to-gender-discrimination-1.6363239

Levy, Yigal. 2010. "The Clash between Feminism and Religion in the Israeli Military: A Multilayered Analysis." *Social Politics* 17, no. 2: 185–209.

Libya: Discriminatory Restriction on Women. Human Rights Watch, February 23, 2017. https://www.hrw.org/news/2017/02/23/libya-discriminatory-restriction-women

Londono, Ernesto. 2011. "Women Bracing for Battle to Protect Qaddafi." *Washington Post,* July 3. Proquest.

Marlowe, Ann. 2011. "Boxed In? The Women of Libya's Revolution." *World Affairs* (September/October): 64–67.

McKernan, Bethan. 2017. "Female Kurdish Fighters Announce New Training Academies for Arab Women to Take on Isis in Syria." *Independent,* January 4. https://www.independent.co.uk/news/world/middle-east/female-kurdish-fighters-ypj-set-up-new-training-academies-arab-yazidi-women-to-fight-isis-a7508951.html

Meddeb, Hamza. 2015. "Conscription Reform Will Shape Tunisia's Future Civil-Military Relations." October 21. https://carnegie-mec.org /diwan/61704

Miller, Judith. 1986. "Libya's Women: Era of Change." *New York Times*, February 3. https://www.nytimes.com/1986/02/03/style/libya-s-women -era-of-change.html

Moghadam, Valentine M. 2014. "Democratization and Women's Political Leadership in North Africa." *Journal of International Affairs* 68, no. 1: 59–78. http://www.jstor.org/stable/24461706

Nonoo, Houda. 2012. "Bahrain's Women Pioneers: Women in the Army and Police." https://houdanonoo.wordpress.com/2012/03/27/bahrains -women-pioneers-women-in-the-army-and-police

Nordland, Rod. 2018. "Woman Are Free and Armed in Kurdish Controlled Northern Syria." *NYT* (online), February 24. https://www .nytimes.com/2018/02/24/world/middleeast/syria-kurds-womens -rights-gender-equality.html

Parmelee, Jennifer. 1986. "Libyan Women Defy Tradition to Answer Call to Arms." *LA Times*, January 26. Proquest.

Prince-Gibson, Eetta. 2007. "Chief of Staff Reinstates Women's-Status Post." *The Jerusalem Report*, April 2. Proquest.

Rashad, Marwa, and Stephen Kalin. 2019. *Saudi Arabia Women's Rights Reforms May Still Be Thwarted by Custom.* August 5. https://www .reuters.com/article/us-saudi-women-guardianship/saudi-arabia -womens-rights-reforms-may-still-be-thwarted-by-custom -idUSKCN1UV1Q4

Rosman-Stollman, Elisheva. 2009. "Women of Valor: The Garin Program and the Israel Defense Forces." *Israel Studies* 14, no. 2 (Summer): 158–177.

Salloum, Habeeb. 2003. "Women in the United Arab Emirates." *Contemporary Review* (August): 101–104. Proquest.

Sasson-Levy, Orna. 2001. "Gender Performance in a Changing Military: Women Soldiers in 'Masculine' Roles." *Israel Studies Forum* 17, no. 1: 7–22. JSTOR.

"Saudi Arabia Allows Women to Join Military." 2018. BBC, February 26. https://www.ecoi.net/en/document/1065861.html

Schaefer, Agnes Gereben, Jennie W. Wenger, Jennifer Kavanagh, Jonathan P. Wong, Gillian S. Oak, Thomas E. Trail, and Todd Nichols. 2015. *Implications of Integrating Women into the Marine Corps Infantry.* Santa Monica, CA: RAND.

Sharoni, Simona. 1995. "Gendered Identities in Conflict: The Israeli-Palestinian Case and Beyond." *Women's Studies Quarterly* 23, no. 3/4: 117–135. JSTOR.

Shehadeh, Lamia Rustum. 1999. "Women in the Lebanese Militias." In *Women and War in Lebanon,* edited by Lamia Rustum Shehadeh, 145–166. Gainesville: University Press of Florida.

Sly, L., & Ramadan, A. 2013. "The All-Female Militias of Syria." *Washington Post,* January 25. Proquest.

Van Creveld, Martin. 2000. "Armed but Not Dangerous: Women in the Israeli Military." *War in History* 7, no. 1: 82–98. JSTOR.

Zraick, Karen. 2014. "Arab Women Led Airstrikes over Syria." *New York Times,* September 25. https://www.nytimes.com/2014/09/26/world/middleeast/emirates-first-female-fighter-pilot-isis-airstrikes.html

FIVE

Sub-Saharan Africa

In much of Sub-Saharan Africa, women's roles in security and defense have been dictated by the customs, cultures, and requirements of the nation. In some countries, women have fought to protect themselves and their families or have been forced to serve in conscript militaries. In others, women have risen to the highest ranks of leadership as generals and in civilian positions. In some situations, women have joined small armed groups during wars of independence or civil wars. After these wars, countries have neglected reintegrating women into civil society, often downplaying their contributions during war. Though their service is necessary during hostilities, frequently their expanded role during wartime is reversed after the fighting. Women are pushed back into the home and excluded from disarmament, demobilization, and reintegration programs. Despite fighting a traditional mind-set that encourages women to remain home as primary caregivers, they face high rates of discrimination and harassment. Hope exists in the region as women have reached the highest ranks of leadership in the defense sector and have been admitted into combat roles in many countries.

For the purposes of this chapter, Sub-Saharan Africa includes Angola, Benin, Botswana, Burkina Faso, Burundi, Cameroon, Cape Verde, Central African Republic, Chad, Comoro Islands, Congo Republic, Cote d'Ivoire, the Democratic Republic of Congo, Djibouti, Equatorial Guinea, Eritrea, Ethiopia, Gabon, Gambia, Ghana, Guinea, Guinea-Bissau, Kenya, Lesotho, Liberia, Madagascar, Malawi, Mali, Mauritania, Mauritius, Mozambique, Namibia, Niger, Nigeria, Rwanda, São Tomé and Principe, Senegal,

Seychelles, Sierra Leone, Somalia, South Africa, South Sudan, Sudan, Swaziland, Tanzania, Togo, Uganda, Zambia, and Zimbabwe.

Of these nations, only Mauritius lacks a standing army, instead relying on a police force to carry out all military, police, and security functions. In 1945, Mauritius deployed a contingent of 200 women to Egypt to serve with the British Royal Air Force as clerks, telephone operators, and nurses (Jackson 2001, 66).

SOCIETAL VIEWS OF MASCULINITY AND WARFARE

War's conduct in Sub-Saharan Africa remains a gendered phenomenon, with many men protecting the nation or group, while women serve in the home. Women have joined in independence fights, either through necessity or motivated by a cause. In Africa, women are often forced to join military efforts through recruitment or the threat of sexual violence. Many ultimately had served as laborers, servants, or sexual slaves, while others were combatants (Honwana 2005, 5). Baez and Stern found that many women have been victims of gender-based violence in Africa, with rape used frequently as a weapon of war. They also note that many women join in armed factions to protect themselves from abuse (Baaz and Stern 2012, 712).

Several historical legends exist championing the role of African women in battles. However, these events are few and far between, as in most societies in the region, men are viewed as connected to warfare with women's primary responsibility in the home. With that said, Queen Zhinga of Matamba, located in Angola, ruled over her kingdom in the seventeenth century, fighting several wars against the Portuguese. She is reported to have sacrificed male prisoners before entering battle and kept a harem of male concubines (Edgerton 2000, 140). Women in the Kingdom of Asante, now Ghana, often taunted men into fighting, though declined to fight themselves (Edgerton 2000, 137). The Kingdom of Dahomey, located in current-day Benin, used women as soldiers in 1729 after heavy losses of men in battle (Alpern 1998, 20). European accounts of these Amazon warriors describe women who were mistaken for men, with loose tunics fastened around their waist with belts (Alpern 1998, 54). The women trained in combat pursuits, physical endeavors, and moral and religious instruction, much as men would (Edgerton 2000, 28). The women never served in mixed-gender units, though competition between the all-male and all-female units was reportedly fierce (Edgerton 2000, 153).

European accounts convey that Dahomey women were among the most determined adversaries. A final battle against French troops armed with superior weaponry killed all but fifty of the 1,500 women who attacked (Dash 2011). These women were among the most feared warriors, and they paved the way for women to serve in Benin's army today. Women are only required to register for service and may volunteer (Zeldin 2007). Beninese youth who want to enter the military are required to have a higher education diploma, eliminating many who may otherwise be qualified and interested in service.

Often, cultural change trails legal modifications. Deeply held traditions and attitudes take time to adjust. While many national constitutions in Africa explicitly guarantee women equal rights, including property rights,

The Natives of Dahomey are featured in this from an exposition in 1900 in Paris, France. The Kingdom of Dahomey, located in present-day Benin, was home to trained female fighters. European accounts suggest that the women were fierce, often fighting to the death. (Library of Congress)

educational rights, and civil liberties, the African Union (AU) found that many of these rights are not guaranteed in practice. As such, the AU advocates for full-gender equality, both before the law and in reality (*AU Strategy for Gender Equality & Women's Empowerment 2018–2028* 2018, 10). For example, in Zimbabwe, Mali, and Ghana, women do not always inherit property, confining them to their family's protection and control and fewer economic opportunities than men (Gaddis, Lahoti, and Li 2018, 9).

South Africa leads the way for gender integration, although traditional attitudes regarding women's place in society persist. Nosiviwe Mapisa-Nqakula is the longest-serving defense minister on the continent, holding the position since 2012. She recalls an incident when she attended a conference for defense ministers and took her seat at the table. Initially, other ministers were shocked that she sat down, thinking that she was South Africa's defense minister's assistant. She admonished her male counterparts to allow women to "take their rightful places," noting that women "don't want to be patronized, they want to be recognized for what they do" (Ighobor 2019).

In many countries, African women are subject to gender-based violence, early marriage, and female genital mutilation (World Health Organization

---

WOMEN IN POLITICS IN SUB-SAHARAN AFRICA

In 2018, a few women became part of a small group of women to rise to the highest ranks of leadership in Sub-Saharan Africa. Ethiopian President Sahle-Work Zewde assumed her role as head of state with a speech emphasizing the importance of equality. She joins Saara Kuugongelwa-Ahmadhila, prime minister of Namibia, in reaching for the highest ranks of government service. Women, particularly in Africa, are more likely to serve in positions that oversee social roles, rather than government and defense. Ethiopia boasts a Cabinet that is 50 percent female, including the country's first minster for defense. Rose Christiane Raponda became the first female defense minister in Gabon in 2019. As women join the political ranks, their role in the military often grows, leading many scholars to look forward to women assuming more positions throughout the militaries of Sub-Saharan Africa (Turkington 2018).

FURTHER READING

Turkington, Rebecca. 2018. "A Step Forward for Women in African Politics." *Council on Foreign Relations,* October 25. https://www.cfr.org/blog/step-forward-women-african-politics

Regional Office for Africa n.d.). These factors confine their independent choices significantly in many African nations. Additionally, high rates of HIV/AIDs affect more women than men in the region, and many countries lack the capacity to stop their spread or treat those who have been infected (Rupp, Diallo, and Phillipps 2012, 9). Patrick Cammaert, a retired Dutch general who served as a peacekeeper in the Democratic Republic of the Congo, remarked that "it has probably become more dangerous to be a woman than a solider in armed conflict" (Ham 2014, 120).

Young girls have also participated in conflicts in the Democratic Republic of the Congo (DRC), Sierra Leone, and Uganda (Quénivet 2008, 219). Haer and Bomhelt found that up to 40 percent of some nonstate armed groups in Africa were children, including girls (Haer and Bohmelt 2018, 395). While these girls are often forced into service by nonstate-sponsored armed groups, occasionally government troops recruited or kidnapped girls to serve with them. Younger girls were more likely to be assaulted than older women, due to fears that older women had HIV/AIDs. Many girl soldiers continued their service after they became legal adults at eighteen. They served as cooks, porters, messengers, or active combatants (Haer and Bohmelt 2018, 397). Though the focus of this chapter is not on child soldiers, many young women do serve in the armed factions of their state, often not by choice.

The region's history of colonialism and abrupt transition from colonial rule allowed many foundational elements, such as diversity in the armed forces and the purpose of the military, to be overlooked in the transition to independence (Mazrui 2011). The emergence of change is slow, though women may now serve in some capacity in most armed forces. In many postconflict African countries, governments have developed quota systems to ensure equality for minority groups, including women. Human rights groups contend that including women in the military may increase women's opportunities throughout society (Louw-Vaudran 2015). Placing women on par with men in military positions has the potential to raise their status in political, social, and economic realms (Mophuting 2003, 7). Critics note that quota systems must balance both gender and ethnic groups, a difficult task. Quota systems often marginalize previously privileged groups, leading to complaints of unfairness (Gjelsvik 2013, 3). Advocates of quotas believe they should be supported for real policy change to be effective (Louw-Vaudran 2015).

While women have been guaranteed the right to serve in public institutions in many African countries over the years, including the military, at

130   Women and the Military

least two states cited the cost of appropriate accommodations and uniforms as a primary reason for an earlier refusal to integrate. Both Malawi and Botswana were among the last militaries to permit women in the armed forces with Malawi recruiting women around the turn of the twenty-first century (Sharp and Fisher 2005, 50). Even with their late entry into the military, one female officer attended and graduated Sandhurst, the Royal Military Academy in Great Britain, and women now serve as paratroopers and marines, placing them on the frontlines of combat (IPS Correspondents 1999). Similarly, the Botswanan government declined to integrate the Botswanan Defense Forces until 2007, citing a lack of funding to revamp training locations (Sharp and Fisher 2005, 50). Reports from 2014 suggest that recruiting women is slow, and they comprise less than 10 percent of the force (Lucas 2014). The Botswanan military struggles with challenges of integration, including patriarchal attitudes, marginalization, inequality, and abuse of women (Pheage 2016). Some servicewomen allude to confusing practices in dealing with fraternization issues and sexual assault, along with a promotion system that rejects meritocracy, as barriers to continued service (Pheage 2016).

FACTORS INFLUENCING CHANGE

Several factors have led to changes for women in society, particularly relating to military service. Conscription of women may lead to increased status in society, while women's participation in civil wars have often led to exclusion from political processes after the war. Women's participation in peacekeeping operations and a recognition of their value in deescalating violence, ability to work in conservative societies with strict gender separation and their successes on the ground have begun to modify their position in African society.

Several nations in Sub-Saharan Africa use conscription to fill their ranks. This conscription is either universal service or selective service, and the level of enforcement varies. Universal service requires everyone in a certain population to serve, while selective service allows the military to choose recruits based on the needs of the military (Desilver 2019). A recent study about conscription found women are drafted as part of universal service requirements in Eritrea and Mali, while Benin, Cape Verde, and Mozambique have selective service (Desilver 2019). Women in Sudan may be drafted, though only men have served as part of this program (Desilver 2019). Other states maintain inactive conscription services but may choose to institute them during a period of national emergency. Chad and the Ivory Coast have indicated that they would include both men and women if they were to implement their conscription programs. Chad requires women to serve for one year in either compulsory military or civil service, but these stipulations have never been fully enforced (Desilver 2019). Equatorial Guinea has selective compulsory service for eighteen-year-old men and women, though similar to Chad, this draft is rarely imposed.

Of those countries that enforce conscription laws, Eritrea stands out. The Eritrean constitution guarantees gender equality, allowing men and women to be drafted into direct combat units. The constitution also allows for indefinite extensions of service in times of emergency. The Eritrean government contends that the ongoing tensions with neighboring Ethiopia constitute a national emergency and has kept much of the population on active or reserve duty status as a result (Maclean 2018). Both men and unmarried women are required to serve for up to eighteen months. Six months of that time is training, while the other twelve may be devoted to military duties or other national development projects. Many Eritreans continue to search for ways to avoid this indefinite service. Human rights groups cite the frequent unwritten extension of service (sometimes for years), as a major driver for individuals to flee the country, across the Sahara or the Mediterranean Sea (Human Rights Watch 2019).

Possible draftees may be excused for health reasons. For women, pregnancy will exempt them from service. However, those who do not participate in national service are unable to finish secondary school, as the final year of schooling is spent in Sawa, a remote military camp training for service (Maclean 2018). Reports indicate that women serve as domestic servants during their service, while others describe forced relationships with senior officers. Women who enter sexual relationships with superior officers are often provided easier training regimens or more food (Human Rights Watch 2019). Some women have reportedly been held in shipping containers for refusing to engage in sexual relations with their commanding officers during their service (Human Rights Watch 2009).

INDEPENDENCE AND CIVIL WARS

Women have participated in national wars of independence and civil wars throughout Africa. Although still excluded from many areas of the military and political life, their service in these seminal battles have influenced some countries in Africa to include women in their militaries and

132 Women and the Military

afford them higher roles in political life. In many African states, women served in both official government militaries and in armed factions. These wars were often brutal, subjecting women to rape and other forms of gender-based violence. Women were sometimes conscripted and forced to serve, while others joined to protect themselves and their families. After the violence, women were often excluded from disarmament, demobilization, and reintegration programs, which created further issues for women who had grown up fighting and were used to certain levels of equality. These women had few other tangible skills, given the years they had spent fighting.

In the 1960s, during Mozambique's War for Independence, women were in the Destacamento Femenino (DF), or the women's military wing. They learned to handle weapons and when deployed in combat were responsible for guarding the camp, conducting reconnaissance, or looting missions (Honwana 2005, 79). Others served as intelligence officers or in support positions. Currently, the laws in Mozambique do not distinguish between men and women, so all women are eligible for conscription. Women are usually not on the frontline, but often train at the Moamba garrison and serve in support and administrative roles (Honwana 2005, 92).

Similarly, during the struggle for Angola's liberation, women were conscripted in the People's Armed Forces of Liberation of Angola (FAPLA). After the Bicesse Accords in 1993, the FAPLA and the Armed Forces of Liberation of Angola became the Angolan Armed Forces (Leão and Rupiya 2005, 28). Currently, both men and women may join the Angolan military, with men required to register for the draft at the age of eighteen and women between the ages of twenty and twenty-four serving voluntarily. Former chief of staff, General Geraldo Sachipengo Nunda, told a group of soldiers that citizens in uniform have more duties than rights. He continued by encouraging them to remain on guard to defend the nation by remaining loyal to the constitution, commander in chief, the people, and the armed forces, suggesting a significant shift in the role of the military in the country (*Agencia Angola Press* 2014).

Women in Ethiopia and Eritrea often fought each other during the decades-long Ethiopian Civil War (1974–1991). About 4 percent of the military forces of the Derg, the Provisional Military Government of Ethiopia, were women (Burgess 2013, 99). Women reportedly made up about 30 percent of the rebel Tigrean People's Liberation Front in 1991 (Burgess 2013, 101). Women fought alongside men, and both shared equal housekeeping duties during the conflict. When the war ended, women on both sides of the conflict were quickly demobilized and often disappointed that they were no longer considered equal to men. As they were occupied with learning military skills, their families criticized their limited household management abilities (Veale 2005, 116). In an effort to maintain some gender equality in the military, in early 2020, five women in the Ethiopian army were promoted to general ("Ethiopia Promotes 65 Military Officers, Including Five Women" 2020).

Women in Eritrea were recruited to fight for independence, rather than conscripted as they are today. The Eritrean People's Liberation Front recruited both men and women as the group fought for independence from Ethiopia between 1973 and 1993 (Bernal 2001, 132). Believing that women were vital to the effort, they campaigned with the slogan "no liberation without women's participation" (Wood 2019, 11). The combatants who answered the call to serve spent six months in single-gender training but served in mixed-gender units. All combatants shared similar work, including camp chores and serving on the frontlines of the guerrilla struggle (Bernal 2001, 134). Many women were eventually trained as mechanics, drivers, and doctors. The thirty years of war disrupted traditional societal norms and at the cessation of violence, women returned home to more traditional spheres, yet struggled to reacclimate (Bernal 2001, 137).

During Sudan's second civil war, women formed the Katibat Banat, an all-women battalion, which fought for the Southern People's Liberation Movement/Army (Elamin and Ismail 2019). A recent report from South Sudan details the rise of a female colonel, who raised seven children while serving in the military. Though she fought for her country for many years, she wants "a situation where women have the right to own property, such as land when their husbands die. Women's rights are not respected" (Sackitey 2020). This particular case reflects the difficulty in changing societal attitudes.

To heal rifts after civil wars, some militaries have changed the structure of their armed forces, recruiting women to service. These women bring new perspectives, and the military provides a steady source of income after violent conflicts. After the end of hostilities in Liberia, President Ellen Johnson-Sirleaf implemented rigorous vetting panels, rejecting those who committed atrocities during the war. She announced her goal of building an army that was 20 percent female (Harsch 2010, 11). Liberia reconstituted its military in 2006 after temporary demobilization in 2003 and recruited ethnic minorities and women to serve. However, many women were unable to meet the qualification of a high school education, and estimates from 2016 suggest that less than 4 percent of the military is female (Abdulmelik 2016, 26). Johnson and Lidow found that many service members have a close familial tie to the military that encouraged their service, which is in alignment with previous findings in Malawi, Sudan, and South Africa (Johnson and Lidow 2016, 443).

In the Central African Republic, under the watch of a female defense minister, Marie-Noëlle Koyara, the country is actively working to rebuild the army after the civil war in 2012 (Solomon 2019). The history of instability and military intervention in the country has emphasized the need for a military more representative of the people. The Central African Republic's military is currently less than 8 percent female ("Central African Republic Background Note" 2019).

WOMEN AND DISARMAMENT, DEMOBILIZATION, AND REINTEGRATION (DDR)

Many of the disarmament, demobilization, and reintegration programs in Africa were not designed to accommodate women. These programs build capacity for long-term stability, security, and peace in countries after war, while reintegrating former combatants. While men who serve in support fields like medical, communications, and supply are considered soldiers, most women who serve in similar positions are not perceived as such (MacKenzie 2009, 257). As a result, many women have been excluded from the DDR process and find themselves isolated after their participation in conflict. Women in Rwanda, Zimbabwe, Eritrea, and Sierra Leone all reported feeling as though the DDR process largely ignored them and left them without options (El-Bushra, Fused in Combat). Some women in Rwanda served as leaders in promoting the genocide in 1994 and made up 6 percent of the detainees by the end of the hostilities (Darden 2015, 458). Others helped to end the genocide (Holmes 2018, 241). Both groups of women have been omitted from the DDR process.

In Zimbabwe, women have served since colonial times. After liberation struggles, women could remain in the armed forces, though many were also excluded from the DDR process (Sharp and Fisher 2005). Zimbabwe has made some progress connected with women in the military and society. Zimbabwe's 2013 constitution requires parity in all public institutions, though few women have attained high ranks in government or military service (Morna, Makamure, and Glenwright 2018, 238). In 2016, Ellen

Chiweshe assumed the number three position in the air force when she became air commodore. Upon her promotion, she shared the challenge of breaking into a man's world (Mutsaka 2016).

Recent research focused on Sierra Leone's DDR process noted that women were treated as though their only roles in the conflict were as wife, camp follower, or sex slave, rather than as female soldiers (MacKenzie 2009, 243). Though women were often victims, many identified as former soldiers, sharing their rank, name of their military unit, and occupation during war. Interviews with women in Sierra Leone suggested that over 75 percent believed they served in active combat by leading lethal attacks, screening and killing prorebel civilians. They also reported serving as combatants, poisoning captured war prisoners with lethal drugs, as well as gun trafficking, killing, and fighting (MacKenzie 2009, 249). Some estimates suggest that women may have comprised between 10 to 50 percent of some armed groups (MacKenzie 2009, 245).

When the civil war concluded, many communities and families expressed concern about the marriageability of female soldiers due to the "assumption they had been raped or they had given birth to children out of wedlock" (MacKenzie 2009, 257). Women were encouraged to allow grandparents to raise their children or to marry their rapists, in order to blend into the community. In this way, women continued to function as chattel. The community often encouraged women to return to their former places in society, stripping away any authority or positions they had earned during the war. Any opportunity to "rethink and reshape gender stereotypes and hierarchies" was destroyed when the women were defined as victims of war, rather than as soldiers (MacKenzie 2009, 258). The lack of protection for women after the conflict impeded women's progress in an already patriarchal society, that constrained them by custom, practice, and law.

Though the status of women in Sierra Leone after the civil war was precarious, a gender policy was introduced ensuring equal opportunities that has allowed women to serve in the Republic of Sierra Leone Armed Forces since 2010. Of the estimated 8,500 soldiers in the military, about 300 of them were women (Fofanah 2010). To further encourage women to join, women served as platoon commanders, and promotion boards were realigned to give women a more equitable opportunity for promotion. Sierra Leone sent seven women to Darfur with UN peacekeeping operations and committed to increasing that number to twenty.

However, even with these improvements, recruitment remains a challenge less than a decade after the end of the civil war. Many women in

Sierra Leone lack the basic school certificate required to join the military, and even fewer have a senior secondary school certificate necessary for officer posts. Even as women earn admission into security forces, some families object to their participation. Working with international organizations and the United Kingdom, Sierra Leone launched the Special Female Recruitment Program, asserting that the presence of women in national security is beneficial to national peace, cohesion, and development. By 2019, more women joined the ranks of the armed forces, with a recent commissioning ceremony including over 300 combined women officer cadets and recruits at the Armed Forces Training Center (Thomas 2019).

Sierra Leone's first female brigadier general, Kestoria Kabia, joined the service in the 1978 recruitment drive. She is one of the first generals in Africa who did not come from the medical services field. BG Kabia was selected as Sierra Leone's Military Officer of the Year in 2008 and now manages assignments, personnel, training, education, recruitment, and promotions for the armed forces (Thatcher 2010).

EQUALITY FOR WOMEN

Legal changes in society can sometimes lead to culture change over time. In many nations, newly written constitutions and founding documents have guaranteed equality of opportunity in education, jobs, and rights to women. This equality is sometimes slow in coming, with military women still confined to logistics and support roles. In some states, women's participation in the armed forces is so low that they are almost invisible. However, any participation is an improvement from earlier militaries, which excluded women completely. Some countries, such as South Africa, have taken meaningful steps, often aiding other regional countries through peacekeeping and security cooperation, to expand roles throughout the continent to women.

In many ways, South Africa has improved women's military roles, serving as an example for other nations to follow. The country emerged from a brutal history of apartheid, a system that separated whites from blacks (Africans, Coloreds, and Indians), into a system that accepts previously disenfranchised minorities into larger roles in society (Heinecken 2007). The end of apartheid led the armed forces to more fully integrate both ethnic and gender minorities, with gender integration becoming less controversial than race integration (Heinecken 2007, 86).

Prior to the end of apartheid, only white women were recruited into the South African Defense Forces, a precursor organization to the current South African National Defense Force (SANDF). In 1970, white women joined the South African Defense Forces due to a shortage of white male soldiers. Women were limited to support roles that included military intelligence and more traditional jobs in personnel, logistics, and medical services (Heinecken 2002, 719).

The Umkhonto we Sizwe (MK), on the other hand, allowed women to serve in many frontline roles. Originally launched as an armed wing of the African National Congress in 1962, the Umkhonto we Sizwe employed women for unconventional warfare since 1976 after women convinced members of the African National Congress (ANC) that they could function as soldiers (Makau 2009, 36). More strongly tied to raising children and running families, women's participation rates in the MK remained lower than men's and were likely between 15 to 20 percent (Makau 2009, 29). The MK had strict policies to create a safe environment for women who joined the struggle. Rules dictated that women should be treated in a dignified manner as friends and comrades. Despite this, women were expected to perform domestic housekeeping around the camps, including cooking and washing.

A 1996 White Paper on National Defense for the Republic of South Africa noted that education and training are an integral part of building and maintaining a professional army and emphasized facilitating equal opportunities for women soldiers (Minister of Defence, South Africa 1996, 13). Importantly, this paper also established the right of women to serve in any rank or position, including combat roles. Published after apartheid and the integration of South African forces, the Department of Defense was keenly aware that the military's composition was not yet representative of South Africa's population and required affirmative action and equal opportunity programs. These programs emphasized education, training, and development for women, black officers, and other previously disadvantaged personnel. Citing the need for combat readiness, the report asserted that the SANDF could not perform effectively if capable individuals were excluded from senior posts solely because of race or gender (Minister of Defence, South Africa 1996, 28).

There are no legislative limitations for women in the SANDF, and women serve in all frontline roles as well as study at the military academy. Despite the positive legal changes pushing for gender equality, women are not fully accepted in certain roles. Surveys conducted from 1996 and 1998 reflect society's split between those who favored women's role in combat and those who continued to support a combat exclusion (Heinecken 2002, 721). In 2002, Portia Sibiya became the first female commander of the Air Command Unit. While many believed that only a man should occupy that post, her success led to her promotion to brigadier general and appointment as the defense attaché in France. In 2010, South Africa increased the quota for women in the security forces to 40 percent to speed up gender mainstreaming, though has not yet reached this goal.

As part of Mapisa-Nqakula's role as the minister of defense in South Africa, she focused on promotion processes, making them equitable, along with recruitment strategies to attract men and women of the highest caliber to join the military. The number of senior ranking women in the SADNF expanded from one to forty-three in just over two decades, even boasting the first black woman combat pilot, a huge achievement in a country that saw bitter and institutionalized racism less than thirty years ago (Ighobor 2019).

Other countries in Africa are making progress integrating women. Burundi has made great strides since 1993, when women first joined the military. Women now make up 10 percent of the force (Abdulmelik 2016, 22). The country provided gender training to about 1,200 members of the military, paving the way for additional female recruits (Abdulmelik 2016, 22). The country remains committed to improving gender equality and opportunity. Similarly, in Lesotho, the military is committed to gender equality, though it has often fallen short of this goal. A 2014 law that prohibits women from becoming pregnant within five years of their enlistment forced three women from service (Mohloboli 2018). The soldiers were eventually reinstated after bringing their case to the high court, which ruled that the standing order was illegal because women have the right to reproduce. Women make up 13 percent of the Lesotho Armed Forces, though very few have earned the rank of major or higher. In 2017, some military members realized that to attract and retain women, the country needed to adapt its physical standards to allow women to serve based on varied standards, rather than on the male standard (Matope 2017).

In the Seychelles People's Defense Force, women have been held to the same standard as their male peers, regardless of their job. Margaret Louise, the first woman to join the Seychelles military, joined in 1979, earning the rank of major after thirty-seven years in uniform (Louise 2016). Five second lieutenants, including three women, from the Seychelles People's

Defense Force recently graduated from the Indian Army Officer Training Academy (OTA) in Chennai, India. The three women were the first to be trained at OTA ("Seven Young Officers Join the SPDF Officer Corps" 2019).

Increasing the number of women in the military may not lead to gender equality. Women make up almost a quarter of service members in Tanzania, with the highest-ranking woman, Brigadier General Sara Rwambali, serving as the director of the Army's Social Affairs section (Morna, Makamure, and Glenwright 2018, 238). In this role, she planned several events on gender integration, bringing together representatives from across the continent to discuss best practices (Mcnamara 2015). However, recent statements made by the president of Tanzania, John Magufuli, portend decreasing opportunities for women in the country. In 2018, he suggested that women should eschew birth control, having as many children as possible, and that women who become pregnant may no longer attend school (Busari 2018).

Other countries also appear to have regressed in their efforts towards gender equality. Nigeria has a complicated relationship with women in the military. Women were admitted into Nigerian's officer training course in 2011, eventually graduating near the top of their class as members of both the noncombat and combat course. Two women also enrolled at the U.S. Military Academy at West Point as cadets. A 2017 decision by President Muhammadu Buhari to ban women from the Nigerian academy was widely reported, although the army denied these reports (Obi 2017). Later reports suggested that women joined the Nigerian Air Force as fighter pilots, yet it remains unclear if women are still permitted to attend the defense academy (*The Guardian* 2019).

Many countries have integrated their militaries, while Nigeria established a separate Nigerian Army Women's Corps in 2018. This unit, designed to deal with ongoing tensions with Boko Haram, a terrorist group, allows women to contribute to national development and security by serving as bodyguards, intelligence officers, and election oversight officials (Ahovi 2019). The country also established a gender unit, committed to a zero-tolerance policy for sexual harassment and abuse (Abdulmelik 2016, 28).

In 2015, Major General Fatuma Ahmed became the first woman to earn that rank, after serving as a member of the Kenyan Air Force for thirty-two years (Njeru 2018). Women were first eligible to join the Women Service Corps in 1971, though the force was disbanded in 2000. As members of the women's only institution, they were prohibited from marrying or

140   Women and the Military

having children while serving. The Kenyan constitution mandates that 30 percent of the armed forces should be female, though official numbers are scarce and estimates suggest that Kenya has not achieved this goal (Bouka and Sigsworth 2016, 9). For example, female officers only represent about 8 percent of the force (Bouka and Sigsworth 2016, 11). Kenyan society remains patriarchal, expecting women to care for the home and family, making a military career an unappealing choice (Bouka and Sigsworth 2016, 11). Existing policies allow women to serve on the frontlines, though the masculine military culture has turned women away from recruitment drives (Gitonga 2015).

Other countries, such as Burkina Faso, have made efforts to integrate women, by changing laws and creating gender-monitoring offices (Abdulmelik 2016, 22). The first women joined in 2007, and recent reports suggested that women are subjected to "specific psychological difficulties," including physical violence, sexual assault and harassment, and musculoskeletal injuries (Goumbri et al. 2018, 2). Scholars have found that 84 percent of women interviewed did not feel fulfilled in military life, with a number expressing that they were not recognized for their service in the armed forces (Goumbri et al. 2018, 6). About a third of the women interviewed admitted that they had been harassed, though less than 8 percent believed that they had been sexually harassed (Goumbri et al. 2018, 7). Furthermore, women had a difficult time with work-life balance, a common complaint among women serving in the military around the world (Goumbri et al. 2018, 7).

Gender mainstreaming was implemented to increase women's roles in state institutions, including the military, and enhance gender equality. Reports on gender mainstreaming's progress have emphasized contradictions in the Senegalese military. Many people assert that women cannot "handle seeing death," which would limit their military positions; however, women are often nurses, constantly exposed to death (Oliphant 2014, 12). In Senegal, women joined the military in 1984 as nurses and doctors. In 2010, they gained additional opportunities due to President Abdoulaye Wade's emphasis that the military should mirror society (Oliphant 2014, 2). However, strong traditional norms often keep women in the homes, responsible for the success of their husbands. Women make up around 13 percent of the military and are extremely successful. While women might outperform the men with whom they train, this success does not lead to increased promotion opportunities, suggesting that women still face inherent bias in the armed forces (Oliphant 2014, 16).

Women in the Somali military comprise just under 8 percent of the force, and some have found themselves fighting against the terrorist group Al-Shabab, commanding male soldiers. Other female soldiers have been confined to administrative roles (Gaffey 2016). Iman Elman fought against the gender stereotype that required her to wear a skirt, arguing that as a commander, she would be on the frontlines with her soldiers, something not easily done in a skirt. Elman was raised in Canada and enlisted in the Somali National Army to provide a role model for other women. She is one of two women in her unit and the first to serve on the frontlines (Goldbaum 2017).

Women were recruited in the 1960s to form an all-woman brigade in the Zairian Armed Forces. Though this plan never came to fruition, women were trained around the world as soldiers and parachutists (Baaz and Stern 2012, 717). After the civil war in the late 1990s, various armed groups formed the Congolese national army. Some of the former warring factions included as many as 20 percent women, and many continue to serve in the Congolese national army today (Puechguirbal 2003, 1273). More women joined the military after widespread recruitment campaigns but reportedly have less education and training than previous recruits (Baaz and Stern 2012, 717). Though women were targeted during recruitment campaigns, estimates from 2012 suggest that less than 2 percent of service members are women (Baaz and Stern 2012, 717). This number is down from the 5 percent in 2003 just after the various armed factions in DRC came together to form the Congolese national army (Baaz and Stern 2012, 717).

Though women are equal before the law in DRC, women report a gap between law and treatment (Puechguirbal 2003, 1272). Many women convey that they are viewed by men as "objects of pleasure" and "flowers who should serve them tea" (Baaz and Stern 2012, 719). Some men argue that physical and psychological weaknesses led to women serving as "feminine support" (Baaz and Stern 2012, 718). As of 2012, there were fewer than twenty senior female officers, and most women served in support roles such as administration, medical care, intelligence, and logistics. By 2015, some progress was made when three women were appointed to the rank of general (Abdulmelik 2016, 23).

In other countries, few women serve in any notable capacity. In Gambia, women may join the military at eighteen, though it is unclear how prevalent they are in the military. In 2011, a woman was reportedly promoted to the rank of general (Fadera 2011). Women serve only nominally in Guinea-Bissau, according to a 2015 report from the UN Integrated Peacebuilding Office in Guinea-Bissau. In 2011, the first female officer from Djibouti graduated from the U.S. Army's Transportation Basic Officer Leader Course. First Lieutenant Amina Moussa served in the army for eleven years, making up part of the 2 percent of the military that is female, before earning a place as an officer (Bell 2011).

Though Madagascar's military has committed to recruiting 10 percent women, official records are unclear as to how many women actually serve (Morna, Makamure, and Glenwright 2018, 237). Freedom House suggests that urban women often serve in equal roles to men, though rural women are often found in more traditional roles (Freedom House 2011). Mauritanian President Mohamed Ould Ghazouani ran on a platform stressing the need for women in the military prior to his successful election in 2019 (Melly 2019, 26). He has not yet made any changes that would encourage women to serve in greater numbers.

WOMEN AND PEACEKEEPING

Women's increasing participation in peacekeeping operations is enhancing their status in the military and society. Many African nations support United Nations and African Union peacekeeping efforts and emphasize women's roles as peacekeepers. Women provide value in nations where strong gender segregation norms exist or where rape, trafficking, and sexual slavery are used as tactics of war (Cobiskey 2018). Although Gjelsvik notes that most African nations make little effort to recruit women, they are beginning to play important roles in these operations. Women usually serve at lower ranks and in support roles, rather than in decision-making positions (Gjelsvik 2013, 4). Some nations, such as Ethiopia, South Africa, Ghana, Nigeria, and Rwanda, have contributed significantly to missions on the continent ("GHANBATT Female Engagement Team Boosts Image of Ghana in UN Operations in DRC" 2019).

Many conflicts in Africa are armed independence struggles where rebel groups vie for power with established, often corrupt, governments; others are conflagrations between warring groups from within states. As countries have emerged from these struggles, frequently with new governments, they have committed to assisting neighboring states in peacekeeping efforts led by the United Nations or the African Union. These peace operations and stabilization efforts have deliberately included increased numbers of women,

Female soldiers drill at an event marking the fiftieth anniversary of the country's independence in Accra, Ghana, in 2007. The Ghanian military is recruiting more women to support ongoing peacekeeping missions on the continent. (David Snyder/Dreamstime.com)

recognizing that women can leverage parts of the population that men cannot (Bigio and Vogelstein 2018). Local populations in Namibia, Rwanda, and South Africa report that women serving as peacekeepers deescalated violent situations better than men, while appearing more receptive to civilian complaints (Bigio and Vogelstein 2018). Karim and Beardsley found that bolstering the proportion of women in peacekeeping forces and "recruiting more individuals with higher values for gender equality" helped decrease the reports of sexual violence against peacekeepers (Karim and Beardsley 2016, 109). Although increasing the number of women in peace operations is not a panacea, Karim and Beardsley find that contributing nations with strong records of gender equality have fewer civilian reports of sexual violence (Karim and Beardsley 2016, 109). Gender equality is measured in the level of primary school education for girls and labor force participation rates (Karim and Beardsley 2016, 112). Rwanda, Ghana, and South Africa have all expanded the number of women in their peacekeeping missions.

144 Women and the Military

PEACEKEEPERS IN SUB-SAHARAN AFRICA

The commander of the South African battalion of the Force Intervention Brigade in the Democratic Republic of Congo, LTC Tiisetso Sekgobela, is a South African woman, the first to command an infantry battalion. She is among the 102 women deployed to the DRC as part of this peacekeeping effort. The brigade is the only UN unit that may engage in military offensives. It is also responsible for engagements with women and children, Ebola prevention, and other programs for the protection of civilians. Joining the military in 2004, she was often selected as a top performer, including in a subunit commander's course and in a junior command and staff course.

FURTHER READING

Cronjé, Justin. 2020. "Lieutenant Colonel Tiisetso Sekgobela: A Leader amongst Men." *DefenceWeb,* January 27. https://www.defenceweb.co.za/sa-defence /lieutenant-colonel-tiisetso-sekgobela-a-leader-amongst-men

---

In South African peacekeeping contingents, women make up about 14 percent of total personnel (Pather 2017). Although the South African government would increase the number of women in peacekeeping operations, the total number of women in the military is a limiting factor. During the country's tenure as president of the United Nations Security Council in October 2019, a rotating position, the country focused on women's involvement in peace and security initiatives ("Support for Women Peacekeepers, Civil Society Leaders Crucial in Horn of Africa Peace Efforts, Top Officials Tell Security Council" 2019).

Rwanda's experience with the genocide in 1994 that killed millions of men, women, and children has impacted Rwanda's role in regional conflagrations and in peacekeeping missions. Rwanda saw a rise in violence against women in the years leading up to the genocide (Holmes 2018, 223). Women were often oppressed and marginalized, with few property rights and little protection from gender-based violence. Many were uneducated with few employment opportunities outside the home (Holmes 2018, 228). In the aftermath of the genocide, the traditional perception of women is being challenged by a more modern culture that explicitly advocates for women's rights, with women occupying 64 percent of the seats in Parliament in 2018 (Holmes 2018, 228). The genocide reshaped the population in Rwanda, and women now comprise over 50 percent of the population (Burnet 2008, 384).

To increase its domestic and international legitimacy, the Rwandan Defense Force has recruited more women and pushed against traditional Rwanda culture that marginalizes women. Many women in Rwanda still believe that the military is a man's job, requiring them to be "aggressive and uncomfortably masculine" (Holmes 2018, 239). Other women note that their parents tried to dissuade them from joining the military. They believe that women in the military are viewed as less competent than their male counterparts and might be used as sexual servants to the men in the RDF (Holmes 2018, 240).

Despite these views, Rwanda has included women in the ranks of its peacekeeping missions. The Rwandan military has adopted difficult roles throughout the African continent, sending peacekeepers to Sudan and South Sudan, implementing lessons learned during the 1990s (Kuehnel and Wilen 2018, 163). Between 2004 and 2014, the number of women serving increased from 241 to 633 (Holmes 2018, 237). Most women joined for patriotic or practical reasons as the RDF provides security and a steady salary, along with maternity leave and educational opportunities (Holmes 2018, 239). The military is also working toward gender mainstreaming by creating a Gender Desk to train military personnel to understand gender-based violence (Kuehnel and Wilen 2018, 161).

As part of the African Union Mission in Somalia (AMISOM), Burundi, Djibouti, Kenya, Sierra Leone, and Uganda deployed military peacekeepers to Somalia. Though women made up around 1.5 percent of the military personnel, Uganda's contingent included 3 percent women in its total force (Gjelsvik 2013, 3). A 2016 report on progress in the region noted that of the fifty-two officers from Uganda serving abroad in peacekeeping missions, twelve were women (Abdulmelik 2016, 30). This increase is encouraging, as women can interact with segments of the population sometimes forgotten in peace operations. However, a 2007 Ugandan policy calls for women to comprise at least 30 percent of the armed forces, and a report from 2014 suggests that women still make up less than 15 percent of the force ("Uganda: Ugandan Women Military, Police Officers Demand Greater Equality" 2014).

A UN peacekeeping effort in the Central African Republic (CAR) includes more women proportionally than any other current peacekeeping operation, including a small female engagement team from the Zambian battalion (Howard 2019). Women make up about 10 percent of the Zambian Defense Force (Morna, Makamure, and Glenwright 2018, 238). The Zambian unit in the CAR includes 59 women out of a unit of 930 ("Civil-Military

146   Women and the Military

Activities with MINUSCA Peacekeepers" 2018). These women patrol markets and provide needed medical care for women in the CAR.

PARTNERSHIP EFFORTS

A key factor influencing the changing role of women in African militaries is the impact of external relations. The history of instability in the region has encouraged a sense of cooperation with partners from around the world, with many sharing lessons related to gender issues. The United States cooperates with many nations across Africa, assisting in training and professionalization of the armed forces. In addition to hosting conferences that allow soldiers to share best practices, the countries cooperate to build stronger relationships. USAFRICOM is heavily involved in assisting many African nations with efforts to "recruit, train, and retain women to build more representative military forces" (Ham 2014, 117). Much of the training has focused on how women can be integrated into a military, with an emphasis on cultural and societal factors that determine women's roles in society. Additionally, some of the training has focused on specialty skills, such as communications and intelligence.

As part of a partnership with the Benin and Togolese Army, the North Dakota National Guard hosts senior military and embassy personnel. Both nations prioritize recruiting, retaining, and further integrating women into the military. Officially banned from the military in Togo in 1963, women rejoined in 2007 and have attended several partnership events on the continent and in the United States (Joyce 2015). A 2018 Women's Communication Symposium, hosted by AFRICOM in Stuttgart, Germany, hosted fourteen women in the communications field from Angola, Botswana, Burkina Faso, Chad, Ghana, Morocco, Nigeria, Senegal, and Sierra Leone as part of the women's military-to-military engagement program (Jones 2018). This conference allowed women to better understand the challenges faced by their peers, as well as sharing best practices for providing communications support to their militaries. In 2019, women from Cameroon, Chad, Niger, Nigeria, Mali, and Senegal participated in an all-women military intelligence training course, held at the Nigerian Defense Intelligence College (Loch 2020). The women learned to analyze information and provide better intelligence to prepare for a range of military operations.

Women in Sub-Saharan Africa have largely made progress in integration in armed forces, though no country has achieved true equality. Independence and civil wars have allowed women to push for the constitutionally guaranteed equality, yet women are still subjected to gender-based violence that may constrain their roles in the region. There is hope for the region, however, with an increasing number of women serving in peacekeeping roles to help protect vulnerable populations.

FURTHER READING

Abdulmelik, Semiha. 2016. *Implementation of the Women, Peace, and Security Agenda in Africa.* Addis Ababa, Ethiopia: Office of the Special Envoy on Women, Peace, and Security of the Chairperson of the African Union Commission.

Affram, Robert Yaw. 2011. *Gender and the Ghana Armed Forces: An Examination of Women's Integration and Operational Effectiveness.* Master's thesis, University for Development Studies.

Agencia Angola Press. 2014. "Men and Women in Military Have More Duties than Rights—FAA Staff Chief." December 16. http://m .portalangop.co.ao/angola/en_us/noticias/politica/2014/11/51/Men -and-women-military-have-more-duties-than-rights-FAA-Staff -Chief,b32d89b6-1cf9-4e11-a97d-9e8215e45683.html

Ahovi, Isa Abdulsalami. 2019. "Nigerian Army Women's Corps Hold Training Week." *The Guardian*, April 6.

Alpern, Stanley B. 1998. *Amazons of Black Sparta: The Women Warriors of Dahomey.* New York: New York University Press.

AU Strategy for Gender Equality & Women's Empowerment 2018–2028. 2018. Addis Ababa, Ethiopia: African Union Headquarters.

Baaz, Maria Eriksson, and Maria Stern. 2012. "Fearless Fighters and Submissive Wives: Negotiating Identity among Women Soldiers in the Congo (DRC)." *Armed Forces & Society* 39, no. 4: 1–29.

Bell, T. Anthony. 2011. "LogU Student Is Djibouti's First Female Officer." *Fort Lee Traveler*, January 27.

Bernal, Victoria. 2001. "From Warriors to Wives: Contradictions of Liberation and Development in Eritrea." *Northeast African Studies* 8, no. 3: 129–154.

Bigio, Jamille, and Rachel Vogelstein. 2018. *Increasing Female Participation in Peacekeeping Operations.* New York: Council on Foreign Relations.

Bouka, Yolande, and Romi Sigsworth. 2016. *Women in the Military in Africa: Kenya Case Study.* East Africa report. Addis Ababa, Ethiopia: Institute for Security Studies.

Burgess, Gemma. 2013. "A Hidden History: Women's Activism in Ethiopia." *Journal of International Women's Studies* 14, no. 3: 96–107.

Burnet, Jennie E. 2008. "Gender Balance and Governance in Rwanda." *African Affairs* 107, no. 428: 361–386.

Busari, Stephanie. 2018. "'Don't Use Birth Control,' Tanzania's President Tells Women in the Country." *CNN,* September 11. Accessed February 2, 2020. https://www.cnn.com/2018/09/11/africa/tanzania-birth -control-magufuli-intl/index.html

"Central African Republic Background Note." 2019. *Geneve Centre for Security Sector Governance,* January 10. Accessed February 1, 2020. https://issat.dcaf.ch/Learn/Resource-Library/Country-Profiles /Central-African-Republic-Background-Note

"Civil-Military Activities with MINUSCA Peacekeepers." 2018. *United Nations News & Media Photo,* October 10. Accessed February 2, 2020. https://www.unmultimedia.org/s/photo/detail/787/0787444 .html

Cobiskey, Olivia. 2018. "Female Participation Strengthens Peacekeeping Protection Efforts." *United States Army Africa,* August 21. Accessed February 20, 2020. https://www.usaraf.army.mil/media-room/article /28894/female-participation-strengthens-peacekeeping-protection -efforts

Darden, Jessica Trisko. 2015. "Assessing the Significance of Women in Combat Roles." *International Journal* 70, no. 3: 454–462.

Dash, Mike. 2011. "Dahomey's Women Warriors." *Smithsonian Magazine*, September 23.

Desilver, Drew. 2019. *Fewer Than a Third of Countries Currently Have a Military Draft; Most Exclude Women.* Washington, DC: Pew Research Center.

Edgerton, Robert B. 2000. *Warrior Women: The Amazons of Dahomey and the Nature of War.* Boulder, CO: Westview Press.

Elamin, Nisrin, and Tahani Ismail. 2019. "The Many Mothers of Sudan's Revolution." *Al-Jazeera*, May 4.

"Ethiopia Promotes 65 Military Officers, Including Five Women." 2020. *Fana Broadcasting Company,* January 18. https://www.fanabc .com/english/ethiopia-promotes-military-officers

Fadera, Hatab. 2011. "Gambia: Nation's First Female Army General Decorated." *AllAfrica,* May 12. Accessed January 17, 2019. https://allafrica.com/stories/201105120709.html

Fofanah, Mohamed. 2010. "A Place for Women in Sierra Leone's Military." *Inter Press Service News Agency*, September 23.

Freedom House. 2011. "Madagascar: Countries at the Crossroads 2011." *Freedom House.* Accessed February 2, 2020. https://freedomhouse.org/report/countries-crossroads/2011/madagascar

Gaddis, Isis, Rahul Lahoti, and Wenjie Li. 2018. *Gender Gaps in Property Ownership in Sub-Saharan Africa.* Policy Research Working Paper, World Bank Group.

Gaffey, Conor. 2016. "Meet the Female Somali Military Captain Fighting Al-Shabab." *Newsweek*, February 28.

"GHANBATT Female Engagement Team Boosts Image of Ghana in UN Operations in DRC." 2019. *United Nations Peacekeeping,* January 22. Accessed January 17, 2020. https://peacekeeping.un.org/en/ghanbatt-female-engagement-team-boosts-image-of-ghana-un-operations-drc

Gitonga, Antony. 2015. "Brown Teeth Keep Aspiring KDF Soldiers Off Recruitment." *Standard Digital,* September 29. Accessed January 17, 2020. https://www.standardmedia.co.ke/article/2000177920/brown-teeth-keep-aspiring-kdf-soldiers-off-recruitment

Gjelsvik, Ingvild Magnæs. 2013. "Women, Peace and Security in Somalia: A Study of AMISOM." *Norwegian Institute for International Affairs* 16: 1–5.

Goldbaum, Christina. 2017. "Female Peacekeepers Fight Militants and Prejudice in Somalia." *World Policy Journal*, April 10.

Goumbri, P., D. Nanema, B. Bague, Z. Ilboudo, L. Ganou, and A. Ouedraogo. 2018. "Psychosocial Risks among Female Military Personal in Burkina Faso." *Journal of Psychiatry and Psychiatric Disorders* 2, no. 1: 1–8.

The Guardian. 2019. "NAF's Remarkable Gender Inclusion." November 10. Accessed February 2, 2020. https://guardian.ng/opinion/nafs-remarkable-gender-inclusion

Haer, Roos, and Tobias Bohmelt. 2018. "Girl Soldiering in Rebel Groups, 1989–2013: Introducing a New Dataset." *Journal of Peace Research* 55, no. 3: 395–403.

Ham, Carter. 2014. "Working with African Nations to Support the Role of Women as Agents of Peace and Security." In *Women on the*

Frontlines of Peace and Security, 113–125. Washington, DC: National Defense University Press.

Harsch, Ernest. 2010. "Security Reform Key to Protecting Women." *Africa Renewal* (January): 9–11.

Heinecken, Lindy. 2002. "Affirming Gender Equality: The Challenges Facing the South African Armed Forces." *Current Sociology* 50, no. 5: 715–728.

Heinecken, Lindy. 2007. "Diversity in the South African Armed Forces." In *Cultural Diversity in the Armed Forces: An International Comparison*, edited by Joseph Soeters and Jan van der Meulen. New York: Routledge.

Holmes, Georgina. 2018. "Gender and the Military in Post-Genocide Rwanda." In *Women and Genocide: Survivors, Victims, Perpetrators*, edited by Elissa Bemporad and Joyce W. Warren, 223–249. Bloomington: Indiana University Press.

Honwana, Alcinda. 2005. *Child Soldiers in Africa*. Philadelphia: University of Pennsylvania Press.

Howard, Lise. 2019. *Assessing the Effectiveness of the UN Mission of the Central African Republic*. New York: International Peace Institute.

Human Rights Watch. 2009. *Service for Life: State Repression and Indefinite Conscription in Eritrea*. Special, HRW.

Human Rights Watch. 2019. *"They Are Making Us into Slaves, Not Educating Us" How Indefinite Conscription Restricts Young People's Rights, Access to Education in Eritrea*. Special, HRW.

Ighobor, Kingsley. 2019. "Reshaping the Forces." *Africa Renewal*, November.

IPS Correspondents. 1999. "Rights: Malawi: Army to Recruit First Women Soldiers." *IPS News Agency,* September 4. Accessed December 2, 2019. http://www.ipsnews.net/1999/09/rights-malawi-army-to-recruit -first-women-soldiers

Jackson, Ashley. 2001. *War and Empire in Mauritius and the Indian Ocean*. New York: Palgrave.

Johnson, Tim, and Nicholai Lidow. 2016. "Band of Brothers (and Fathers and Sisters and Mothers . . .): Estimating Rates of Military Participation among Liberians Living with Relatives in the Military; a Research Note." *Armed Forces & Society* 42, no. 2: 436–448. https://doi.org/10.1177%2F0095327X14562858

Jones, Grady. 2018. "AFRICOM J6 Holds Annual Women's Communication Symposium." *United States Africa Command,* July 3.

Accessed July 9, 2019. https://www.africom.mil/media-room/Article/30968/africom-j6-holds-annual-womens-communication-symposium

Joyce, Jennifer. 2015. "North Dakota National Guard Hosts Representatives from Republic of Benin and Togolese Republic." *National Guard,* May 12. Accessed July 9, 2019. https://www.nationalguard.mil/News/Article/588392/north-dakota-national-guard-hosts-representatives-from-republic-of-benin-and-to

Karim, Sabrina, and Kyle Beardsley. 2016. "Explaining Sexual Exploitation and Abuse in Peacekeeping Missions: The Role of Female Peacekeepers and Gender Equality in Contributing Countries." *Journal of Peace Research* 53, no. 1: 100–115. https://doi.org/10.1177%2F0022343315615506

Kuehnel, Josefine, and Nina Wilen. 2018. "Rwanda's Military as a People's Army: Heroes at Home and Abroad." *Journal of Eastern African Studies* 12, no. 1: 154–171. https://doi.org/10.1080/17531055.2018.1418168

Leão, Ana, and Martin Rupiya. 2005. "A Military History of the Angolan Armed Forces from the 1960s Onwards—as Told by Former Combatants." In *Evolutions and Revolutions: A Contemporary History of Militaries in Southern Africa*, edited by Martin Rupiya, 7–42. Pretoria, South Africa: Institute for Security Studies.

Loch, Patrick. 2020. *All-Female Military—Intelligence Training in Nigeria Supports Peace, Security Initiatives,* January 3. Accessed February 15, 2020. https://www.africom.mil/media-room/article/32525/all-female-military-intelligence-training-in-nigeria-supports-peace-security-initiatives

Louise, Margaret, interview by Genevieve Morel and Betymie Bonnelame. 2016. *Military Not Just Any Other Job, Says Seychelles' Newly Promoted—and Only—Female Major,* March 13.

Louw-Vaudran, Liesl. 2015. "African Women Are Increasingly Part of the Military and Police, but These Remain Strongly Male-Dominated Institutions." *Institute for Security Studies,* June 10. Accessed February 2, 2020. https://issafrica.org/iss-today/women-in-africas-top-brass-its-not-just-about-the-numbers

Lucas, Julie M. 2014. "Barriers Break Down at African Gender Integration Seminar." *United States Africa Command,* July 8. Accessed January 13, 2020. https://www.africom.mil/media-room/Article/23286/barriers-break-down-at-african-gender-integration-seminar

MacKenzie, Megan. 2009. "Securitization and Desecuritization: Female Soldiers and the Reconstruction of Women in Post-Conflict Sierra Leone." *Security Studies* 18, no. 2: 241–261. https://doi.org/10.1080/09636410902900061

Maclean, Ruth. 2018. "'It's Just Slavery': Eritrean Conscripts Wait in Vain for Freedom." *The Guardian*, October 11.

Makau, Kongko Louis. 2009. "Aspects of Some Experiences for Women in the Struggle for Liberation in the MK: 1976–1988: A Case Study of 10 Women." Master's thesis, University of Johannesburg.

Matope, Tsitsi. 2017. "'Female Officers Up to Task of Leading Army.'" *Lesotho Times,* October 7. Accessed January 20, 2020. http://lestimes.com/female-officers-up-to-task-of-leading-army

Mazrui, Ali, interview by Susan Enuogbope Majekodunmi. 2011. *Gender Mainstreaming in the Senegalese Armed Forces,* April 21.

Mcnamara, Mickie. 2015. "Initial Planning Begins for Tanzania Gender Integration Seminar." *United States Africa Command,* February 2. Accessed February 2, 2020. https://www.africom.mil/media-room/Article/25145/initial-planning-begins-for-tanzania-gender-integration-seminar

Melly, Paul. 2019. *Mauritania's Unfolding Landscape Elections, Hydrocarbons and Socio-Economic Change.* Research paper. London: Chatham House.

Minister of Defence, South Africa. 1996. "White Paper on National Defence for the Republic of South Africa." White paper.

Mohloboli, Keiso. 2018. "Female Soldiers Reinstated." *Lesotho Times,* February 17. Accessed February 2, 2020. http://lestimes.com/female-soldiers-reinstated

Mophuting, Mpho C. 2003. *Expanding the Shield and Facing the Challenges: Integration of Women in the Botswana Defence Force.* Master's thesis. Monterey, CA: Naval Postgraduate School.

Morna, Colleen Lowe, Lucia Makamure, and Danny Glenwright. 2018. *SADC Gender Protocol 2018 Barometer.* Johannesburg: Southern Africa Gender Protocol Alliance.

Mutsaka, Farai. 2016. "Woman Gets a Top Post in Zimbabwe's Air Force." *AirForce Times*, January 5.

Njeru, Betty. 2018. "Meet Fatuma Ahmed Kenya's First Female Major General." *Standard Digital,* July 14. https://www.standardmedia.co.ke/article/2001287935/who-is-major-general-fatuma-ahmed

Obi, Paul. 2017. "Nigeria: We've Not Stopped Training of Female Cadets, Says Army." *AllAfrica,* November 15. Accessed February 2, 2020. https://allafrica.com/stories/201711150040.html

Oliphant, Valerie. 2014. *Gender Mainstreaming in the Senegalese Armed Forces.* Case study. Washington, DC: Partners for Democratic Change.

Pather, Raeesa. 2017. "SA Deploys More Women UN Peacekeepers to Curb Sexual Abuse." *Mail & Guardian,* September 17. Accessed February 2, 2020. https://mg.co.za/article/2017-09-19-sa-deploys-more-women-peacekeepers-in-bid-to-curb-sexual-abuse

Pheage, Tefo. 2016. "Army Women Shake-Up BDF." *Mmegioonline,* September 2.

Puechguirbal, Nadine. 2003. "Women and War in the Democratic Republic of the Congo." *Signs* 28, no. 4 (Summer): 1271–1281. https://doi.org/0.1086/368319

Quénivet, Noëlle. 2008. "Girl Soldiers and Participation in Hostilities." *African Journal of International and Comparative Law* 16: 219–235. https://doi.org/10.3366/E0954889008000182

Rupp, Emily, Assitan Diallo, and Sharon Phillipps. 2012. *Mali Gender Assessment.* Gender Assessment, USAID.

Sackitey, Gideon. 2020. *Female Soldiers Rising Up South Sudan's Military Ranks Call for Greater Respect for Human Rights.* UN Mission in South Sudan.

"Seven Young Officers Join the SPDF Officer Corps." 2019. *Seychelles People's Defence Forces,* September 23. Accessed January 17, 2020. https://www.spdf.sc/seven-young-officers-join-the-spdf-officer-corps

Sharp, Paul, and Louis Fisher. 2005. "Inside the 'Crystal Ball': Understanding the Evolution of the Military in Botswana and the Challenges Ahead." In *Evolutions and Revolutions: A Contemporary History of Militaries in Southern Africa*, 43–62. Pretoria, South Africa: Institute for Security Studies.

Solomon, Salem. 2019. "African Women Surmount Obstacles to Redefine Their Countries' Militaries." *VOA News,* February 24. Accessed February 1, 2020. https://www.voanews.com/africa/african-women-surmount-obstacles-redefine-their-countries-militaries

"Support for Women Peacekeepers, Civil Society Leaders Crucial in Horn of Africa Peace Efforts, Top Officials Tell Security Council." 2019.

United Nations Meeting Coverage, November 4. Accessed February 2, 2020. https://www.un.org/press/en/2019/sc14010.doc.htm

Thatcher, Amelia. 2010. "Sierra Leone and Brig. Gen. Kabia: A Progressive Voice for African Military Women." *U.S. Army,* May 17. Accessed February 2, 2020. https://www.army.mil/article/39230/sierra_leone_and_brig_gen_kabia_a_progressive_voice_for_african_military_women

Thomas, Abdul Rashid. 2019. "President Bio Warns Newly Recruited Female Soldiers to Stay Away from Politics." *The Sierra Leone Telegraph,* September 8. Accessed February 2, 2020. https://www.thesierraleonetelegraph.com/president-bio-warns-newly-recruited-female-soldiers-to-stay-away-from-politics

"Uganda: Ugandan Women Military, Police Officers Demand Greater Equality." 2014. *PeaceWomen,* August 6. Accessed May 19, 2019. http://peacewomen.org/content/uganda-ugandan-women-military-police-officers-demand-gender-equality

Veale, Angela. 2005. "Collective and Individual Identities: Experiences of Recruitment and Reintegration of Female Excombatants of the Tigrean People's Liberation Army, Ethiopia." In *Invisible Stakeholders: Children and War in Africa*, edited by Angela McIntyre, 105–126. Pretoria, South Africa: Institute for Security Studies.

"Women Are Still Underrepresented in All Areas of Decision-Making in Guinea-Bissau." 2015. *United Nations Integrated Peacebuilding Office in Guinea-Bissau,* April 20. Accessed January 17, 2020. https://uniogbis.unmissions.org/en/women-are-still-underrepresented-all-areas-decision-making-guinea-bissau

Wood, Reed M. 2019. *Female Fighters: Why Rebel Groups Recruit Women for War.* New York: Columbia University Press.

World Health Organization Regional Office for Africa. n.d. "Women's Health." *World Health Organization Regional Office for Africa.* Accessed February 1, 2020. https://www.afro.who.int/health-topics/womens-health

Zeldin, Wendy. 2007. "Benin: Military Service Law." *Library of Congress,* November 2. Accessed February 1, 2020. https://www.loc.gov/law/foreign-news/article/benin-military-service-law

SIX

Central and East Asia

Central and East Asia is a region full of contradictions. Over history, women were drafted into militaries to support war efforts, then forced out of militaries without pensions or recognition after the cessation of hostilities. Most women who served in the military were sheltered from the front, acting in traditionally noncombat roles. Currently, many countries are actively recruiting women into militaries across the region to support national security efforts against revisionist states. Others continue to advance the role of women in accordance with UN Resolution 1325 and other modernization efforts. In Central and East Asia, women have played traditional roles in the home, while men have protected the family and the nation. With the rise of communism, women have ventured outside the home at the behest of governments who need workers. Although some women assumed more equitable roles, these were often short-lived or nominal in nature.

The socialist ideology dominating much of the region encourages quota systems, leading to relatively equal levels of representation by women in some Parliaments. This equality in representation has not translated to true gender equality, and women trail their male counterparts in representation and treatment across the military and other professions. This chapter explores Central and East Asian countries encompassing Armenia, Azerbaijan, China, Georgia, Hong Kong, Japan, Kazakhstan, Kyrgyzstan, Mongolia, North Korea, Russia, South Korea, Tajikistan, Taiwan, Turkmenistan, and Uzbekistan.

SOCIETAL VIEWS OF MASCULINITY AND WARFARE

Religion and social norms in Central and East Asia often influence perceptions of expected roles of women in family and society. Islam, principally practiced in much of Central Asia before and after the rule of the Soviet Union, expected women to maintain the household and educate children. As such, they find themselves restricted to more domestic pursuits. Orthodox Christianity, practiced in much of Russia, encourages women to maintain a strong sense of family in the home. Officially, communism downplayed the role of religion, though the norms of the religion proved to be resilient. Although communist ideology encouraged women to pursue equal status in society, conflicting views held that women could not assume all roles in society, including those of combat. Confucianism, a tradition practiced in many Chinese, Taiwanese, Korean, and Japanese communities, encouraged women to follow their husbands and tend to domestic chores. Buddhism, practiced in northern Asia, championed women's critical role in the family and allowed women to make decisions in the home. These religions influenced the social cultures of Central and East Asia, at times charging women with tending to home and family, while men served as community protectors.

A statue of Hua Mu-Lan, the inspiration behind the Disney movie *Mulan*, shows one of China's most famous women warriors. Disguising herself as a man, she joined the military to serve in her father's place. Her deception went undetected, and she retired quietly to her hometown. (Sim Kay Seng/Dreamstime.com)

Women in Central and East Asia are often lauded for their roles in the home, though early myths about women fighters are not uncommon in the region. Hua Mu-Lan, depicted in the Disney movie *Mulan,* was one of China's most famous women warriors known for serving in her father's stead. Cutting her hair short, her deception went undiscovered though she allegedly fought for at least ten years before retiring to her hometown. Known to be a great fighter, her general even offered his daughter's hand in marriage (Jones 1997, 24). One of Mongolia's most vicious khan, Genghis Khan was known to accept the counsel of Sorghaqtani Khatun, his daughter-in-law, about military affairs. Another daughter is rumored to have participated in the conquest of the Persian city of Nushapur and Qutulun, defeating every man she fought. These women, while rarer, still play a role in the collective understanding of women's roles in the region (De Nicola 2017, 41).

Under communist influence, most notably in China and the states of the former Soviet Union, women were encouraged to pursue jobs outside the home, including military service to replace men who had been killed during World War II, yet in reality, they were also charged with taking care of the home and children. As such, women were held to high and challenging expectations. They were expected to be "free and equal participants in the society, supportive wives, and nurturing mothers who taught their children to be model Soviet citizens" (Clements 2012, 212).

China and North Korea both strive to have 30 percent female representation in their Parliaments, ostensibly promoting gender equality (BBC News 2017; Bjarnegård and Melander 2013, 559). Neither has reached the threshold, with China's Parliament at 23 percent and North Korea's at 16 percent female representatives (CIA 2020). Chinese society has historically been male-dominated and women were often treated as property, forced to undergo foot binding and other practices that kept them in the home sphere. The one-child policy enforced in China has allowed a significant gender imbalance to develop, though the Kuomintang, the Chinese Nationalist Party, publicly advocates for gender equality. Additionally, increased maternity protection laws have limited women's choices and kept them from reaching gender equality because employers prefer not to pay the cost of maternity leave (Neuman and Schmitz 2018). Women in North Korea still struggle against an ingrained culture that once saw women restricted to the home. The heavily patriarchal attitudes of North Korea's society allow for both sexual abuse in the military, along with a reliance on women to perform more domestic duties, even in their role as soldiers (Lim 2018).

158 Women and the Military

Women in both Azerbaijan and Armenia are encouraged to select jobs that are "gender appropriate" and allow them flexibility to care for children. Women in Armenia face a socially conservative society, expecting women to remain in the domestic sphere. Most women in Armenia select occupations that offer flexible working hours, without travel and in sectors that are perceived as "safer and less open to moral judgements about being mainly with male colleagues" (McLaughlin, Armenia Country Gender Assessment 2019, 23). In nearby Azerbaijan, women serve in the National Assembly and up to 90 percent of women reportedly graduate from secondary school, though women's participation in politics is largely a result of quota systems from the Soviet period (Mandl 2011, 16). While Azerbaijan began to establish many programs to reaffirm the importance of women in society, after the breakup of the Soviet Union, the State Committee for Women's Issues was renamed the State Committee on Family, Women and Children's Affairs (SCFWCA), implicitly shifting the focus from women to the family. Azerbaijan's labor laws also protect pregnant women and prohibit women from serving in workplaces with difficult or potentially harmful labor conditions. These laws, combined with the existing patriarchal structure, serve to maintain gender divisions that make it more difficult for women to serve in the military. The Asian Development Bank noted that many women gravitate toward occupations with more flexibility to accommodate the demands on their time from the home, often leading them away from the military (McLaughlin, Azeerbaijan Country Gender Assessment 2019, 21).

Japan enacted the Basic Law for a Gender Equal Society in 1999, to promote gender equality across all sectors of society. Additionally, Japan established the National Action Plan on Women, Peace, and Security in 2015 with an emphasis on participation, conflict prevention, protection, humanitarian and reconstruction assistance, and the framework to monitor, evaluate, and review ("National Action Plan on Women, Peace, and Security" 2015, 6). These policy efforts influenced women to work outside the home. Even with official emphasis on a more equal society, women face ingrained norms that require them to divide their attention between a profession and a family. There are several major barriers unique to Japanese society that hamper the integration of women into the Japanese military (World Economic Forum in Collaboration with McKinsey & Company 2014). One of these is the women's double burden of working outside the home and being the primary caregiver in the home. Data from the Organization for Economic Co-operation and Development (OECD) suggests that Japanese men spend on average forty-one minutes on unpaid work, while women spend four hours on domestic duties and caring for children.

Additionally, Japanese culture emphasizes the "anytime/anywhere" performance model, demanding that workers are available twenty-four hours a day, seven days a week. This requirement disproportionally affects women who are already responsible for many duties in the home. Historically, Japanese culture has not provided many public and societal support mechanisms—most glaring is the dearth of child care. Finally, women often lack role models and opportunity. While many Japanese companies, including the military, are adapting by providing support such as more flexible work programs and parental leave programs, cultural change trails behind. Even when women serve, they are often marginalized and their contributions to national security ignored.

Language reflects cultural beliefs and can impact how people perceive the world. The word for soldier in Georgian is "jarisk'atsi," which translates to "army man." In a similar manner, "er" the word for "man" in traditional Kyrgyz culture, may also be translated as "warrior." These elements of language shape the traditional roles of men as warriors and women as caregiver (Blakkisrud and Kyzy 2017). In Russia, the tsar and other leaders of Russia are the Fathers of the Nation, while the land is known as Mother Russia, a reference to the nurturing role that women are thought to play in Russian society (Roudakova and Ballard-Reisch 1999). Even in North Korea, where women are drafted and serve alongside men, women are required to conduct daily cleaning chores and cooking duties during their service. They are still called "ttukong unjeongsu," which translates as "cooking pot lid drivers" (Mohan 2017). Women in North Korea also report high levels of rape and sexual harassment, despite the military's harsh punishment of up to seven years jail time for men found guilty of rape. The heavily patriarchal attitudes of North Korean society allow for both sexual abuse in the military and a reliance on women to perform domestic duties, even in their role as soldiers (Lim 2018).

MAKEUP UNDER CAMOUFLAGE

Central and East Asian cultures emphasize women's appearance, and this belief carries over to the military. Some militaries in Central and East Asia hold beauty competitions to showcase servicewomen, claiming that these contests help with recruiting efforts. Others require women to interview,

160   Women and the Military

highlight their culinary skills, or perform other talents to join the military. Though not unusual to see militaries showcasing the real lives of their members, beauty contests and other events may perpetuate gender stereotypes rather than emphasizing professional skills necessary for service.

In 2005, the Russian military organized an annual beauty pageant for women in the Russian Ground Forces. In 2006, Major General Niolai Burbyga, the head of the judging committee, noted that "our sociologists studied opinions in the forces in different regions, and came to the conclusion that such a contest is needed," because everyday life could be monotonous while serving (Bigg 2005). This tradition continues today; women from the Russian Strategic Missile Forces recently competed in a 2018 beauty contest called "Makeup Under Camouflage" in Russia's Yaroslavl region. The women not only showcased their military skills, but also their creative and culinary talents. A Russian daily military newspaper features a "Miss Red Star" every week, with a picture and short biography of a woman serving in the Armed Forces as a soldier or civilian. Women are often "treated as women first, and soldiers second" (Grau and Bartles 2016, 23).

Though women serve throughout the Russian military, they are often not perceived as real women. Bolstering the perception that women's appearance is important, a photo shoot in Russia to celebrate International Women's Day did not feature any of the 45,000 women serving in the Russian Armed Forces. Instead, the men of the Armed Forces surrounded ballerinas, a nod to a woman's role in the home as a delicate and beautiful thing. Women have served in the Russian military since World War I, though they have rarely been allowed to celebrate this role as soldiers. It was not until 2016 that women could take part in the Victory Day Parades, held annually to commemorate the defeat of the Nazi threat during World War II.

Several other regional countries use beauty contests to enhance their enlistment numbers. To counter the perception that the Kazakh military is not a profession for women, the Ministry of Defense hosted Batyr Arular (Warrior Women) in 2015 and 2016, a nationwide beauty contest and a test of military skills (D. Lee n.d.). The competition was used to attract Internet users to military service (Wheaton 2015). About 120 women competed, showcasing their beauty, moral, and spiritual qualities with the top twelve recognized by the Ministry of Defense (Tomlinson 2015). The contest featured personal profiles with pictures in uniform and civilian clothing. The service members also highlighted their prowess with combat skills by throwing grenades, shooting weapons, driving military vehicles, and swimming. Defense Minister Imangali Tasmagambetov noted that the contest exemplified that women could serve their native land and be role models. Women were showcased online, while users from Kazakhstan, Russia, the United States, Germany, Indonesia, and India voted. One voter said that while there were some attractive women, he was not sure if he would sign up to serve based on their beauty (Tomlinson 2015). The Kazakh government and some voters also suggested that the contest could help improve the image of Kazakhstan after the popular movie *Borat* cemented negative stereotypes of Kazakhs.

In 2009, women were selected to fly fighter jets for the Chinese People's Liberation Army (PLA), and reports began to circulate that women were being selected to join the military based on their talent and beauty. Young women joining the PLA were asked to sing, dance, or highlight other artistic abilities as part of the selection process. The PLA interview included a 30-second self-introduction, a 2.5-minute question and answer period, and a 2-minute talent show. A *China Daily* report wrote that one of the interview judges believed that these tryouts would help to ensure that the "right people" were selected for the military though the talent tests only applied to women recruits (Kania 2016).

CHINA

Gao Yuan, an entertainer in the People's Liberation Army of China, became famous for her smile after she appeared at a National Day Parade. She is also one of the first female musicians in the Chinese military. She is the deputy director of the female military ensemble. Chinese women often found that the song and dance troupe of the PLA were welcoming workplaces and the women were given equal status as male veterans after the end of their service.

FURTHER READING

"Female Chinese Soldier Stuns Millions after Appearing at the Military Parade to Mark the Nation's 70th Anniversary." 2019. *Daily Mail*, October 2. https://www.dailymail.co.uk/news/article-7529221/Female-soldier-stuns -millions-appearing-Chinas-National-Day-parade.html

FACTORS INFLUENCING CHANGE

Early myths and stories of women in battle illustrate that women have held roles outside the home throughout history. However, connected with cultural views of gender, official government policy sometimes assists in the marginalization of women. Increasing technology, demographic changes, gender mainstreaming, and external influences have all impacted women's roles in the Central and East Asian militaries.

In the early nineteenth century, Captain Ching Yih, one of the most successful Chinese naval captains, wanted to marry Hsi Kai, a woman captured in one of his raids. When brought before him for his inspection, Hsi Kai attacked him and refused to marry him. When offered golds, silks, slaves, and property to comply, Hsi Kai agreed on the condition that she obtain joint command of his naval fleet. She took command of two of his six fleets after their marriage. Upon his death a few years later, she commanded the entire fleet (Jones 1997, 28). Known to be a formidable naval tactician, the Chinese government finally paid her to allow the Mandarin Navy to pass safely.

Women served in significant roles during the Chinese Civil War (1927–1949) and the Second Sino-Japanese War (1937–1945), though were often demobilized quickly after hostilities. Most served in support and logistics roles. When the PLA downsized in the 1950s, women were often the first to be sent home, though the PLA began to recruit women in 1967 again. Between 1934 and 1935, over 3,000 women served in combat and non-combat roles in China's thirteenth-month, 12,500-km Long March (Li 1994, 67). The Red Army, the precursor to the PLA, began a series of retreats, determined to evade the Kuomintang army. As they retreated, women organized stretcher teams to move the sick and wounded, recruited troops, foraged for food, and acted as nurses and medics. The Women's Independence Brigade supplied the Red Army, and the Women's Engineer Battalion brought precious metals to pay for the military. Women continued to serve in logistical support roles, and eventually the all-women units were disbanded with members integrated into mixed-gender units (Li 1994, 68).

Today, China has the largest armed forces in the Asia-Pacific region and the highest number of women in uniform. The PLA continues to implement restructuring initiatives to become a force capable of conducting joint complex operations. China has also made significant strides in allowing women to serve in many combat roles. The PLA, like many militaries, has acknowledged the changing character of war with an increasing reliance on technology that has permitted women to serve in a greater variety of roles. In addition, the efforts to build a high-quality force have encouraged PLA leadership to address the possible human capital issue driven by the one-child policy. China's large population negates the need for increased recruitment of women and instead, many women who would be identified as high quality, are being urged to have children (Kania and Allen 2016).

Because the military is considered a prestigious organization with capacity to enhance a person's position in society, only the most qualified recruits (both men and women) are admitted every year. Military members receive nice housing, and families often get special treatment. Women, enticed by better jobs, improved housing, attractive pensions, and an elevated social status, have joined the PLA in increased numbers. Women are offered three months maternity leave after the birth of their children and receive a small stipend every month until a child turns fourteen. If both parents serve, the stipend is doubled.

The PLA provides an annual quota for recruitment, divided among the provinces by population. About 1 to 2 percent of the annual quota is reserved for women who wish to join (Nelsen 2019, 19). All men are required to register for conscription at the age of eighteen and may be conscripted until they are twenty-two. Women may volunteer but are not required to register, though they may serve according to the military's needs (Kaufman and Mackenzie 2009, 5). In 2007, a recruitment campaign focused on eighteen- and nineteen-year-old women in an attempt to showcase gender equality.

Conscripts undergo physical exams, as well as other health and psychological exams. All who serve must undergo both military skills and political training. The political training may differ by rank and military branch though it reportedly involves military discipline and law, as well as ideology, and the "glorious traditions of the PLA" (Blasko 2008, 108). Women are occasionally recruited after finishing their civilian college degrees to become NCOs. This relatively new program allows for better disciplined and broadened NCOs, as well as conscripts. Both men and women take advantage of this opportunity, particularly when they cannot find other employment. This recruitment program permits them to serve in localities close to their homes. These NCOs comprise a small fraction of the overall NCOs corps; most NCOs are recruited from conscripts who want to extend their service.

164   Women and the Military

While few women hold high-ranking leadership roles in the Chinese Communist Party in China, female soldiers and officers have seen their roles in the PLA expanded. Until relatively recently, women served mostly in support and logistics roles, along with political and propaganda units. They also participate as part of the PLA's performing arts troupes. In addition to their service in the Army, Navy, Air Force, and Rocket Force, scholars believe that women serve in the new Strategic Support Force (Kania 2016). Some units are all female, though others allow women to train alongside their male counterparts. Women have served as part of artillery and air defense units, often in female-only units. These units have been recognized as competing well against mixed-gender units.

In addition to China's army, women serve in navigation and sonar roles aboard ships, although they are explicitly banned from serving on submarines. In 2014, twenty women graduated from the Dalian Naval Ship Academy, including the first Uighur female officer (Kania and Allen 2016). Dilihumar Aburat graduated from Xinjiang University with a degree in electrical engineering and chose to follow in her father's footsteps, serving in the PLA (Lei 2014). After passing a series of tests and interviews, she earned a place at Dalian Naval Ship Academy, joining a small cohort of forty-one cadets studying radar electronics (Lei 2014). Women have also served across the Air Force, with additional plans to recruit women from sixteen provinces. In March 2010, the PLA recruited for a female missile launch unit in the Second Artillery Force (SAF), which has responsibility for both nuclear and conventional missiles. There are some signs within Chinese news media that women are being groomed for positions of greater responsibilities (Kania and Allen 2016). Women still face a traditional glass ceiling in China. A guide for company commanders instructs commanders to help women understand how to comport themselves by refraining from crying while being corrected or trained (Kania 2016).

The Chinese news media has reported successes in integration with frequent comparisons to the United States and its own struggles with integration into some billets. Women have deployed as part of a peacekeeping infantry battalion to South Sudan and as part of medical teams in the Congo, Lebanon, and Mali. They also serve in specialized units, including acrobatic flying units and special forces units. A 2016 incident in China went widely underreported when a Chinese J-10 fighter pilot, Yu Xu, died during training. She ejected from her aircraft and was hit by another in midair. The woman was among the first sixteen women qualified to fly fighter jets, and just the fourth qualified on the J-10. Yu Xu was training to be a member of the Bayi acrobatic team, like the U.S. Navy's Blue Angels. Sources reported that standards for women were lowered to earn spots in combat units, though this claim may not be entirely true (Radio Free Asia 2016).

In China, while many women must demonstrate their poise and beauty to join the PLA, an elite squad of women in the 82nd Group Army's Special Warfare Brigade is selected for their ability to run, ruck, and compete with the best. The women reportedly complete challenging daily physical training regimens and train in parachuting operations, rappelling, weapon shooting, and scuba diving. The women also undergo several weeks of sea training every year in swimming and diving courses alongside men of other special operations units (Wanli 2017). Their lives are more structured than in many parts of the Chinese military, though the fighters have earned the respect of many of their peers and are devoted to serving (Wanli 2017). Women in China may face traditional gender bias as they seek to join the military, though some women have proven that they can compete and succeed in the most elite roles.

Women's roles in Russia have shifted due to necessity, allowing women to serve in elite units, though they were often confined to more traditional roles, as in China. During World War I, women held noncombat roles to make men available for combat on the frontlines. While imperial rules technically barred women from combat, many circumvented this issue by simply enlisting as men far from home and without required medical examinations that would have exposed the deception. By 1917, at least 6,000 Russian women served as soldiers in various capacities, many as doctors or nurses. Occasionally, these traditional female roles put them on or close to the frontline, though many served in hospitals far from the front. Schischkina Yavein, the president of the Russian Women's Rights Society, established a hospital for soldiers and trained female nurses for service at the front (Jensen 2012, 192). Elsa Winokurow served as head physician in an all-female Moscow hospital throughout the war.

In one case, the Russian government formed the First Women's Battalion of Death in 1917, headed by Maria Bochkareva, contending that women who could fight would both inspire and shame men into fighting harder (Jensen 2012, 209). Bochkareva was well known for volunteering for scouting missions and rescuing wounded soldiers from no-man's land. This new unit received at least 3,000 applicants, though only 300 were accepted. Russian military records indicate that the unit had little effect on military morale, largely due to the ongoing revolution and Russia's exit

166   Women and the Military

from the war. The women were often attacked by Russian mobs at home and feared for their safety. After the Russian Revolution in 1917, the unit was disbanded and Bochkareva was executed by the Bolsheviks in 2018 as an enemy of the people (Goodridge 2018). This experiment laid the foundation for units staffed with women during World War II.

Demographic changes impacted women's roles in the military. During World War II in the Soviet Union, millions of men left the civilian workforce in 1941 and died on the frontlines. The affected populations were from what is now Russia, Armenia, Azerbaijan, Georgia, Kazakhstan, Kyrgyzstan, Tajikistan, Turkmenistan, and Uzbekistan, as well as many of the former Soviet Union Republics located in Europe. After Hitler's refusal to honor the 1939 Molotov-Ribbentrop Non-Aggression Pact, women replaced men in the ongoing war effort to defeat Fascist Germany. Some estimates place the total number of drafted women in the Soviet Union at around one million. In 1943, at the height of their participation, they accounted for about 8 percent of the regular army, almost double the number that served in the U.S. and German militaries (Nazemroaya 2014). Women's acceptance in the military proved short-lived, as many women resumed more traditional gender roles after the end of World War II in 1945. In 1946, there were twenty million more working-age women than men in the Soviet Union, and by the mid-1970s women still outnumbered men in the overall Soviet workforce (Women's International Network News 1997).

Communist ideology encouraged gender equality, yet war planners believed that women preferred to remain at home, replacing men who were drafted in their civilian roles and assisting with civil defense. This proved to be a miscalculation, as the military turned away thousands of volunteers. Women joined for patriotic reasons. Vera Malakhova, a medical student at the time of the German invasion, enlisted to defend her country, believing that it was her duty to go to the front. She and her classmates helped to make up the approximately 40 percent of female physicians who served (Clements 2012, 239).

In the military, women needed to prove their competence since many men perceived female soldiers as disrupting the good order and discipline of units. Many female Soviet veterans describe rampant sexual harassment, but in many cases, declined to label assaults as rape. They often highlight "front marriages" where commanders "married" women from their units. These field wives often got better rations and lighter workloads (Clements 2012, 244). Though they had to fight for recognition in their units, women were eligible for promotion and benefits as well as equal pay during hostilities.

Officially, women were banned from combat roles in Russia, but unofficially, they served close to the front and came under enemy fire often. According to some estimates, one hundred and twenty thousand women served in combat units, as armorers, artillery and antiaircraft soldiers, gunners, pilots, and snipers, in addition to more traditional support roles (Young 2016). These more traditional roles often involved nursing and other medical positions, as well as communications and engineers. Women comprised 70 percent of the personnel in communications and transport units (Clements 2012, 239). They also served as part of the partisan forces operating in Eastern Europe, cutting communication lines, serving as snipers, and collecting intelligence, often after parachuting into hostile areas. They were expected to assist in housekeeping duties where they were stationed, a situation that often rankled both the women and men who saw the double duty that women were doing.

In contrast to other militaries that allowed women to serve, the Soviets did not set up separate military institutions. The Soviet Union had some all-female units, along with others that were gender integrated. Three units, the 46th Guards Night Bomber, the 125th Guards Bomber, and the 586th Fighters, sent women into air combat, flying plywood and fabric biplanes, navigating with maps when available and by sight when unable to obtain maps. Their Western counterparts allowed women to fly transport missions. While the 125th and 586th both had male commanders, the 46th was led by Lieutenant Colonel Evdokia Bershanskaia, a woman. All three regiments shared the same missions and flew the same aircraft as their male counterparts. The women of the 46th Guards Night Bomber were known as the "night witches" by the Germans. Flyers from all three units performed daring feats, cutting their engines as they approached their targets and dropping their payloads on their targets. After that, they climbed as fast as they could away from enemy fire, but about 27 percent of the women who served on flight crews died (Clements 2012, 241).

After the war, women left the army as soon as they could, striving to build a more stable life. Many were forcibly removed from the military, though they had served honorably. Women often found it hard to readjust to civilian life as rumors of their turning to lesbianism circulated. Unlike the male veterans of World War II, the women did not get preferential treatment in education, employment, and recruitment into the Communist

168   Women and the Military

RUSSIA

Women in the Soviet Union served in many frontline combat roles during World War II, including as fighter pilots, tank drivers, and gunners. The grudging acceptance of the Soviet state was largely due to the heavy losses of men, though women were often eager to defend their nation and so pushed for expanded roles during the war. This agreement to allow women to serve proved short-lived, and women were often demobilized quickly after the end of hostilities. The Germans were so impressed by the skills of the 588th Night Bomber Regiment that they called the women the "Night Witches." The women often flew without maps or radios, and their planes were old training biplanes that were small enough that they didn't appear on radar. The unit was the most highly decorated by the end of the war, though was disbanded just months after the end of World War II.

FURTHER READING

"Meet the Night Witches, the Daring Female Pilots Who Bombed Nazis by Night." 2019. *History.com,* June 7. https://www.history.com/news/meet-the -night-witches-the-daring-female-pilots-who-bombed-nazis-by-night

---

Party after their service and were often looked on with suspicion by those who knew they had served.

EXTERNAL EVENTS AND INTERNAL POLITICS

External events and politics influenced women's military service. Just as women were once accepted in the Soviet Armed Forces as a means of necessity during World War II, the Russian Army began to recruit women heavily after the fall of the Soviet Union in 1989, a move that coincided with the increase in short-term (two- or three-year) conscripted soldiers. By 2005, the Russian Federation estimated that about 40 percent of the armed forces were women (Eifler 2006, 3). The military offers service women a comparable salary, health care, and maternity leave. Research reflects that higher earning potential in the military, travel benefits, holiday checks, and housing services encouraged single mothers to serve. Military women surveyed in 2005 wanted to serve at least until they reach the age limit or until retirement, allowing them a secure future (Eifler 2006, 6).

In 2013, estimates suggested that around 29,000 women served in the Russian armed forces. In 2018, around 45,000 served in the armed forces. There are about 1,000 female members of the Cadet Corps in Russia. Women defend the Russian Homeland as part of the Ground Forces, the Air Force, and the Strategic Missile Forces. None have attained the rank of general or higher, and women are banned from garrison and sentry duties, as well as combat roles on the frontlines. While women do want the opportunity to serve, most reject compelling women to join. According to polls from 2013, most of the country believes that expanding conscription to young women would be problematic (McDermott 2013).

To join the military, women must be at least twenty, while men are eligible to be drafted at the age of eighteen. Women often serve between three and ten years, depending on the specialty that they join (Russian Army

Young women from the all-Russian military-Patriotic movement "Yunarmiya" on Red Square during a rehearsal for Victory Day Parades on May 6, 2018. Women served in both world wars, even flying biplanes and dropping bombs during World War II. However, women were forbidden from participating in the Victory Day Parades until 2016. (Vladgalenko/Dreamstime.com)

170   Women and the Military

2019). The wives of contract NCOs and officers from the Russian military often enlist to serve as cooks, administrative support, and communications operators. Some observers assert that "without the work of women, some forces would not be operational" (Eifler 2006, 3). However, women still comprise less than 10 percent of the force. Women are eligible to serve as officers and soldiers, and many do serve as junior noncommissioned officers. Most women are still in communications, staff jobs, and medical specialties, a divide that corresponds with many other Central and East Asian nations. Recently, however, the Defense Ministry opened roles as pilots to women, including for combat aircraft. Women also serve in the Spetsnaz, the Russian special forces, in coed or female-only units. The female-only detachments conduct intelligence-gathering missions or serve as beacons in assault forces during a foreign incursion. Women also train at the Russian airborne academy at Ryazan as officers in charge of Russian paratrooper units and instructors. Russia initially considered opening positions to women on submarines by 2018, though the country was reportedly influenced by the issues from the U.S. Navy in halting expansion (Korolkov 2015).

Sandwiched between Russia and China, Mongolia relies heavily on diplomacy to maintain peaceful relations with its neighbors. The country's goal is to create and maintain a small but efficient and professional armed force for defense and peacekeeping missions. Women participate in both ground and air forces of the Mongolian military. In 2017, the first female noncommissioned officer from Mongolia attended and completed the U.S. Army SFC Christopher R. Brevard Non-Commissioned Officer Academy, in Alaska. Muncunchimeg Nyamaajav joined the Mongolian Army at the age of nineteen and is now part of the 17 percent of the Mongolian Armed Forces that is female (Harris 2015). She completed the Basic Leader Course in Alaska, participating in field exercises as well as sharing her unique experiences with her classmates. Women are deeply integrated into Mongolian contributions to UN peacekeeping missions, including in Sudan, where they have served as medical professionals, and in Sierra Leone, where they were guards protecting the Special Court for Sierra Leone. In Sudan, the hospital consisted of sixty-eight people; half of them were women (United Nations 2018).

Tension on the Korean Peninsula has forced both North and South Korea to consider how and where women serve. The two countries have adopted opposite strategies toward the situation. In 2015, the North Korean government made conscription mandatory for both men and women. Women are gradually being recognized as more equal by the government.

Central and East Asia 171

In North Korea, women are drafted for up to seven years, while men are drafted for up to eleven. They often perform similar daily routines, though women's physical training regimens are shorter. Many women in North Korea cite the expected daily meal as part of the reason they volunteered to join the military, as well as the sense of patriotism (Lim 2018).

Women in South Korea are not required to participate in mandatory military service, called *gundae*, contributing to a gender divide in the country. A petition launched in South Korea called on the South Korean government to require women to serve instead of perpetuating the stereotype that women should give birth, rather than fight. This petition went viral, getting over 70,000 signatures in just three days. The government refrained from acting on the petition, though it has generated additional discussion as to women's standing in society (M. Y. Lee 2017). The petition mentioned may not have expanded conscription, but it helped in another way. The Ministry of National Defense decided to end restrictions on women serving on the frontlines. This is a sharp turn from the early 1990s when women served in the separate Women's Army Corps. By 2020, women serve throughout the three services, as both officers and NCOs. With over 10,000 women on active duty, they make up about 5.5 percent of the armed forces (Yonhap 2017).

A country's security situation also impacts whether women are recruited into the military. Japan's three closest neighbors—Russia, North Korea, and China—present a significant threat to the country and have led the Japanese government to entice more people to join the military. Prime Minister Shinzo Abe pushed to recruit additional women to the military, largely as an economic boost, though women also proved their worth during peacekeeping missions. Japan cited both national security threats and a declining birthrate as key reasons to reimagine recruiting and retention efforts for its military, with a special emphasis on women (Nishimura 2019).

Women first joined the Japan Ground Self-Defense Force in 1954 with just 144 female service members. That number has since grown to about 15,000 or about 6.5 percent of the total force. The military's goal over the next fifteen years is to raise the total percentage to 10 percent (Jozuka and Wakatsuki 2019). The Japan Ground Self-Defense Force missed recruiting goals for several years, and the average age is thirty-five, though the target age of recruitment is between eighteen and thirty-two (Copp 2019). A white paper, commissioned by the Japanese government, also notes reforms that the military is implementing to promote work-life balance.

172   Women and the Military

The military is allowing telework in the Ministry of Defense (MoD) as well as providing additional workplace nurseries. Finally, to recruit personnel who left midcareer for child rearing, the SDF is expanding programs for reemployment opportunities (Ministry of Defense 2018, 23).

Japan's peacekeeping missions, heavily watched at home and in the press, have served as an opportunity for women to prove their worth to an organization. Japan, known for its pacifist stance on the use of its military abroad amid post–World War II restrictions, has started to deploy soldiers abroad while allowing them to use weapons in self-defense. However, a 2016 law allowed peacekeepers to use their weapons to protect innocent civilians (Hornung 2019).

Japan lifted all restrictions on women in combat units in 2018, except where maternal protection is required by law (Jozuka and Wakatsuki 2019). Women are otherwise allowed to serve in infantry, reconnaissance, engineering, aviation, and even submarine units. In November 2015, the Japan Air Self-Defense Force lifted the ban on women operating fighter jets and reconnaissance aircraft. Once thought to have such extreme g-forces that women could not operate effectively, the Japanese Air Force commissioned Japan's first female fighter jet pilot, Misa Matsushima. Women are still restricted from positions in ground tunnel units and biological and chemical weapon defense units. In biological and chemical weapon defense units, service members handle dangerous substances and risk inhaling hazardous dust particles. Restrictions for women exist due to the domestic Labor Standards Law, which protects women from substances that could affect pregnancies (*The Japan Times* 2018).

In 2013, two women took command of the naval destroyers, *JS Shimayuki* and *JS Setoyuki,* for the first time since Japan's modern navy began. Commander Miho Otani and Commander Ryoko Azuma were responsible largely for training missions but could be called upon for surveillance, anti-submarine warfare and anti-ship missions, as well as detecting and shooting down aircraft and ballistic missiles (Spitzer 2013). Just a few years after her successful command of the naval training destroyer, Commander Otani took command of the *Yamagiri* destroyer, overseeing a crew of 220. Just ten of those crew members were women. She was also one of the first female graduates at the National Defense Academy. After seeing images of the Gulf War on the news and a newspaper ad for the National Defense Academy, she joined the military, expecting some resistance. She quickly realized that opposition would emanate much closer to home. Her father was reluctant for her to join the military. Her path to success was challenging and after her marriage, she was asked when she would be leaving her job. She is currently married to a fellow destroyer captain and has been forced to make hard decisions about who would care for her daughter when both are out to sea (Demetriou 2016). Women in the Japanese military can take up to three years off after the birth of a child, though the Japanese culture has discouraged women from taking that time.

Similarly, Commander Azuma assumed command of a warship squadron, including the flagship Izumo helicopter carrier in 2016. The four-ship squadron includes about 1,000 crew members, with just thirty women. Azuma joined the military in 1996, when women were still banned from serving on warships, though were able to join warships in 2008. At her official change of command ceremony, Azuma assured the men and women assembled that her gender should not be a concern as she would concentrate her energy on her duties as a commander (Japan Defense Focus 2018).

Though the Japanese government is actively recruiting women, challenging issues of integration remain. Many training sites, including the National Defense Academy, suffer from a lack of women's facilities, limiting the total number of women who can serve. There are only sixty places at the Academy (out of a total of 480 positions) for women, though women have been attending the school since 1992 (*The Japan Times* 2018). Even the basic training units in Japan are stretched thin. In 2018, 219 women went to Yokosuka training base, a location designed to hold just 120 women bound for the Japanese navy in a typical year. There are three other locations for maritime training, though none can accommodate women at this time. The Air Self-Defense Force only allows women to train in one of its two training locations, although women may be allowed to train at both soon. Finally, the Ground Self-Defense Force allows women only at Camp Asaka and is considering forming a new unit to assist in training (Burke and Ichihashi 2018).

In many post-Soviet countries, the states' newfound independence created new security concerns and have affected women's roles in the military. About 8,000 women serve in the Kazakh military, comprising about 30 percent of the total end strength. The military has struggled to attract volunteers, instead relying on drafted soldiers. To bolster recruiting efforts in Kazakhstan, both girls and boys in their teens are invited to participate in military clubs and activities that simulate military life, with classroom instruction, physical training, and field-training exercises. These clubs are meant to encourage service and have young people see the armed forces as a possible profession. Ultimately, Kazakhstan's goal is to recruit more volunteers, eschewing an overreliance on drafted soldiers (Stein 2016, 3).

Similar to other countries, women in Kazakhstan hold positions in medical, communications, and women's support units. They serve in military education, science, and patriotic education programs (Zhalil 2018). Women are also accepted into military departments in civilian universities. Standards for their entrance are lower than for their male counterparts, though they are expected to pass a medical evaluation and will commission as reserve lieutenants. The women can later choose to serve in the military. In a recent effort to increase opportunities for women, they have been appointed as deputy commanders in companies, battalions, and brigades. Women from Kazakhstan have deployed as military observers to UN peacekeeping operations and are eligible to serve in the Kazbrig peacekeeping brigade, part of the airmobile Ground Forces (Zhalil 2018).

In 2013, during the annual Defender of the Fatherland Day, the commander-in-chief, President Nazarbayev, promoted chairperson of the Committee for Legal Statistics and Special Recordkeeping of Kazakhstan Prosecutor General's Office, Saule Aitpayeva, to the rank of general. She is the first female general since Kazakhstan became independent after the fall of the Soviet Union. She later briefly served as the commissioner for children's rights. The rank largely appears to be symbolic and tied to her government service.

In Armenia, clashes in the enclave of Nagorno-Karabakh remain common between Azerbaijani and Armenian forces. Estimates suggest that as many as 2,000 women now serve in the Armenian military, the majority in clerical, medical, and communications roles (Danielyan 2017). Some women reportedly serve as snipers and sappers. Women attend the Vazgen Sarkisian Military University and the Marshal Khanperiants Aviation Institute, as well as the Stepanakert Military High School in preparation for future service. The aviation institute trains women to serve in aviation and air defense units.

As part of ongoing efforts within the Council of Europe, a UK-sponsored project aims to better human rights protections in the military, with a focus on equal service conditions for women officers, allowing them to work toward positive change ("Human Rights and Women in the Armed Forces in Armenia" 2019). Armenian human rights activist, Armen Tatoyan, proposed several changes to make military service more appealing to women, including allowing women to serve in more roles, stationing married couples on posts close to one another, and an increased public affairs campaign highlighting women's contributions.

As Armenia considers new protections for women, Azerbaijan continues to emphasize a history of women's equality, often touting Ziba Ganiyeva's accomplishments. Ganiyeva served as a sniper in World War II and reportedly killed 129 enemy soldiers. During her career, she also served as a scout and radio operator. The country reportedly trains women as snipers. The government estimates that as many as 1,000 women serve on active military duty in this Muslim-majority nation, though they do so as volunteers, rather than conscripts. A young, elite special forces trooper, who recently wrote a book about her experiences, served in Azerbaijan's military and posed as a pinup model (Lomsadze 2018).

Like Armenia and Azerbaijan, wars drove women to serve in the Georgian military. Women served on the frontlines, particularly as doctors and nurses during the 2008 Russo-Georgian War. For years, the country placed men in roles as warriors and protectors, while women served in nurturing roles. These ingrained cultural attitudes have made it difficult for women to integrate into the military more broadly. The Georgian minister of defense is heading a program to understand the current experiences of men and women in the Georgian Armed Forces, with a special emphasis on building a diverse force with as few barriers to service as possible. The country is working to improve its standing within the international community and achieve the highest level of professional accountability ("Improving Gender Equality in Georgia's Armed Forces" 2018).

Several reports from Georgian servicewomen reflect the challenge of serving in a culture where gender roles are clearly defined. One Georgian woman felt she needed to hide her service and her deployment from her parents, fearing their disapproval in a nation that reinforces gender stereotypes. Georgia has committed to assisting in NATO's operations in Afghanistan and women continue to deploy, with at least thirty-three serving in Afghanistan. Current restrictions constrain women to administrative, medical, and humanitarian work, though like other women who have deployed to Afghanistan, Georgian women participate in base defense, street patrols, and training Afghan soldiers. While men are required to serve for eighteen months as conscripts, women in Georgia are not, and this fact seems to limit their motivation for careers in security fields (Corso 2013).

Despite changes on the ground, cultural attitudes concerning women's place in society remain. The former Georgian minister of defense, Retired Lieutenant General Davit Tevzadze, believes that "killing is not a woman's job," and that a "woman's job is creating life and caring for life" (Corso 2013). His daughter, Ketovan Tevzadze, trained as a member of Georgia's special forces and was the only woman in a class of 162 people. She found herself sharing both living accommodations and restrooms with men. Though she had trained to serve as a member of Georgia's special forces, she was relegated to office jobs.

Kyrgyzstan, like many other Central Asian nations, began to support peacekeeping operations by increasing the number of women serving as members of United Nations contingents. The country also released its first National Action Plan on Women, Peace, and Security in 2013, with a follow-up plan in 2018. Though women's roles in defense and security are specified as priority areas for the country, analysts note that the country neglected to allocate money and additional resources to the plan without much information on time line (Miller, Pournik, and Swaine 2014). Kyrgyzstan has about 4,000 women serving in its armed forces, though reports conflict. Women may volunteer at the age of nineteen, unlike their male counterparts, who are subject to twelve months of conscription.

Under Soviet rule in Tajikistan, women enjoyed significant progress in their rights and opportunities. However, as the poorest country in Central Asia, Tajikistan has not invested in their educational system with women as the hardest hit population. Women fought in World War II and were active participants in the military training of the youth organizations of the Communist Party (Direnberger 2016, 5). Additionally, women fought in the 1992–1997 civil war but do not serve in any official numbers. State ideology encourages strong gender norms, with women serving as mothers and "bearers of traditions" (Direnberger 2016, 10).

Women have made significant strides in Uzbekistan's civil service and military. Female representation at all levels of the government grew from 3.4 percent in 2005 to 17.1 percent in 2016 (Yeniseyev 2017). Not subject to the draft, they may sign up as professional soldiers in noncombat units though families encourage women to serve in more "female sectors such as: sewing, teaching, or nursing" (Uzbek Bureau for Human Rights and Rule of Law 2015, 12). Uzbekistan's defense doctrine, approved in 2018, may expand roles for women. The doctrine emphasizes air defense measures to better protect the homeland, though the doctrine is so new that it is unclear what its effect will be on the military (Ibragimov 2019, 51).

While women work outside the home in Uzbekistan, prior to an International Women's Day event in 2017, the Uzbek president, Shavkat Mirziyoyez, lauded women for their domestic work, particularly in keeping alien ideas and social threats away from the children of Uzbekistan (Yeniseyev 2017). This statement reflects a perpetuation of the social norm that women's priority should be the home.

Until late 2018, the Republic of China (Taiwan) maintained the unpopular policy of conscription to bolster its internal defense against the People's Republic of China (China). Taiwan's position in the world is an uncertain one. China believes that Taiwan is a wayward province, while Taiwanese leaders want to make the island an "indigestible porcupine" and believe that a well-trained military will help in that endeavor (Chung-Yuan 2018). From Taiwan's perspective, this "porcupine strategy" makes Taiwan a less appealing target to invaders, with bunkers throughout the country, tanks hidden in civilian neighborhoods, and lighter weight cruise missiles (*The Economist* 2019). This conscription policy required women from the outlying islands of Fuchien to serve in a civil defense role. After the end of conscription, the Taiwanese military continues to struggle to find enough volunteers to fill the ranks, even with incentives of 110 days of leave a year, a state-sponsored education, and a comfortable salary. Taiwanese leaders pledged to end mandatory service to cut costs and boost the professionalism of the armed forces.

In 2013, Taiwanese President Ma Ying-Jeou canceled the island's 8 percent quota for women, suggesting that women should comprise more of the total armed force. At the time, the Taiwanese military had about 7.6 percent women (Taiwan to Cancel Quotas for Women in the Military: President 2013). Additionally, he noted that Taiwan was ranked fourth in the world for gender equality, just behind Sweden, the Netherlands, and Denmark, and that his goal was to improve Taiwanese women's social status while eliminating lingering gender discrimination. Women now make up about 14 percent of the all-volunteer military, serving in combat units in all three forces (Chung-Yuan 2018). Women are still barred from the navy's submarine squadron. However, of the nearly 300 serving generals and admirals in Taiwan, just two are women, suggesting a lingering glass ceiling. In recent years, the first all-woman artillery squad participated in the Han Kuang military exercises. The soldiers practiced a variety of drills testing weapons effectiveness to boost combat readiness. The all-woman squad met all training standards required of them and surpassed many expectations (DeAeth 2018).

OTHER ISSUES: MILITARY STRESS

A recent study exploring the effects of stress and anxiety on men and women in the Chinese military found that women have better coping strategies than their civilian female counterparts. All the participants in the study were students at a ten-month training course, with 470 women and 379 men participating. All were members of the Infantry Division and unmarried. The officers were spending about ten hours a day training, with a focus on parading, physical training, and comprehensive training. The results showed that women reported less social support than men in training and experienced higher rates of negative coping styles, including avoidance and self-reproach (Jiang et al. 2013). However, the study found that both men and women coped significantly better than their civilian counterparts. The study is unclear whether those surveyed had always had better coping strategies or if their military service and training had taught them those skills.

The PLA using surveys found that female PLA service members report mental distress at higher rates than their male counterparts (Yang 2019). This rise is a change from previous studies, where women have typically shown less signs of distress. Women have increasingly joined in more combat-focused roles without lessening the burdens of their family obligations. The study also found that cadets and officers experience less stress than their enlisted and noncommissioned officer counterparts; women are more prevalent in lower ranks and given far less responsibility to make decisions in the PLA. General Han Weiguo wrote an article advocating for service members to return home to support ill family members, those who are about to give birth, and when children take school entrance exams, going so far as to propose that service members who fail to care for families should be investigated. If enacted, these reforms would suggest a significant shift in the mentality of the PLA (Yang 2019). Additional flexibility may allow women, who often bear higher responsibilities for their families, to care for them without losing their jobs as well as help shift the culture to allow women to continue to serve even as they strive to maintain a personal and professional balance.

While women continue to make strides toward gender equality across Central and East Asia, societal cues often keep them from full integration. Women are still largely restricted from serving in submarine units and units that deal with hazardous chemicals. Many of the countries of Central and East Asia have allowed women to serve due to wartime necessity or ongoing threats, though others remain male-dominated organizations.

FURTHER READING

BBC News. 2017. "Reality Check: Does China's Communist Party Have a Woman Problem?" *BBC News*, October 25.

Bigg, Claire. 2005. "Russia; Army Puts on a Pretty Face." *Radio Free Europe*, June 22.

Bjarnegård, Elin, and Erik Melander. 2013. "Revisiting Representation: Communism, Women in Politics, and the Decline of Armed Conflict in East Asia." *International Interactions* 39, no. 4: 558–574.

Blakkisrud, Helge, and Nuraida Abdykapar Kyzy. 2017. "Female Heroes in a Man's World: The Construction of Female Heroes in Kyrgyzstan's Symbolic Nation-Building." *Demokratizatsiya: The Journal of Post-Soviet Democratization* (Spring): 113–136.

Blasko, Dennis J. 2008. "PLA Conscript and Noncommissioned Officer Individual Training." In *The "People" in the PLA: Recruitment, Training, and Education in China's Military*, edited by Travis Tanner, Andrew Scobell, and Roy Kamphausen, 99–138. Carlisle, PA: Strategic Studies Institute.

Burke, Matthew M., and Aya Ichihashi. 2018. "Japan's Self-Defense Forces Consider All-Female Training Units to Accommodate Growing Recruit Numbers." *Stars and Stripes*, December 12.

Chung-Yuan, Yao. 2018. "Bettering the Military for Women Will Recruit More." *Taipei Times*, May 31.

CIA. 2020. "CIA, the World Factbook." *North Korea,* February 7. https://www.cia.gov/library/publications/the-world-factbook/geos/kn.html#Govt

Clements, Barbara Evans. 2012. *A History of Women in Russia: From the Earliest Times to the Present.* Bloomington: Indiana University Press.

Copp, Tara. 2019. "How Will Japan Defend Itself, If It Can't Get Its Youth to Serve?" *The Miltary Times*, January 30.

Corso, Molly. 2013. "Georgia: Women Soldiers Fight for the Right to Fight Like Men." *Eurasianet,* March 8. Accessed June 5, 2019. https://eurasianet.org/georgia-women-soldiers-fight-for-the-right-to-fight-like-men

Danielyan, Emil. 2017. "Armenia: Boosting Female Presence in Army." *Eurasianet*, January 4.

DeAeth, Duncan. 2018. "First Taiwanese All-Female Artillery Squad Takes Part in Military Drills in Penghu." *Taiwan News*, May 24.

180   Women and the Military

Demetriou, Danielle. 2016. "Meet Japan's First Female Warship Captain." *The Telegraph*, June 5. https://www.telegraph.co.uk/news/2016/06/05/meet-japans-only-female-warship-captain

De Nicola, Bruno. 2017. *Women in Mongol Iran: The Khatuns, 1206–1335*. Edinburgh, Scotland: Edinburgh University Press.

Direnberger, Lucia. 2016. "Representations of Armed Women in Soviet and Post-Soviet Tajikistan: Describing and Restricting Women's Agency." *The Journal of Power Institutions in Post-Soviet Societies* 17.

The Economist. 2019. "China's Might Is Forcing Taiwan to Rethink Its Military Strategy." January 26.

Eifler, Christine. 2006. "Underestimated Potential: Women Soldiers in the Russian Armed Forces." *The Journal of Power Institutions in Post-Soviet Societies* 4/5.

Focus Taiwan News Channel. 2013. "Taiwan to Cancel Quotas for Women in the Military: President." (March 8): 1.

Goodridge, Elisabeth. 2018. "Overlooked No More: Maria Bochkareva, Who Led Women into Battle in WWI." *The New York Times*, April 25.

Grau, Lester W., and Charles K. Bartles. 2016. *The Russian Way of War.* Fort Leavenworth, KS: Foreign Military Studies Office (FMSO).

Harris, Sachel. 2015. "Mongolian Soldier Blazes Trail for Fellow Females." (December 1): 1. https://www.army.mil/article/159315/mongolian_soldier_blazes_trail_for_fellow_females

Hornung, Jeffrey W. 2019. "With Little Fanfare, Japan Just Changed the Way It Uses Its Military." *Foreign Policy*, May 3.

"Human Rights and Women in the Armed Forces in Armenia." 2019. *Council of Europe,* June 1. Accessed October 1, 2019. https://www.coe.int/en/web/yerevan/human-rights-and-women-in-the-armed-forces-of-armenia

Ibragimov, M. M. 2019. "Priorities of the Construction of the Armed Forces of the Republic of Uzbekistan in the Conditions of Development of Forms and Methods of Contemporary Armed Struggle." *Military Review,* 47–55.

"Improving Gender Equality in Georgia's Armed Forces." 2018. *North Atlantic Treaty Organization,* February 21. Accessed March 3, 2019. https://www.nato.int/cps/en/natohq/news_152461.htm

Japan Defense Focus. 2018. "First-Ever JMSDF Female Escort Division Commander." *JDF*, May, no. 99 ed. https://www.mod.go.jp/e/jdf/no99/specialfeature.html

The Japan Times. 2018. "Women Taking on More Front-Line Roles in Japan's Military." October 18. https://www.japantimes.co.jp/news /2018/10/18/national/social-issues/women-taking-front-line-roles -japans-military/#.XP6LlIhJHcs

Jensen, Kimberly. 2012. "Volunteers, Auxiliaries, and Women's Mobilization." In *A Companion to Women's Military History*, edited by Barton Hacker and Margaret Vining, 189–231. Leiden, Netherlands: Brill.

Jiang, Yuan, Yun F. Sun, Ye B. Yang, Jing J. Tang, Sheng J. Wu, and Dan M. Miao. 2013. "Gender Differences in Coping Styles of Chinese Military Officers Undergoing Intensive Training." *Military Psychology* 25, no. 2: 124–135. https://doi.org/10.1037/h0094954

Jones, David E. 1997. *Woman Warriors: A History.* Dulles, VA: Brassey's.

Jozuka, Emiko, and Yoko Wakatsuki. 2019. "Answering the Call: The Women on the Front Lines of Japan's Defense." *CNN,* February 3. https://www.cnn.com/2019/01/23/asia/japan-self-defense-force -recruitment-intl/index.html

Kania, Elsa. 2016. "Holding Up Half the Sky? (Part 1: The Evolution of Women's Roles in the PLA)." *China Brief* 16, no. 15.

Kania, Elsa, and Kenneth Allen. 2016. "Holding Up Half the Sky? (Part 2)—Women in Combat Roles in the PLA." *China Brief,* 13–20.

Kaufman, Alison A., and Peter W. Mackenzie. 2009. *Field Guide: The Culture of the Chinese People's Liberation Army.* Field Guide, CNA China Studies.

Korolkov, Alexander. 2015. "Women to Serve in Russian Navy Submarines?" *Russia Beyond,* March 27. https://www.rbth.com/economics /2015/03/27/women_to_serve_in_russian_navy_submarines _42237

Lee, Dmitry. n.d. *Kazakh Army Women Balance Gender and Responsibilities.* Accessed June 15, 2019. https://www.edgekz.com/kazakh -army-women-balance-gender-and-responsibilities

Lee, Michelle Ye Hee. 2017. "South Korea Exempts Women from the Draft. Is That Fair?" *The Washington Post*, September 18.

Lei, Zhao. 2014. "Uygur Women Are Navy's Latest Wave." *China Daily*, August 1.

Li, Xiaolin. 1994. "Chinese Women Soldiers: A History of 5,000 Years." *Social Education* 58, no. 2: 67–71.

Lim, Hyun-Joo. 2018. "What Life Is Like for North Korean Women— According to Defectors." *Independent*, September 9.

Lomsadze, Giorgi. 2018. "Azerbaijan's Model Soldier: Pinup, Writer and Fighter." *Eurasianet,* January 22. Accessed June 5, 2019. https://eurasianet.org/azerbaijans-model-soldier-pinup-writer-and-fighter

Mandl, Sabine. 2011. *Women in AZERBAIJAN Peace, Security and Democracy from a Women's Rights Perspective.* Desk Research, Ludwig Boltzmann Institute of Human Rights.

McDermott, Roger. 2013. "The Role of Women in Russia's Armed Forces." *Eurasia Daily Monitor.*

McLaughlin, Kathleen. 2019. *Armenia Country Gender Assessment.* Country Gender Assessment, Manila, Philippines: Asian Development Bank.

McLaughlin, Kathleen. 2019. *Azeerbaijan Country Gender Assessment.* Country Gender Assessment, Manila, Philippines: Asian Development Bank.

Miller, Barbara, Milad Pournik, and Aisling Swaine. 2014. *Kyrgyzstan National Action Plan Analysis.* Online, PeaceWomen, Women's International League of Peace and Freedom.

Ministry of Defense. 2018. "Defense of Japan 2018." Annual military report.

Mohan, Megha. 2017. "Rape and No Periods in North Korea's Army." *BBC News*, November 21.

"National Action Plan on Women, Peace, and Security." 2015. https://www.mofa.go.jp/files/000101798.pdf

Nazemroaya, Mahdi Darius. 2014. "The Historic Role That Soviet Women Played in Defeating the Nazis in World War II." *Global Research,* March 8. Accessed November 1, 2019. https://www.globalresearch.ca/how-the-west-ignores-women-as-actors-in-otherized-societies-a-sociological-unraveling-of-the-logos-of-the-soviet-amazons/5372529

Nelsen, Harvey W. 2019. *The Chinese Military System: An Organizational Study of the Chinese People's Liberation Army.* New York: Routledge.

Neuman, Scott, and Rob Schmitz. 2018. "Despite the Ends of China's One-Child Policy, Births Are Still Lagging." *NPR*, July 16.

Nishimura, Kumi. 2019. "The Japan Self-Defense Force: A Crisis in the Ranks." *National Interest*, September 11.

Organization for Economic Co-operation and Development. 2014. "Balancing Paid Work, Unpaid Work and Leisure." http://www.oecd.org/gender/data/balancingpaidworkunpaidworkandleisure.htm

Radio Free Asia. 2016. "Female Fighter Pilot's Death Came after Propaganda Drive by China's Military." https://www.rfa.org/english/news/china/military-women-11142016125029.html

Roudakova, Natalia, and Deborah S. Ballard-Reisch. 1999. "Femininity and the Double Burden: Dialogues on the Socialization of Russian Daughters into Womanhood." *Anthropology of East Europe Review* 17, no. 1: 21–34.

Russian Army. 2019. *Woman in the Army (Translated)*. Accessed December 1, 2019. http://russianarmya.ru/sluzhba-dlya-zhenshhin-po-kontraktu.html

Spitzer, Kirk. 2013. "Japanese Women Take Command, Finally." *Time Magazine*, March 22.

Stein, Matthew. 2016. *Transition in the Armed Forces of Kazakhstan—From Conscripts to Contract Soldiers*. Fort Leavenworth, KS: Foreign Military Studies Office.

Tomlinson, Simon. 2015. "Borat's Call of Beauty? Kazakhstan Military Unveils Its 123 'Prettiest Soldiers' in Bid to Attract More People to Sign Up." *Daily Mail*, April 10.

United Nations. 2018. *Service and Sacrifice: Mongolia Continues to Strengthen Its Contribution to UN Peacekeeping*, March 9. Accessed May 2019. https://news.un.org/en/story/2018/03/1004552

United Nations Security Council Coverage. 2019. "Deployment of Female Personnel Boosts Effectiveness, Says Secretary-General, as Security Council Holds Open Debate on Women in Peacekeeping." April 11.

Uzbek Bureau for Human Rights and Rule of Law. 2015. *Uzbekistan's Implementation of the CEDAW*. Responses to list of issues CEDAW/C/UZB/Q/5. Tashkent, Uzbekistan: UBHRRL.

Wanli, Yang. 2017. "All Female Fighting Force Wins All Around Respect." *China Daily*, July 31.

Wheaton, Oliver. 2015. "Kazakhstan's Army Is Holding a Beauty Competition for Its Female Recruits." *Metro*, April 23.

Women's International Network News. 1997. "Russian Business Women Are Moving Up Slowly." *Newsweek* (December 8): 1.

World Economic Forum in Collaboration with McKinsey & Company. 2014. *Closing the Gender Gap in Japan*. Insight Report, World Economic Forum.

Yang, Zi. 2019. "Assessing Mental Health Challenges in the People's Liberation Army, Part 1: Psychological Factors Affecting Service Members, and the Leadership Response." *China Brief* 14.

Yeniseyev, Maksim. 2017. "Role of Women Grows in Uzbekistani Society." *Central Asia News*, March 21. Accessed June 5, 2019. https://central.asia-news.com/en_GB/articles/cnmi_ca/features/2017/03/21/feature-02

Yonhap. 2017. "Korea to Expand Women's Role in Military." *The Korea Herald*, December 20.

Young, Marissa. 2016. *Changing the Face of War in Russia: Women in the Russian Armed Forces,* May 17. Accessed March 2019. http://natoassociation.ca/the-changing-face-of-war-in-russia

Zhalil, Madina. 2018. "Kazakh Army to Plan to Actively Involve Women." *The Qazaq Times*, April 9. https://qazaqtimes.com/en/article/37953

SEVEN

South and Southeast Asia

There is extraordinary diversity in South and Southeast Asia regarding women's participation in the armed forces. Some countries have a long history of participation, while others continue to exclude women from service. For example, in Vietnam the Trung sisters from 40 CE are known for leading a rebellion against the Chinese Han dynasty. Another Vietnamese heroine, Lady Trieu, also confronted the Chinese in a popular revolt in 60 CE (Anderson 2011, 297). In 1880, during the battle of Maiwand in Afghanistan, a woman named Malalai died fighting the British and became a national hero. More countries globally are allowing women to execute combat roles whether in combat support services, combat support, nondirect combat, and ground close combat (GCC). Nondirect combat roles refer to those that "stop short of 'direct' killing" (Suresh and Matthews 2017, 28). This includes serving on submarines, warships, and combat aircraft.

In Asia, women have been permitted this nondirect combat role in South Korea (2002), Singapore (2012), China (2013), and Pakistan (2013). Despite the traditional view of women in many Asian countries, women are beginning to play a greater role in the armed forces across the region. In Bangladesh, women began serving in the military in 2003 and continue to serve in support roles. Women entered the Sri Lankan Armed Forces in the 1970s and serve in most positions, including on the frontline. However, they cannot serve in the Special Forces or fast attack squadrons (Suresh and Matthews 2017, 32). This chapter details several countries in South and Southeast Asia where women have played important roles in the military and where transformations in societal views of gender roles are

186 Women and the Military

occurring. This chapter includes Afghanistan, Bangladesh, Bhutan, Brunei, Cambodia, East Timor, India, Indonesia, Laos, Malaysia, Maldives, Myanmar, Nepal, Pakistan, Philippines, Singapore, Sri Lanka, Thailand, and Vietnam.

SOCIETAL VIEWS OF MASCULINITY AND WARFARE

Although there is great diversity of views in South and Southeast Asian countries regarding women's role in society, and in warfare specifically, many contend that the military is a man's domain with a woman's central obligation to the family. Others argue that society is not prepared for women to die on the battlefield and highlight women's physical and mental weaknesses as reasons to bar women from some positions in the armed forces. These perceptions, in part, lead to low participation rates of women in military positions across the region. Additionally, Islam holds an important position in several countries in the region, impacting relations between the sexes and perceptions of women's roles in society and abilities.

As in many of the South and Southeast Asian countries, during the colonial period in Sri Lanka, the role of women was "traditional" as reproducers, homemakers. "Sri Lankan women, be they Sinhala, Tamil or Muslim, continue to be constructed as the reproducers, nurturers and disseminators of "tradition," "culture," "community," and "nation" (De Alwis 2002, 675–676). Sri Lanka has been marked by violence due to ethnic tensions between Tamil separatists and the Sri Lankan state. Consequently, women have assumed various roles in this culture of violence including as warriors. Women participated in youth riots that lasted from 1987 to 1989, and Tamil women's participation in combat has increased. The militant group, the Liberation Tigers of Tamil Eelan (LTTE), has a women's wing that gained worldwide attention following the assassination of Rajiv Ghandi, the prime minister of India in 1993, by a female suicide bomber (De Alwis 2002, 682).

In India, despite Indian President Pranab Mukherjee's pronouncement in February 2016 that all military positions would be open to women, the reality on the ground did not materialize. Women are barred from being noncommissioned officers and are not permitted to attend military academies, which impacts their ability for future promotions (Suresh and Matthews 2017, 31). Despite their service in the military for eighty-eight years, women comprise only 5 percent of military officers and cannot serve in

South and Southeast Asia   187

combat either on land, sea, or air (Mallapur 2015). Combat positions are still closed to women because society is not prepared for women to be taken as prisoners during combat (Bhattacharyya 2012, 321). The military also claims that warships have not yet been configured to provide separate accommodations for men and women.

Connected with Indian culture, men have difficulty accepting female officers and taking orders from them. Many male soldiers come from rural areas and have not experienced women in positions of authority (Munshi and Pandey 2017, 144). According to Bhattacharyya, the patriarchic structure of Indian society, despite the Indian constitution's provision protecting women's rights, led to women's dependence on men and a societal belief that women's roles are associated with the home and family (Bhattacharyya 2012, 318). Women comprise less than half a percent of the Indian military out of the 1.3 million personnel in the Armed Forces. They first joined the military in 1927, serving as nurses in the Military Nursing Service, and eventually as doctors in 1943 as part of the Army Medical Corps (Munshi and Pandey 2017, 140). Some women have played significant military roles in India's history. For example, during India's War of Independence against the British, Lakshmi Sahgal led 1,000 women in the Jhansi regiment, which was formed in 1943 (Bhattacharyya 2012, 318).

By 1992, the Indian cabinet opted to expand jobs for women in the armed forces. The Cabinet Committee on Parliamentary Affairs approved the introduction of female officers into the military. Although the numbers are small, female officers make up 4 percent of the Indian Army and 5 percent of the Navy (Kaur 2016, 182). A crucial debate regarding women in the Indian Armed Forces centered on permanent commissions where women would serve a minimum of twenty years and receive a pension commensurate with their male counterparts. Most women, except those in the medical and legal corps, received temporary commissions called short service commissions that lasted for ten years with an option to extend, while men procured permanent commissions. Women who served in the Judge Advocate General's office or Army Education Corps were granted permanent commissions in 2008 (Kaur 2016, 182). Prior to 2015, due to the rule on permanent commissions, women were unable to receive a pension, although in specific cases, the Supreme Court decided whether women could receive a permanent commission (Munshi and Pandey 2017, 140). For example, in 2015, the Delhi High Court ruled that female naval officers will be granted rights similar to male counterparts (Kaur 2016, 183). By 2019, the India government approved all women receiving the

Female soldiers in India gather in a park to exercise. Women have served in the Indian military for over ninety years. Women first joined the military in 1927, serving as nurses in the Military Nursing Service and eventually as doctors in 1943 as part of the Army Medical Corps. (MACHPhotography/Dreamstime.com)

same permanent commissions as men (*India Today* 2019). The fact that women had not been afforded the same benefits as men reflected the cultural view that women's importance in the military was unequal to that of men.

Despite the inclusion of women in the military, Pakistan espouses a contradictory position toward women. Although a woman, Benazir Bhutto held the highest political position as prime minister twice (1988–1990, 1993–1996), Pakistan remains a male-dominated, patriarchal society that often resists advances in women's rights. Pakistan's policies toward women in the military have been confusing with some branches being open, only to be closed after a short while. When Pakistan declared its independence in 1947 after its partition with India, the government allowed women to serve in the armed forces. There are 4,000 women in a military of 550,000, comprising less than 1 percent of the forces (Pennington 2006). By 2015, Pakistan had promoted three women to the rank of general; however, although women can serve in combat support positions, they cannot serve on the frontlines. Modeling its Air Force after the British Royal Air Force and then the U.S. Air Force, Pakistan allowed women to serve in Air Force medical positions. When Benazir Bhutto was in power in 1995, she convinced Air Chief Marshal Abbas Khattak to allow women to serve in positions other than medical (Shah 2015). They began serving as air traffic controllers, engineers, and in information technology.

Despite their success in Pakistan, the expectation that women are responsible for the home and children remains (Shah 2015). Additionally, given the low literacy rate of women in Pakistan, far fewer women than men are qualified for military positions. Despite this, by 2002, the Pakistani government permitted women to become pilots, and in 2005 the first women were inducted into the Pakistani Air Force (Shah 2015). In 2006, four women completed the fighter pilot course at the Pakistani Air Force Academy at Risalpur, and one woman, Saira Amin, graduated first in her class (Shah 2015). This success, along with others, impacted a key change in the Pakistani Armed Forces as they integrated women into some combat arms (Abbas 2006). By 2015, 339 women served in the Air Force with twenty-one women serving as pilots, although most women continue to enter the Air Force in medical positions. In 2006, the Pakistani Army also allowed women to serve in the signal, engineering, computing, and legal branches (Pennington 2006).

Other parts of Asia, such as Vietnam, also reflect traditional gender roles, influenced by the Chinese Confucian tradition, which holds that women are subservient to men and are required to obey men. Despite these perceptions of women's subservience and primary domestic role, there is a saying in Vietnamese culture, that during times of invasion "even the women must fight." This perception reflects a tradition of women's militarization during times of strife and a cultural perception that women possess a role in family protection (Anderson 2011, 298). In Vietnam, women provided domestic services to the Army, including cooking, doing laundry, and tending to husbands and sons who were involved in fighting. In some cases, women followed male family members to camps, similar to camp followers of many other countries. From 1965 to 1975, many South Vietnamese men brought female family members close to where they were based. In addition to fulfilling domestic chores, in some cases, women radioed messages about artillery fire when an operator was killed or handed their husbands ammunition (Anderson 2011, 300). However, most activities were domestic, and the government in Saigon perceived these tasks as patriotic even though many women participated out of economic need and family security rather than as a symbol of patriotism.

Women who did not bear sons could be divorced by their husbands, or a man could take another wife or concubine, reflecting the premier value placed on men in society. With this said, Vietnam, prior to Chinese influence, held women to a higher standard than women in China (Anderson 2011, 299). Similarly, women have had a relatively high status in Burmese (Myanmar) society. Historically, even the British colonizers recognized this higher status relative to Muslim and Hindu women in areas such as property rights and other areas of economics. In Burmese society, women were considered industrious businesswomen (Aung 2015, 536–537). During colonial times, the British implemented free trade, which modernized rice production and facilitated imported labor from India and China. These workers were willing to accept lower wages than some of the Burmese women, who had been instrumental in all aspects of rice cultivation. Resenting the use of imported labor, this situation led to Burmese women's participation in the nationalist movement (Aung 2015, 537).

When the British withdrew from Burma in 1942 after the Japanese invasion, Chinese and Indian workers left. Burmese women returned to their traditional roles in the economy dealing with small-scale domestic production. The Anti-Fascist People's Freedom League (AFPFL) was established in 1944 to oppose the Japanese occupation. The Communist Party called for women to join the resistance, and in February 1945 the Women's Regiment of the Burma Independence Army (BIA) was established. Although women did not serve in combat, they were trained in espionage, intelligence, and military tactics. Many served in villages mobilizing the population, gathering intelligence, and providing food and assistance to military men. Due to a lack of scholarship on this issue, it is unknown whether women excelled at mobilizing village support or whether they were given these responsibilities since men were occupied on the frontlines. The women's regiment was disbanded only three months after its creation, perhaps alluding to the fact that men found women's abilities "limited" (Aung 2015, 539–540).

In Southeast Asia, the Philippines has one of the more gender equitable policies regarding women in the military. The Women Auxiliary Corps was established in 1963 by the Republic Act 3835 and permitted women to serve in "non-combat/administrative duties and such other functions and services as may be prescribed by the Secretary of National Defense" (http://pcw.gov.ph/law/republic-act-3835). In 1992, Republic Act No. 7192 declared women as "full and equal partners of men" (Suresh and Matthews 2017, 32). In April 1993, the first group of women entered the military academies, but were limited to comprising up to 5 percent of the total number of cadets. Although women can be two inches shorter than men to be admitted, all other entrance tests are the same for both genders. Women were successful at the Academy, and by 1999 Arlene A. Dela Cruz graduated first in her class. According to the Philippine Academy website, the reason for the low percentage of women in the institution relates to the lack of adequate facilities.

Aside from admission into the military academies, increased gender equality was bolstered by the 2010 Magna Carta in the Philippines, which stated that there should be nondiscrimination in employment, including the military and police. Following the legislative changes, women's military roles expanded. In 2013, a Philippine woman commanded the

Soldiers train at the Special Action Force School in Fort Sto. Domingo, Philippines. In Southeast Asia, the Philippines has one of the more gender equitable policies regarding women in the military. Women were permitted in ground combat in 2015, serving in a combat unit, the Kampilan division, in Central Mindanao. (Hrlumanog/Dreamstime.com)

peacekeeping operation in Haiti, and in 2014, the Philippines appointed the first woman to command a naval ship. Women were then permitted in ground combat in 2015, serving in a combat unit, the Kampilan division, in Central Mindanao, although their numbers were very small (Suresh and Matthews 2017, 32).

In India, a critical issue regarding women's military service, along with the granting of permanent commissions, centers around integration into the combat arms. Since the 1990s, women have served as officers in combat support arms and services. The ninety-four pilots and fourteen female navigators have not held combat roles and work mostly in transport and helicopter units (Suresh and Matthews 2017, 30). Women can be in frontline assignments, such as border patrol or riot control in the Indian paramilitary forces, but cannot serve in the infantry, armor, or artillery (Munshi and Pandey 2017, 140). In India, Vice Chief Air Marshal P. K. Barbora argued that training women fighter pilots yields a poor return on the investment, implying that women are less competent than men (Mathers 2013, 141).

The country of Bhutan has a small military with approximately ten thousand people in the Royal Bhutan Army (Munshi and Pandey 2017, 140). In 2000, the Army began commissioning women as officers, but the majority have served in the medical, dental, and legal field. In 2017, twenty of the twenty-one female officers serving in the Army were serving in one of those three fields (Munshi and Pandey 2017, 140).

FACTORS INFLUENCING CHANGE

As in many other countries and regions, several factors led to a push for increased recruitment of women into the military in South and Southeast Asian countries. Women's participation in wars against colonial powers and for independence have changed women's roles in society and the military. Additionally, more women are being recruited into the military because of an increase in peacekeeping missions, which often require women to conduct body searches or interact with women in conservative areas of the world. Another factor impacting women in the military is the technological revolution that negates, in some military jobs, the need for physical strength. Moreover, demographic changes affect the number of women in the military. For example, with the decline of the Japanese birthrate, the government is encouraging women to join the military (Suresh and Matthews 2017, 29). Countries such as China, Indonesia, and India, which continue to have high birthrates, have been slower to open more areas to women. Finally, a country's economic situation influences the number of women in the military. For many women in war-torn Sri Lanka, where conflict was raging from 1983 to 2009, joining the military was a way out of severe economic depression (Mathers 2013, 134).

WAR OF INDEPENDENCE AND PEACEKEEPING

Countries' experiences with wars of national liberation have influenced women's roles in society and the armed forces. In Vietnam, the war against both the French and Americans in the 1960s and 1970s "was indeed part of the struggle to protect and save the family" (Anderson 2011, 298). Women in both the North and South participated actively for their countries, and according to one scholar, their participation is the reason for North Vietnam's victory against the United States (Anderson 2011, 298). Although women in Vietnam held traditional responsibilities as mothers and homemakers, the concept of family protection was also prominent. This concept of protection is reflected in the 1981 Vietnamese government announcement that it would not conscript women, although they could be mobilized during wartime (Woods 1985, 149).

During the Vietnam War, Ho Chi Minh, the president of communist North Vietnam, rallied women and expected them to participate in the fight for their country ("The Vietnamese Women Who Fought for Their Country" 2016). During that period, women served as nurses, while others participated in combat as part of the Vietnamese People's Army in the North or in the Viet Cong in South Vietnam. Although only sixty thousand women served in the North Vietnamese Army when it admitted them in 1969, almost one million more served in militias and other professional activities in support of the war effort. The Youth Corps, whose responsibility included keeping the Ho Chi Minh trail open, was 70 percent female (Anderson 2011, 298). One million women participated in the National Liberation Front (NLF) in South Vietnam with sixty thousand women participating as soldiers in the Viet Cong (Anderson 2011, 299).

The Women Armed Forces Corps was established in 1964 in South Vietnam and had 1,800 members who were part of the Army of the Republic of Vietnam (ARVN). They did not serve in combat, although in some exceptional cases they were in battles. Some women served as officers in

194   Women and the Military

intelligence in the Police Special Group. South Vietnam's President Ngo Dinh Diem's sister-in-law, Ngo Dinh Nhu, created a small military unit called the Vietnamese Women's Solidarity Movement, which she referred to as "little darlings" (Anderson 2011, 301). Although some women learned to shoot pistols, the unit was mainly for show and lasted only from 1955 to 1963. This contrasts with North Vietnam's women of the National Liberation Front (NLF), who fought against the United States and South Vietnamese. The NLF had two women among its initial founders, Nguyen Thi Binh and Duong Quynh Hoa. The NLF had both military and political functions, but the People's Liberation Armed Forces (PLAF), the organization's fighting force, was created in 1961. The North's PLAF inducted large numbers of women into the organization (Anderson 2011, 302).

Connected with North Vietnam's National Liberation Front, the Women's Liberation Association founded also in 1961, recruited women to oppose the U.S. and South Vietnam forces. Many women from the South, who joined the NLF or the Women's Liberation Association, were searching for women's equality and "denounced both the historic inequality of women and their exploitation under the South Vietnamese government" (Anderson 2011, 303). Female guerillas were difficult to identify as they blended in with other Vietnamese peasants. After 1965 when there was a shortage of North Vietnamese soldiers, more women participated in armed combat, but usually supported the combatants with food, clothing, and nursing. The NLF claims that over one million women were members of their organization by 1965 (Anderson 2011, 303).

In 1965, in the South, an all-female fighting unit called C3 was established and operated in the district of Cu Chi, known for its guerilla activity. One woman, Vo Thi Mo, who began fighting when she was a teen, led attacks on U.S. tanks and participated with the South's Viet Cong members in other operations (Anderson 2011, 308). In many cases, women fought alongside men. Vietnamese culture is influenced heavily by Confucianism, which champions male superiority. This view made it challenging for men to accept women's roles in the fight. In some cases, women disguised themselves as men to be accepted in a unit.

Due to Ho Chi Minh's acceptance and fight for women's equality, women in the North had a different experience than those in the South. Whereas many women in both the North and South were illiterate, Ho Chi Minh encouraged women's education, their right to vote, equal work opportunities, and the abolition of polygamy. In the North, there was an almost complete mobilization of the population, and women were trained to fight, although they were not drafted into the military. Ho believed that for national liberation to succeed, women also needed to be liberated. The Indochinese Communist Party recruited women from its foundation and pushed for gender equality, although men made up its leadership (Anderson 2011, 309). Despite this, most women in North Vietnam received military and combat training, although women were not required to serve in the People's Army of Vietnam. Those who served provided medical care and other noncombat positions. Women also worked under terrible conditions to maintain the Ho Chi Minh trail so that troops and supplies could be transported to the South.

Indonesia's experience with foreign powers also influenced perceptions and policies on women in the armed forces. In Indonesia, after the Japanese defeated the Dutch and occupied the country from 1942 to 1945, the Japanese created women's organizations that were required to support the war effort. For example, women who joined the Srikandi Brigade learned how to administer first aid and prepare food for the volunteer army (Blackburn 2004, 21). Although Indonesia has incorporated women into the military, they have not necessarily reached equality with their male counterparts. There is a gendered division of labor within the armed forces. In 1949, when President Sukarno ruled Indonesia, he believed that a modern nation should be egalitarian, and he pointed to women's integration into the armed forces as proof of Indonesia's progress (Sunindyo 1998, 8). Despite their service, women continued to be represented in the Indonesian culture in contradictory ways. Even within the Indonesian military in the 1990s, women were not equal partners to men, with a sexual division of labor reflecting women serving in more domestic roles. According to Sunindyo, state-sponsored publications have sexualized portrayals of military women.

VIRGINITY TESTS REQUIRED FOR INDONESIAN FEMALE RECRUITS

Indonesia requires that female recruits for the National Armed Forces and police, along with fiancées of military officers, undergo "virginity tests." The UN has called for the end of these invasive and degrading actions. Others have questioned the rationale of these tests and argued they have no connection to a state's national security. The World Health Organization weighed in, explaining that the tests are not accurate nor grounded in science.

196 Women and the Military

A coffee table book from 1992 has a photo of a woman in uniform and describes her important role in "enhancing the smooth running and efficiency" of the military, a way that men are never described (Sunindyo 1998, 12). For some, the fact that women serve in the military reflects a gender equality that might not actually exist. Indonesia requires that female military recruits, along with fiancées of military officers, undergo "virginity tests." The UN has called for the end of these invasive actions. As Nisha Varia, a woman rights advocacy director said, "The Indonesian armed forces should recognize that harmful and humiliating 'virginity tests' on women recruits does nothing to strengthen national security" (Human Rights Watch 2015). The World Health Organization has argued that the tests have no scientific grounding or accuracy.

In Nepal, the Maoist insurgency lasting from 1996 to 2006, was a key factor influencing change for women in the Nepali Armed Forces. From 1996 to 2006, the Communist Party of Nepal with its Maoist guerilla movement, battled the Nepalese military. Women were recruited to technical jobs in the military beginning in 1961, and in 2004, the military opened more positions to them. The military plans to increase the percentage of women in the military to 9 percent. In 2017, there were 4,094 women serving in the Nepalese military with 163 officers in general services and 191 in technical fields (My Republica). Despite the traditional Nepalese culture where women's main role is in the domestic domain, they were recruited to be active fighters for the Maoist rebels.

For women, life in Nepal reflected the lack of an education, an early arranged marriage, and "a repetitive pattern of reproductive activities" (Bogati 2015). The insurgency gave women, particularly those from lower socioeconomic statuses, the opportunity for more gender equality, working and fighting alongside men. Former female insurgents held that their main reason for joining the insurgency was in support of Maoist support for gender equality and female empowerment. Postinsurgency Nepal has seen improvements in women's rights. For example, in the political structure, 33 percent of parliamentary seats are reserved for women. In the postconflict environment, the Nepalese Army is moving toward increased inclusiveness by incorporating not only former Maoist insurgents, but women and other minorities groups (Bogati 2015). The Directive on Gender Conduct and the Women Military Directive, both issued in 2014, intends to create a zero-tolerance toward violence against women and to facilitate the recruitment of more women into the military. Whereas prior to 2004, women served mostly in medical or engineering positions, currently most positions are open to them.

Although Indian women do not serve in combat, they have participated in peacekeeping operations, specifically in Monrovia, Liberia, and this activity is enhancing women's status in the armed forces. Their deployment to Liberia emanated from the passage of UN resolution 1325 in 2000. The resolution recognized that armed conflict affects women differently than men and, in response, the UN created female peacekeeping units to create a safe space for female victims of violence (Basu 2010). The units are also tasked with assisting local security institutions to build capacity and execute their own security.

Aside from helping women in host nations, the addition of more women in peacekeeping forces is moving toward greater gender equality within United Nations agencies. The Indian peacekeepers are part of an all-female unit trained in combat tactics, crowd control, and counterinsurgency (Basu 2010). The first unit arrived in Liberia in 2007 to help police combat the rampant sexual violence plaguing the country in connection with the civil war. "Conflict is linked to the way genders are socially constructed; this requires analysis of the different roles of women and men in violence" (Pruitt 2016, 17). Part of the FFPU's job is to ensure that the socially constructed concepts of masculinity and femininity connected to violence are not perpetuated in the postconflict arena.

There is a pervasive belief that for women to succeed in the military or traditionally masculine institutions, they must embrace masculine traits. These all-female units allow women to approach peacekeeping in a way that might not require the adoption of these traits (Pruitt 2016, 19). Aside from providing security, the unit mentored local women in health care and family issues (Basu 2010). They taught women self-defense, conducted classes on sexual violence and AIDS, and provided medical treatment ("Hailed as 'Role Models'" 2016). India has provided the third largest number of women to police operations behind Bangladesh and Nepal.

One of the reasons for women's incorporation into peacekeeping operations, aside from the issue of rights and equality, stems from the argument that gendered institutions such as the military can be transformed by changing the social composition of societal institutions. In other words, permitting women to participate in the military or police forces that are traditionally hegemonic masculine domains, can lead to changed gender roles (Pruitt 2016, 18). The all-female Indian unit has served as a role model for Liberian women who comprised only 6 percent of Liberia's security sector prior to the Indian peacekeeping force's arrival. By 2016, this percentage increase to 17 percent. Although other factors might account for this jump, having a female unit patrolling Liberia made a positive impact on Liberia's women ("Hailed as 'Role Models'" 2016).

According to Lesley Pruitt, in an all-women unit, women can "pursue structural and procedural changes that give serious attention to women's needs and motivations" (2016, 2). Peacekeeping forces have proven more acceptable to host countries than introducing foreign militaries to contain internal conflict, although the operations usually contain police, military, and humanitarian dimensions. These forces agree to remain impartial, must be accepted by all parties in dispute, and forego the use of force except in self-defense (Pruitt 2016, 15).

In contemporary Afghanistan, both foreign intervention and domestic politics have impacted women's roles in society and the military. When the extremely conservative Taliban assumed control of the country in 1995, women were forbidden from leaving their homes without a male escort and without being covered from head to toe in a Burqa, their traditional dress. Having been doctors, lawyers, and employed outside the home prior to this time, the Taliban relegated women to the private and domestic realm. In more recent years, the Afghan Defense Ministry wants to increase the percentage of female soldiers in the armed forces. As of 2017, there were 1,575 women in the military comprising only 3 to 4 percent of the armed forces. The ministry announced a goal of reaching 10 percent women, yet Afghanistan continues to struggle with gender

---

AFGHAN FEMALE PILOT RECEIVES DEATH THREATS

Niloofar Rahmani became the first female military pilot in Afghanistan since the Taliban were ousted from power. She received asylum in the United States in 2018 after receiving death threats, although military officials in Afghanistan denied the allegations and offered that Rahmani had lied (Sukhanyar 2016). Rahmani's situation reflects the traditional culture of Afghanistan regarding women working outside the home and a profound belief that employment in the public realm is a masculine domain.

FURTHER READING

Sukhanyar, Jawad. 2016. "Afghan Response to Female Pilot's U.S. Asylum Case: 'I Am Sure She Lied.'" *New York Times*, December 25. https://www.nytimes .com/2016/12/25/world/asia/afghanistan-niloofar-rahmani-asylum-air-force -pilot.html

equality. Niloofar Rahmani became the first female military pilot in Afghanistan since the Taliban were ousted from power, but she sought asylum in the United States after receiving death threats ("Afghanistan Seeks More Women to Join Its Army" 2017). Rahmani's situation reflects the traditional culture of Afghanistan regarding women working outside the home and a profound belief that employment in the public realm is a masculine domain. To entice women to serve, despite constraining cultural views, the ministry announced that it was creating a new salary scale to incentivize women's recruitment.

Some women have been assigned to the Special Forces and to the Special Mission Wing of the Afghan Special Security Forces, an aviation unit. Afghan president Ashraf Ghani's desire to expand the Special Mission Wing has increased women's recruitment. The women are trained to assist on night raids of insurgents to fill the void left by departing international forces. Even with foreign forces in Afghanistan, then President Hamid Karzai objected to foreigners entering Afghan homes. When Afghan troops enter a home to capture insurgents, Afghan culture forbids men from searching women. Furthermore, the raids usually occur when women and children are at home. Female soldiers are tasked with rounding up women and children and guard against female suicide bombers (Faiez 2013).

Khatool Mohammadzai had been in the Afghan army for over thirty years, but she could not serve after the Taliban takeover in 1996. After the coalition forces removed the Taliban from power in 2001, she was reinstated and was promoted to brigadier general in that same year. Mohammadzai was the first female paratrooper in Afghan history, logging 500 jumps (Najibullah 2010). In 2018, there were ten women working in the unit in logistics, medical, intelligence, and security. The government's goal is to expand that number to forty women by 2020 ("Women of the SMW" 2018).

After the U.S. invasion of Afghanistan in 2001, the Marshal Fahim Military Academy admitted women, although men and women train separately in weapons, physical fitness, and medical care (VOA news). Like Mohammdzai, women have begun to play more important roles in the security environment of postconflict Afghanistan by drawing support away from insurgents. However, women have made very limited progress integrating into the Afghan Security Forces due to the traditional male-dominated society and the strict separation required in Islam. The Afghan government planned to open training academies for women in rural areas, but these more conservative areas make recruitment extremely challenging.

After the overthrow of the Taliban in 2001, the Afghan government recruited both men and women into the country's new police force. In Afghanistan, there was a critical need to have women police officers to search and guard women given the conservative Afghan society separating men and women in the public realm. Despite their training, women did not gain access to leadership roles in the police forces due to male opposition to women working in what they perceived as a male profession. German police trainers, who arrived in Kabul in 2002, were responsible for preparing police instructors. However, the U.S. government was dissatisfied with the pace of training and the number of police officers trained (Benard et al. 2008, 31). The United States began to instruct recruits in a variety of training centers across Afghanistan. Additionally, the government contracted with DynCorp, an independent contractor, to build new training facilities and instruct police.

One of the United States' main responsibilities was to train the Afghan National Army (ANA) with assistance from other coalition countries. By 2006, there were only 200 women in the ANA serving in medical, logistics, and communications. At that stage, the United States did not advocate for the integration of women into the military due to the belief that their incorporation must fit with the norms and culture of the host country (Benard et al. 2008, 32). However, in 2016, the United States budgeted approximately $93.5 million to increase the number of Afghan women serving. The percentage of women remained low, never rising above 1 percent of the security forces (Faizy 2017). Women's inclusion in the security sector has been challenging, with conservative groups threatening women who participate in public life. For example, in 2006, the provincial head of the Ministry of Women's Affairs, Safinye Amajan, was assassinated. In 2008, the highest-ranking female police officer was assassinated on her way to work in Kandahar ("Helmand's Top Policewoman Dies After Attack" 2013). The Taliban frequently targeted soldiers and police, so despite the increased salary and transportation offered to women, few enlisted.

After the Taliban took control of Afghanistan in 1996, women were forbidden to practice medicine and forced to remain home. Although the military medical school trained men, it was forced to close, reopening its doors only in 2009. When the school reopened, women were admitted and make up 25 percent of the students. The United States committed to providing ten years of funding to the school. The students train for seven years, with the first year at the National Military Academy of Afghanistan, learning basic military skills. They then attend the Kabul Medical

University (KMU). As such, all candidates must meet stringent academic and physical requirements. Since women were deprived an education under the Taliban, by 2009, only nine women met all the physical and educational requirements for the program (Hampton 2009).

DEMOGRAPHIC CHANGE AND WOMEN'S INTEGRATION

In Singapore, demographic issues led to a change in women's recruitment. Singapore allows women to serve in most positions except in ground close combat. Women began serving in the Singaporean Armed Forces in 1986 and have served in combat roles including artillery, as pilots flying both F-15s and F-16s, and since 2004, as mortar platoon leaders in infantry units. In 2015, Gan Siow Huang was appointed the first female brigadier general and head of air intelligence (Chow 2015). The Singapore Armed Forces wants to increase the number of women to replace the dwindling number of male recruits, due to declining birthrates. In 2013, 1,500 women served in jobs including in artillery, as pilots and intelligence officers and comprised 7.5 percent of the military. The SAF is recruiting women in specific roles including cyber, military intelligence, and air warfare surveillance (Chow 2015).

As a test case in 2004, the Singapore Armed Forces allowed women to lead motor platoons in an infantry unit. One reason the military permitted women's participation in the infantry is connected to the cultural stigma attached to serving in the infantry. The SAF has trouble recruiting officers for the infantry and decided to assess women's abilities. Given Singapore's geography as a small landmass surrounded by water, Navy and Air Force's prestige outweighs that of the infantry, and as such, women are closed out of many positions in those branches (Mathers 2013, 138; Walsh 2007, 277). Despite opening more roles to women, public sentiment opposes the use of women in combat, and this factor affects the roles women can hold in the military. Similar to female service members in other countries, women in the SAF contend that they must work harder than men as any mistake is attributed to their gender (Walsh 2007, 278).

According to Walsh, Singapore has one of the strongest militaries in Southeast Asia due to its technological advances, yet suffers from several institutional weaknesses, including limiting women's roles in the armed forces (Walsh 2007, 266). He recommends recruiting women specifically to augment the declining military population and to take advantage of the

202 Women and the Military

highly educated female population. Additionally, Walsh argues that the SAF should include women in more positions, including combat divers and pilots, giving Singapore a larger pool of qualified recruits from which to select (Walsh 2007, 278).

As Singapore is increasing its participation in global and regional deployments, Walsh argues that its weaknesses will have profound effects on its national security (Walsh 2007, 266). Women, as both soldiers and officers, have been underutilized and contribute to the weakness of the military. The training for most women is considerably shorter than that of men due, in part, to the fact that most women are not trained in combat skills. In the Army, much of the training is conducted separately from men, and female officers train for twelve months, while men train for more. In the Navy, basic training for women is only two weeks, while it is ten for men (Walsh 2007, 277). Certain advance courses for officers reintegrates women with men.

The Singapore military has a system of scholarship awards, and it was only in 1993 that women could compete for the Merit Scholarship for Women, which equates with the second highest scholarship for men and allows women to study overseas. Attaining one of these scholarships is critical for promotion and assignment, although many assignments are still closed to women (Walsh 2007, 277). Very few women are promoted beyond the rank of captain, and it was only in 1999 that two women obtained the rank of lieutenant colonel.

In 2011, after the government of Myanmar transitioned from military to civilian rule, the government declared that women between the ages of eighteen to twenty-seven could be drafted in times of national emergency (Hodal 2013). Women had served as nurses, but in 2013, the government advertised that they were looking for women to serve as second lieutenants and train in Yangon, although they would not be sent to the frontlines. A military career appeals to some women since it pays better than many other jobs in a country that has low wages. In 2014, the military appointed two female officers to serve as the representatives to Myanmar's lower house of Parliament fulfilling part of the 25 percent quota of military officials in the legislature. Women only comprise 5 percent of the seats in Parliament (Radio Free Asia 2014). Although women were selected for the parliamentary positions, concerns exist as to whether any of the military representatives hold actual authority to make decisions (Radio Free Asia 2014). Although women have served in the military since 1954, the Burmese military ceased recruiting women for nonmedical positions in 1961. The first women to graduate from officer's training school since 1961 occurred in 2014 (Mclaughlin 2014).

Countries in South and Southeast Asia have diverse social and political cultures leading to various perspectives on women's roles in society and the military. Wars of independence, foreign interventions, and globalization, along with domestic economic and political transformation, have led to changing roles for women in some regional militaries.

FURTHER READING

Abbas, Zaffar. 2006. "Pakistan Gets Women Combat Pilots." *BBC*, March 30. http://news.bbc.co.uk/2/hi/south_asia/4861666.stm

"Afghanistan Seeks More Women to Join Its Army." 2017. *Military.Com*, January 27. https://www.military.com/daily-news/2017/01/27/afgha nistan-seeks-more-women-join-its-army.html

Anderson, Helen E. 2011. "Vietnamese Women and the American War." In *The Columbia History of the Vietnam War,* edited by David L. Anderson, 297–316. New York: Columbia University Press. JSTOR.

Aung, Zin Mar. 2015. "From Military Patriarchy to Gender Equity: Including Women in the Democratic Transition in Burma," *Social Research* 82, no. 2 (Summer): 531–551.

Basu, Moni. 2010. "Indian Women Peacekeepers Hailed in Liberia." March 2. http://www.cnn.com/2010/WORLD/africa/03/02/liberia .women/index.html

Benard, Cheryl, Seth G. Jones, Olga Oliker, Cathryn Quantic Thurston, Brooke K. Stearns, and Kristen Cordell. 2008. "Women and Nation-Building." RAND. https://doi.org/10.7249/MG579

Bhattacharyya, Arundhati. 2012. "Women in Military in India: The Cry for Parity." *Mediterranean Journal of Social Sciences* 3, no. 2 (May): 317–325.

Blackburn, Susan. 2004. *Women and the State in Modern Indonesia.* Cambridge: Cambridge University Press.

Bogati, Subindra. 2015. "Assessing Inclusivity in the Post-War Army Integration Process in Nepal." *Inclusive Political Settlements Paper* 11 (July). https://www.berghof-foundation.org/nc/en/publica tions/publication/assessing-inclusivity-in-the-post-war-army -integration-process-in-nepal

Chow, Jeremy. 2013. "SAF Aims to Recruit at Least 500 More Women by 2018." *Straits Times,* July 21. https://www.straitstimes.com/singapore /saf-aims-to-recruit-at-least-500-more-women-by-2018.

Chow, Jermyn. 2015. "SAF Gets Its First Female General." *Straits Times*, June 26. https://www.straitstimes.com/singapore/saf-gets-its-first -female-general

De Alwis, Malathi. 2002. "The Changing Role of Women in Sri Lankan Society." *Social Research* 69, no. 3: 675–691.

Faiez, Rahim. 2013. "Afghan Army Is Training Women for Special Forces: They Fill Key Role on Night Raids, Corralling Women and Children." *St. Louis Post*, February 15, A.10.

Faizy, Sultan. 2017. "An Elite Officer Battles Sexism and the Taliban; Sergeant Is One of 83 Afghan Women in Special Unit." *Los Angeles Times,* May 3, A.4. https://www.latimes.com/world/la-fg -afghanistan-female-police-2017-story.html

"Hailed as 'Role Models,' All-Female Indian Police Unit Departs UN Mission in Liberia." 2016. *UN News,* February 12. https://news.un .org/en/story/2016/02/522102-feature-hailed-role-models-all -female-indian-police-unit-departs-un-mission

Hampton, Tracy. 2009. "Afghan Military Medical School Reopens Enrolls Women in First Class of Cadets." *JAMA* 302, no. 19 (November 18): 2081–2082.

"Helmand's Top Policewoman Dies After Attack." 2013. *Radio Free Europe Radio Liberty*, September 13. https://www.rferl.org/a/afghanistan -top-policewoman-nigar-slain/25107054.html

Hodal, Kate. 2013. "Burmese Army Recruits Female Soldiers as It Struggles to Tackle Rebel Groups." *The Guardian* (U.S. Edition), October 16. https://www.theguardian.com/world/2013/oct/16/burmese -army-recruits-female-soliders-rebels

Human Rights Watch. 2015. *Indonesia: Military Imposing "Virginity Tests."* May 13. https://www.hrw.org/news/2015/05/13/indonesia-military -imposing-virginity-tests#

India Today. 2019. "Women Officers to Get Permanent Commission in All 10 Branches of Indian Army: Defence Ministry." March 5. https:// www.indiatoday.in/india/story/women-officers-to-get-permanent -commission-in-all-10-branches-of-indian-army-defence-ministry -1470967-2019-03-05

Kaur, Mukhwindeer. 2016. "Employment of Women in Indian and Hungarian Armed Forces: A Comparative Study." *AARMS* 15, no. 2: 181–186. https://folyoiratok.uni-nke.hu/document/uni-nke-hu/aarms -2016-2-kaur.original.pdf

Mallapur, Chaitanya. 2015. "88 Years On, 5% Military Officers Are Women." *IndiaSpend*, March 10. https://archive.indiaspend.com /cover-story/88-years-on-5-military-officers-are-women-68416

Mathers, Jennifer G. 2013. "Women and State Military Forces." In *Women and Wars*, edited by Carol Cohn, 124–145. Boston: Polity Press.

Mclaughlin, Tim. 2014. "First Women Graduate from Officer Training School." *Myanmar Times*, August 30. https://www.mmtimes.com /national-news/11487-first-women-graduate-from-officer-training -school.html

Munshi, Anupama, and Suruchi Pandey. 2017. "Attitude of Men Towards Inclusion of Women in Bhutanese and Indian Army: A Literature Review." *South Asian Journal of Human Resources Management* 4, no. 2: 139–148. doi:10.1177/2322093717733401

Najibullah, Farangis. 2010. "Afghan Women Joining Armed Forces in Greater Numbers, Challenging Convention." *Radio Free Europe Radio Liberty*, November 1. https://www.rferl.org/a/Women_Joining _Afghan_Armed_Forces_In_Greater_Numbers_Challenging _Convention/2207468.html

Pennington, Matthew. 2006. "Women Make Gains in Pakistan's Military." *Sunday Gazette,* June 18. Proquest.

Pruitt, Lesley J. 2016. *The Women in Blue Helmets Gender, Policing, and the UN's First All-Female Peacekeeping Unit.* Oakland: University of California Press.

Radio Free Asia. 2014. *Myanmar Military's First Women Representatives Join Parliament.* January 14. https://www.ecoi.net/en/document /1065861.html

Shah, Bina. 2015. "How High Can Pakistan's Air Force Women Fly?" *New York Times*, June 8. https://www.nytimes.com/2015/06/09 /opinion/bina-shah-high-can-pakistans-air-force-women-fly .html

Sunindyo, Saraswati. 1998. "What the Earth Is Female and the Nation Is Mother: Gender, the Armed Forces and Nationalism in Indonesia." *Feminist Review* no. 58 (Spring): 1–21.

Suresh, Lekshmi, and Ron Matthews. 2017. "Asia's Women Warriors." *Jakarta Defense Review Asia* (May/June): 28–32. https://fitribintang .com/2017/05/27/asias-women-warriors

"The Vietnamese Women Who Fought for Their Country." 2016. *BBC News*, December 6.

Walsh, Sean P. 2007. "The Roar of the Lion City: Ethnicity, Gender and Culture in the Singapore Armed Forces." *Armed Forces and Society* 33, no. 2: 265–285.

"Women of the SMW—Afghan Special Mission Wing." 2018. *SOF News,* March 24. https://sof.news/afghanistan/women-of-the-smw

Woods, Dorothea. 1985. "The Conscription of Women for National Defense, the Militarization of Women, and Some Ethical Perspectives on Women's Involvement in the Military." *Current Research on Peace and Violence* 8, no. 3/4: 149–159. JSTOR.

EIGHT

Oceania

Women serve in a wide variety of roles in militaries across Oceania, largely due to the diversity of cultures in the region. Women are generally permitted to serve in all security forces, though several states do not have their own militaries, instead relying on cooperative security agreements with the United States, Australia, or New Zealand.

Australia and New Zealand fully opened their ranks to women, allowing women to serve across the full range of combat specialties earlier than either the United States or the United Kingdom. New Zealand welcomed women in all roles just after the turn of the twenty-first century. Australia allowed women to compete for many combat positions in 2013 with all roles fully opened in 2016. On many of the smaller islands, the predominantly patriarchal governance structures of the Pacific have often stopped women from fully integrating into formal decision-making structures and the military. Kiribati, Nauru, Palau, and the Marshall Islands rely on mutual security agreements with Australia, New Zealand, or the United States without full military forces of their own. Still others have small coast guards or police forces that often nominally allow women to serve. For this chapter, the following countries are included in Oceania: Australia, Fiji, Kiribati, the Marshall Islands, Micronesia, Nauru, New Zealand, Palau, Papua New Guinea, Samoa, the Solomon Islands, Tonga, Tuvalu, and Vanuatu.

SOCIETAL VIEWS OF MASCULINITY AND THE MILITARY

The women of the region occupy different roles in society. In Australia and New Zealand, women often work outside the home, though still bear a higher responsibility for unpaid, domestic labor than men. In other countries, women primarily serve in domestic roles in the home or the informal economy. Though women's roles in society are changing, the debate on women in Australia's armed forces was temporarily hampered after the publication of an article on the integration of women in the Australian Defense Force (ADF). The article noted that much of the resistance to opening all combat roles to women was colored by the idea that young women would be subject to death and injury, harming the future population of Australia (Smith 1990, 141). Additionally, those who serve, even away from the front lines, are portrayed differently than men by the media. In May 1998, four members of the Royal Australian Navy (RAN) were killed, including one woman. The men were portrayed as loyal and trustworthy mates, while Midshipman Megan Pelly was noted to be "spirited, strong, and independent and career minded but at the same time she was quite domesticated" (Dargaville 1998).

The tension between the professional lives of women and their role in the home impacts women's service. While attitudes toward gender are changing, the issue of the public and domestic roles of women continue to emerge. Even in the countries where women are permitted in all specialties, the cultural inclination placing the bulk of child care and other unpaid domestic labor on women remains strong (Australian Human Rights Commission 2012, 102). Like many service members throughout the world, women struggle to balance children and career, along with the physical demands of the military. Many women cite increased stress in frontline roles and a lack of flexibility in careers as factors that force them out of the most highly regarded combat specialties.

Australian society concentrates on providing a more diverse and inclusive workplace "with a focus on gender equality in professional development and progression opportunities" (Commonwealth of Australia 2016). Recent reports from Australia have shed light on the gender divide present within the Australian Parliament, with many senators claiming that sexism remains endemic within political culture (Mao 2019). While women earned the right to run in federal elections around the turn of the twentieth century, no woman won election until around 1940. Over the past twenty years, Australia has fallen from fifteenth in the world to fiftieth in parliamentary

A female officer leads Australian soldiers during a promenade at Anzac parade, Canberra, Australia. Both Australia and New Zealand commemorate all Australians and New Zealanders who served and died in all wars during Anzac Day. Women served as nurses during both world wars, helping to support these service members. (Rorem/Dreamstime.com)

gender diversity. The women who have attained the highest ranks of political office in Australia have all had one thing in common—they were childless. Recently, several members of Parliament quit, claiming that the job, requiring a posting to remote Canberra, is incompatible with family life. While the Australian military has made many strides in closing the gender divide, there are still issues within the services that closely mirror societal rifts.

As of 2014, the New Zealand military proportionally had higher female representation than the United States, the United Kingdom, Canada, and Australia, although these numbers did not continue to rise as expected in the following years. Reports showed that women were entering the military, but often left at higher rates than their male counterparts. Though this statistic is worrisome, it is in line with the turnover for the New Zealand Public Service (Defence 2014, 21). To combat the declining representation of women in the military, New Zealand began to implement active recruiting and retention strategies in 2014, rather than the passive ones that the military had previously relied on. This included women-only career fairs with an emphasis on defense industries as well as outreach at girls' schools.

Balancing work and home, coupled with the perception that women continue to bear responsibility for most of domestic work, has a strong impact on women's participation in the armed forces. The military identified that as people have children later in life, they are forced to make choices between two "greedy" organizations, family and military. People who have children at an older age are likely to be in demanding and higher-level positions in the military. Men and women who left the New Zealand military often noted that they were given little notice for travel or moves, impacting their ability to plan for their family's future.

Across the region, efforts to encourage gender equality are promising. A joint venture between UN Women and Oceania Rugby teaching women and girls to play the sport across the region is promoting both gender equality and the prevention of violence against women. Eight women's military and police rugby teams participated in the Pacific Military Cup in 2018. Teams from Australia, New Zealand, Fiji, Tonga, Samoa, Vanuatu, Solomon Island, and the Cook Islands competed, allowing the nations to use friendly competition to showcase the strength of the women in the military and police forces. The tournament fostered community engagement, with service members and athletes teaching elementary school students basic rugby skills. Though not all the women in the competition serve in the armed forces, all contribute to stability efforts through their work in external and internal security (*Women's Rugby Sevens Brings Pacific Nations Together* 2019).

The rugby tournament served a dual purpose. Women participated in athletic competition while leading discussions about women's roles in the region, along with attitudes regarding gender, power, and violence. Domestic violence, sexual harassment, and discrimination remain widespread in parts of the region, particularly in Papua New Guinea, with about two in three women reportedly suffering from intimate partner abuse (Bouscaren 2018). The country remains largely patriarchal, with women expected to serve their fathers and husbands. Women are generally expected to raise children, while men make most decisions about land and marriage. These attitudes influence perspectives on women and the military.

While Fiji's constitution explicitly provides protection from discrimination on the basis of gender and sexual orientation, the reality is that recent estimates suggest that 66 percent of women have experienced physical abuse, many from within their own family ("UN Women—Fiji" n.d.). Often, women who do experience this violence refuse to report it because of their belief in reprisal and their general belief that their culture allows for violence against women.

FACTORS INFLUENCING CHANGE

While women serve in small numbers in many countries in Oceania, governments of these nations are proud of efforts made to integrate women. Shifting attitudes regarding gender impacted by both external and domestic factors have led to important changes for women's participation in militaries across Oceania. Women's integration is often coupled with increased educational and professional opportunities. The first women to join their country's militaries have also understood the burden they bear as they pave the way for others to follow in their footsteps.

Responsible for the overall security and well-being of Fijians, the Republic of the Fiji Military Forces (RFMF) has both a land force and a maritime component. The Land Force Command maintains war-fighting capabilities that include nation-building, humanitarian assistance, and disaster relief, with a limited ability to provide a light infantry company for Peacekeeping Operations (Fiji n.d.). Women joined the RFMF in 1988, aware of their roles as pioneers, often citing the professionalism and discipline that came with the force as their inspiration for joining (Bolatiki, Why WOI Officer Chandra Joined the RFMF 2018). Like many militaries, women have different physical standards than men, making some skeptical of their ability to perform vital work.

As members of the Land Force Command, women have served their local communities and on overseas deployments to the Middle East. Fijian women play key roles in peacekeeping missions, and several have attended the UN Female Military Officer's Course in India, where they were exposed to an understanding of conflict-related sexual violence. This training prepares them for their roles in peacekeeping by teaching them how best to assist the most vulnerable women and children in those conflict societies ("In the Words of Captain Anaseini Navua Vuniwaqa: 'There Is a Need for Female Peacekeepers'" 2018).

Rear Admiral Viliame Naupoto, commander of the RFMF, suggested that recruiting women into the navy would also allow women to achieve

FIJI

Major Amelia Tadu is one of nine women serving in the Republic of Fiji Military Forces and one of the original seven women who joined the military in 1988. She is a logistic staff officer and participated in Pacific Pathways, a security cooperation effort with the United States military in 2015. Fiji continues to devote additional funding to recruiting women because of the important role that they play in security cooperation and peacekeeping operations. Women from Fiji have served around the world in peacekeeping missions, including on the Syria-Israel border as part of the United Nations Disengagement Observer Force in the Golan Heights.

FURTHER READING

"PP15 Women, Peace and Security—A Night with the Woman of RFMF." 2015. *NavyLive,* July 27. https://navylive.dodlive.mil/2015/07/27/pp15-women -peace-and-security-a-night-with-the-woman-of-rfmf

---

equal opportunity in education and other government services, making up for the earlier lack of state and social services (George 2016, 88). In 2018, women were recruited to join the Maritime Component for the first time and with just six women in the class of 1979, the women were pioneers. In addition to receiving state services, these newly opened roles promised women a zero-tolerance policy on violence against women and children (Naqelevuki 2018). The first woman to join the navy as a commissioned officer was Silipa Tagicaki Kubuabola, a specialist in maritime law, who is now serving as a lawyer (Bolatiki, Navy to Recruit Women 2018).

Progress was slower for women in Papua New Guinea, who were barred from service in the army until 2009. The first twenty-one women graduated training in December 2009 (Anis 2009). In addition to their admittance into the ground forces of the PNGDF, women have also joined naval forces, in units largely responsible for defending the local waters of the island nation. The nation is still adapting policies to ensure that women can serve in both branches of the military safely (Sefe 2017).

Members of New Zealand's military assisted in officer-training sessions held in Papua New Guinea, the first such training in over a decade. In 2013, the first women enrolled in officer training and, just a few months later, three more women graduated. An army captain from New Zealand, Anika Tiplady, trained women for the unique difficulties they face as military women in a male-dominated environment (*ABC News AU* 2013). The women she mentored were put under physical and mental pressure with limited sleep and food to learn to cope with pressure and maintain their leadership abilities under stress (Quilliam 2013). This training and this integration marked an important step for women in the armed forces in the region, as well as for cooperation efforts between the two countries. Tiplady served for eight years in the New Zealand Defense Force as both a soldier and an officer, deploying to the Middle East in 2011. She continued to serve as an Army reservist while still playing competitive rugby and studying to become a doctor (Stevens 2014, 34).

By 2018, there were still only 170 women in the PNGDF, though the defense minister expressed hope that women would continue to join the service. The defense minister suggested that the increased inclusion of women into the force would be useful to show the world that the defense force is strengthened by the women who have joined (*Papua New Guinea Post-Courier* 2018).

During a recent exchange with the U.S. Nevada National Guard, women from His Majesty's Armed Forces from Tonga joined their male counterparts to discuss women, peace, and security efforts. The team also drafted a national action plan for the Kingdom of Tonga. This action plan brings women into the conversation of prevention and resolution of conflicts, peace negotiations, peacekeeping, and postconflict reconstruction. Captain Siulolo Tapueluelo, who has served in the HMAF for two years as a lawyer, conveyed that the exchange program has helped Tonga's military to realize how vital women are to peace and security efforts. She also noted that her experience has become more positive since the beginning of this effort (Riley 2019).

AUSTRALIA AND NEW ZEALAND

Australia and New Zealand have made the most progress towards full integration, with women able to earn admission into any military position. The two countries also collaborate frequently, exploring women's contributions to the force and issues of recruitment and retention. In addition, the countries work throughout the region and world training soldiers and participating in peacekeeping operations. Both countries continue to reflect on where they have fallen short on integration, especially regarding sexual harassment and assault.

214 Women and the Military

Australia Pre–World War II: A Culture of Selfless Service

In the early years of their independence, neither Australia or New Zealand encouraged women's participation in the military, though many women wanted to serve their nation or the British Commonwealth by following troops abroad to fight wars. In both Australia and New Zealand, young women supported the Boer Wars in South Africa between 1899 and 1902, paying for their own passage to help wounded and sick soldiers.

In 1898, the Australian Army Nursing Service was founded in New South Wales with just one female superintendent and twenty-four nurses. These women cared for soldiers in South Africa, although they returned home without veterans' benefits. In 1903, the director general of medical services in Australia, Surgeon General Williams, set up a federalized nursing service, the Australian Army Nursing Service (AANS), capitalizing on the success of the nurses in South Africa to petition for this expansion. Designed primarily as a reserve force, it consisted of volunteer civilian nurses who could be called on in cases of national emergency. By 1914, the system had expanded to include a female superintendent from each state, along with matrons who oversaw the daily work of the nurse corps.

After the outbreak of World War I, nurses left Australia in September 1914, bound to serve anywhere that Australia troops were stationed as part of the First Australian Imperial Force (AIF). In total, 2,139 Australian women served abroad between 1914 and 1918 in locations as far-flung as France, Greece, Egypt, and India, while another 423 served in Australia ("Australian Army Medical Corps: Australian Army Nursing Service in World War I" n.d.). Additionally, women organized the Australian Women's Services Corps in November 1916. They worked in the fields, fulfilled medical roles, completed military administrative tasks, trained swimmers, and practiced drills. Australian women also formed the Khaki Girls in 1917, conducting drills and paramilitary training (Jensen 2012, 207). In 1916, the unit gained a matron in chief, later given the rank of colonel. These women were generally extended the same customs and courtesies as officers, though held no formal rank. The nurses earned a variety of awards for their service, including Commander of the Order of the British Empire and Officer and Member of the Order of the British Empire, and twenty-three foreign awards. Twenty-five women died overseas during this time.

Many women were demobilized quickly after their return home from overseas. Between the world wars, the AANS maintained a reserve status and women who had volunteered were kept on the rolls, though they were largely unoccupied in the interwar period. The protocols and military rules frustrated many women since they were not given formal military training by the Australian military (Nelson and Rabach 2002, 79).

World War II: Limited Recognition for Women

When Germany invaded Poland in 1939, the women of the Nursing Service were alerted, and volunteers joined the fight against the Axis powers. For the first three and half years of World War II, women in the AANS served in Australia, the Middle East, Europe, and the Pacific without official rank, in base and field hospitals and casualty clearing stations (Jensen 2012, 202). Prior to 1943, the women were treated much like officers, but called pips. In 1944, women were given rank, and those who were majors and above attended army administrative training, learning about army organizations and how to operate within the military structure, helping to assuage some of the frustration that they felt during the interwar period and the early years of World War II.

During World War II, 3,477 women served as members of the AANS. At least seventy-one died overseas, fifty-three of whom died due to hostile action, and eighteen from accidents and illness ("Second World War Nurses" n.d.). During the fall of Singapore in 1942, many nurses were killed in action, and others were taken as prisoners of war after several Australian general hospitals were captured. Women continued to prove themselves in service, earning two George Medals, an award for gallantry "not in the face of the enemy," as well as over one hundred other decorations (Australian Army Staff 2007, 50). Members of the AANS were deactivated along with other military members between 1945 and 1949, with many AANS nurses on call to provide needed care if hospitals were short-staffed.

During World War II, in addition to performing traditionally feminine roles as nurses and domestic service corps, Australian women served in the Women's Auxiliary Air Force (WAAAF), the Australian Women's Army Service (AWAS), the Australian Army Medical Women's Service (AAMWS), and the Women's Royal Australian Naval Service (WRANS). The WAAAF provided ground crew support as wireless and teleprinter operators, administrative, cipher, and domestic roles. Women could only serve for an enlistment of twelve months, earning just two-thirds that of what their male counterparts did (Gillson 1962, 99–100). Women in the

AAMWS served in many of the same locations as the women of the AANS, and the two organizations merged to form the Royal Australian Army Nursing Corps in 1949.

The Australian Women's Army Service (AWAS), formed in 1941, allowed women to replace men in some noncombat military roles. Women were employed in clerical roles and as cooks but also found work in more atypical roles, including drivers, signaleers, provosts, and cipher clerks. By the end of the war, over 679 women had served as officers and 24,026 women had enlisted in the AWAS ("Australian Women's Army Service (AWAS)" 2017). The women of the AWAS served abroad in New Guinea during the war. These women had committed to serve for the duration of the war, passing both medical and security checks. Stood up in 1941, the AWAS was demobilized by 1947, though many of the women who served in the AWAS would serve in the Women's Royal Australian Army Corps (WRAAC), an eventual successor to the many organizations formed during World War II. The first and only commander of the AWAS, Sybil Howry Irving, was later given the rank of honorary colonel in the WRAAC.

The Women's Royal Australian Naval Service (WRANS) was initially created as an Australia-based auxiliary service responsible for wireless communications for the Navy. Florence Violet McKenzie had initially proposed that the women should join the Royal Australian Navy (RAN) to allow more men to serve abroad, though her idea was rejected. Hired as civilian employees of RAN, the women eventually started to conduct training for men. After a successful recruitment campaign, the leadership of the RAN saw the need for an officer corps for women, creating the WRANS. Activated in 1942, it was deactivated in 1947.

Portrayals of the ADF from World War I and World War II primarily focused on men who were rough, crude, ill-mannered, unsophisticated, but were fighters (Spurling 2000, 83). As women participated in the Defense Force Women's Auxiliaries, the public was concerned that women would adopt those "masculine traits," acting less like women and more like the stereotypes of male warriors. The media portrayed women primarily in two ways. Women were "scatter-brained, emotional, and often promiscuous, stereotypical feminine model" (Spurling 2000, 84). The other depiction was that of a "masculine, formidable, domineering woman with no redeeming feminine attributes and implicit innuendo of lesbianism" (Spurling 2000, 84). These images further discouraged women from serving. The stereotypes also allowed men to classify military women in negative ways, perpetuating these labels.

Post–World War II: Societal Change and Full Service for Women

While the end of the fighting in 1945 allowed the Australian government to shut down the various women's corps, the Cold War forced the government to reconsider how and when women could contribute. The Women's Royal Australian Army Corps (WRAAC) was established in April 1951, as Australia faced a manpower shortage and the country supported the Korean War effort. The WRAAC was officially disbanded in 1984, and women were permitted to serve in the ADF, albeit in limited positions.

The Australian government reestablished the WRANS in 1951, and it was designated a permanent part of the Australian military in 1959, though women were unable to serve if they were married or pregnant. The marriage restriction lasted until 1969. Just five years later, women who were pregnant could remain on active duty (Mitchell 2010). Women were permitted to serve on ships in 1983 for the first time. In 1985, all remaining members of the WRANS joined the Royal Australian Navy after the WRANS was officially disbanded.

By 1992, women were eligible to participate in about 85 percent of the total specialties, a jump from about 50 percent in 1979 (Barrie 2000, 4). Though women could serve in 93 percent of jobs prior to lifting the combat ban in 2011, women made up just 4.5 percent of the senior ranks in the defense establishment (Topping 2011). They served in the navy as clearance divers, took command of warships, and boarded submarines. Women flew attack helicopters and fighter jets as members of the Royal Australian Air Force (RAAF). Additionally, Australian women served as members of task forces in Iraq and Afghanistan and in UN peacekeeping operations around the world.

Though the RAAF opened most pilot jobs to women in 1987, the role of fighter jet pilot was closed to women until 2016. Prior to that, at least forty-two women graduated from flight school between 1987 and 2016, going on to serve as pilots in C-17 Globemasters, C-130 Hercules, and Wedgetail Airborne, which were early warning and control planes. These aircraft were transport or intelligence and surveillance collection platforms and were less likely to place women in combat. Air Marshall Davies suggested that generational changes in gender attitudes were helpful to recruiting women, noting that the "big blokey fighter pilot attitude is starting to dilute a little" (Wroe 2016).

218   Women and the Military

Initially, the defense ministry planned to exclude men and women under 62 kg from entering the F-35 program, due to the increased risk of neck injury during ejection. As most women weigh less than men, this rule impacted women disproportionately. Initial tests suggested that helmets used in testing would throw the pilots' head forward at unacceptable levels during emergency ejections (Wroe 2015). The restriction was eventually lifted, and women are training to participate in the first operational squadrons of the F35, expected in 2021 ("F-35A Lightning II" n.d.).

In 2011, the Australian minister of defense, Stephen Smith, announced that all positions would soon be open to anyone who could earn admission, effectively ending the previous policy of excluding women from direct ground combat. Australian society was divided on the integration of women into combat. Smith emphasized that the decision was about putting the best people on the line, regardless of gender and that all soldiers would compete based on abilities. As a large country geographically with a small population, Australians quickly realized that making the military "better educated, more adaptable, more innovative—and more inclusive" would be a necessity to protect Australia and support partners and allies around the world (Barrie 2000, 2). Despite this realization, many Australians believed that women would suffer high casualty rates once fully exposed to the dangers of combat. Some critics argued that even as the services opened their ranks to anyone who could meet the standards, the "punishing hours, dangerous activities, and long periods away from home would still make it difficult for many more women to reach the top" (Topping 2011).

From their countries' own experiences with integration, senior defense ministers from Canada and New Zealand observed no major issues with women serving in all roles. The Australian Defense Association, a security think tank in Australia, countered that differences in muscle distribution, centers of gravity, and rate of recovery from physical exertion would likely make women more vulnerable in combat (Topping 2011). Initial fears that opening all roles to women would weaken standards in combat specialties were likely overstated because of a historical reluctance to allow women into the roles.

Recent publications from the Australian Defense Association suggest that no operational standards will be lowered to encourage women's participation. From their perspective, there are no physiological, emotional, or "insurmountable teamwork" barriers to employing women (Australia

Defence Association 2019). The ADF is developing leaders from across all military specialties, rather than simply relying on combat and operations corps. The current system of career management within the Army, for example, "has a bias towards generalist male, combat corps, regimental soldiers, whose partner is normally the primary caregiver of the children" (Australian Human Rights Commission 2014, 28). Targeted recruitment programs have proven effective, yet sometimes have been accompanied by backlash. Some researchers and observers have noted that women who earn admission to combat specialties may face accusations of lowered standards and special treatment, undermining merit in the promotion process (Australian Human Rights Commission 2014, 9).

The Australian Defense Association notes that Australia employs women in combat roles at or above the rates of other Western countries. With the opening of all roles to women, the percentage of women in the ADF increased from 13.8 percent in 2011 to 15.5 percent in 2016 to 17.9 percent in 2017 (Fitriani, Suresh, and Matthews 2017, 29). Separated into three distinct branches, the Army, Navy, and Air Force each have their own cultures and as such, treatment of women varies significantly across services. Each has set targets for representation by women in the military by 2023. The Navy and Air Force's targets are 25 percent while the Army is 15 percent (Australian Human Rights Commission 2014, 22).

AUSTRALIA

Captain Chloe Dray, a descendent of the Gungurri people of Western Queensland, followed in a family tradition when she joined the Australian Army. Both her grandfathers served in the military; one grandfather served in the Army during World War II, serving in New Guinea and the Dutch East Indies. The other served in Korea as part of the Royal Australian Navy. Her father also served as an instrument fitter in the Air Force. Though she comes from a small community, she noted that being part of the Army means that everyone has the same opportunities and is treated equally.

FURTHER READING

"Captain Chloe Dray—a Third-Generation Servicewoman." 2015. *Indigenous .Gov.Au,* April 24. https://www.indigenous.gov.au/news-and-media/stories /captain-chloe-dray-third-generation-servicewoman

Challenges to Integration

Even as official policy opened combat roles to women, cultural norms slowed full integration. Once known for a "tight" culture with stark differences between the "in group," and the "out group," the Australian military expected that women, ethnic minorities, and those of different sexual orientations would be unable to conform appropriately to the norms, role requirements, and shared identities of the predominantly male culture (Fitriani, Suresh, and Matthews 2017).

In 1997, Bronwyn Grey's *Report of the Review into Policies and Practices to Deal with Sexual Harassment and Sexual Offences at the Australian Defense Force Academy (ADFA)* was published. The ADFA was forced to respond to claims of sexual harassment of women at the institution, along with significant levels of inappropriate sexual behavior in the ADFA (Australian Human Rights Commission 2011, 19). To combat the "high level of tolerance of the unacceptable behavior among the cadets and the members of the military staff," the ADFA made a number of policy changes, including increased awareness training (Australian Human Rights Commission 2011, 7).

By 2011, when the Australian Human Rights Commission conducted another independent review of the ADFA, investigators found the academy was an improved place, although widespread, low levels of sexual harassment endured, with inadequate levels of supervision. The ADFA was criticized for the high level of staff turnover and lack of training given to supervisors when they arrived for this assignment, rendering them unable to best counsel and lead young adults. Many of the military staff had not encountered mixed-gender environments previously.

As with many military organizations, women's varying physical needs were not well understood, with women experiencing higher levels of injury than men. Women also confronted pressures to conform to the masculine environment to succeed as cadets and military officers. The 2011 report noted that women and men were often held to the men's standards for physical fitness and that women should "toughen up" and should know that "men will always be associated with that whole macho killing people" attitude (Australian Human Rights Commission 2011, 29). Though the 2011 report highlighted many similar issues that the 1998 Grey Report did, the ADFA had clearly made progress. Cadets often repeated that "[women] get treated like people," and "everyone is given equal opportunities to achieve and perform at their best" (Australian Human Rights Commission 2011, 27).

One of the key recommendations from this 2011 report highlighted the need to match all cadets with mentors to provide support and advice. This mentorship program was modeled on workplace-based mentoring programs that other universities, including the University of New South Wales, already implemented (Australian Human Rights Commission 2011, 22). In the same year that the ADFA was commended for its progress, reports of a Skype affair began (Senate Foreign Affairs, Defence and Trade Committee 2014, 4). A male and female cadet were engaged in consensual sexual activities in the barracks while the male cadet, Cadet Daniel MacDonald, filmed and live-streamed the activity to other male cadets without the woman's permission. Found guilty of the charge, Cadet MacDonald was sentenced to two twelve-month probationary periods by the Supreme Court and was cleared to continue his course of studies at the ADFA. However, the Australian Army expelled him shortly after he was sentenced, claiming that his conduct was inconsistent with the values of the Australian military (Australian Associated Press 2013). This incident also prompted reviews into the use of alcohol and other personal conduct of personnel at the ADF (Senate Foreign Affairs, Defence and Trade Committee 2014, 5).

This affair also raised questions about graduates of the ADFA and their conduct when they matriculated, with investigations finding that there may have been 700 "plausible cases of abuse" dating back to the 1950s (Norman 2014). In response to the 2012 review into possible issues at the ADFA, the government established the Defense Abuse Response Taskforce (DART) and discovered that several allegations implicated officers serving in the military. By 2016, DART had received 2,439 complaints, finding that 1,751 of those were plausible (Defence Abuse Response Taskforce 2016, 14). At least 1,726 of these complaints were settled through reparation payments. These payments acknowledged that the abuse occurred, rather than serving as compensation for the abuse. Other victims were provided counseling support, with the clear majority of those receiving counseling coming from the Army and Navy (Defence Abuse Response Taskforce 2016, 22). Many of those who lodged complaints did so for bullying and harassment, physical abuse, sexual abuse, and sexual harassment cases (Defence Abuse Response Taskforce 2016, 24).

In response to complaints of mismanaged sexual assault reports, the ADF set up the Sexual Misconduct Prevent and Response Office (SeMPRO) (Senate Foreign Affairs, Defence and Trade Committee 2014). This office, first fully operational in 2013, has reportedly assisted with making victims of sexual assault comfortable to report their abuse and get help (Senate Foreign Affairs, Defence and Trade Committee 2014, 50). Australia removed the reporting and management of sex crimes from the military chain of command to make women more likely to report. While the system remained under the chain of command, many did not report due to fear of repercussions and damage to future career prospects. In addition, to encourage victims to get the help they needed after a sexual assault, the ADF set up a restricted reporting mechanism, where victims could get medical help without needing to formally begin an investigation (*Sexual Misconduct Prevention and Response Office Supplement* 2018, 3).

The ADF continues to make progress on full and fair treatment of all people. This progress was recognized in a 2014 report that suggested that enduring cultural change was slow, but coming. However, challenging the "most deeply held 'sacred cows' of the ADF's culture" proved to be a much harder bridge to cross. Previously, the ADF culture reflected a belief that "to be equal is to be the same" and that "senior leadership should be drawn from the arms corps," and that promotion on merit "should have no regard to the question of gender" (Australian Human Rights Commission 2014, 25).

Working Mothers and Families

Once forced to leave the service when pregnant, women are now entitled to maternity leave. Their choices are no longer dictated by policy, though societal expectations still drive women's choices in the ADF. Women who have served for at least twelve months of qualifying service and give birth while on active duty in the ADF may be entitled to up to fourteen weeks of paid maternity leave. Each woman is also entitled to another thirty-eight weeks of unpaid leave. Women are required to be off work in the six weeks prior to the birth. Importantly, maternity leave is an entitlement, and while members of the ADF are required to apply for it, their supervisors are also required to approve it (Australian Defence Force 2016/19, 5.6.12).

Among the most challenging issues for the Australian military, as it struggled with opening all jobs to women and encouraging more women to serve, is that the military lifestyle is not conducive to a stable family life. The successful women in the ADF are often those without children. A 2012 report from the Australian Human Rights commission identified that

88.9 percent of men who are general officers have children, while just 22.2 percent of women general officers have children (Australian Human Rights Commission 2012, 22). The Australian Human Rights Commission Review of 2012 noted that many women, and some men, were practicing informal flexible work arrangements that allowed parents to be present for important events in their children's lives. This review asserted that while informal arrangements could entice individual members to stay in the military, formalized agreements would guarantee members the ability to attend family events (Australian Human Rights Commission 2012, 32).

Though women are entitled to maternity leave, their careers often suffer due to family obligations. One member of an Australian focus group commented that she planned her conception time line to make sure that she could attend the Australian Command and Staff College to remain competitive for senior military ranks (Australian Human Rights Commission 2012, 147). Other women agreed that they would have more career flexibility in nontechnical support roles, including administration, human resources, and logistics. While all specialties were open to them, some required passage through an old boy's club to succeed (Australian Human Rights Commission 2012, 173).

To maintain flexibility in its workforce, the ADF allows members to transfer between the Permanent ADF and Reserves to best fit their individual needs using a flexible workforce model called Project Suakin. This is a major step forward for all service members, but overwhelmingly benefits women, who often feel the need to choose between family and career. The military is concentrating on attracting and retaining women and Indigenous Australians, although their recruitment continues to be a challenge (*Women in the ADF Report 2017–2018* 2019, 15).

NEW ZEALAND: VOLUNTEERING FOR SERVICE

Like most militaries, the bulk of New Zealand's earliest female military members served in the medical field. During the Boer Wars between 1899 and 1902, women from New Zealand were selected based on age, their first-rate nursing skills, and the "vocal insistence of the nurses and pressure from the New Zealand Government" (Kendall and Corbett 1990, 5). Eager to serve their country, nurses were not issued distinctive uniforms and were paid by public subscription. At least thirty women from New Zealand served in the Boer Wars and upon their return home, the women were not afforded the same rights as their English counterparts. For example, at least two applied for the monetary bounty given to English nurses, but they were told that colonial nurses were not entitled to it. Though the women from New Zealand did not officially serve in the military, the women were often eligible for and awarded military decorations, including the Queens' South Africa Medal.

The Defense Act of 1886, amended in February 1906 and in May 1908, allowed for the nurses to serve officially as members of the New Zealand Medical Corps Nursing Reserve. While this was a step forward for the professionalization of nursing in the military, it still proved to be insufficient, particularly at the outbreak of World War I. Only with the advent of the New Zealand Army Nursing Service were up to one hundred women allowed to volunteer, sworn to "fulfill any duties in time of war which the Director may require. . . . Provided that for service outside New Zealand, only voluntary service will be required" (Kendall and Corbett 1990, 29).

The New Zealand matron in chief, Hester Maclean, suggested that women should accompany the troops heading overseas in support of the war, but was informed that no nurses would be sent with New Zealand Expeditionary Forces (NZEF). Within days, however, six nurses were called up and sent overseas as members of New Zealand's Army Nursing Service Reserve (NZANSR). In 1915, the Australian government accepted New Zealand's offer of nurses to serve with the AANS, and twelve nurses from New Zealand served as members of the AANS in Egypt. A limited number of women from both Australia and New Zealand also supported British medical units as part of the Commonwealth system.

Eventually, about 600 women served overseas as members of the New Zealand Army Nursing Service, attached to the Expeditionary Force, for as long as five years during World War I (McRae, "New Zealand Nurses at War" 2015). When the nursing service was established, the women were treated as officers in every respect, ranking just below medical officers, though they had no official rank. In October 1915, a transport ship was torpedoed by a German submarine in the Aegean Sea, and ten women from the New Zealand Nursing Service died (McRae, "'All of a Sudden There Was This Bang'" 2015).

While the war ended, the military hospitals in New Zealand continued operations and were phased into civilian control by 1922. When Matron-in-Chief Hester Maclean tendered her resignation, she spoke of "How proud I have been to have had the privilege of forming the NZ Army Nursing Service. Much work for the Defense Department has devolved on me and while willing to carry on during the war in addition to my usual duties without extra payment, I feel that the time has come when the position should be no longer an honorary one" (Kendall and Corbett 1990, 89).

World War II: Additional Recognition for Women

While women served honorably during World War I, they were given limited recognition during the interwar period. As early as 1939, women approached the government with plans for a women's service modeled after the British land army, complete with a uniform to acknowledge their direct contribution to the war effort. These suggestions were largely rejected, though the beginning of World War II led to some changes for women.

Nurses placed on the reserve list after World War I were called for service between 1939 and 1940, and hundreds of civilian nurses volunteered to serve in the NZANS. The nurses received the World War I badge of the NZANS and a real military uniform, but each nurse had to order her own. The women were still not afforded rank, though they were treated as officers. This treatment varied and by 1942, all nurses wore badges of rank similar to, but smaller than, those of commissioned officers in the Army. While the NZANS operated with other members of the British Commonwealth Force, trained nurses were also appointed to the Royal New Zealand Air Force in 1940. Five ex-NZANS were selected on a temporary basis to serve with the air force.

Women in New Zealand served in the Women's War Service Auxiliary (WWSA) to coordinate nationwide efforts during World War II, as servers in canteens on military bases and in clerical roles throughout the country (Taylor 1986, 1064). These women did not wear standard uniforms or have ranks, though their efforts allowed additional men to serve at home and abroad. Women also replaced men in the farming industry (Taylor 1986, 1070). In contrast to Australia and the United States where women often joined manufacturing sectors, women replaced men in New Zealand's farming industry. Women largely remained in traditionally feminine roles, including retail and clerical jobs and served infrequently as tram conductors and signalers (Montgomerie 1989, 2).

After the war, New Zealand's government rejected the need for the NZANS, though some nurses supported units at Army Camp Hospitals, Air Force Station Hospitals, and the Devonport Naval Base. Within a few years, women would once again be considered for service, when the New Zealand Army Act defined officers and soldiers "as including women," making this the first time that women were legally recognized as members of the Army. Nurses served in Korea until 1953, with less pay than other women in the military. The nurses of the RNZN and RNZAF eventually integrated into the New Zealand Nursing Corps, assuming the same Army rank, a common uniform, and equal pay to the women serving in other roles.

By 1947, only 561 women remained in military service, after they were demobilized following the end of World War II. The separate women's services were retained, with the Royal New Zealand Nursing Corps (RNZNC) and the New Zealand Women's Royal Army Corps (NZWRAC) both accepting women. The NZWRAC required women between eighteen and thirty who had an endorsed school certificate and could serve as junior officers. Women also joined the Women's Royal New Zealand Air Force (WRNZAF) for periods of three years, if they were single, widowed, or legally separated and without dependent children. Women served in the Women's Royal New Zealand Naval Service (WRNZNS) between 1917 and 1977, though their jobs were limited to typing and educational roles. Women were not allowed to marry while remaining on active duty.

The NZDF Today: Full Service for Women

The NZDF became an integrated force in July 1977 when all the separate women's corps became part of the NZDF (*Wahine Toa Women in Defence* n.d.). Women were still restricted from serving in many combat-related roles, though many prohibitions were gradually lifted. A paper directed by the commandant of the RNZNS published in 1981 suggested that women's roles had evolved from that of wife and mother to those of full employment and that the NZDF should adapt accordingly (*Changes to Defence Policy Regarding Employment of Women* n.d.). This paper coincided with an ongoing discussion regarding the need for women to work in the defense forces to fill ongoing manpower shortages. Ultimately, the paper recommended that women serve on survey and research ships. Previously, women filled many roles in supply, administration, and communications.

In 1998, Clare Burton asserted that the NZDF needed to change policies and attitudes toward women serving, to allow them to serve safely and successfully (*Changes to Defence Policy Regarding Employment of Women* n.d.). She found that women were subjected to widespread gender harassment, a lack of family-friendly policies, and a general lack of acceptance of women in military roles. Shortly after Burton's report, the NZDF formally removed all combat restrictions on women, allowing them to compete for any role in the military. Women were first admitted to the infantry in 2001, and the first female platoon commander of a rifle platoon deployed to East Timor by 2002, serving as a peacekeeper.

The NZDF reviewed the progress of gender integration, and in 2005 the Hanson Burns Report found that the military was making significant progress in creating a more family-friendly institution, along with lowering instances of sexual harassment, and integrating women into the service. Many women reported that they felt a growing sense that women could and did make important contributions to the NZDF.

In 2014, New Zealand produced another report that specifically assessed the extent to which women were treated equitably, able to achieve their

Male and female soldiers of the New Zealand army cluster around a Mercedez-Benz Unimog truck. Women serve across the military in New Zealand but often leave active duty earlier than men. The New Zealand Defense Force continues to actively recruit women who are often able to engage parts of society that men are not. (Michael Williams/Dreamstime.com)

full potential, and free from harassment, bullying, and assault (Defence 2014, 3). This report found that the NZDF faced steep competition from domestic and international sources to recruit and retain the best person for each job in the military, with many young men and women leaving New Zealand to work in Australia (Defence 2014). While previous missions of the NZDF were exclusively combat based, Future35, the main strategy document for the NZDF, identified the need for a wide range of people to perform both traditional and nontraditional roles, including humanitarian assistance and peacekeeping (Defence 2014, 9). During operations, men cannot engage effectively with all members of a population, especially those with strict gender separation.

New Zealand also recruits and retains diversity outside of gender, with an emphasis on native populations. The former chief of the Defense Force, Lieutenant General Rhys Jones, noted that highlighting diversity in both gender and ethnicity overcomes ethnic divisions in New Zealand's bicultural framework and may help to model cooperation in other locations that have divided populations.

Like the Australian Defense Force, women are often subjected to a combat glass ceiling and underrepresented in command positions, particularly those in senior command. In 2011, about 16 percent of the armed forces were women. In 2019, that number had risen to 17.5 percent, with the Navy at 23.8 percent, the Air Force at 19.2 percent, and the Army with 13.6 percent (Mark 2019). Women make up about 6 percent of the combat and operations branches (New Zealand Ministry of Defence n.d.). A member of a senior promotion board conveyed that to reach the highest levels of the military, an officer should be a warrior, though few requirements for this formally exist. Historical recruitment documents in the NZDF made clear that to reach the top of the organization, a recruit must serve in a combat operations branch: Armored Corps, Infantry, Pilots, Navigators, or those who commanded a large ship in the General List Executive Branch of the Navy. Though these restrictions are no longer explicit, they still influence those who are selected for promotion (Defence 2014, 29).

While women recognize their opportunities to attend trainings that assist in promotion, courses that require extended periods away from home make family commitment challenging (Defence 2014, 29). The NZDF has offered a variety of more family-friendly policies, including part-time work. However, career managers have found it difficult to allow service members to take advantage of these career placement opportunities, particularly in smaller fields with fewer military members.

In contrast to both Australia and the United States, New Zealand's military has not yet set up a centralized system accounting for and responding to sexual harassment. Some cases are handled by the police force, while others are handled internal to the NZDF. The NZDF also does not use a service-wide survey to capture the prevalence of sexual assaults in the service. However, surveys conducted after recruit training suggest that women in the Army are two to three times more likely than men to report bullying, discrimination, and harassment by staff (Defence 2014, 40).

COOPERATIVE SECURITY EFFORTS IN OCEANIA

Several states in Oceania rely on cooperative security agreements to support their national security interests. These are some of the poorest nations in the world and often have small populations with few natural exportable resources available. The Solomon Islands has no regular military forces, though they have various paramilitary elements that constitute a de facto navy. Samoa maintains informal defense ties with New Zealand under a 1962 Treaty of Friendship. Tuvalu trains a national police force to maintain order on the island, while Vanuatu has a small force of volunteers that is designed to assist with the Vanuatu Police Force.

With no independent military, Kiribati relies on Australia and New Zealand for its defense as does Nauru, the smallest island nation in the world. The two nations signed memoranda of understanding on security cooperation issues. The Compact of Free Association, a compact between the United States, the Federated States of Micronesia, the Marshall Islands, and Palau, allows the United States to provide for the area's defense and control of the surrounding air and sea ("The Compact of Free Association" n.d.).

The series of thirty-two low-lying atolls that make up Kiribati are most threatened by natural disasters, technological issues, and human-caused disasters. As part of the security agreement between Australia and Kiribati, Australia provides Kiribati maritime surveillance and broader security cooperation (*Kirbati Country Brief* n.d.). Kiribati and Australia maintain three-year Aid Partnership Arrangements based on a Memorandum of Understanding on Development Cooperation first signed in April 1994; the most recent one, signed in August 2016, promised that the Australian and Kiribati government would "enhance security cooperation, coordination and information sharing, including on health, identity, and border security" ("Australia-Kirbati Aid Partnership Arrangement" 2016–2019).

230   Women and the Military

As part of the Compact of Free Association, the United States has defense-operating rights in the area around the Federated States of Micronesia, the Marshall Islands, and Palau. Micronesia also maintains a small paramilitary force, part of the Division of Maritime Surveillance (Micronesia 2017). The citizens of these three independent nations may serve in the U.S. military, though they are not citizens of the United States and are restricted from becoming officers. A recent documentary, *Island Soldier,* suggested that the men and women who volunteer from these nations largely do so because of the economic opportunities afforded by the military, even if their service is limited. The average salary for a young person from the independent nation of Micronesia is approximately $2,000 a year, while the average salary for a private in the U.S. military is about $19,000 (Fitch 2017). Less than 6 percent of all enlisted U.S. military members come from these small nations (Office of the Under Secretary of Defense, Personnel and Readiness 2016).

The Republic of the Marshall Islands, known for the U.S. military base on Kwajalein Atoll, is a secluded island chain with an independent Sea Patrol, a division of the Marshall Islands Police. The Sea Patrol is primarily responsible for inspections and rapid response to major issues near the Marshall Islands. The Compact of Free Association requires the United States to provide aid to the Marshall Islands in exchange for continued rights to maintain a secure military presence in the area.

According to the Palau Compact of Free Association and Subsidiary Agreements, the United States has the full authority and responsibility for security and defense matters in and relating to Palau through 2044. In the event of an attack on Palau, the United States would aid the government and citizens of Palau (Gootnick 2012). The U.S. military currently counts around 500 Palauan soldiers as members of the military. During a 2017 International Women's Day Celebration, the U.S. Embassy reached out to Palauan women in the military, receiving almost seventy replies. These women cited the life-changing nature of service and the confidence built as the most important parts of their service in the U.S. military ("Ambassador Hyatt Honors Palauan Women's Service in US Military #BeBoldForChange" 2017).

Women in Oceania continue to prove their desire to serve in the military; the earliest volunteers were those who often paid their own way and were put into harm's way with little or no formal military training, to protect men from disease and injury. Currently, women can often serve in any position for which they qualify, though they must continue to fight against societal norms, sometimes choosing between the greedy institutions of family and the military.

FURTHER READING

ABC News AU. 2013. "Papua New Guinea's First Female Army Officers Set to Graduate Next Year." September 23. https://www.abc.net.au/news/2013-09-24/an-png-first-female-troops/4977140

"Ambassador Hyatt Honors Palauan Women's Service in US Military #BeBoldForChange." 2017. *U.S. Embassy in the Republic of Palau,* March 23. Accessed February 15, 2020. https://pw.usembassy.gov/palauan-womens-us-military-service

Anis, Alison. 2009. "Women Recruits Take Up Duties as Soldiers." *The National,* December 7. https://www.thenational.com.pg/women-recruits-take-up-duties-as-soldiers

Australia Defence Association. 2019. *Women in Combat: Operational Capability Must Always Be the Prime Determinant of ADF Employment Policy.* Canberra: Australia Defence Association.

"Australia-Kirbati Aid Partnership Arrangement." 2016–2019. Partnership arrangement, Tarawa.

"Australian Army Medical Corps: Australian Army Nursing Service in World War I." n.d. *ANZAC Portal.* Accessed February 12, 2020. https://anzacportal.dva.gov.au/wars-and-missions/ww1/military-organisation/australian-imperial-force/australian-army-nursing-service

Australian Army Staff. 2007. *The Australian Army at War: An Official Record of Service in Two Hemispheres, 1939–1944.* Bennington, VT: Merriam Press.

Australian Associated Press. 2013. "Daniel McDonald, Cadet in Skype Sex Affair, Kicked Out of Army." *The Guardian,* November 8. https://www.theguardian.com/world/2013/nov/09/daniel-mcdonald-skype-sex-affair-kicked-out-army

Australian Defence Force. 2016/19. "Australian Defence Force Pay and Conditions Manual." *ADF Pay and Conditions Manual.* Canberra, Australia. http://www.defence.gov.au/PayAndConditions/ADF/Members-Guide/Leave/MaternityLeave.asp

Australian Human Rights Commission. 2011. *Treatment of Women in the Australian Defence Force.* Phase 1 Report. Sydney: Australian Human Rights Commission.

Australian Human Rights Commission. 2012. *Review into the Treatment of Women in the Australian Defence Force*. Phase 2 Report. Sydney: Australian Human Rights Commission.

Australian Human Rights Commission. 2014. *Review into the Treatment of Women in the Australian Defence Force*. Sydney: Australian Human Rights Commission.

"Australian Women's Army Service (AWAS)." 2017. *Australian War Memorial*, November 13. Accessed November 20, 2018. https://www.awm.gov.au/articles/encyclopedia/awas

Barrie, Chris. 2000. "The Integration of Women into the Australian Defence Force." In *Women in Uniform: Perceptions and Pathways*, edited by Kathryn Spurling and Elizabeth Greenhalgh, 1–9. Canberra, Australia: School of History, University College, UNSW.

Bolatiki, Maika. 2018. "Navy to Recruit Women." *Fiji Sun Online*, January 9.

Bolatiki, Maika. 2018. "Why WOI Officer Chandra Joined the RFMF." *Fiji Sun Online*, March 31.

Bouscaren, Durrie. 2018. "For Survivors of Domestic Abuse in Papua New Guinea, Volunteers Offer Safe Havens." *NPR*, June 6.

Changes to Defence Policy Regarding Employment of Women. n.d. Accessed November 1, 2019. http://navymuseum.co.nz/changes-to -defence-policy-regarding-employment-of-women

Commonwealth of Australia. 2016. *2016 Defence White Paper*. Annual. Canberra, Australia: Department of Defence.

"The Compact of Free Association." n.d. Government document. Signed between U.S. government (Department of Interior) and Federated States of Micronesia, and Republic of Marshall Islands. First signed in 1986.

Dargaville, Jane. 1998. "Friends Say Farewell to a Loyal and Trustworthy Mate." *Canberra Times*, May 9.

Defence Abuse Response Taskforce. 2016. *Report of Abuse in Defence— Final Report*. Canberra: Government of Australia. https://apo.org .au/sites/default/files/resource-files/2016/09/apo-nid67232 -1205506.pdf

Defence, Evaluation Division Ministry of. 2014. *Maximizing Opportunities for Military Women in the New Zealand Defence Force*. Wellington, New Zealand: Evaluation Division Ministry of Defence.

"F-35A Lightning II." n.d. *Air Force*. Accessed February 16, 2020. https://www.airforce.gov.au/technology/aircraft/strike/f-35a-lightning-ii

Fiji, Government of. n.d. *Republic of Fiji Military Forces.* Accessed August 18, 2018. http://www.rfmf.mil.fj

Fitriani, Lekshmi Suresh, and Ron Matthews. 2017. "Asia's Women Warriors." *Defence Review Asia* (May/June): 28–32.

George, Nicole. 2016. "'Lost in Translation': Gender Violence, Human Rights and Women's Capabilities in Fiji." In *Gender Violence & Human Rights: Seeking Justice in Fiji, Papua New Guinea and Vanuatu*, edited by Aletta Biersack, Margaret Jolly, and Martha Macintyre, 81–125. Acton, Australia: ANU Press.

Gillson, Douglas. 1962. *Royal Australian Air Force 1939–1942*. Adelaide, Australia: The Griffin Press.

Gootnick, David. 2012. "Proposed U.S. Assistance to Palau through Fiscal Year 2024." *Government Accountability Office*. Government Accountability Office, September 10.

"In the Words of Captain Anaseini Navua Vuniwaqa: 'There Is a Need for Female Peacekeepers.'" 2018. *UN Women,* December 19. Accessed January 23, 2019. http://www.unwomen.org/en/news/stories/2018/12/in-the-words-of-captain-anaseini-navua-vuniwaqa

Island Soldier. 2017. Directed by Nathan Fitch. Documentary film. http://www.islandsoldiermovie.com

Jensen, Kimberly. 2012. "Colunteers, Auxiliaries, and Women's Mobilization." In *A Companion to Women's Military History*, edited by Barton Hacker and Margaret Vining, 189–231. Leiden, Netherlands: Brill.

Kendall, Sherayl, and David Corbett. 1990. *New Zealand Military Nursing: A History of the RNZNC Boer War to Present Day*. Auckland, New Zealand: Sherayl Kendall and David Corbett.

Kirbati Country Brief. n.d. Accessed January 23, 2019. https://dfat.gov.au/geo/kiribati/Pages/kiribati-country-brief.aspx

Mao, Frances. 2019. "2019 Election: Why Politics Is Toxic for Australia's Women." *BBC News*, May 16.

Mark, Ron. 2019. *Defence Minister Salutes Our Military Women on Women's Day,* March 8. https://www.scoop.co.nz/stories/PA1903/S00055/defence-minister-salutes-our-military-women-on-womens-day.htm

McRae, Andrew. 2015. "'All of a Sudden There Was This Bang.'" *RNZ,* October 23. Accessed February 26, 2020. https://www.rnz.co.nz/news/national/287792/'all-of-a-sudden-there-was-this-bang'

McRae, Andrew. 2015. "New Zealand Nurses at War." *RNZ,* October 24. Accessed February 26, 2020. https://www.rnz.co.nz/news/national/287897/new-zealand-nurses-at-war

234 Women and the Military

Micronesia, Government of the Federated States of. 2017. *Department of Transportation, Communications & Infrastructure.* http://www.ict.fm/index.html

Mitchell, Rhett. 2010. "Australian Maritime Issues 2010: SPC-A Annual." *Papers in Australian Maritime Affairs.*

Montgomerie, Deborah. 1989. "Men's Jobs and Women's Work: The New Zealand Land Service in World War II." *Agricultural History* 63, no. 3 (Summer): 1–13.

Naqelevuki, Viliaina. 2018. "Women in the Navy." *The Fiji Times,* May 18.

Nelson, Sioban, and Jennifer Rabach. 2002. "Military Experience—the New Age of Australian Nursing & Other Failures." *Health and History* 4, no. 1: 79–87.

New Zealand Ministry of Defence. n.d. *Military Women.* Accessed November 10, 2019. https://www.defence.govt.nz/what-we-do/assessing-the-defence-system/military-women

Norman, Jane. 2014. "Defence Force Abuse Review Chief Says 'Shadow of Doubt' over Every Male ADFA Cadet Who Graduated between 1986 and 1998." *ABC News,* August 13. https://www.abc.net.au/news/2014-08-13/shadow-of-doubt-over-male-adfa-graduates-between-86-and-98/5668528

Office of the Under Secretary of Defense, Personnel and Readiness. 2016. *Population Representation in the Military Services: Fiscal Year 2016 Summary Report.* Arlington, VA: CNA.

Papua New Guinea Post-Courier. 2018. "The Increasing Role of Women in the Military." February 21. https://postcourier.com.pg/increasing-role-women-military

Quilliam, Rebecca. 2013. "New Zealand Trains First Female PNG Army Officers." *New Zealand Herald,* September 23.

Riley, Jonnie. 2019. "National Guard Program Emphasizes Women's Role in Peace, Security." *U.S. Army,* January 18. https://www.army.mil/article/216345/national_guard_program_emphasizes_womens_role_in_peace_security.

"Second World War Nurses." *Australian War Memorial.* n.d. Accessed November 11, 2019. https://www.awm.gov.au/visit/exhibitions/nurses/ww2

Sefe, Jerry. 2017. "Women Encouraged to Enlist in Navy." *Papua New Guinea Post-Courier,* October 20. https://postcourier.com.pg/women-encouraged-enlist-navy

Senate Foreign Affairs, Defence and Trade Committee. 2014. *Processes to Support Victims of Abuse in Defence*. Canberra: Commonwealth of Australia.

Sexual Misconduct Prevention and Response Office Supplement. 2018. Supplement. Canberra: Commonwealth of Australia.

Smith, Hugh. 1990. "Women in the Australian Defence Force: In Line for the Front Line?" *The Australian Quarterly* 62, no. 2 (Winter): 125–144.

Spurling, Kathryn. 2000. *Women in Uniform: Perceptions and Pathways*. Canberra, Australia: School of History, University College, UNSW.

Stevens, Sam. 2014. "Running with the Ball." *University of Otago Magazine* (February): 34–35.

Taylor, Nancy M. 1986. "The Home Front Volume II." In *The Official History of New Zealand in the Second World War 1939–1945*. Wellington, New Zealand: Historical Publications Branch.

Topping, Alexandra. 2011. "Australia to Send Women into Frontline Combat: Military Removes All Gender Barriers to Service; Thinktank Says Female Troops More Vulnerable." *The Guardian*, September 28.

"UN Women—Fiji." n.d. *UN Women—Asia Pacific*. Accessed January 20, 2019. http://asiapacific.unwomen.org/en/countries/fiji/co/fiji

Wahine Toa Women in Defence. n.d. Accessed November 20, 2019. https://www.airforcemuseum.co.nz/whats-on/wahine-toa-women-in-defence

Women in the ADF Report 2017–2018. 2019. Supplement. Canberra: Commonwealth of Australia.

Women's Rugby Sevens Brings Pacific Nations Together. 2019. Media release. Canberra: Australian Government, Department of Defense.

Wroe, David. 2015. "Joint Strike Fighter Ejector Seat Could Break Lightweight Pilot's Neck." *The Sydney Morning Herald*, October 23. Accessed August 3, 2018. https://www.smh.com.au/politics/federal/joint-strike-fighter-ejector-seat-could-break-lightweight-pilots-neck-20151023-gkh480.html

Wroe, David. 2016. "Women Poised to Start Flying RAAF Fighter Jets." *The Sydney Morning Herald*, February 5. Accessed August 3, 2018. https://www.smh.com.au/politics/federal/women-poised-to-start-flying-raaf-fighter-jets-20160205-gmmt7s.html

Bibliography

Abbas, Zaffar. 2006. "Pakistan Gets Women Combat Pilots." *BBC*, March 30. http://news.bbc.co.uk/2/hi/south_asia/4861666.stm

ABC News AU. 2013. "Papua New Guinea's First Female Army Officers Set to Graduate Next Year." September 23. https://www.abc.net.au/news/2013-09-24/an-png-first-female-troops/4977140

Abdulmelik, Semiha. 2016. *Implementation of the Women, Peace, and Security Agenda in Africa.* Implementation. Addis Ababa, Ethiopia: Office of the Special Envoy on Women, Peace, and Security of the Chairperson of the African Union Commission.

Affram, Robert Yaw. 2011. *Gender and the Ghana Armed Forces: An Examination of Women's Integration and Operational Effectiveness.* Master's thesis, University for Development Studies.

"Afghanistan Seeks More Women to Join Its Army." 2017. *Military.Com*, January 27. https://www.military.com/daily-news/2017/01/27/afghanistan-seeks-more-women-join-its-army.html

Afshar, Haleh. 2003. "Women and Wars: Some Trajectories towards a Feminist Peace." *Development in Practice* 13, no. 2/3: 178–188. http://www.jstor.org/stable/4029590

Agencia Angola Press. 2014. "Men and Women in Military Have More Duties Than Rights—FAA Staff Chief." December 16. http://m.portalangop.co.ao/angola/en_us/noticias/politica/2014/11/51/Men-and-women-military-have-more-duties-than-rights-FAA-Staff-Chief,b32d89b6-1cf9-4e11-a97d-9e8215e45683.html

Ahovi, Isa Abdulsalami. 2019. "Nigerian Army Women's Corps Hold Training Week." *The Guardian*, April 6, 2019.

Ahronheim, Anna. 2017. "1 in 6 Female Soldiers Report Sexual Harassment in IDF." *The Jerusalem Post*, September 10. Proquest.

238 Bibliography

Alpern, Stanley B. 1998. *Amazons of Black Sparta: The Women Warriors of Dahomey.* New York: New York University Press.

"Ambassador Hyatt Honors Palauan Women's Service in US military #BeBoldForChange." 2017. *U.S. Embassy in the Republic of Palau,* March 23. Accessed February 15, 2020. https://pw.usembassy.gov /palauan-womens-us-military-service

Anderson, Helen E. 2011. "Vietnamese Women and the American War." In *The Columbia History of the Vietnam War,* edited by David L. Anderson, 297–316. New York: Columbia University Press. JSTOR.

Anis, Alison. 2009. "Women Recruits Take Up Duties as Soldiers." *The National,* December 7. https://www.thenational.com.pg/women -recruits-take-up-duties-as-soldiers

Arabsheibani, G. Reza, and Lamine Manfor. 2002. "From Farashia to Military Uniform: Male-Female Wage Differentials in Libya." *Economic Development and Cultural Change* 50, no. 4 (July): 1007–1019.

Arakji, Dina. 2019. "Females in the Ranks." Carnegie Middle East Center. June 19. https://carnegie-mec.org/diwan/79306

Arieff, Alexis. 2011. "Tunisia: Recent Developments and Policy Issues." January 18. Accessed November 7, 2019. https://digital.library.unt .edu

Asefnia, Nakisa, Lisa Cowan, and Rose Werth. 2017. "HIV Risk Behavior and Prevention Considerations among Military Personnel in Three Caribbean Region Countries: Belize, Barbados, and the Dominican Republic." *Current HIV Research* 15, no. 3: 154–160. https:// doi: 10.2174/1570162X15666170517121316

Augustine, Marlene. 2019. "Defence Force Needs More Women." *Trinidad and Tobago Newsday,* February 15.

Aung, Zin Mar. 2015. "From Military Patriarchy to Gender Equity: Including Women in the Democratic Transition in Burma," *Social Research* 82, no. 2 (Summer): 531–551.

Australia Defence Association. 2019. *Women in Combat: Operational Capability Must Always Be the Prime Determinant of ADF Employment Policy.* Canberra: Australia Defence Association.

"Australia-Kirbati Aid Partnership Arrangement." 2016–2019. Partnership arrangement, Tarawa.

"Australian Army Medical Corps: Australian Army Nursing Service in World War I." n.d. *ANZAC Portal.* Accessed February 12, 2020.

https://anzacportal.dva.gov.au/wars-and-missions/ww1/military
-organisation/australian-imperial-force/australian-army-nursing
-service

Australian Army Staff. 2007. *The Australian Army at War: An Official Record of Service in Two Hemispheres, 1939–1944.* Bennington, VT: Merriam Press.

Australian Associated Press. 2013. "Daniel McDonald, Cadet in Skype Sex Affair, Kicked Out of Army." *The Guardian,* November 8. https://www.theguardian.com/world/2013/nov/09/daniel-mcdonald -skype-sex-affair-kicked-out-army

Australian Defence Force. 2016/19. "Australian Defence Force Pay and Conditions Manual." *ADF Pay and Conditions Manual.* Canberra, Australia. http://www.defence.gov.au/PayAndConditions/ADF /Members-Guide/Leave/MaternityLeave.asp

Australian Defence Force Academy. 1998. *Report of the Review into the Policies and Practices to Deal with Sexual Harassment and Sexual Offences.* Canberra, Australia: Department of Defence.

Australian Human Rights Commission. 2011. *Treatment of Women in the Australian Defence Force.* Phase 1 Report. Sydney: Australian Human Rights Commission.

Australian Human Rights Commission. 2012. *Review into the Treatment of Women in the Australian Defence Force.* Phase 2 Report. Sydney: Australian Human Rights Commission.

Australian Human Rights Commission. 2014. *Review into the Treatment of Women in the Australian Defence Force.* Sydney: Australian Human Rights Commission.

"Australian Women's Army Service (AWAS)." 2017. *Australian War Memorial,* November 13. Accessed November 20, 2018. https:// www.awm.gov.au/articles/encyclopedia/awas

AU Strategy for Gender Equality & Women's Empowerment 2018–2028. 2018. Addis Ababa, Ethiopia: African Union Headquarters.

Baaz, Maria Eriksson, and Maria Stern. 2012. "Fearless Fighters and Submissive Wives: Negotiating Identity among Women Soldiers in the Congo (DRC)." *Armed Forces & Society* 39, no. 4: 711–739. https:// doi.org/10.1177%2F0095327X12459715

Badaro, Maximo. 2014. "'One of the Guys': Military Women, Paradoxical Individuality, and the Transformations of the Argentine Army." *American Anthropologist* 117, no. 1: 86–99. https://doi.org/10.1111 /aman.12163

Bahry, Louay, and Phebe Marr. 2005. "Qatari Women: A New Generation of Leaders?" *Middle East Policy* 12, no. 2 (Summer): 104–119. EBSCO HOST.

Barrie, Chris. 2000. "The Integration of Women into the Australian Defence Force." In *Women in Uniform: Perceptions and Pathways*, edited by Kathryn Spurling and Elizabeth Greenhalgh, 1–9. Canberra, Australia: School of History, University College, UNSW.

Barry, Ben. 2013. "Women in Combat." *Survival* 55, no. 2: 19–30.

Basu, Moni. 2010. "Indian Women Peacekeepers Hailed in Liberia." March 2. http://www.cnn.com/2010/WORLD/africa/03/02/liberia.women/index.html

"Belize Super-Women Compete in Grueling Match." 2019. March 25. http://www.reporter.bz/2019/03/25/belize-super-women-compete-in-grueling-match

Bell, T. Anthony. 2011. "LogU Student Is Djibouti's First Female Officer." *Fort Lee Traveler*, January 27.

Benard, Cheryl, Seth G. Jones, Olga Oliker, Cathryn Quantic Thurston, Brooke K. Stearns, Kristen Cordell. 2008. "Women and Nation-Building." Santa Monica, CA: RAND. https://doi.org/10.7249/MG579

Bengio, Ofra. 2016. "Game Changers: Kurdish Women in Peace and War." *The Middle East Journal* 70, no. 1: 30–46. https://dx.doi.org/10.3751/70.1.12

Bernal, Victoria. 2001. "From Warriors to Wives: Contradictions of Liberation and Development in Eritrea." *Northeast African Studies* 8, no. 3: 129–154. https://www.jstor.org/stable/41931273

Bhattacharyya, Arundhati. 2012. "Women in Military in India: The Cry for Parity." *Mediterranean Journal of Social Sciences* 3, no. 2 (May): 317–325.

Bigg, Claire. 2005. "Russia; Army Puts on a Pretty Face." *Radio Free Europe*, June 22.

Bigio, Jamille, and Rachel Vogelstein. 2018. *Increasing Female Participation in Peacekeeping Operations.* New York: Council on Foreign Relations.

Bjarnegård, Elin, and Erik Melander. 2013. "Revisiting Representation: Communism, Women in Politics, and the Decline of Armed Conflict in East Asia." *International Interactions* 39, no. 4: 558–574. https://doi: 10.1080/03050629.2013.805132

Blackburn, Susan. 2004. *Women and the State in Modern Indonesia.* Cambridge: Cambridge University Press.

Blakkisrud, Helge, and Nuraida Abdykapar Kyzy. 2017. "Female Heroes in a Man's World: The Construction of Female Heroes in Kyrgyzstan's Symbolic Nation-Building." *Demokratizatsiya: The Journal of Post-Soviet Democratization* 25, no. 2 (Spring): 113–136. https://www.muse.jhu.edu/article/657199

Blasko, Dennis J. 2008. "PLA Conscript and Noncommissioned Officer Individual Training." In *The "People" in the PLA: Recruitment, Training, and Education in China's Military*, edited by Travis Tanner, Andrew Scobell, and Roy Kamphausen, 99–138. Carlisle, PA: Strategic Studies Institute.

Bogati, Subindra. 2015. "Assessing Inclusivity in the Post-War Army Integration Process in Nepal." *Inclusive Political Settlements Paper* 11 (July). https://www.berghof-foundation.org/nc/en/publica tions/publication/assessing-inclusivity-in-the-post-war-army -integration-process-in-nepal

Bolatiki, Maika. 2018. "Navy to Recruit Women." *Fiji Sun Online*, January 9.

Bolatiki, Maika. 2018. "Why WOI Officer Chandra Joined the RFMF." *Fiji Sun Online*, March 31.

Bouka, Yolande, and Romi Sigsworth. 2016. *Women in the Military in Africa: Kenya Case Study*. East Africa Report. Addis Ababa, Ethiopia: Institute for Security Studies.

Boulègue, Jean. 1991. "Feminization and the French Military: An Anthropological Approach." *Armed Forces and Society* 17, no. 3: 343–362.

Bouscaren, Durrie. 2018. "For Survivors of Domestic Abuse in Papua New Guinea, Volunteers Offer Safe Havens." *NPR*, June 6.

Braw, Elizabeth. 2016. "Norway's 'Hunter Troop.'" *Foreign Affairs*, February 8.

"Bronze Medal for BDF." 2019. *DF,* October 30. https://www.bdfbarbados .com/cism-games

Brooke-Holland, Louisa. 2016. Women in Combat, Briefing Paper Number 7521, March 4. https://researchbriefings.files.parliament.uk /documents/CBP-7521/CBP-7521.pdf

Brown, Lucy, and David Romano. 2006. "Women in Post-Saddam Iraq: One Step Forward or Two Steps Back?" *NWSA Journal* 18, no. 3: 51–70. http://www.jstor.org/stable/40071181

Burgess, Gemma. 2013. "A Hidden History: Women's Activism in Ethiopia." *Journal of International Women's Studies* 14, no. 3: 96–107.

Burke, Hilary. 2007. "Women Defense Ministers Chip at Latin America's Macho Image." *Reuters* (January 31): 1.

Burke, Matthew M., and Aya Ichihashi. 2018. "Japan's Self-Defense Forces Consider All-Female Training Units to Accommodate Growing Recruit Numbers." *Stars and Stripes*, December 12.

Burnet, Jennie E. 2008. "Gender Balance and Governance in Rwanda." *African Affairs* 107: 361–386.

Busari, Stephanie. 2018. "'Don't Use Birth Control,' Tanzania's President Tells Women in the Country." *CNN*, September 11. Accessed February 2, 2020. https://www.cnn.com/2018/09/11/africa/tanzania -birth-control-magufuli-intl/index.html

Byrd, Miemie Winn. 2019. "Integration of Women and Gender Perspective into the Myanmar Armed Forces to Improve Civil-Military Relations in Myanmar." *Military Review* (November/December): 35–39.

Campbell, Meagan. 2016. "Detonating the Glass Ceiling." *Maclean's* 129, no. 23 (June 13): 21–23.

Carreiras, Helena. 2002. "Women in the Portuguese Armed Forces: From Visibility to 'Eclipse.'" *Current Sociology* 5, no. 5 (September): 687–714. https://doi.org/10.1177/0011392102050005005

Cawkill, Paul, Alison Rogers, Sarah Knight, and Laura Spear. 2009. "Women in Ground Close Combat Roles: The Experiences of other Nations and a Review of the Academic Literature." *Defense Science and Technology Laboratory*. https://assets.publishing.service .gov.uk/government/uploads/system/uploads/attachment_data/file /27406/women_combat_experiences_literature.pdf

"Central African Republic Background Note." *Geneve Centre for Security Sector Governance*, January 10. Accessed February 1, 2020. https://issat.dcaf.ch/Learn/Resource-Library/Country-Profiles /Central-African-Republic-Background-Note

Chandler, Adam. 2017. "Why Sweden Brought Back the Draft." *The Atlantic*, March 3. https://www.theatlantic.com/international/archive /2017/03/sweden-conscription/518571

Changes to Defence Policy Regarding Employment of Women. n.d. Accessed November 1, 2019. http://navymuseum.co.nz/changes-to -defence-policy-regarding-employment-of-women

Chapman, Krystal, and Maya Eichler. 2014. "Engendering Two Solitudes? Media Representations of Women in Combat in Quebec and the Rest of Canada." *International Journal* 69, no. 4: 594–611.

Chow, Jermyn. 2015. "SAF Gets Its First Female General." *Straits Times*, June 26. https://www.straitstimes.com/singapore/saf-gets-its-first-female-general

Chow, Jeremy. 2018. "SAF Aims to Recruit at Least 500 More Women by 2018." *Straits Times*, July 21. https://www.straitstimes.com/singapore/saf-aims-to-recruit-at-least-500-more-women-by-2018

Chung-Yuan, Yao. 2018. "Bettering the Military for Women Will Recruit More." *Taipei Times*, May 31.

CIA. 2020. "CIA, the World Factbook." *North Korea,* February 7. https://www.cia.gov/library/publications/the-world-factbook/geos/kn.html#Govt

"Civil-Military Activities with MINUSCA Peacekeepers." 2018. *United Nations News & Media Photo,* October 10. Accessed February 2, 2020. https://www.unmultimedia.org/s/photo/detail/787/0787444.html

Clements, Barbara Evans. 2012. *A History of Women in Russia: From the Earliest Times to the Present.* Bloomington: Indiana University Press.

Cobiskey, Olivia. 2018. "Female Participation Strengthens Peacekeeping Protection Efforts." *United States Army Africa,* August 21. Accessed February 20, 2020. https://www.usaraf.army.mil/media-room/article/28894/female-participation-strengthens-peacekeeping-protection-efforts

Commonwealth of Australia. 2016. *2016 Defence White Paper.* Annual. Canberra, Australia: Department of Defence.

Copp, Tara. 2019. "How Will Japan Defend Itself, if It Can't Get Its Youth to Serve?" *The Military Times*, January 30.

Corso, Molly. 2013. "Georgia: Women Soldiers Fight for the Right to Fight Like Men." *Eurasianet,* March 8. Accessed June 5, 2019. https://eurasianet.org/georgia-women-soldiers-fight-for-the-right-to-fight-like-men

Cox, Ashlee. 2016. "Female Quota Full." *Nation News*, January 23. https://www.nationnews.com/nationnews/news/76989/female-quota

Crowley, Kacy, and Michelle Sandhoff. 2017. "Just a Girl in the Army: U.S. Iraq War Veterans Negotiating Femininity in a Culture of Masculinity." *Armed Forces & Society* 43, no. 2: 221–237. https://doi.org/10.1177%2F0095327X16682045

Dalton, Jane. 2018. "Qatar Allows Military Women to Do Service for the First Time." *The Independent*, April 6. https://www.independent

244 Bibliography

.co.uk/news/world/middle-east/qatar-women-military-service-allow-gender-saudi-arabia-a8291451.html

Dandeker, Christopher, and Mady Wechsler Segal. 1996. "Gender Integration in Armed Forces: Recent Policy Developments in the United Kingdom." *Armed Forces and Society* 23 (Fall): 29–47.

Danielyan, Emil. 2017. "Armenia: Boosting Female Presence in Army." *Eurasianet*, January 4.

Darden, Jessica Trisko. 2015. "Assessing the Significance of Women in Combat Roles." *International Journal* 70, no. 3: 454–462. https://doi.org/10.1177/0020702015585306

Dargaville, Jane. 1998. "Friends Say Farewell to a Loyal and Trustworthy Mate." *Canberra Times*, May 9.

Dash, Mike. 2011. "Dahomey's Women Warriors." *Smithsonian Magazine*, September 23. https://www.smithsonianmag.com/history/dahomeys-women-warriors-88286072

DeAeth, Duncan. 2018. "First Taiwanese All-Female Artillery Squad Takes Part in Military Drills in Penghu." *Taiwan News*, May 24.

De Alwis, Malathi. 2002. "The Changing Role of Women in Sri Lankan Society." *Social Research* 69, no. 3: 675–691.

Decew, Judith Wagner. 1995. "The Combat Exclusion and the Role of Women in the Military." *Hypatia* 10, no. 1 (Winter): 56–73.

Defence. n.d. *Royal Australian Army Nursing Corps (RAANC)*. Historical. Canberra: Government of Australia.

Defence Abuse Response Taskforce. 2016. *Report of Abuse in Defence—Final Report*. https://apo.org.au/sites/default/files/resource-files/2016/09/apo-nid67232-1205506.pdf Canberra: Government of Australia.

Defence, Evaluation Division Ministry of. 2014. *Maximizing Opportunities for Military Women in the New Zealand Defence Force*. Wellington, New Zealand: Evaluation Division Ministry of Defence.

Degroot, Gerard J. 2001. "A Few Good Women: Gender Stereotypes, the Military and Peacekeeping." *International Peacekeeping* 8, no. 2 (June): 23. doi:10.1080/13533310108413893

Demetriou, Danielle. 2016. "Meet Japan's First Female Warship Captain." *The Telegraph*, June 5. https://www.telegraph.co.uk/news/2016/06/05/meet-japans-only-female-warship-captain

De Nicola, Bruno. 2017. *Women in Mongol Iran: The Khatuns, 1206–1335*. Edinburgh, Scotland: Edinburgh University Press.

Department of Defense. "2017 Demographics: Profile of the Military Community." http://download.militaryonesource.mil/12038/MOS /Reports/2017-demographics-report.pdf

Desilver, Drew. 2019. *Fewer Than a Third of Countries Currently Have a Military Draft; Most Exclude Women.* Washington, DC: Pew Research Center.

Dharmapuri, Sahana. 2011. "Just Add Women and Stir?" *Parameters* (Spring): 56–70.

Dialogo. 2013. "Uruguay: Women Make Great Strides in the Military." *Dialogo: Digital Military Magazine*, October 8.

Direnberger, Lucia. 2016. "Representations of Armed Women in Soviet and Post-Soviet Tajikistan: Describing and Restricting Women's Agency." *The Journal of Power Institutions in Post-Soviet Societies.* https://doi.org/10.4000/pipss.4249

Donadio, Marcela, ed. 2016. *A Comparative Atlas of Defence in Latin America and Caribbean: 2016 Edition.* Ciudad Autonoma de Buenos Aires: RESDAL.

Ducloux, Anne. 2016. "A Muslim Woman Officer in the Soviet Army during the Soviet-Afghan War: A Soviet 'Anti-Hero.'" *The Journal of Power Institutions in Post-Soviet Societies* 17. https://doi.org/10 .4000/pipss.4157

Dussán, Yolima. 2018. "WIMCON 2018: Armed Forces Need More Women in All Branches." *Diálogo Digital Military Magazine*, December 21.

Düzgün, Meral. 2016. "Jineology: The Kurdish Women's Movement." *The Journal of Middle East Women's Studies* 12, no. 2 (July): 284–287. Project Muse.

The Economist. 2019. "China's Might Is Forcing Taiwan to Rethink Its Military Strategy." January 26, 2019.

Edgerton, Robert B. 2000. *Warrior Women: The Amazons of Dahomey and the Nature of War.* Boulder, CO: Westview Press.

Eichler, Maya. 2014. "Militarized Masculinities in International Relations." *Brown Journal of World Affairs* XXI, no. 1 (Fall/Winter): 81–93.

Eifler, Christine. 2006. "Underestimated Potential: Women Soldiers in the Russian Armed Forces." *The Journal of Power Institutions in Post-Soviet Societies* 4/5. https://doi.org/10.4000/pipss.4157

Elamin, Nisrin, and Tahani Ismail. 2019. "The Many Mothers of Sudan's Revolution." *Al-Jazeera*, May 4.

Ellingsen, Dag, Ulla-Britt Lilleaas, and Michael Kimmel. 2016. "Something Is Working—But Why? Mixed Rooms in the Norwegian

246   Bibliography

Army." *Nordic Journal of Feminist and Gender Research* 24, no. 3: 151–164.

Ember, Carol R., and Melvin Ember. 2011. *Cultural Anthropology*. 13th ed. New Jersey, NJ: Prentice Hall.

English, Allan D. 2004. *Understanding Military Culture: A Canadian Perspective*. Montreal: McGill-Queen's University Press. http://www.jstor.org/stable/j.ctt80gt7.11

Estrada, Armando X., and Anders W. Berggren. 2009. "Sexual Harassment and Its Impact for Women Officers and Cadets in the Swedish Armed Forces." *Military Psychology* 21: 162–185. https://doi.org/10.1080/08995600902768727

"Ethiopia Promotes 65 Military Officers, Including Five Women." 2020. *Fana Broadcasting Company,* January 18. https://www.fanabc.com/english/ethiopia-promotes-military-officers

Eulriet, Irene. 2012. *Women and the Military in Europe: Comparing Public Cultures*. New York: Palgrave.

"F-35A Lightning II." n.d. *Air Force*. Accessed February 16, 2020. https://www.airforce.gov.au/technology/aircraft/strike/f-35a-lightning-ii

Fadera, Hatab. 2011. "Gambia: Nation's First Female Army General Decorated." *AllAfrica,* May 12. Accessed January 17, 2019. https://allafrica.com/stories/201105120709.html

Faiez, Rahim. 2013. "Afghan Army Is Training Women for Special Forces: They Fill Key Role on Night Raids, Corralling Women and Children." *St. Louis Post*, February 15, A.10.

Faizy, Sultan. 2017. "An Elite Officer Battles Sexism and the Taliban; Sergeant Is One of 83 Afghan Women in Special Unit." *Los Angeles Times,* May 3, A.4. https://www.latimes.com/world/la-fg-afghanistan-female-police-2017-story.html

Feaver, Peter D., and Richard H. Kohn. 2001. *Soldiers and Civilians: The Civil-Military Gap and American National Security*. Cambridge, MA: MIT Press.

Fiji, Government of. n.d. *Republic of Fiji Military Forces*. Accessed August 18, 2018. http://www.rfmf.mil.fj

Fitriani, Lekshmi Suresh, and Ron Matthews. 2017. "Asia's Women Warriors." *Defence Review Asia* (May/June): 28–32.

Fitrani, Randall, G. S. Cooper, and Ron Matthews. 2016. "Women in Ground Close Combat." *RUSI Journal* 161, no. 1 (February/March): 14–24.

Focus Taiwan News Channel. 2013. "Taiwan to Cancel Quotas for Women in the Military." March 8: 1.

Fofanah, Mohamed. 2010. "A Place for Women in Sierra Leone's Military." *Inter Press Service News Agency*, September 23.

Ford, Stanley P. 2012. *Core Values: A Soldier's Story*. Bloomington, IN: iUniverse.

"Four JDF Senior Officers Promoted." 2019. *Jamaica Observer*, February 8. http://www.jamaicaobserver.com/news/four-jdf-senior-officers-promoted-rocky-meade-antonette-wemyss-gorman-create-history_156671

Fox, Mary-Jane. 2004. "Girl Soldiers: Human Security and Gendered Insecurity." *Security Dialogue* 35, no. 4: 465–479. https://doi.org/10.1177%2F0967010604049523

Frederic, Sabina. 2015. "Women's Integration into the Argentine Armed Forces and Redefinition of Military Service. What Does Military Democratization Mean?" *Dynamiques Internationales Revue de Relations Internationales* 11: 1–23. EBSCO HOST.

Frederic, Sabina, and Sabrina Calandron. 2015. "Gender Policies and Armed Forces in Latin America's Southern Cone." *Res Militaris Ergomas Issue, Women in the Military* 1: 1–15.

Frederic, Sabina, and Laura Masson. 2015. "Profession and the Military Family in the Argentine Armed Forces." In *Military Families and War in the 21st Century: Comparative Perspectives*, edited by Rene Moelker, Manon Andres, Gary Bowen, and Philippe Manigart, 73–84. New York: Routledge.

Freedom House. 2011. "Madagascar: Countries at the Crossroads 2011." *Freedom House*. Accessed February 2, 2020. https://freedomhouse.org/report/countries-crossroads/2011/madagascar

Fuentes, Andres Resendez. 1995. "Battleground Women: Soldaderas and Female Soldiers in the Mexican Revolution." *The Americas* 51 (April): 525–553. https://www.jstor.org/stable/1007679

Gaddis, Isis, Rahul Lahoti, and Wenjie Li. 2018. *Gender Gaps in Property Ownership in Sub-Saharan Africa*. Policy Research Working Paper, World Bank Group.

Gaffey, Conor. 2016. "Meet the Female Somali Military Captain Fighting Al-Shabab." *Newsweek*, February 28.

Gallardo, Natalia. 2016. "A Committed Peacekeeper Woman from Uruguay." United Nations Organization Stabilization Mission in the DR Congo, May 26. https://monusco.unmissions.org/en/committed-peacekeeper-woman-uruguay

García-Moreno, Claudia, Christina Pallitto, Karen Devries, Heidi Stöckl, Charlotte Watts, and Naeemah Abrahams. 2013. *Global and*

248 Bibliography

Regional Estimates of Violence against Women: Prevalence and Health Effects of Intimate Partner Violence and Non-Partner Sexual Violence. Geneva: World Health Organization.

George, Nicole. 2016. "'Lost in Translation': Gender Violence, Human Rights and Women's Capabilities in Fiji." In *Gender Violence & Human Rights: Seeking Justice in Fiji, Papua New Guinea and Vanuatu*, edited by Aletta Biersack, Margaret Jolly, and Martha Macintyre, 81–125. Acton, Australia: ANU Press.

"GHANBATT Female Engagement Team Boosts Image of Ghana in UN Operations in DRC." 2019. *United Nations Peacekeeping,* January 22. Accessed January 17, 2020. https://peacekeeping.un.org/en /ghanbatt-female-engagement-team-boosts-image-of-ghana-un -operations-drc

Ghanem, Dalia. 2015. "Women in the Men's House: The Road to Equality in the Algerian Military." November 4. https://carnegie-mec.org /2015/11/04/women-in-men-s-house-road-to-equality-in-algerian -military-pub-61463

Ghanem, Dalia. 2018. "Women at Arms." December 3. https://carnegie -mec.org/diwan/77852

Giannini, Renata, Mariana Lima, and Pérola Pereira. 2016. "Brazil and UN Security Council Resolution 1325: Progress and Challenges of the Implementation Process." *PRISM* (March 1): 178–197.

Gillson, Douglas. 1962. *Royal Australian Air Force 1939–1942.* Adelaide, Australia: The Griffin Press.

Gitonga, Antony. 2015. "Brown Teeth Keep Aspiring KDF Soldiers Off Recruitment." *Standard Digital,* September 29. Accessed January 17, 2020. https://www.standardmedia.co.ke/article/2000177920 /brown-teeth-keep-aspiring-kdf-soldiers-off-recruitment

Gjelsvik, Ingvild Magnæs. 2013. "Women, Peace and Security in Somalia: A Study of AMISOM." *Norwegian Institute for International Affairs,* 1–5.

Glick, P., and S. Fiske. 2010. "An Ambivalent Alliance: Hostile and Benevolent Sexism as Complementary Justification for Gender Inequality." *American Psychologist* 56: 109–118.

Goldbaum, Christina. 2017. "Female Peacekeepers Fight Militants and Prejudice in Somalia." *World Policy Journal* (April 10).

Goldstein, Joshua S. 2001. *War and Gender.* Cambridge: Cambridge University Press.

Goodridge, Elisabeth. 2018. "Overlooked No More: Maria Bochkareva, Who Led Women into Battle in WWI." *The New York Times*, April 25.

Gootnick, David. 2012. "Proposed U.S. Assistance to Palau through Fiscal Year 2024." *Government Accountability Office.* Government Accountability Office, September 10.

Goumbri, P., D. Nanema, B. Bague, Z. Ilboudo, L. Ganou, and A. Ouedraogo. 2018. "Psychosocial Risks among Female Military Personal in Burkina Faso." *Journal of Psychiatry and Psychiatric Disorders* 2, no. 1: 1–8.

Grau, Lester W., and Charles K. Bartles. 2016. *The Russian Way of War.* Fort Leavenworth, KS: Foreign Military Studies Office (FMSO).

The Guardian. 2019. "NAF's Remarkable Gender Inclusion." November 10. Accessed February 2, 2020. https://guardian.ng/opinion/nafs-remarkable-gender-inclusion

Gustavsen, Elin. 2013 "Equal Treatment of Equal Opportunity: Male Attitudes towards Women in the Norwegian and US Armed Forces." *Acta Sociologica* 56, no. 4: 361–374.

Guyana Times. 2019. "GDF Women's Corp Celebrates 52nd Anniversary." February 2.

Hacker, Barton C. 1981. "Women and Military Institutions in Early Modern Europe: A Reconnaissance." *Signs* 6 (Summer): 643–671.

Hacker, Barton C., and Margaret Vining. 2012. *A Companion to Women's Military History.* Leiden, Netherlands: Brill.

Haer, Roos, and Tobias Bohmelt. 2018. "Girl Soldiering in Rebel Groups, 1989–2013: Introducing a New Dataset." *Journal of Peace Research* 55, no. 3: 395–403. https://doi.org/10.1177/002234331 7752540

Haltiner, Karl W. 1998. "The Definite End of the Mass Army in Western Europe?" *Armed Forces and Society* 25, no. 1 (Fall): 7–36.

Ham, Carter. 2014. "Working with African Nations to Support the Role of Women as Agents of Peace and Security." In *Women on the Frontlines of Peace and Security*, 113–125. Washington, DC: National Defense University Press.

Hampton, Tracy. 2009. "Afghan Military Medical School Reopens Enrolls Women in First Class of Cadets." *JAMA* 302, no.19 (November 18): 2081–2082.

Haring, Ellen L. 2013. "What Women Bring to the Fight." *Parameters* 43, no. 2 (Summer): 27–32.

Harries-Jenkins, Gwyn. 2002. "Women in Extended Roles in the Military: Legal Issues." *Current Sociology* 50, no. 5 (September): 745–769. doi:10.1177/0011392102050005008

250 Bibliography

Harris, Hermione. 1988. "Women and War: The Case of Nicaragua." In *Women and the Military System*, edited by Eva Isaksson, 190–209. New York: St. Martin's Press.

Harris, Sachel. 2015. "Mongolian Soldier Blazes Trail for Fellow Females." December 1: 1. https://www.army.mil/article/159315/mongolian _soldier_blazes_trail_for_fellow_females

Harsch, Ernest. 2010. "Security Reform Key to Protecting Women." *Africa Renewal* (January): 9–11.

Heinecken, Lindy. 2002. "Affirming Gender Equality: The Challenges Facing the South African Armed Forces." *Current Sociology* 50, no. 5: 715–728. https://doi.org/10.1177%2F0011392102050005006

Heinecken, Lindy. 2007. "Diversity in the South African Armed Forces." In *Cultural Diversity in the Armed Forces: An International Comparison*, edited by Joseph Soeters and Jan van der Meulen, 77–94. New York: Routledge.

Hendricks, Cheryl, and Lauren Hutton. 2008. "Defence Reform and Gender." In *Gender and Security Sector Reform Toolkit*, edited by Megan Bastick and Kristin Valasek, Tool Number 3, 1–24. Geneva: DCAF, OSCE/ODIHR, UN-INSTRAW.

Herrmann, Irene, and Daniel Palmieri. 2010. "Between Amazons and Sabines: A Historical Approach to Women and War." *International Review of the Red Cross* 92, no. 877 (March): 19–30.

Hill, Michael. 2019. "West Point to Graduate Record Number of Black Female Cadets." *The Army Times*, May 23. https://www.armytimes .com/news/your-army/2019/05/23/west-point-to-graduate-record -number-of-black-female-cadets

Hirst, Monica, and Reginaldo Mattar Nasser. 2014. *Brazil's Involvement in Peacekeeping Operations: The New Defence-Security Foreign Policy Nexus*. Oslo, Norway: Norwegian Peacebuilding Resource Centre.

Hodal, Kate. 2013. "Burmese Army Recruits Female Soldiers as It Struggles to Tackle Rebel Groups." *The Guardian* (U.S. Edition), October 16. https://www.theguardian.com/world/2013/oct/16/burmese -army-recruits-female-soliders-rebels

Holliday, Janet R. 2012. "Female Engagement Teams." *Military Review* (March–April): 90–95.

Holmes, Georgina. 2018. "Gender and the Military in Post-Genocide Rwanda." In *Women and Genocide: Survivors, Victims, Perpetrators*, edited by Elissa Bemporad and Joyce W. Warren, 223–249. Bloomington: Indiana University Press.

Honwana, Alcinda. 2005. *Child Soldiers in Africa.* Philadelphia: University of Pennsylvania Press.

Hornung, Jeffrey W. 2019. "With Little Fanfare, Japan Just Changed the Way It Uses Its Military." *Foreign Policy,* May 3.

Howard, Lise. 2019. *Assessing the Effectiveness of the UN Mission of the Central African Republic.* New York: International Peace Institute.

"Human Rights and Women in the Armed Forces in Armenia." 2019. *Council of Europe,* June 1. Accessed October 1, 2019. https://www.coe.int/en/web/yerevan/human-rights-and-women-in-the-armed-forces-of-armenia

Human Rights Watch. 2009. "Service for Life: State Repression and Indefinite Conscription in Eritrea." Special, HRW.

Human Rights Watch. 2019. "'They Are Making Us into Slaves, Not Educating Us.' How Indefinite Conscription Restricts Young People's Rights, Access to Education in Eritrea." Special, Human Rights Watch.

Ibragimov, M. M. 2019. "Priorities of the Construction of the Armed Forces of the Republic of Uzbekistan in the Conditions of Development of Forms and Methods of Contemporary Armed Struggle." *Military Review* (January/February): 47–55.

Ighobor, Kingsley. 2019. "Reshaping the Forces." *Africa Renewal,* November. http://www.ipsnews.net/1999/09/rights-malawi-army-to-recruit-first-women-soldiers

"Improving Gender Equality in Georgia's Armed Forces." 2019. *North Atlantic Treaty Organization,* February 21. Accessed March 3, 2019. https://www.nato.int/cps/en/natohq/news_152461.htm

International Labour Office. 2016. *Women at Work: Trends 2016.* Geneva: International Labour Office.

"In the Words of Captain Anaseini Navua Vuniwaqa: 'There Is a Need for Female Peacekeepers.'" 2018. *UN Women,* December 19. Accessed January 23, 2019. http://www.unwomen.org/en/news/stories/2018/12/in-the-words-of-captain-anaseini-navua-vuniwaqa

IPS Correspondents. 1999. "Rights: Malawi: Army to Recruit First Women Soldiers." *IPS News Agency,* September 4. Accessed December 2, 2019.

Ishaq, Mohammed. 2014. "Advancing the Equality and Diversity Agenda in Armed Forces: Global Perspectives." *International Journal of Public Sector Management* 27, no. 7: 598–613. https://doi.org/10.1108/IJPSM-01-2013-0005

Island Soldier. 2017. Directed by Nathan Fitch. Documentary film. http://www.islandsoldiermovie.com

Ivarsson, Sophia, Armando X. Estrada, and Anders W. Berggren. 2005. "Understanding Men's Attitudes towards Women in the Swedish Armed Forces." *Military Psychology* 17, no. 4 (October): 269–282.

Jackson, Ashley. 2001. *War and Empire in Mauritius and the Indian Ocean.* New York: Palgrave.

Jacoby, Tami Amanda. 2002. "Gender Relations and National Security in Israel." In *Redefining Security in the Middle East,* edited by Tami Amanda Jacoby and Brent E. Sasley, 83–104. Manchester, UK: Manchester University Press.

Japan Defense Focus. 2018. "First-Ever JMSDF Female Escort Division Commander." *JDF*, May, no. 99 ed. https://www.mod.go.jp/e/jdf/no99/specialfeature.html

The Japan Times. 2018. "Women Taking on Tore Front-Lines Roles in Japan's Military." October 18. https://www.japantimes.co.jp/news/2018/10/18/national/social-issues/women-taking-front-line-roles-japans-military/#.XP6LlIhJHcs

Jensen, Kimberly. 2012. "Volunteers, Auxiliaries, and Women's Mobilization." In *A Companion to Women's Military History*, edited by Barton Hacker and Margaret Vining, 189–231. Leiden, Netherlands: Brill.

Jervis, Rick. 2005. "Army Women Defy Insurgents, Taboo; General Says Iraqi Military Needs Female Soldiers, but They Face Opposition from Foes—and Even Family: FINAL Edition." *USA Today,* July 25. Proquest.

Jiang, Yuan, Yun F. Sun, Ye B. Yang, Jing J. Tang, Sheng J. Wu, and Dan M. Miao. 2013. "Gender Differences in Coping Styles of Chinese Military Officers Undergoing Intensive Training." *Military Psychology* 25, no. 2: 124–135. https://doi.org/10.1037/h0094954

Johnson, Tim, and Nicholai Lidow. 2016. "Band of Brothers (and Fathers and Sisters and Mothers . . .): Estimating Rates of Military Participation among Liberians Living with Relatives in the Military; a Research Note." *Armed Forces & Society* 42, no. 2: 436–448. https://doi.org/10.1177%2F0095327X14562858

Johnston, Jake. 2018. "Meet the New Haitian Military—It's Starting to Look a Lot Like the Old One." *Center for Economic and Policy Research,* March 16. https://cepr.net/meet-the-new-haitian-military-it-s-starting-to-look-a-lot-like-the-old-one

Jones, David E. 1997. *Woman Warriors: A History.* Dulles, VA: Brassey's.

Jones, Grady. 2018. "AFRICOM J6 Holds Annual Women's Communication Symposium." *United States Africa Command,* July 3. Accessed July 9, 2019. https://www.africom.mil/media-room/Article/30968/africom-j6-holds-annual-womens-communication-symposium

Joyce, Jennifer. 2015. "North Dakota National Guard Hosts Representatives from Republic of Benin and Togolese Republic." *National Guard,* May 12. Accessed July 9, 2019. https://www.nationalguard.mil/News/Article/588392/north-dakota-national-guard-hosts-representatives-from-republic-of-benin-and-to

Jozuka, Emiko, and Yoko Wakatsuki. 2019. "Answering the Call: The Women on the Front Lines of Japan's Defense." *CNN,* February 3. https://www.cnn.com/2019/01/23/asia/japan-self-defense-force-recruitment-intl/index.html

Kaieteur News. 2017. "Women's Army Corps Celebrates Golden Jubilee." February 6.

Kania, Elsa. 2016. "Holding Up Half the Sky? (Part 1: The Evolution of Women's Roles in the PLA)." *China Brief* 16, no. 14. https://jamestown.org/program/holding-half-sky-part-1-evolution-womens-roles-pla

Kania, Elsa, and Kenneth Allen. 2016. "Holding Up Half the Sky? (Part 2)—Women in Combat Roles in the PLA." *China Brief* 16, no. 16: 13–20. https://jamestown.org/program/holding-half-sky-part-2-evolution-womens-roles-pla

Karamé, Kari. 1995. "Girls Participation in Combat: A Case Study from Lebanon." In *Children in the Muslim Middle East,* edited by Elizabeth Warnock Fernea, 378–391. Austin: University of Texas Press.

Karim, Sabrina, and Kyle Beardsley. 2016. "Explaining Sexual Exploitation and Abuse in Peacekeeping Missions: The Role of Female Peacekeepers and Gender Equality in Contributing Countries." *Journal of Peace Research* 53, no. 1: 100–115. https://doi.org/10.1177%2F0022343315615506

Katzman, Kenneth. 2015. "The United Arab Emirates: Issues for US Policy." *Current Politics and Economics of the Middle East* 6, no. 1: 89–129.

Kaufman, Alison A., and Peter W. Mackenzie. 2009. *Field Guide: The Culture of the Chinese People's Liberation Army.* Field Guide, CNA China Studies.

Kaur, Mukhwindeer. 2016. "Employment of Women in Indian and Hungarian Armed Forces: A Comparative Study." *AARMS* 15, no. 2: 181–186. https://folyoiratok.uni-nke.hu/document/uni-nke-hu/aarms-2016-2-kaur.original.pdf

Kawar, Jumana. 2017. "Jordanian Women's Evolving Role in the Armed Forces." In *Women in International Security,* November 28. http://wiisglobal.org/2017/11/28/jordanian-womens-evolving-role-in-the-armed-forces

Kazman, Mia. 2019. *Women of the FARC*. Perry Center Occasional Paper. Washington DC: William J. Perry Center for Hemispheric Defense Studies, National Defense University.

Kendall, Sherayl, and David Corbett. 1990. *New Zealand Military Nursing: A History of the RNZNC Boer War to Present Day.* Auckland, New Zealand: Sherayl Kendall and David Corbett.

Kennedy-Pipe, Caroline. 2000. "Women and the Military." *The Journal of Strategic Studies* 23, no. 4: 32–50. doi:10.1080/01402390008437811

King, Anthony. 2013. "The Female Soldier." *Parameters* 43, no. 2 (Summer): 13–25.

King, Anthony. 2013. "Women in Combat." *The RUSI Journal* 158, no. 1: 4–11. doi:10.1080/03071847.2013.774634

King, Anthony. 2015. "Women Warriors: Female Accession to Ground Combat." *Armed Forces & Society* 41, no. 4: 379–387.

Kirbati Country Brief. Accessed January 23, 2019. https://dfat.gov.au/geo/kiribati/Pages/kiribati-country-brief.aspx

Kobavitz, Yaniv. 2018. "Israeli General: Army Should Have Reacted Stronger When Paratroopers Turned Back on Female Instructor." *Haaretz*, August 9. https://www.haaretz.com/israel-news/.premium-israeli-general-army-should-react-stronger-to-gender-discrimination-1.6363239

Koolaee, Elaheh. 2014. "The Impact of Iraq-Iran War on Social Roles of Iranian Women." *Middle East Critique* 23, no. 3, 277–291. doi:10.1080/19436149.2014.949937

Kozerawski, Dariusz. 2017. "The Gender Issue in the Polish Armed Forces on the Example of Peace and Stabilization Operations." *Science and Military* 1: 55–60.

Kronsell, Annica, and Erika Svedberg. 2001. "The Duty to Protect: Gender in the Swedish Practice of Conscription." *Cooperation and Conflict* 36, no. 2: 153–176.

Kuehnel, Josefine, and Nina Wilen. 2018. "Rwanda's Military as a People's Army: Heroes at Home and Abroad." *Journal of Eastern African Studies* 12, no. 1: 154–171. https://doi.org/10.1080/17531055.2018.1418168

Kummel, Gerhard. 2002. "Women in the Bundeswehr and Male Ambivalence." *Armed Forces and Society* 28, no. 4 (Summer): 555–573.

Kussrow, Samanta. 2018. *Primary and Secondary Roles of the Armies: Comparative Case Studies from Latin America.* Buenos Aires, Argentina: RESDAL.

Lane, Andrea. 2017. "Special Men: The Gendered Militarization of the Canadian Armed Forces." *International Journal* 72, no. 4: 463–483. doi:10.1177/0020702017741910

Leão, Ana, and Martin Rupiya. 2005. "A Military History of the Angolan Armed Forces from the 1960s Onwards—As Told by Former Combatants." In *Evolutions and Revolutions: A Contemporary History of Militaries in Southern Africa*, edited by Martin Rupiya, 7–42. Pretoria, South Africa: Institute for Security Studies.

Lee, Dmitry. n.d. *Kazakh Army Women Balance Gender and Responsibilities.* Accessed June 15, 2019. https://www.edgekz.com/kazakh-army-women-balance-gender-and-responsibilities

Lee, Michelle Ye Hee. 2017. "South Korea Exempts Women from the Draft. Is That Fair?" *The Washington Post*, September 18.

Lei, Zhao. 2014. "Uygur Women Are Navy's Latest Wave." *China Daily*, August 1.

Levy, Yigal. 2010. "The Clash between Feminism and Religion in the Israeli Military: A Multilayered Analysis." *Social Politics* 17, no. 2: 185–209.

Li, Xiaolin. 1994. "Chinese Women Soldiers: A History of 5,000 Years." *Social Education* 58, no. 2: 67–71.

Lim, Hyun-Joo. 2018. "What Life Is Like for North Korean Women—According to Defectors." *Independent*, September 9.

Llubani, Megi. 2014. "Women Representation in the Security Sector in Albania." *Albanian Institute for International Studies,* October 2014 downloaded. https://dgap.org/sites/default/files/article_downloads/policy_brief_aiis_albania_-_women_representation_in_the_security_sector.pdf

Loch, Patrick. 2020. *All-Female Military—Intelligence Training in Nigeria Supports Peace, Security Initiatives,* January 3. Accessed February 15, 2020. https://www.africom.mil/media-room/article

256   Bibliography

/32525/all-female-military-intelligence-training-in-nigeria-supports -peace-security-initiatives

Lodge, Alyssa, and Simone Bak. 2015. "The Role of Female Personnel in National Security and Peacekeeping: Alumni Share Their Perspective." *International Student Management Office, National Defense University,* August 25. https://ismo.ndu.edu/About/News/Article /614630/the-role-of-female-personnel-in-national-security-and -peacekeeping-alumni-share

Lomsadze, Giorgi. 2018. "Azerbaijan's Model Soldier: Pinup, Writer and Fighter." *Eurasianet,* January 22. Accessed June 5, 2019. https:// eurasianet.org/azerbaijans-model-soldier-pinup-writer-and-fighter

Londono, Ernesto. 2011. "Women Bracing for Battle to Protect Qaddafi." *Washington Post,* July 3. Proquest.

Louise, Margaret, interview by Genevieve Morel and Betymie Bonnelame. 2016. *Military Not Just Any Other Job, Says Seychelles' Newly Promoted—and Only—Female Major,* March 13.

Louw-Vaudran, Liesl. 2015. "African Women Are Increasingly Part of the Military and Police, but These Remain Strongly Male-Dominated Institutions." *Institute for Security Studies,* June 10. Accessed February 2, 2020. https://issafrica.org/iss-today/women-in-africas-top -brass-its-not-just-about-the-numbers

Lucas, Julie M. 2014. "Barriers Break Down at African Gender Integration Seminar." *United States Africa Command,* July 8. Accessed January 13, 2020. https://www.africom.mil/media-room/Article /23286/barriers-break-down-at-african-gender-integration-seminar

Lusher, Adam. 2017. "RAF Regiment Starts Accepting Women for Ground Close Combat Roles." *Independent*, September 1. https://www .independent.co.uk/news/uk/home-news/women-in-combat-roles -british-armed-forces-raf-regiment-first-to-recruit-ban-lifted -frontline-a7924701.html

MacKenzie, Megan. 2009. "Securitization and Desecuritization: Female Soldiers and the Reconstruction of Women in Post-Conflict Sierra Leone." *Security Studies* 18, no. 2: 241–261. https://doi.org/10.1080 /09636410902900061

MacKenzie, Megan H. 2012. "Let Women Fight: Ending the U.S. Military's Female Combat Ban." *Foreign Affairs* 91, no. 6 (November/ December): 32–42. JSTOR.

Maclean, Ruth. 2018. "'It's Just Slavery': Eritrean Conscripts Wait in Vain for Freedom." *The Guardian*, October 11.

Makau, Kongko Louis. 2009. "Aspects of Some Experiences of Women in the Struggle for Liberation in the MK: 1976–1988: A Case Study of 10 Women." Master's thesis, University of Johannesburg.

Mallapur, Chaitanya. 2015. "88 Years On, 5% Military Officers Are Women." *IndiaSpend*, March 10. https://archive.indiaspend.com/cover-story/88-years-on-5-military-officers-are-women-68416

Mandl, Sabine. 2011. *Women in Azerbaijan Peace, Security and Democracy from a Women's Rights Perspective*. Desk research. Vienna, Austria: Ludwig Boltzmann Institute of Human Rights.

Mao, Frances. 2019. "2019 Election: Why Politics Is Toxic for Australia's Women." *BBC News*, May 16.

Marin, Nefretery. 2019. *Military Strategy to Fully Include Women*, March 22. https://liberationvoice.com/belize-politics/no-excuses-military-strategy-to-fully-include-women/

Mark, Ron. 2019. *Defence Minister Salutes Our Military Women on Women's Day*, March 8. https://www.scoop.co.nz/stories/PA1903/S00055/defence-minister-salutes-our-military-women-on-womens-day.htm

Marlowe, Ann. 2011. "Boxed In? The Women of Libya's Revolution." *World Affairs* (September/October): 64–67.

Masson, Laura E. 2017. "Women in the Military in Argentina: Nationalism, Gender, and Ethnicity." In *Gender Panic, Gender Policy*, edited by Vasilikie Demos and Marcia Texler Segal, 23–43. Bingley, UK: Emerald Publishing.

Mathers, Jennifer G. 2013. "Women and State Military Forces." In *Women and Wars: Contested Histories, Uncertain Futures*, edited by Carol Cohn, 124–145. Boston: Polity Press.

Matheson, Ian, and Ellyn Lyle. 2017. "Gender Bias in Canadian Military Leadership Training." *Journal of Ethnographic and Qualitative Research* 12: 18–28.

Matope, Tsitsi. 2017. "Female Officers Up to Task of Leading Army." *Lesotho Times,* October 7. Accessed January 20, 2020. http://lestimes.com/female-officers-up-to-task-of-leading-army

May, R. J. 1993. *The Changing Role of the Military in Papua New Guinea*. Canberra, Australia: Strategic and Defence Studies Centre Research School of Pacific Studies.

Mazrui, Ali, interview by Susan Enuogbope Majekodunmi. 2011. *Gender Mainstreaming in the Senegalese Armed Forces,* April 21.

McCone, Dave R., Cynthia J. Thomsen, and Janice H. Laurence. 2018. "Introduction to Special Issue on Sexual Harassment and Sexual

Assault in the US Military." *Military Psychology* 30, no. 1: 175–180. doi:10.1080/08995605.2018.1479550

McDermott, Roger. 2013. "The Role of Women in Russia's Armed Forces." *Eurasia Daily Monitor.*

McKernan, Bethan. 2017. "Female Kurdish Fighters Announce New Training Academies for Arab Women to Take on Isis in Syria." *Independent,* January 4. https://www.independent.co.uk/news/world/middle -east/female-kurdish-fighters-ypj-set-up-new-training-academies -arab-yazidi-women-to-fight-isis-a7508951.html

McLaughlin, Kathleen. 2019. *Armenia Country Gender Assessment.* Country Gender Assessment. Manila, Philippines: Asian Development Bank.

McLaughlin, Kathleen. 2019. *Azerbaijan Country Gender Assessment.* Country Gender Assessment. Manila, Philippines: Asian Development Bank.

Mclaughlin, Tim. 2014. "First Women Graduate from Officer Training School." *Myanmar Times,* August 30. https://www.mmtimes.com /national-news/11487-first-women-graduate-from-officer-training -school.html

Mcnamara, Mickie. 2015. "Initial Planning Begins for Tanzania Gender Integration Seminar." *United States Africa Command,* February 2. Accessed February 2, 2020. https://www.africom.mil/media-room /Article/25145/initial-planning-begins-for-tanzania-gender-integration -seminar

McNeish, John-Andrew, Gabriel Rojas Andrade, and Catalina Vallejo. 2015. *Striking a New Balance? Exploring Civil-Military Relations in Colombia in a Time of Hope.* CMI Working Paper. Bergen, Norway: CMR Michelsen Institute.

McRae, Andrew. 2015. "'All of a Sudden There Was This Bang.'" *RNZ,* October 23. Accessed February 26, 2020. https://www.rnz.co.nz /news/national/287792/'all-of-a-sudden-there-was-this-bang'

McRae, Andrew 2015. "New Zealand Nurses at War." *RNZ,* October 24. Accessed February 26, 2020. https://www.rnz.co.nz/news/national /287897/new-zealand-nurses-at-war

McSally, Martha E. 2011. "Defending America in Mixed Company: Gender in the U.S. Armed Forces." *Daedalus* 140, no. 3 (Summer): 148–164.

Meddeb, Hamza. 2015. "Conscription Reform Will Shape Tunisia's Future Civil-Military Relations." October 21. https://carnegie-mec.org /diwan/61704

Melly, Paul. 2019. *Mauritania's Unfolding Landscape Elections, Hydrocarbons and Socio-Economic Change.* Research paper. London: Chatham House.

Micronesia, Government of the Federated States of. 2017. *Department of Transportation, Communications & Infrastructure.* http://www.ict.fm/index.html

Miller, Barbara, Milad Pournik, and Aisling Swaine. 2014. *Kyrgyzstan National Action Plan Analysis.* Online, PeaceWomen, Women's International League of Peace and Freedom.

Miller, Judith. 1986. "Libya's Women: Era of Change." *New York Times,* February 3. https://www.nytimes.com/1986/02/03/style/libya-s-women-era-of-change.html

Minister of Defence, South Africa. 1996. "White Paper on National Defence for the Republic of South Africa." White paper.

Ministry National Security. 2019. "Belize Coast Guard Recruiting Women for Leadership Positions." *Ministry National Security,* December 5. https://mns.gov.bz/press-releases/belize-coast-guard-recruiting-women-for-leadership-positions

Ministry of Defense. 2018. "Defense of Japan 2018." Annual military report.

Mitchell, Rhett. 2010. "Australian Maritime Issues 2010: SPC-A Annual." *Papers in Australian Maritime Affairs.*

Moelker, Rene, and Jolanda Bosch. 2008. "Women in the Netherlands Armed Forces." In *Women in the Military and in Armed Conflict,* edited by Helena Carreiras and Gerhard Kümmel, 81–127. Wiesbaden, Germany: VS Verl. für Sozialwiss. doi.org/10.1007/978-3-531-90935-6_5

Moghadam, Valentine M. 2014. "Democratization and Women's Political Leadership in North Africa." *Journal of International Affairs* 68, no. 1: 59–78. http://www.jstor.org/stable/24461706

Mohan, Meghan. 2017. "Rape and No Periods in North Korea's Army." *BBC News,* November 21.

Mohloboli, Keiso. 2018. "Female Soldiers Reinstated." *Lesotho Times,* February 17. Accessed February 2, 2020. http://lestimes.com/female-soldiers-reinstated

Montano, Sonia, and Maria Nieves Rico. 2007. "Women's Contribution to Equality in Latin America and the Caribbean." *Economic Commission for Latin America and the Caribbean (ECLAC).* ECLAC, 1–130.

Montgomerie, Deborah. 1989. "Men's Jobs and Women's Work: The New Zealand Land Service in World War II." *Agricultural History* 63, no. 3 (Summer): 1–13.

Mophuting, Mpho C. 2003. *Expanding the Shield and Facing the Challenges: Integration of Women in the Botswana Defence Force.* Master's thesis. Monterey, CA: Naval Postgraduate School.

Morna, Colleen Lowe, Lucia Makamure, and Danny Glenwright. 2018. *SADC Gender Protocol 2018 Barometer.* Johannesburg: Southern Africa Gender Protocol Alliance.

Moskos, Charles. 2001. "What Ails the All-Volunteer Force: An Institutional Perspective." *Parameters* 31, no. 2 (Summer): 29–47.

Moyano, Inigo Guevara. 2011. Report. Strategic Studies Institute, US Army War College. http://www.jstor.org/stable/resrep11788

Mulinari, Diana. 1998. "Broken Dreams in Nicaragua." In *The Women and War Reader*, edited by Lois Ann Lorentzen and Jennifer Turpin, 157–163. New York: New York University Press.

Munshi, Anupama, and Suruchi Pandey. 2017. "Attitude of Men towards Inclusion of Women in Bhutanese and Indian Army: A Literature Review." *South Asian Journal of Human Resources Management* 4, no. 2: 139–148. doi:10.1177/2322093717733401

Mutsaka, Farai. 2016. "Woman Gets a Top Post in Zimbabwe's Air Force." *Air Force Times*, January 5.

Nantais, Cynthia, and Martha F. Lee. 1999. "Women in the United States Military: Protectors or Protected?" *Journal of Gender Studies* 8, no. 2: 181–191.

Naqelevuki, Viliaina. 2018. "Women in the Navy." *The Fiji Times*, May 18.

"National Action Plan on Women, Peace, and Security." 2015. https://www.mofa.go.jp/files/000101798.pdf

Nato Summary of the National Reports. 2016. Accessed September 18, 2018. https://www.nato.int/nato_static_fl2014/assets/pdf/pdf_2017_11/20171122_2016_Summary_of_NRs_to_NCGP.pdf

Nazemroaya, Mahdi Darius. 2014. "The Historic Role That Soviet Women Played in Defeating the Nazis in World War II." *Global Research,* March 8. Accessed November 1, 2019. https://www.globalresearch.ca/how-the-west-ignores-women-as-actors-in-otherized-societies-a-sociological-unraveling-of-the-logos-of-the-soviet-amazons/5372529

Nelsen, Harvey W. 2019. *The Chinese Military System: An Organizational Study of the Chinese People's Liberation Army.* New York: Routledge.

Nelson, Sioban, and Jennifer Rabach. 2002. "Military Experience—the New Age of Australian Nursing & Other Failures." *Health and History* 4, no. 1: 79–87.

Neuman, Scott, and Rob Schmitz. 2018. "Despite the End of China's One-Child Policy, Births Are Still Lagging." *NPR*, July 16.

New Zealand Ministry of Defence. n.d. *Military Women.* Accessed November 10, 2019. https://www.defence.govt.nz/what-we-do/assessing-the-defence-system/military-women

Nielsen, Vicki. 2002. "Women in Uniform." *NATO Review* (Summer): 30–33.

Nishimura, Kumi. 2019. "The Japan Self-Defense Force: A Crisis in the Ranks." *National Interest*, September 11.

Njeru, Betty. 2018. "Meet Fatuma Ahmed Kenya's First Female Major General." *Standard Digital,* July 14. https://www.standardmedia.co.ke/article/2001287935/who-is-major-general-fatuma-ahmed

Nonoo, Houda. 2012. "Bahrain's Women Pioneers: Women in the Army and Police." https://houdanonoo.wordpress.com/2012/03/27/bahrains-women-pioneers-women-in-the-army-and-police

Norman, Jane. 2014. "Defence Force Abuse Review Chief Says 'Shadow of Doubt' over Every Male ADFA Cadet Who Graduated between 1986 and 1998." *ABC News,* August 13. https://www.abc.net.au/news/2014-08-13/shadow-of-doubt-over-male-adfa-graduates-between-86-and-98/5668528

Obi, Paul. 2017. "Nigeria: We've Not Stopped Training of Female Cadets, Says Army." *AllAfrica,* November 15. Accessed February 2, 2020. https://allafrica.com/stories/201711150040.html

Office of Economic Cooperation and Development. 2014. "Balancing Paid Work, Unpaid Work and Leisure." http://www.oecd.org/gender/data/balancingpaidworkunpaidworkandleisure.html

Office of the Under Secretary of Defense, Personnel and Readiness. 2016. *Population Representation in the Military Services: Fiscal Year 2016 Summary Report.* Arlington, VA: CNA.

Oliphant, Valerie. 2014. *Gender Mainstreaming in the Senegalese Armed Forces.* Case study. Washington, DC: Partners for Democratic Change.

Osoba, Ermina. 2003. "Women in Management and Decision-Making Processes in Antigua and Barbuda: A Statistical Analysis." *Antigua and Barbuda Country Conference.* The University of West Indies.

Papua New Guinea Post-Courier. 2018. "The Increasing Role of Women in the Military." February 21. https://postcourier.com.pg/increasing-role-women-military

Parmelee, Jennifer. 1986. "Libyan Women Defy Tradition to Answer Call to Arms." *LA Times*, January 26. Proquest.

Pather, Raeesa. 2017. "SA Deploys More Women UN Peacekeepers to Curb Sexual Abuse." *Mail & Guardian,* September 17. Accessed February 2, 2020. https://mg.co.za/article/2017-09-19-sa-deploys -more-women-peacekeepers-in-bid-to-curb-sexual-abuse

Pennington, Matthew. 2006. "Women Make Gains in Pakistan's Military." *Sunday Gazette,* June 18. Proquest.

Pheage, Tefo. 2016. "Army Women Shake-Up BDF." *Mmegio Online*, September 2.

Phillips, Dion E. 1988. "The Creation, Structure, and Training of the Barbados Defense Force." *Caribbean Studies* 21, no. 1/2 (January–June): 124–157. www.jstor.org/stable/25612931

Phillips, Dion E. 1997. "The Trinidad and Tobago Defence Force: Origin, Structure, Training, Security and Other Roles." *Caribbean Quarterly* 43, no. 3: 13–33. https://doi.org/10.1080/00086495.1997.116 72099

Phillips, Dion E. 2002. "The Military of Belize." *Belize Country Conference,* University of West Indies.

Polga-Hecimovich, John. 2019. *Ecuadorian Military Culture 2019.* Miami: Florida International University Steven J. Green School of International & Public Affairs.

Prasad, Neelam. 2019. "Women in the Mix as Authority Recruits 70 More Firefighters." *Fiji Sun Online*, January 16.

Pratt, Nicola. 2013. "Reconceptualizing Gender, Re-Inscribing Racial-Sexual Boundaries in International Security: The Case of UN Security Council Resolution 1325 on 'Women, Peace and Security.'" *International Studies Quarterly* (December): 772–783.

Prince-Gibson, Eetta. 2007. "Chief of Staff Reinstates Women's-Status Post." *The Jerusalem Report*, April 2. Proquest.

Pruitt, Lesley J. 2016. *The Women in Blue Helmets Gender, Policing, and the UN's First All-Female Peacekeeping Unit.* Oakland: University of California Press.

Puebla, Teté. 2003. *Marianas In Combat: Teté Puebla and the Mariana Grajales Women's Platoon in Cuba's Revolutionary War, 1956–58.* eds. Mary-Alice Waters, Luis Madrid, and Martín Koppel. Atlanta, GA: Pathfinder.

Puechguirbal, Nadine. 2003. "Women and War in the Democratic Republic of the Congo." *Signs* 28, no. 4 (Summer): 1271–1281. https:// doi .org/0.1086/368319

Quénivet, Noëlle. 2008. "Girl Soldiers and Participation in Hostilities." *African Journal of International and Comparative Law* 16: 219–235. https://doi.org/10.3366/E0954889008000182

Quilliam, Rebecca. 2013. "New Zealand Trains First Female PNG Army Officers." *New Zealand Herald*, September 23.

Radio Free Asia. 2016. "Female Fighter Pilot's Death Came after Propaganda Drive by China's Military." October 14.

Ramos, Alex. 2019. "SOCSOUTH, Guatemalan Female Engagement Platoon Exchange Information." *U.S. Southern Command,* October 1. https://www.southcom.mil/MEDIA/NEWS-ARTICLES/Article/1975846/socsouth-guatemalan-female-engagement-platoon-exchange-information

"Reality Check: Does China's Communist Party Have a Woman Problem?" 2017. *BBC News*, October 25.

Riley, Jonnie. 2019. "National Guard Program Emphasizes Women's Role in Peace, Security." *U.S. Army,* January 18. https://www.army.mil/article/216345/national_guard_program_emphasizes_womens_role_in_peace_security

Robert, Krisztina. 2013. "Constructions of 'Home,' 'Front,' and Women's Military Employment in First-World-War Britain: A Spatial Interpretation." *History and Theory* 52 (October): 319–343.

Ross, Jen. 2005. "In Traditional Chile, Meet the Soldiers with Pearl Earrings." *The Christian Science Monitor,* November 7.

Roudakova, Natalia, and Deborah S. Ballard-Reisch. 1999. "Femininity and the Double Burden: Dialogues on the Socialization of Russian Daughters into Womanhood." *Anthropology of East Europe Review* 17, no. 1: 21–34.

Rupp, Emily, Assitan Diallo, and Sharon Phillipps. 2012. *Mali Gender Assessment.* Gender Assessment, USAID.

Russian Army. 2019. *Woman in the Army (Translated).* Accessed December 1, 2019. http://russianarmya.ru/sluzhba-dlya-zhenshhin-po-kontraktu.html

Sackitey, Gideon. 2020. *Female Soldiers Rising Up South Sudan's Military Ranks Call for Greater Respect for Human Rights.* UN Mission in South Sudan.

Salkever, Stephen G. 1986. "Women, Soldiers, Citizens: Plato & Aristotle on the Politics of Virility." *Polity* 19, no. 2 (Winter): 232–253. http://www.jstor.org/stable/3234912

Salloum, Habeeb. 2003. "Women in the United Arab Emirates." *Contemporary Review* (August): 101–104. Proquest.

The San Pedro Sun. 2019. "Belizean Coast Guard Female Lieutenant Makes History." June 21. https://www.sanpedrosun.com/community-and -society/2019/06/22/belize-coast-guard-lieutenant-alma-pinelo -receives-honor-graduate-award-at-us-training-center

Sasson-Levy, Orna. 2001. "Gender Performance in a Changing Military: Women Soldiers in 'Masculine' Roles." *Israel Studies Forum* 17, no. 1: 7–22. JSTOR.

Schaefer, Agnes Gereben, Jennie W. Wenger, Jennifer Kavanagh, Jonathan P. Wong, Gillian S. Oak, Thomas E. Trail, and Todd Nichols. 2015. "Lessons Learned from the Experiences of Foreign Militaries." In *Implications of Integrating Women into the Marine Corps Infantry*, 43–90. Santa Monica, CA: RAND. http://www.jstor.org /stable/10.7249/j.ctt19gfk6m.13

Seck, Hope Hodge. 2015. "Mixed-Gender Teams Come Up Short in Marines' Infantry Experiment." *Marine Corps Times*, September 10. https:// www.marinecorpstimes.com/news/your-marine-corps/2015/09 /10/mixed-gender-teams-come-up-short-in-marines-infantry -experiment

"Second World War Nurses." *Australian War Memorial.* Accessed November 11, 2019. https://www.awm.gov.au/visit/exhibitions /nurses/ww2

Sefe, Jerry. 2017. "Women Encouraged to Enlist in Navy." *Papua New Guinea Post-Courier,* October 20. https://postcourier.com.pg/women -encouraged-enlist-navy

Senate Foreign Affairs, Defence and Trade Committee. 2014. *Processes to Support Victims of Abuse in Defence.* Canberra: Commonwealth of Australia.

Service Women's Action Network (SWAN). 2019. *Women in the Military: Where They Stand.* 10th ed. https://www.servicewomen.org/wp -content/uploads/2019/04/SWAN-Where-we-stand-2019-0416 revised.pdf

"Seven Young Officers Join the SPDF Officer Corps." 2019. *Seychelles People's Defence Forces,* September 23. Accessed January 17, 2020. https://www.spdf.sc/seven-young-officers-join-the-spdf-officer-corps

Sexual Misconduct Prevention and Response Office Supplement. 2018. Supplement. Canberra: Commonwealth of Australia.

Shah, Bina. 2015. "How High Can Pakistan's Air Force Women Fly?" *New York Times*, June 8. https://www.nytimes.com/2015/06/09 /opinion/bina-shah-high-can-pakistans-air-force-women-fly.html

Sharoni, Simona. 1995. "Gendered Identities in Conflict: The Israeli-Palestinian Case and Beyond." *Women's Studies Quarterly* 23, no. 3/4: 117–135. JSTOR.

Sharp, Paul, and Louis Fisher. 2005. "Inside the 'Crystal Ball': Understanding the Evolution of the Military in Botswana and the Challenges Ahead." In *Evolutions and Revolutions: A Contemporary History of Militaries in Southern Africa*, edited by Martin Rupiya, 43–62. Pretoria, South Africa: Institute for Security Studies.

Shehadeh, Lamia Rustum. 1999. "Women in the Lebanese Militias." In *Women and War in Lebanon,* edited by Lamia Rustum Shehadeh, 145–166. Gainesville: University Press of Florida.

Siebold, Guy L. 2007. "The Essence of Military Group Cohesion." *Armed Forces & Society* 33, no. 2 (January): 286–295.

Skare, Mari. 2014. "NATO's Commitment to Women, Peace, and Security." In *Women on the Frontlines of Peace and Security*, 53–63. Washington, DC: National Defense University Press.

Skjelsbaek, Inger, and Torunn L. Tryggestad. 2009. "Women in the Norwegian Armed Forces: Gender Equality or Operational Imperative?" *Minerva Journal of Women and War* 3, no. 2 (Fall): 34–51.

Sloan, Kathryn A. 2011. *Women's Roles in Latin America and the Caribbean.* Santa Barbara, CA: ABC-CLIO.

Sly, L., & Ramadan, A. 2013. "The All-Female Militias of Syria." *Washington Post,* January 25. Proquest.

Smith, Hugh. 1990. "Women in the Australian Defence Force: In Line for the Front Line?" *The Australian Quarterly* 62, no. 2 (Winter): 125–144.

Solomon, Salem. 2019. "African Women Surmount Obstacles to Redefine their Countries' Militaries." *VOA News,* February 24. Accessed February 1, 2020. https://www.voanews.com/africa/african-women-surmount-obstacles-redefine-their-countries-militaries

Song, Sophie. 2013. "Myanmar's Military Now Recruiting Women for the First Time in History." *International Business Times*, October 25. http://www.ibtimes.com/myanmars-military-now-recruiting-women-first-time-history-1441700

Spero, Kerri. 2016. "Honduran Sapper Leadership Course Graduates First Female Combat Engineer." *Joint Task-Force Bravo,* December 21. https://www.jtfb.southcom.mil/News/Article-Display/Article/1036269/honduran-sapper-leadership-course-graduates-first-female-combat-engineer

Spitzer, Kirk. 2013. "Japanese Women Take Command, Finally." *Time Magazine*, March 22.

Spurling, Kathryn. 2000. *Women in Uniform: Perceptions and Pathways.* Canberra, Australia: School of History, University College, UNSW.

Steder, Frank Brundtland. 2014. "Is It Possible to Increase the Share of Military Women in the Norwegian Armed Forces?" *International Relations and Diplomacy* 2, no. 5 (May): 293–309.

Stein, Matthew. 2016. *Transition in the Armed Forces of Kazakhstan— From Conscripts to Contract Soldiers.* Fort Leavenworth, KS: Foreign Military Studies Office.

Stevens, Sam. 2014. "Running with the Ball." *University of Otago Magazine* (February): 34–35.

Stiehm, Judith Hicks. 1985. "The Generations of Enlisted Women." *Signs* 11, no. 1 (Autumn): 155–175.

St. Kitts & Nevis Observer. 2017. "The St. Kitts–Nevis Defence Force Adds 19 Recruits." August 19.

Strønen, Iselin Åsedotter. 2015. *Servants of the Nation, Defenders of La Patria: The Bolivarian Militia in Venezuela.* CMI Working Paper. Bergen, Norway: Chr. Michelsen Institute (CMI)/ University of Bergen.

Strønen, Iselin Åsedotter. 2016. "'*A Civil-Military Alliance': The Venezuelan Armed Forces before and during the Chávez Era.*" CMI Working Paper. Bergen, Norway: Chr. Michelsen Institute/University of Bergen.

Sunindyo, Saraswati. 1998. "When the Earth Is Female and the Nation Is Mother: Gender, the Armed Forces and Nationalism in Indonesia." *Feminist Review*, no. 58 (Spring): 1–21.

"Support for Women Peacekeepers, Civil Society Leaders Crucial in Horn of Africa Peace Efforts, Top Officials Tell Security Council." 2019. *United Nations Meeting Coverage,* November 4. Accessed February 2, 2020. https://www.un.org/press/en/2019/sc14010.doc.htm

Suresh, Lekshmi, and Ron Matthews. 2017. "Asia's Women Warriors." *Jakarta Defense Review Asia* (May/June): 28–32. https://fitribintang .com/2017/05/27/asias-women-warriors

Symons, Ellen. 1991. "Under Fire: Canadian Women in Combat." *CJWL/ RFD* 4: 477–511.

Szayna, Thomas S., Eric V. Larson, Angela O'Mahony, Sean Robson, Agnes Gereben Schaefer, Miriam Matthews, J. Michael Polich et al. 2016. *Consideration for Integrating Women into Closed Occupations in U.S. Special Operations Forces.* Santa Monica, CA: RAND. https://www.rand.org/pubs/research_reports/RR1058.html

Taylor, Nancy M. 1986. "The Home Front Volume II." In *The Official History of New Zealand in the Second World War 1939–1945.* Wellington, New Zealand: Historical Publications Branch. https://natlib.govt.nz/records/21612107?search%5Bi%5D%5Bcategory%5D=Books&search%5Bi%5D%5Bsubject%5D=World+War%2C+1939-1945+--+Social+aspects+--+New+Zealand&search%5Bpath%5D=items

Tegel, Simeon. 2015. "A Bolivian Is Thought to Be the First Woman General in Latin America Commanding Combat Troops." *www.pri.org,* March 17.

Thatcher, Amelia. 2010. "Sierra Leone and Brig. Gen. Kabia: A Progressive Voice for African Military Women." *U.S. Army,* May 17. Accessed February 2, 2020. https://www.army.mil/article/39230/sierra_leone_and_brig_gen_kabia_a_progressive_voice_for_african_military_women

Thomas, Abdul Rashid. 2019. "President Bio Warns Newly Recruited Female Soldiers to Stay Away from Politics." *The Sierra Leone Telegraph,* September 8. Accessed February 2, 2020. https://www.thesierraleonetelegraph.com/president-bio-warns-newly-recruited-female-soldiers-to-stay-away-from-politics

Thomas-Woodward, Tiffany A. 2003. "'Towards the Gates of Eternity': Celia Sánchez Manduley and the Creation of Cuba's New Woman." *Cuban Studies* 34: 154–280. doi:10.1353/cub.2004.0030

Thu, Kyaw, Myo Thant Khine, and Rachel Vandenbrink. 2014. "Myanmar Military's First Women Representatives Join Parliament." *Radio Free Asia News and Information,* January 14.

Tomlinson, Simon. 2015. "Borat's Call of Beauty? Kazakhstan Military Unveils Its 123 'Prettiest Soldiers' in Bid to Attract More People to Sign Up." *Daily Mail,* April 10.

"Uganda: Ugandan Women Military, Police Officers Demand Greater Equality." 2014. *Peace Women,* August 6. Accessed May 19, 2019. http://peacewomen.org/content/uganda-ugandan-women-military-police-officers-demand-gender-equality

United Nations. 2006. *Women's Anti-Discrimination Committee Takes Up Report of Eritrea; Told Gender Equality Efforts Hindered by*

Stereotypes, Poverty, War. UN press release. Washington, DC: U.S. Federal News Service.

United States Military Academy at West Point. 2018. "West Point Class Profile." *United States Military Academy at West Point,* July 6. https://www.westpoint.edu/admissions/class-profile

"UN Women—Fiji." *UN Women—Asia Pacific.* Accessed January 20, 2019. http://asiapacific.unwomen.org/en/countries/fiji/co/fiji

U.S. Embassy Paramaribo. 2015. "Military Women Exchange Experiences during International Women's Week." *U.S. Embassy in Suriname,* March 20. https://sr.usembassy.gov/military-women-exchange -experiences-international-womens-week

Van Creveld, Martin. 2000. "Armed but Not Dangerous: Women in the Israeli Military." *War in History* 7, no. 1: 82–98. JSTOR.

Van Meter, Spencer. 2014. "Partnering with Chile to Strengthen International Peacekeeping." *U.S. Department of State Official Blog,* June 4. http://2007-2017-blogs.state.gov/stories/2014/06/04/partnering -chile-strengthen-international-peacekeeping.html

Varoglu, A. Kadir, and Adnan Bicaksiz. 2005. "Volunteering for Risk: The Culture of the Turkish Armed Forces." *Armed Forces and Society* 31, no. 4 (Summer): 583–598.

Veale, Angela. 2005. "Collective and Individual Identities: Experiences of Recruitment and Reintegration of Female Excombatants of the Tigrean People's Liberation Army, Ethiopia." In *Invisible Stakeholders: Children and War in Africa*, edited by Angela McIntyre, 105–126. Pretoria, South Africa: Institute for Security Studies.

"The Vietnamese Women Who Fought for their Country." 2016. *BBC News*, December 6.

Wahine Toa Women in Defence. Accessed November 20, 2019. https:// www.airforcemuseum.co.nz/whats-on/wahine-toa-women-in-defence

Walsh, Sean P. 2007. "The Roar of the Lion City: Ethnicity, Gender and Culture in the Singapore Armed Forces." *Armed Forces and Society* 33, no. 2: 265–285.

Weissensteiner, Nina. 2016. "Austrian Army Aims to Recruit Up to 10,000 Volunteers by 2020." *BBC Monitoring European*, September 16. Proquest.

Wilson-Harris, Nadine. 2019. "JDF Focuses on Recruiting More Women." *The Jamaica Gleaner,* March 19. http://jamaica-gleaner.com/article /news/20190319/jdf-focuses-recruiting-more-women

Winslow, Donna, and Jason Dunn. 2002. "Women in the Canadian Forces: Between Legal and Social Integration." *Current Sociology* 50, no. 5 (September): 641–667.

"Women Are Still Underrepresented in All Areas of Decision-Making in Guinea-Bissau." 2015. *United Nations Integrated Peacebuilding Office in Guinea-Bissau,* April 20. Accessed January 17, 2020. 2https://uniogbis.unmissions.org/en/women-are-still-underrepre sented-all-areas-decision-making-guinea-bissau

Women in the ADF Report 2017–2018. 2019. Supplement. Canberra: Commonwealth of Australia.

"Women to Serve in Close Combat Roles in the British Military." 2016. *BBC,* July 8. https://www.bbc.com/news/uk-36746917

Women's Rugby Sevens Brings Pacific Nations Together. 2019. Media release. Canberra: Australian Government, Department of Defense.

Wood, Reed M. 2019. *Female Fighters: Why Rebel Groups Recruit Women for War.* New York: Columbia University Press.

Woods, Dorothea. 1985. "The Conscription of Women for National Defense, the Militarization of Women, and Some Ethical Perspectives on Women's Involvement in the Military." *Current Research on Peace and Violence* 8, no. 3/4: 149–159. JSTOR.

Woodward, Rachel, and Claire Duncanson. 2017. *The Palgrave International Handbook of Gender and the Military.* London: Macmillan Publishers.

World Health Organization Regional Office for Africa. n.d. "Women's Health." *World Health Organization Regional Office for Africa.* Accessed February 1, 2020. https://www.afro.who.int/health-topics /womens-health

Wroe, David. 2015. "Joint Strike Fighter Ejector Seat Could Break Lightweight Pilot's Neck." *The Sydney Morning Herald,* October 23. Accessed August 3, 2018. https://www.smh.com.au/politics/federal /joint-strike-fighter-ejector-seat-could-break-lightweight-pilots -neck-20151023-gkh480.html

Wroe, David. 2016. "Women Poised to Start Flying RAAF Fighter Jets." *The Sydney Morning Herald,* February 5. Accessed August 3, 2018. https://www.smh.com.au/politics/federal/women-poised-to -start-flying-raaf-fighter-jets-20160205-gmmt7s.html

Zeldin, Wendy. 2007. "Benin: Military Service Law." *Library of Congress,* November 2. Accessed February 1, 2020. https://www.loc.gov/law /foreign-news/article/benin-military-service-law

Zhalil, Madina. 2018. "Kazakh Army to Plan to Actively Involve Women." *The Qazaq Times*, April 9. https://qazaqtimes.com/en/article/37953

Zraick, Karen. 2014. "Arab Women Led Airstrikes over Syria." *New York Times,* September 25. https://www.nytimes.com/2014/09/26/world/middleeast/emirates-first-female-fighter-pilot-isis-airstrikes.html

Index

Note: An italicized *f* following a page number indicates a figure.

Aberdeen Proving Ground, 16
Afghanistan, 13, 14–15, 198–201
Africa
  child soldiers, 129
  conscription, 125, 130–131
  customs and cultures, 125
  Dahomey women, 127, 127*f*
  equality, 136–142
  factors influencing, 130–131
  historical legends, 126–127
  independence movements and
    civil wars, 126, 131–134
  integration of women, 128
  partnership efforts, 146–147
  in peacekeeping operations,
    142–146
  quota systems, 129
  See also Sub-Saharan African
    countries
African National Congress (ANC),
  137
African Union (AU), 128
African Union Mission in Somalia
  (AMISOM), 145
Aisha, Princess, 110

Albanian armed forces, 92
alcohol consumption, 53, 221
Algerian armed forces, 100–101
Algerian war of independence, 100
Amal (Shia militia group), 102
Amin, Saira, 189
Angola, 132
Anti-Fascist People's Freedom
  League (AFPFL), 190
Antigua and Barbuda Defense
  Force, 49
apartheid, 136–137
Arab Human Development Report
  (AHDR), 97
Arab Spring, 98
Arab world, 97, 99, 101–102, 108
Ardjoune, Fatima Zohra, 100–101
Argentine armed forces, 33–34,
  46–48
Argentine government, 34
Armed Forces of Liberation of
  Angola, 132
Armenian forces, 158, 174–175
Army of the Republic of Vietnam
  (ARVN), 193

272 Index

Army Physical Fitness
  Test (U.S.), 9
Asante, Kingdom of, 126
Assad, Bashar al-, 105, 106
Assad, Hafiz al-, 105
Australian armed forces, 207,
  208–209, 210, 213–219,
  220–222
Australian Army Medical
  Women's Service (AAMWS),
  215, 216
Australian Army Nursing Service
  (AANS), 214–215
Australian Defense Force Academy
  (ADFA), 220–221
Australian Human Rights
  Commission, 220–221
Australian Imperial Force (AIF),
  214
Australian Parliament, 208–209
Australian society, 208, 218
Australian Women's Army Service
  (AWAS), 215, 216
Azerbaijan, 158

Baez, Gladys, 35
Bahamas, 49–50
Bahrain Defense Forces, 105
Bangladesh armed forces, 185
Barbados Defense Force, 41, 53
Basic Law for a Gender Equal
  Society, 158
Belgium armed forces, 60, 76, 92
Belize, 41
Ben Ali, Zine al-Abidine, 98
Benghazi, 101
Benin, 127, 130, 146
Bhutan, 192
Bhutto, Benazir, 188, 189

Binh, Nguyen Thi, 194
Bobadilla, Rosa, 37
Bochkareva, Maria, 165
Boer Wars, 223
Boko Haram, 139
Bolivarian Armed Forces, 35
Bolivarian Revolution, 1999, 35
Borge, Tomas, 39
Botswana government, 130
Botswanan Defense Forces, 130
Boudouani, Fatima, 101
Boumediene, Houari, 100
Braga, Marcia Andrade, 44
Brazilian armed forces, 43–45
British Army, 52, 65, 113
Buddhism, 156
Bulgarian Armed Forces, 77, 92
Bulgarian Armed Forces Women's
  Association (BUAFWA), 77
Burkina Faso, 140, 146
Burma, 190
Burton, Clare, 226
Burundi, 138
Bush, George H. W., 11

Cameron, David, 72
camp followers, 1, 2, 62, 98, 135,
  189
Canada
  change, factors influencing,
    18–19
  masculinity and warfare, views
    on, 17–18
  women's integration into combat
    arms, 20–27
Cape Verde, 130
Caribbean forces, 49–51, 52
Carignan, Jennie, 26–27
Carter, Jimmy, 6–7

Carter, Nick, 72
Catholocism, 32
Central African Republic (CAR), 134, 145–146
Central and East Asia, 155
  appearance, 159–161
  external events and internal politics, 168–177
  factors influencing, 162–168
  masculinity and warfare, 156–159
  military stress, 178
  myths about women fighters, 157
  religion influence on social cultures of, 156
Chad, 131
Chavez, Hugo, 35
Chen, 113
child soldiers, 129
Chilean armed forces, 45–46, 46*f*
Chilean Ministry of Defense, 45
China, 157
Chinese Civil War, 162
Chinese People's Liberation Army (PLA), 161, 162–165
Clinton, Bill, 7
cognitive intelligence, 12
Colegio Militar de la Nacion (CMN), 46
Collège Interarmeés de la Défense (CID), 68
Colombia armed forces, 40
combat arms
  European armed forces, 70–72
  female commander in, 26–27
  women's integration into, 12–16, 20–27, 70, 71, 72, 75, 115, 118, 189, 192

combat aviation exclusion, 13, 14
combat exclusion of women
  arguments for, 6–7, 10, 20–21, 73
  in IDF, 115
  in NZDF, 226
  opposition to, 15
  policy recommendations regarding, 14, 15
  removal of, 9, 13
  in United Kingdom, 70–71, 74
combat pay to women, 14
combat positions, 4, 13, 21, 25–26, 59, 60, 73, 81, 91, 100, 115, 117, 187, 207
combat readiness and effectiveness, 10–11, 16, 137
combat zones, U.S. women in, 12, 13–15
communism, 156
Communist Party of Nepal, 196
Compact of Free Association, 229–230
compulsory military service, 81, 112, 117, 131
confidence-building measures, 43
Confucianism, 156
Congolese national army, women in, 141
conscription
  gender roles and, 33
  in Germany, 82–83
  in Kyrgyzstan, 176
  move away from, 45, 59, 81, 83
  in Mozambique, 130
  in Russia, 169
conscription of women
  attitudes concerning, 81, 169
  and citizenship obligations, 84
  in Israel, 112, 114, 117

conscription of women (*cont.*)
in Ivory Coast, 131
on Korean Peninsula, 170–171
in Mexico, 36
in Norway, 81–82
rejection of, 82–83
in Sub-Saharan Africa, 125,
130–131
in Sudan, 130
in Sweden, 81
in Taiwan, 177
in Tunisia, 99
Continental Army (U.S.), 1, 2
cooperative security efforts,
229–231
Corbin, Margaret, 2
Costa Rica, 52
coverture, 1
Croatia, 61, 77, 92
Cuban armed forces, 37–38
Cuban Revolution, 35, 37
Czech Republic, 74–75

Dahomey, Kingdom of, 126–127,
127*f*
Dalian Naval Ship Academy, 164
Danish armed forces, 69
Defense Abuse Response Taskforce
(DART), 221
Defense Act of 1886 (New
Zealand), 224
Defense Advisory Committee on
Women in the Services
(DACOWITS), 5
Defense Service Law (Israel), 115
demographic transformations, 90,
118, 166, 192, 201
Denmark, 75
Derg, 132

Desert Storm, 13, 14
Destacamento Femenino (DF)
(Mozambique), 132
Directorate of Women's Military
Affairs (DWMA) (Jordan),
110, 112
disarmament, demobilization, and
reintegration (DDR), 134–136
Dominican Republic, 52–53
Doskozil, Hans-Peter, 79
due process, 5, 6
Duong Quynh Hoa, 194

Ecuador, 33–34
egalitarianism, 67
Egypt, 114
Eisenhower, Dwight David, 5
El Salvador, 40
enlistment standards, 5
"Equality for All" document
(Canada), 19
equality for military women. *See*
gender equality
Equal Opportunities Commission
(United Kingdom), 85
Equal Rights Amendment, 1972, 5
Eritrea, 130, 131, 132–133
Eritrean People's Liberation Front,
133
Estonian armed forces, 92
Ethiopian Civil War (1974-1991),
132–133
European armed forces
combat arms, 70–72
cultural perspectives, 68
demographic and economic
changes impacting, 90
factors influencing role of, 81–84
gender issues, 75

integration issues, 69–73
legal and cultural shifts
   influencing, 84–90
men's attitudes toward women
   in, 66–67
noncombatant functions, 63
peacekeeping operations, 72
recruitment and retention efforts,
   75–81
sexual harassment issues, 91–93
societies' views of women in, 68
statistics, 59–61
support and logistical functions,
   62
technological changes
   impacting, 90
war participation, 61–64
in war zones, 90–91
after World War II, 64–68
European Union (EU), 69

Family Code of 1975, 35
Farabundo Marti National
   Liberation Front (FMLN),
   39*f*, 40
"Far East" (term defined), 97
Federated States of Micronesia,
   229, 230
Female Engagement Team, Quick
   Reaction Force (QRF), 111
Female Engagement Teams
   (FETs), 14
female-only military teams, 14
Fifth Amendment, 5, 6
Fiji, 210–211, 212
France, 59, 60*f*, 68, 81
Free Officer's Revolution, 101
Frontiero v. Richardson (1973), 6
F-35 program, 218

Gallup Canada, 24
Gambia, 141
Ganiyeva, Ziba, 175
Garre, Nilda, 47
Gauthier v. Canada (1989), 24–25
gender-based violence, 126, 128
gender discrimination, 16, 20, 23,
   177
gender equality
   in Albanian society, 89
   in Canada, 19, 20, 22–23
   in Central and East Asia, 178
   in China and North Korea, 157
   in Eritrean constitution, 131
   in Europe, 85
   in European countries, 81
   in Germany, 87
   in Israel, 113, 116–117
   in Japan, 158
   in Kenya, 139–140
   in Lesotho, 138
   in NATO countries, 72, 84
   in Nigeria, 139
   in Norway, 70, 78–79
   in peacekeeping forces, 143, 197,
     210
   in Philippines, 190, 191
   PKK and, 106, 108
   in Seychelles, 138–139
   in South Africa, 136–138
   in South Dakota National
     Guard, 50
   in Sub-Saharan Africa, 136–142
   in Sweden, 66, 81
   in Tanzania, 139
   in Trinidad and Tobago, 51
   in United States, 3, 5–6, 7, 8
Gender Equality Office, 92
gender-free tests, 74

276   Index

gender integration. *See* integration of women
Gender Policy Council for Defense (GPC), 47
genocide, 144
Georgian armed forces, 175–176
German Armed Forces, 64, 82–83
Greek Armed Forces, 92
Grenada, 52
group collaboration, 12
Guatemala, 48–49
Guinea-Bissau, 141–142
Gulf War, first, 7, 65–66, 91
gundae, 171
Guyana Defense Force, 41

Haganah, 113
Haiti, 51–52
Hashomer, 112
HeForShe Campaign, 51
Herrera, Petra, 37
Hezbollah (Shia militia group), 102
Hinan, Tin, 99
His Majesty's Armed Forces from Tonga, 213
HIV/AIDS, 129
Honduras, 41–42
Horchani, Farhat, 99
Hua Mu-Lan, 156*f,* 157
Hultgreen, Kara, 7–8
Hunter, Duncan, 15
Hunter Troop (Jeggertroppen) (Norway), 78

Indian armed forces, 186–188, 188*f,* 192, 197–198
Indochinese Communist Party, 195
Indonesian armed forces, 195–196

integration of women
in Australian Defense Force (ADF), 218, 220–222
in Brazil, 43–44
in Burundi, 138
in Canada, 19, 20, 26
in Canadian armed forces, 20–26
in Chinese People's Liberation Army (PLA), 164–165
into combat arms (*see* combat arms, women's integration into)
in Danish armed forces, 69
in Ecuador armed forces, 34
in European armed forces, 69–73
in Indian armed forces, 192
in Japanese armed forces, 173
in Latin American defense forces, 31–32
in New Zealand Defence Force (NZDF), 227
in Oceania countries, armed forces of, 220–221
in PNGDF, 212–213
in South African armed forces, 128
in Swedish armed forces, 69–70
in U.S. armed forces, 8–12
International Maritime Officer Course, 41
involuntary dismissal, litigation against, 9
Iran, 108–109
Iran-Iraq War, 98
Iraq, 13–15, 108
Iraqi Kurdistan, 108
Islam, 156
Islamic law, 97

Islamic State, 106
Israel
 change, factors influencing,
  118–119
 historic overview, 98, 112–115
 masculinity and the military,
  views on, 116–117
 sexual harassment and assault,
  120
Israel Defense Forces (IDF)
 establishment of, 112, 113
 masculine culture of, 114
 women participation in, 112,
  114, 115, 117, 118–119, 120
Ivory Coast, 131

Jamaican Defense Forces (JDF), 50
Japan Air Self-Defense Force, 172
Japanese armed forces, 158–159,
 171–173, 192
Japanese occupation of Burma, 190
Japan Ground Self-Defense Force,
 171–172
Jeggertroppen (Norway), 78
Jewish settlements, 112
Johnson-Sirleaf, Ellen, 133
Jordanian armed forces, 109–112,
 111*f*

Kabbalah, 107
Kabia, Kestoria, 136
Kahina, 9
Katibat Banat, 133
Kazakh armed forces, 160–161,
 173–174, 176
Kenyan armed forces, 139–140
Kerensky, Alexander, 64
Khan, Genghis, 157
Khanzad, 107

Kiribati, 229
Korb, Lawrence, 11
Koyara, Marie-Noëlle, 134
Kubuabola, Silipa Tagicaki, 212
Kuomintang, 157
Kurdish Regional Government
 (KRG), 107
Kurdish Spring, 107
Kurdish women, 106–108
Kurdistan Workers' Party (PKK),
 106–107
Kuugongelwa-Ahmadhila, Saara,
 128
Kwajalein Atoll, 230

Labor Federation *(Histadrut),* 113
Latin American armed forces,
 women in
 barriers to, 45
 changing battlefield role of,
  43–49
 combat units leaders, 37
 conferences on, 36
 Cuban revolution, 35
 Haitian armed forces, 51–52
 labor force participation, 32–33
 masculinity and warfare,
  societal views on, 32–36
 military specialties, 33–35
 revolution, support roles during,
  31, 34, 36–37
 success of, 40–43
 traditional gender roles of, 32
 violence against, 33
 women's participation, factors
  influencing, 36–40
Latin American countries, 31, 35
Latvian armed forces, 61, 76
leadership, 71

278 Index

Lebanese Armed Forces (LAF), 102–103
Lebanese Military Academy, 103
Lebanon, 101, 102–103, 115
Lesotho Armed Forces, gender equality in, 138
Liberation Tigers of Tamil Eelan (LTTE), 186
Liberia, 133–134, 197
Libya, 101
Lionesses for National Defense, 105
Lithuania Armed Forces, 60, 76, 92
Luxembourg armed forces, 60

Maclean, Hester, 224
Madagascar armed forces, 142
Maduro, Nicolas, 35
"Makeup Under Camouflage" contest, 160
Malalai, 185
Malawi, 130
male bonding and cohesiveness, 12
Mali, universal service requirements in, 130
Manning Report, 73
Mansouri, Miriam al, 104
Maoist guerrilla movement, 196
Mapisa-Nqakula, Nosiviwe, 128
Mariana Grajales Brigade, 37
Marin, Nefretery, 41
Marshal Khanperiants Aviation Institute, 174
Marshall, George C., 4, 5
Marshall Islands, 229, 230
masculinity and warfare, societal views of
  in Algeria, 100–101
  in Argentina, 33–34

in Australia and New Zealand, 208–211
in Bahrain Defense Forces, 105
in Canada, 17–18
in Cuba, 35
in Ecuador, 33, 34
in Iraq, 108–109, 109f
in Israel, 112–120
in Jordan, 109–112
in Kurdish-controlled region of Syria, 106–108
in Lebanon, 101–103
in Libya, 101
in MENA region, 98–99
in Mexico, 32–33
in Nicaragua, 34–35
in Qatar, 104–105
in Saudi Arabia, 105
in South and Southeast Asian countries, 186–192
in Syria, 105–106
in Tunisia, 99–100
in UAE, 103–104
in U.S., 3–8
in Venezuela, 34, 35
Mauritius, 126
McKenzie, Florence Violet, 216
McPeak, Merrill, 6
mental health conditions, 53
Mexican armed forces, 38f
Mexican Revolution, women participation in, 36–37
Mexico, 32, 37
Micronesia, 229, 230
Middle East, 97
Middle Eastern and North African (MENA) armed forces
  Algeria, 100–101
  Bahrain Defense Forces, 105

factors influencing, 99–112
Iran, 108–109
Iraq, 108, 109*f*
Israel, 112–120
Jordan, 109–112
Kurdish-controlled region of Syria, 106–108
Lebanon, 101–103
Libya, 101
Qatar, 104–105
Saudi Arabia, 105
societal views of, 98–99
Syria, 105–106
Tunisia, 99–100
UAE, 103–104
Middle Eastern and North African (MENA) countries, 97, 98, 99
military fitness tests, 9
military occupational specialties (MOS), 65
Military Selective Service Act, 1948, 7
Miller, Alice, 115
Minh, Ho Chi, 193
mixed-gender rooms, 70
mixed-gender training, 25, 118
mixed-gender units
Brazil, 44
Canada, 19, 22
China, 162, 164
Dahomey, Kingdom of, 126
Eritrea, 133
Israel, 113
United Kingdom, 72
U.S., 4, 72
Molotov-Ribbentrop Non-Aggression Pact, 1939, 166
Mongolian armed forces, women in, 170

Mo, Vo Thi, 194
Mozambique, 130, 132

National Bolivarian Militia, 35
National Cadet Corps, 49
National Liberation Front (NLF), 100, 193, 194
NATO Committee on Gender Perspectives (NCGP), 59
NATO member countries, 59–60, 72, 77
NATO Summary of the National Reports, 91
Naupoto, Viliame, 211
Nauru, 229
Nepali Armed Forces, 196
Neri, Margarita, 37
Netherlands armed forces
conscription and, 82
parental leave policies, 77
physical fitness tests for, 74
statistics of, 59, 60, 65
Women's Assistance Corps, 65
New Zealand Defence Force (NZDF), 207, 209–210, 213, 223–229, 227*f*
New Zealand Expeditionary Forces (NZEF), 224
New Zealand Medical Corps Nursing Reserve, 224
New Zealand's Army Nursing Service Reserve (NZANSR), 224–225
New Zealand Women's Royal Army Corps (NZWRAC), 226
Ngo Dinh Diem, 194
Ngo Dinh Nhu, 194
Nicaragua, 34–35, 38–39

280   Index

Nigeria, 139
Nigerian Army Women's Corps, 139
"Night Witches," 168
North Africa, warfare in, 99–112
North Dakota National Guard, 146
North Korea, 157, 170–171
North Vietnam, 193–194
Norway's armed forces
  conscription, 81–82
  cultural perspectives of, 67–68
  diversity and gender equality of, 78–79
  integration views for, 69–70
  low female participation, 69
  parental leave policies, 76
Norwegian Royal Guard, 69

Observation on the Integration of Women in the Armed Forces, 47
Ocalan, Syria Abdullah, 106
Oceania armed forces
  in Australia, 213–223
  cooperative security efforts, 229–231
  factors influencing, 211–213
  integration challenges, 220–221
  masculinity, societal views of, 208–211
  in New Zealand, 213, 223–229
  overview of, 207
  working mothers and families, 222–223
Operation Desert Shield, 14

Pahlavi, Reza, 108–109
Pakistan, 188, 189
Palau, 229, 230

Palestine, 112–113
Palmach, 113
Panama, 13, 52
Panetta, Leon, 15
Papua New Guinea, 210
Papua New Guinea Defence Force (PNGDF), 212–213
Paraguay armed forces, 49
parental leave policies, 76–77
patriarchal Catholic religion, 32
patriarchy and warfare. *See* masculinity and warfare, societal views of
peacekeeping operations
  African countries, 142–143
  Argentine armed forces, 47
  in Brazil, 43–44
  in Central African Republic, 145–146
  European armed forces, 72
  Indian armed forces, 197–198
  Japanese armed forces, 172
  Jordanian armed forces, 110
  Kazakh armed forces, 176
  Philippines, women's military service in, 192
  Polish armed forces, 72–73
  Republic of the Fiji Military Forces (RFMF), 211
  in Rwanda, 144–145
  in Somalia, 145
  South Africa, 144
  South and Southeast Asian countries, 192
  Uganda, 145
Pelly, Megan, 208
People's Armed Forces of Liberation of Angola (FAPLA), 132

People's Army of Vietnam, 195
People's Liberation Armed Forces (PLAF), 194
People's National Army (PNA), 100–101
People's Protection Units (PYD), 106
Peruvian armed forces, 49
Philippines, women's military service in, 190–192, 191*f*
Phillips, Anita, 4
physical differences, male-female
  efforts to close, 9
  as integration barrier, 8–10, 73
  Portugal, women in armed forces of, 74
  United Kingdom, women in armed forces of, 73
Pinelo, Alma, 41
"Policy on the Employment of Women" (Canada), 20
Polish Armed Forces, 72–73, 92
Portuguese Armed Forces
  in Air Force with constrained roles, 65
  conscription, shift away from, 83
  parental leave policies, 77
  physical requirements for, 74
  recruiting and retaining, 78
  statistics of, 61
Portuguese constitution of 1997, 83
pregnancy, 8–9, 25, 73
Presidential Commission on the Assignment of Women in the Armed Forces, 7, 10, 11
Public Law 95-485, 6

Qaddafi, Muammar, 101
Qajar Dynasty, 108

Qatar, women's status in, 104–105
Quebec, 22
Quick Reaction Force Female Engagement Team (QRF), 111
quota systems, 155

racial integration, 10
Rahab, Sayyidah, 102
Raponda, Rose Christiane, 128
Reagan administration, 11
Red Army, 162
regional security, 43
Regional Security System (St. Kitts-Nevis), 50, 52
Report of the Royal Commission on the Status of Women in Canada, 18
Republic of Kurdistan, 109
Republic of the Fiji Military Forces (RFMF), 211, 212
revolutionary struggles, women participation in, 31, 34–35, 36–37, 38–39, 40
Revolutionary War (U.S.), 1, 2
risky sexual behavior, 53
Rojava, 106
Romanian armed forces, 61
Romanian MOD, 92–93
Royal Australian Navy (RAN), 208
Royal Bahamas Defense Force, 49–50
Royal Bhutan Army, 192
Royal Grenada Police Force, 52
Royal Military Academy Sandhurst, 110
Royal New Zealand Nursing Corps (RNZNC), 226
Royal St. Lucia Police Force, 52

282   Index

Russian armed forces, women in
  all-Russian military-Patriotic
    movement, 169*f*
  beauty pageant for, 160
  demographic changes impact on,
    166
  external events and politics
    influence on, 168
  forcible removal of, 167
  "Night Witches," 168
  selection process for, 169
  sexual harassment of, 166–167
  statistics of, 169, 170
  during war, 64, 165
  war zone participation, 167
  Women's Battalion of Death,
    First, 165–166
  in World War II, 166–167
Russian Strategic Missile Forces,
  160
Rwanda, 134, 144–145
Rwandan Defense Force, 145

Sadr, Musa al, 102
Sahgal, Lakshmi, 187
Saint Vincent, 52
Salvadoran Civil War, 40
Salvadoran military Independence
  Day parades, 39*f*
Sampson, Deborah, 2
Sanchez, Celia, 37
Sandinista National Liberation
  Front (FSLN), 34–35, 38
Saudi Arabian armed forces,
  women's status in, 105
Second Artillery Force (SAF),
  164
security cooperation, 43
selective service, 6–7, 130

Senegalese armed forces, gender
  mainstreaming in, 140
Servicewomen in Non-Traditional
  Environments and Roles
  (SWINTER trials), 18–19
Sex Discrimination Act of 1975, 84
sexual behavior, risky, 53
sexual harassment and
  discrimination
  ADFA response to claims of,
    220
  in Belgian Armed Forces, 92
  in Bulgarian Armed Forces, 92
  in Canadian armed forces, 23
  in Croatian Armed Forces, 92
  in Estonian armed forces, 92
  in European armed forces,
    91–93
  in Greek Armed Forces, 92
  in Israel Defense Forces (IDF),
    120
  in Latin America's defense
    forces, 33
  in Lithuania Armed Forces, 92
  in New Zealand Defence Force,
    229
  in Norwegian armed forces, 78
  in Polish Armed Forces, 92
  in Romanian MOD, 92–93
  in Russia, 166–167
  in Swedish Armed Forces,
    79, 91
  in U.S. armed forces, 16
Sexual Misconduct Prevent and
  Response Office (SeMPRO),
  221–222
sexual relationships and unit
  cohesion, 11
Seychelles armed forces, 138–139

Sharia law, 97
Shurland, Errington, 41
Sibiya, Portia, 138
Sierra Leone DDR process,
  135–136
Singaporean Armed Forces (SAF),
  185, 201–203
single-gender units, 72
Six-Day War, 114
Slovenian armed forces, 61, 77–78
Social Policy Directorate of the
  Bulgarian Ministry of
  Defense, 92
"social sensitivity," 12
Solomon Islands, 229
Somalia, 141, 145
South Africa, 128, 136–138, 144
South African Defense Forces, 137
South African National Defense
  Force (SANDF), 137–138
South American Defense Council,
  44
Southern People's Liberation
  Movement, 133
South Korea, 170, 171, 185
South Vietnam, 193–194
Soviet Union, 82, 89, 156, 157,
  166–168, 174
Special Action Force School
  (Philippines), 191f
Special Female Recruitment
  Program, 136
Special Forces Green Beret
  qualification course, 16
Special Reconnaissance Regiment,
  70
Srikandi Brigade, 195
Sri Lankan Armed Forces, 185,
  186, 193

State Committee on Family,
  Women and Children's
  Affairs (SCFWCA), 158
St. Kitts-Nevis Defense Force, 50
St. Lucia, 52
Struck, Susan R., 9
Sub-Saharan African countries
  change, factors influencing,
    130–131
  disarmament, demobilization,
    and reintegration in, 134–136
  equality for women, 136–142
  independence and civil wars,
    131–134
  masculinity and warfare,
    societal views of, 126–130
  overview of, 125–126
  partnership efforts, 146–147
  women and peacekeeping,
    142–146
substance abuse issues, 53
Sudan, 130, 133
Suez Campaign, 114
Suriname Defense Force (SDF),
  50–51
Swedish armed forces
  conscription, 81
  integration views for, 69–70
  men's attitudes toward, 66–67
  mixed-gender rooms, 70
  physical issues, 73–74
  recruiting and retaining, 79
  sexual harassment of, 91
SWINTER (Servicewomen
  in Non-Traditional
  Environments and Roles)
  trials, 18–19
Syria, 105–107
Syrian Democratic Forces, 106

284   Index

Tadu, Amelia, 212
Taiwan, 177
Tajikistan armed forces, women in, 176
Tanzania, gender equality in, 139
Tatoyan, Armen, 174–175
Teran, Gina Reque, 31, 40–41
Togolese Army, 146
Tonga, Kingdom of, 213
"Towards Equality" report (Canada), 19
Treaty of Friendship, 1962, 229
Trieu, Lady, 185
Trinidad and Tobago Defense Force (TTDF), 51
Tripoli Women's Military Academy, 101
Trung sisters, 185
Tunisia, 98, 99–100
Turkish armed forces, 77, 80–81
Tuvalu, 229

Uganda, 145
Umkhonto we Sizwe (MK), 137
unit cohesion
    leadership and, 70, 71
    male bonding and, 12, 20
    operational success and, 22
    programs promoting, 118
    women's impact on, 8, 20, 68
    women's integration and, 11–12
United Arab Emirates, women's status in, 103–104
United Kingdom armed forces, women in
    combat exclusion, 70–71, 74
    demographic and economic changes impacting, 90
    in first Gulf War, 65–66, 91

gender-free physical tests for, 74
in Iraq and Afghanistan, 71, 72, 91
joint training and management, 65
legal and cultural shifts influencing, 84
maternity leave for, 65
national plan, 85
opposition to full integration of, 71–72
physical issues, 73
in RAF and Royal Navy, 66
statistics of, 59, 63
technological changes impacting, 90
unit cohesion and, 71
volunteer for noncombatant roles, 62–63
in WAAF, 63f
war zone participation, 90–91
Women's Royal Army Corps, 65
after World War II, 64
in World War II, 63–64
United Nations Emergency Forces II (UNEF), 72
United States
    countries, other compared to, 229
    historic overview, 1–3
    international agreements, 230
    masculinity and warfare, societal views of, 3–8
United States armed forces
    coding system reevaluation, 11
    combat zones, 12–16
    with Continental Army, 1, 2

cultural perspectives of, 68
in first Gulf War, 7, 66
integration issues, 8–12
mixed-gender units, 4
recruitment efforts, 5, 6
statistics, 2–3, 3*f*, 5, 59–60
in World War II, 4
United States v. Virginia (1996),
14
universal service, 130
UN Resolution 1325, 45
UN Security Council Resolution
1325, 84–85
UN Stabilization Mission to Haiti
(MINUSTAH), 51
UN Women and Oceania Rugby,
210
Uruguayan armed forces, 41
USAFRICOM, 146
U.S. Army Ranger School, 15–16
U.S. Coast Guard Training Center,
41
U.S. Marine's combat effectiveness
study, 72
U.S. Southern Command
(SOUTHCOM), 36
U.S. Supreme Court, 6, 14
Uzbekistan, 176–177

Vanuatu, 229
Venezuela armed forces, 41
Venezuelan Constitution, 34, 35
Vier, Sofia, 47
Vietnamese armed forces, 185,
189–190, 193–195
Vietnamese culture, 194
Vietnamese Women's Solidarity
Movement, 194
Vietnam War, 193

Virginia Military Institute
(VMI), 14
VISION 2010, 25
volunteer forces, 39, 41, 59, 81,
83, 113

Washington, George, 2
Weinberger, Casper, 10–11
West Indies Regiment, 50, 52
Westmoreland, William, 6
Williams, Cathay, 3
Women Accepted for Volunteer
Emergency Service
(WAVES), 4–5
Women Armed Forces Corps, 193
Women Auxiliary Corps, 190
Women in Military and Security
Conferences (WIMCON), 36
Women's Armed Services
Integration Act of 1948, 5
Women's Army Auxiliary Corps
(WAAC), 4
Women's Army Corps (WAC),
4, 42
Women's Assistance Corps, 65
Women's Auxiliary Air Force
(WAAF), 63, 215
Women's Corps of the Royal
Netherlands Indian Army, 65
Women's Integration Act of
1948, 8
Women's Liberation Association,
194
women's military-to-military
engagement program, 146
women's movements, 1, 108
Women's National Service
League, 62
Women's Protection Unit, 106

286 Index

women's rights
  in Libya, 101
  in Middle East and North
    Africa, 107
  in Pakistan, 188
  in Russia, 165
  in Rwanda, 144
  in Saudi Arabia, 105
  in Sub-Saharan Africa, 133
  in U.S., 4, 5–6, 7, 8
Women's Royal Australian Army
  Corps (WRAAC), 216–217
Women's Royal Australian Naval
  Service (WRANS), 215, 216,
  217
Women's Royal New Zealand Air
  Force (WRNZAF), 226
Women's Royal New Zealand Naval
  Service (WRNZNS), 226

Women's Service Military
  (Chile), 45
"Wonder Woman Competition"
  (Belize), 41
World War I, 4, 64, 224
World War II, 4, 63–64, 166–167,
  215–216

Xanim, Adile, 107

Yom Kippur War, 114
Youth Corps, 193

Zairian Armed Forces, 141
Zambian Defense Force,
  145–146
Zewde, Sahle-Work, 128
Zhinga, Queen of Matamba, 126
Zimbabwe, 134–135

About the Authors

Ruth Margolies Beitler, PhD, is a professor of comparative politics at the United States Military Academy, West Point. She is the author of three books, including as coauthor of *Women's Roles in the Middle East and North Africa* (Greenwood Press, 2010).

Sarah M. Gerstein is an assistant professor of international relations at the United States Military Academy, West Point, and is an active duty major in the United States Army.